THE YEAR
BEFORE THE FLOOD

Also by Ned Sublette

Books

The World That Made New Orleans: From Spanish Silver to Congo Square
Cuba and Its Music: From the First Drums to the Mambo

Recordings

Kiss You Down South
Cowboy Rumba
Monsters from the Deep (with Lawrence Weiner)
Ships at Sea, Sailors and Shoes (with Lawrence Weiner
and the Persuasions)

THE YEAR
BEFORE THE FLOOD

A STORY OF NEW ORLEANS

Ned Sublette

Lawrence Hill Books

Library of Congress Cataloging-in-Publication Data

Sublette, Ned, 1951-

   The year before the flood : music, murder, and a homecoming in New Orleans :
a memoir / by Ned Sublette.

     p. cm.

   Includes bibliographical references and index.

   ISBN 978-1-55652-824-8 (hardcover : alk. paper)

1. Popular music—Louisiana—New Orleans—History and criticism. 2. Musicology—
Louisiana—New Orleans. 3. Musicians—Louisiana—New Orleans. 4. Music—
Social aspects—Louisiana—New Orleans—History. 5. Music—Political aspects—
Louisiana—New Orleans—History. 6. New Orleans (La.)—Social conditions. I. Title.

ML3477.8.N44S83 2009
780.9763'35—dc22

                                                                    2009011472

Cover design: Monica Baziuk

Cover photographs: top © Ned Sublette; bottom © Jennifer Zdon/America 24-7/
   Getty Images

Interior design: Scott Rattray

All interior photos by Ned Sublette. Historical images of Comus were photographed
at Tulane University Special Collections.

Published by Lawrence Hill Books
An imprint of Chicago Review Press, Incorporated
814 North Franklin Street
Chicago, Illinois 60610
ISBN 978-1-55652-824-8
Printed in the United States of America
5 4 3 2 1

for Constance

CONTENTS

INTRODUCTION

———————

I knew it was going to happen. I just didn't know when.

On August 26, 2005, I was at home in New York City, working on what turned out to be an early version of this book.

By Saturday morning, August 27, the forecast models had converged. The hurricane was Category Five, headed straight for New Orleans. It was easy to see what was coming. And not because I'm clairvoyant.

Everyone knew what was going to happen.

Not the details. But in the broad outline, we all knew it.

Three weeks before, when I photographed the exterior of Fats Domino's pink-tile-and-yellow-brick house on Caffin Avenue in the Lower Ninth Ward, I didn't know it was about to go underwater, or that my childhood hero's white Steinway grand would be lying upside down in six inches of filth when the water receded, or that Fats would have a diabetic crisis in triage, hallucinating that he was about to go onstage after being rescued by boat from the top of his flooded house.[1] But I knew I was seeing something imperiled.

"You described it to me before it happened," said my friend Peter Gordon. During the weeks after New Orleans was flooded, people said things like this to me repeatedly. When pianist/bandleader Arturo O'Farrill visited New Orleans in spring 2005, I took him to see Rebirth Brass Band uptown at the Maple Leaf. The following year, after the flood, he reminded me that I'd talked about the inevitability of a major disaster as we drove around New Orleans that night. "They're all in denial," he remembers I said to him.

My description had always included what was obvious to everyone in New Orleans: the poor would be left behind to drown.

Everyone knew it. But especially, the poor knew it. Part of the fearsome nihilism of New Orleans was the awareness on the part of the city's poor that they were, and had always been, so expendable that they would be abandoned when it started to rain. But fatalistic as they were, even the poor of

ix

New Orleans might not have realized what might happen if they survived a catastrophic flood.

They were left to dehydrate and putrefy. They were abandoned and imprisoned for days without food or water in what was more than once described by those who experienced the ordeal as a modern-day slave ship. Rescuers were actively kept away while those who remained in the city were treated as dangerous insurgents. New Orleanians' guns were confiscated in a house-to-house search, and finally, those remaining in the city were expelled, at gunpoint if necessary.

In a federally organized airlift, those with nowhere to go were dispersed around the country with one-way tickets to destinations not of their choosing. Children affected by the disaster were enrolled in schools in forty-six different states, except for ten thousand or so child evacuees who were not enrolled in school anywhere.[2]

The programs that were supposed to help the evacuees return and rebuild were set up in such a way as to make it as difficult as possible for them to collect the promised aid. People who lived in the Magnolia, St. Bernard, Lafitte, or Calliope projects saw the homes they had left in a hurry closed up tight—not boarded up, but sealed with lead shields—and bulldozed, as the Speaker of the U.S. House of Representatives had recommended be done for the whole city.

"It was as if all of us were already pronounced dead," said one Convention Center survivor.[3]

They had been pronounced dead long ago.

———————

At the age of fifty-three, after an absence of forty-four years, I found myself unexpectedly living back in Louisiana, a place I'd made my younger self forget, for a one-year dream job.

Nobody who's serious about American music can turn down a year in New Orleans. I hadn't spent time on a college campus in thirty years, but there I was with a fellowship at Tulane University. I had an office, a part-time graduate assistant, and no obligation other than to conduct my historical research. It beat the hell out of singing in barrooms, which is what I used to do. My project was to research musical connections among Louisiana, Cuba, and Saint-Domingue (later known as Haiti) in the eighteenth and nineteenth centuries—a key piece of the making of American music, right there. New Orleans offered the logical continuation of the work I had been doing with Cuban music.

But I also had a personal reason for wanting to go back. I lived in Louisiana until I was nine, and I'd never come to terms with having lived there or with having moved away.

Constance was excited to live in this place she'd been reading and hearing about all her life but never experienced, and she was eager to get out of our tiny, rent-stabilized, 9/11-dusted lower Manhattan tenement apartment for a little while. She's my secret weapon from North Dakota. For the over thirty years we've been a couple, she's been my history teacher and my best critic. She published three novels before I ever thought about writing a book.[4]

We would be in New Orleans only ten months, so we acted as if it wouldn't be there tomorrow. We had no idea how right that attitude was. We couldn't know that we were scrutinizing, day by day, the last year the city would be whole. All year long, we tried to engrave New Orleans into our brains. Meanwhile, we were pulled into the rhythm of the city's year.

I started writing this book over Thanksgiving weekend of 2004. It remained unfinished when we returned to Manhattan—which we did a little ahead of schedule, in May 2005, for reasons I'll narrate later. Then, from our refuge, we experienced the horror of August 29 and its aftermath by Internet, radio, and telephone.

For two months after the flood, I was unable to do anything but follow the news. Then I went back to the beginning and restarted the project. It was like building a new house with bricks from an older one, but at the heart of this book is the book I was going to write: a memoir that tells the story of our year—what happened, what I learned—in that unique and problematic city. Some of this book was written in 2004, some of it in 2009, and some of it in between. I don't always know whether to use present or past tense.

This book is about things New Orleanians maybe took for granted, and non–New Orleanians mostly didn't know about. Beyond that, it traces an arc of history as I've lived it, from the days of the legally enforced segregation of the entire population of the South into two castes known as "races" to the failure of 2005. Along the way, I have to stop and open up windows of history, because you can't talk about all this without making reference to things that happened long ago. In following the multiple threads that wind around this complicated place, I hope the reader will have some patience with me.

Part I, by way of introducing your narrator, is mostly about my boyhood in Louisiana, though not in New Orleans. Part II is the story of the last year New Orleans was whole, the way we experienced it. Part I and Part II (up through chapter 11) were drafted before the flood, though substantially revised afterward, and all but the end of Part II was already projected when the flood knocked the city down. Part III, which takes place after the failure of the levees, was unimaginable until then.

In September 2008, a friend in New Orleans said to me, "I'm just now getting back to what I was doing in 2005." I could say much the same, and I don't even live there. Before the flood, I had thought I would have this book drafted by Christmas 2005. Instead it was November 2008. That's how much life got turned upside down.

Why I was summoned to witness the great American music city up close just before it was scattered to the four winds is a question I can't answer, but I feel obliged to testify. I don't claim to be the guy who knows the most about New Orleans, and I don't claim to speak for New Orleans, but I speak for the New Orleans that's in me. This book is necessarily subjective, because New Orleans demands a point of view. If you've been there, much less lived there, you have your own New Orleans, which I hope you'll recognize somehow in the shattered funhouse mirror of ours.

THE YEAR
BEFORE THE FLOOD

PART I

NACKATISH

1

JUMP JIM CROW

As time passes, people, even of the South, will begin to
wonder how it was possible that their ancestors ever fought
for or justified institutions which acknowledged the right of
property in man.

—Ulysses S. Grant, *Personal Memoirs*[1]

My first grade teacher explained to us why we shouldn't put coins
in our mouths.

"It might have been in the hands of a"—she held up her
hands like they were diseased, and contorted her face—"sick person."

Pause.

"It might have been in the hands of a *colored person*."

We lived a couple of other places before we moved to Natchitoches, but
I don't remember them. I learned to talk in Natchitoches, and to read, and to
tune the radio, in that order. I came to consciousness there, in the northwestern part of Louisiana, sixty-eight miles south-southeast of Shreveport.

As the locals never tire of informing you, Natchitoches, founded in 1714,
is four years older than New Orleans. The town's name, that of a now extinct
group of Indians, is pronounced *Nackatish*—a terrible trick to play on a kid
learning to spell, courtesy of French colonists who tried to write down an
Indian name.

I was born in Lubbock, Texas, where my mother's parents lived. My mom was a flatlander from West Texas, and my dad was a hillbilly from Arkansas. He had polio in the big epidemic when he was a child, and his right arm was withered, so despite his energy he couldn't make a living doing manual work or go into the military. Instead he earned a Ph.D. in freshwater biology, though his brother and two sisters never finished high school. He met my mother in graduate school at the University of Oklahoma, while she was getting a master's in biology. On July 8, 1951, a decent year after they got married, I was the first biological result.

My parents got in on the ground floor of the postwar boom, when higher education was a growth industry. American universities expanded like never before or since, and if you worked hard you could go to college. Part of the broad middle-classification of America that took place in the mid-twentieth century, it represented a dignified form of upward mobility, one that let a country boy grow up to own a home in a small town, buy a new car every few years, and raise four kids. All across the country, children of farmers became professors, bureaucrats, professionals, businessmen, homeowners. As the determination to beat the Russians intensified, science in a small-town college was a good place to be. Compared with what my dad's father had to do raising his family in Arkansas during the Great Depression, it was the life of Riley. One of my first memories of Grandfather Sublette is of him coming home with squirrels he'd shot, and Grandmother fixing them for dinner. They didn't have to do that in the 1950s, but they did it anyway, because that was who they were.

I was born six years after the death of Franklin D. Roosevelt, who, prodded by mass movements, was forced to create a social safety net to save capitalism in its moment of crisis. The Depression had radicalized the American public, which was as close to revolution as it's ever gotten. Then the country went to war against fascism and racism, which cranked up the economy. My generation, the so-called postwar baby boom, enjoyed the benefits. I attended free public school, went to an almost-free state university from which I graduated debt-free, and drank water out of the tap. Income taxes were progressive: Elvis Presley and Fats Domino had to pay 91 percent of their taxable income over four hundred thousand dollars.

My childhood coincided with the United States of America's peak of prosperity. I was born ten years after Henry Luce declared it the "American Century." In the interim, World War II had trashed the United States' major economic competitors. We had the natural resources of a good chunk of the North American continent to exploit, a literate workforce, and a drastically expanded middle class of consumers. We had the reserve currency, did much of the world's manufacturing, produced oil (I can remember seeing gasoline for under twenty cents a gallon), and raised vast surpluses of food on our rich farmland.

The United States' economy grew by an average of almost 4 percent a year between 1948, before I was born, and 1973, when I was twenty-two.[2] Economically, politically, and, whenever it was deemed necessary, militarily, we ruled. When I was a toddler, our new Central Intelligence Agency began destabilizing other countries' governments (Iran when I was two, Guatemala just before I turned three), while denying it was doing so, nor did the newspapers of the time suggest it, nor would Americans have believed it. As a nation, we were as united as never before or again after the effort to defeat Hitler and Tojo (never mind that Stalin and the Soviet Army did the heavy lifting on Hitler).

But there was one group of people to whom this prosperity, feeling of unity, and sense of nation were not extended, and they made up a sizable portion of our town. Laws and force of custom divided Natchitoches, and the state of Louisiana, and the entire former self-declared nation of the South, into two color-coded castes.

Even in slavery days, "white" and "black" children might have personal contact, but in the South of my childhood we were kept as separate as humanly possible. We literally didn't know each other. I lived until I was nine in an approximately half-black town without ever having any social contact with a black kid. I don't mean I didn't have any as close friends. I mean I never had a *single conversation* with an African American child. As people say when they talk about those days, that was just the way it was. I can remember having it explained to me that no, their color didn't rub off when they touched things.

The polite way of describing southern society in those days is to say that it was segregated. But it is also fair, if less polite, to say that it was a white supremacist society. The program of the Ku Klux Klan had been implemented. African Americans were overtly, legally, literally second-class citizens.

When Mrs. Harrison asked us if we knew why our school would always remain all white, I hazarded a guess. "Because the Negroes have schools of their own?"

"Yes, they do," she replied, "and they're just as good as ours!"

———

Bullshit, they were just as good as ours.

She probably believed it. A lot of white people lived in fantasyland. But the push to integrate schools didn't come because black people loved being around white people so much that they wanted to come hang out with them. It was because if there were two separate school systems, the black one would get less of every resource. In 1950, "colored" schools in Shreveport had no electricity, and the students used outhouses.[3]

Which is not to say that no educating took place; African Americans who came up in that system remember heroic teachers. Jerome Smith, born in New Orleans in 1939, told me: "We had the worst books that you can imagine, but we had such dedicated educators that it gave us a kind of readiness. . . . We didn't recognize that [at the time], but in the years that followed, we had a foundation." Not everyone was so lucky, and the deck was stacked against African American children getting an education. Overcrowding was the norm for their schools; the Macarty school in New Orleans's Ninth Ward had 2,536 children in a building designed for 1,200. No wonder Fats Domino dropped out of that school in the fourth grade.

No, Mrs. Harrison explained, the reason Northwestern Elementary would always remain white was that the nuns who deeded it to the state had included that as one of the conditions.

Well, that settled it. The deal had been cut long before we were born.

Our white-forever school was a lovely place. Located on the campus of Northwestern State College, where my dad taught, it had expansive, handsome grounds, with a long, sloping hill that led down toward Lake Chaplin, and big airy classrooms with a piano in every one.

We were raised with the southern ideal of the innocent, indolent child. With its pretensions to aristocracy and perhaps a French aversion to exercise, Louisiana was never big on making kids do calisthenics, so for physical education we played Drop the Handkerchief and singing games. I was what was later called hyperactive—I always had a rhythm, or a rhyme, or a song going on—and visibly bored. The class seemed to work on the alphabet all through the first grade.

My parents, being teachers, had taught me to read and do arithmetic at home, so I was considered a gifted child when I started school. This was surely, presumed my biologist parents, the result of good genes, though I think it was more the amount of attention and care they gave me. It was the era of IQ tests, and I was given batteries of them. When I was seven, in some kind of educational experiment that my parents must have had a hand in promoting, I was placed five grades ahead of my level, into a seventh-grade class, for two weeks. (Elementary schools in Natchitoches included grades one through seven.) I found I could handle the academics pretty well, not because I was a genius but because they weren't that tough. Socially, however, I wasn't prepared to be in a roomful of seventh-graders all day.

That was the year *Attack of the 50 Foot Woman* came out—where is this kind of inspiration today, when our cinema needs it?—and I felt myself surrounded by fifty-foot women. There's nothing as mysterious to a seven-year-old boy as a passel of twelve-year-old girls. To further heighten the eroticism of the experience, they had portable transistor radios, and could summon up rock 'n' roll at recess. I could read better than they could, but so what? They had something else going on.

One of my enduring memories of Natchitoches dates from that surreal stint among the giants and giantesses of the seventh grade. The social studies class was instructed to break up into groups and write, and act out, scenes that were to dramatize . . .

A slave auction.

They had us play *slave auction* in social studies class.

I'm not sure what the purpose of that exercise was. But what it demonstrated for me was that some people lived between the piety of knowing that slavery was bad and the desire of living it once again. It proved something I already knew, even at that age: the white South *loved* to reminisce about slavery days.

Since I wasn't a bona fide seventh-grader, I was an auditor for this event, not a participant. No one interpreted the slave roles. No one would have wanted to. The slaves were imaginary. One kid, playing the role of an auctioneer, read haltingly from the script he had laboriously written himself:

"I. Don't. Like. To. Break. Up. These. Families," he read.

"But. What. Can. I. Do?

"It's. My. Job."

I've been a library rat all my life, and though I've escaped into places where books don't go, sooner or later I always find myself back in the library. My first was the Natchitoches Parish Library, where my parents took me regularly. (Different in everything, Louisiana has parishes instead of counties.) It was a new facility, as pretty as my school, as pretty as the town, with comfortable modern Scandinavian-style blond-wood furniture—there were no other chairs like that anywhere else I ever went—and picture windows overlooking the Cane River Lake. They had big wooden stereoscopes that you could play with, with a vast collection of stereographic photo cards for them—three-dimensional pictures of wondrous long-ago people and places. There was a reading program for children: for every book you read, your clown got another shiny-sticker balloon.

Guess who couldn't go into the library.

In many southern towns, libraries were the first public facilities to desegregate, but back when my clown was getting his balloons, if black people wanted books from the public library they had to get a white person to check them out. All across the South this was the case. It presupposed that any black person who was on the ball enough to read a book had a white sponsor. In some places, African Americans could go to the back door and the library's maid would get the books for them (which meant that she was functioning as a librarian but paid as a maid).[4] They couldn't go to museums. They couldn't take the undergraduate biology course my father taught, let alone get a Ph.D. like he had. Black people were born into a system that was deliberately contrived to keep them poor, ignorant, professionally disadvantaged, and politically disfranchised.

Natchitoches was at the southern end of the tristate corner region known as the Ark-La-Tex, a zone of Confederate nostalgia. Many of our townspeople seemed quite clear that the South was going to rise again. One of my classmates—I'll call him Donnie—spent recess every day running at top speed down the hill with his Stars and Bars flying, followed by the other members of his gang, the Rebels. Donnie wasn't very good in school, but he was a natural leader. He was a good-looking kid, with a full head of dirty blond hair, and even when he was in the second grade he had seventh-graders running with him. Donnie didn't say *Negro*.

I had my own gang, the Texas Rangers—asserting my Texanhood, I guess, knowing even then I didn't belong in Natchitoches. It consisted of me and one other kid, who lived by the cottonseed plant. His clothes smelled strongly of cottonseed, which had to be crushed and deodorized as part of the oil-making process. Not like the smell you might get pouring Wesson Oil over a salad, but an industrial-strength smell. Nobody lived that close to the cottonseed plant if they could help it.

In many southern towns, the stinky old cottonseed plant was located in the colored part of town. You could smell it across a broad area. In Natchitoches, it wasn't all that far from the tiny black business district, where black folks from the country would come on Saturdays. Researching this book, I learned something I didn't know at the time: that the black commons, on Horn Street, was popularly known as . . .

The Ape Yard.

The name was presumably put on it by whites, but black people called it the Ape Yard too.[5] As we say when we talk about those days, that was just how it was.

––––––

Our principal at Northwestern Elementary was a man and all the teachers but one were women, as if that were the natural order of things. My father's few female college teaching colleagues were quite openly, and as a matter of course, paid less than the men. When I found that out, I asked my father why, and he explained it to me: they don't have to support a family like men do.

My second-grade teacher, Mrs. Gimbert (pronounced *Zhawm*-bear), was a sweetheart, almost like a second mother to me, and I never heard her say anything racist. I didn't get along so well with my third-grade teacher, Mrs. Mayeaux (pronounced *Miz My-yoo*, because French vowel combinations, whatever they are, tend to reduce to "oo" in Louisiana, as in *beaucoup* becoming *bookoo*).

Our only male teacher was the music instructor, Mr. Westbrook, who had a hypnotic singing voice. His visits to our class captivated me: he came into the classroom, took out a pitchpipe and played a tone, and had us sing a melody on the syllable, *lu, lu, lu*. His daughters were named Melodye and Harmony. (He had a third musical daughter whose name I don't remember, but it wasn't Rhythm.) Melodye was in my class, and I was entranced by her: she could *sing*. By then singing, for which I exhibited no talent at all, was fully ingrained in my consciousness as a mystical act. I was astounded when the three little Westbrook sisters appeared on a television show in Alexandria singing "May the Good Lord Bless and Keep You." I didn't know real people could appear on television.

Music was an integral part of our school day. The nineteenth-century stage repertoire was still current, so we all knew songs like "Polly Wolly Doodle," "The Blue Tail Fly," and "Old Dan Tucker." Our education included dancing in the classroom, pantomiming as we sang: "Jump down, turn around, pick a bale of cotton."

And Miz My-yoo taught us to Jump Jim Crow.

We kids had no idea that this was one of countless variants of the foundation song of blackface minstrelsy. Nor was I aware, at the age of eight, of the term *Jim Crow* to refer to laws and customs of racial preference, but even after I found out about that meaning, I still heard the tune in my head when I heard people in the civil rights movement talk about Jim Crow.

Miz My-yoo was none too young, but she bent down, leaping around and singing, as all us white kids bent down and hopped around the room, wheeling about and turning about with her just so, singing:

Jump!
Jump!
Jump Jim Crow!

2

ARE YOU A YANKEE OR ARE YOU A REBEL?

I remember my parents saying that people in Natchitoches didn't want to know you if your grandparents weren't from there. Which, I realized, meant me too.

Natchitoches was where we lived, but it wasn't really our home. We didn't belong there, though I didn't have a clue how to belong anywhere else. Between my parents' two different ways of talking, I spoke Southern, but not the same dialect as the kids in school. Some of them thought I was a Yankee, though I'd never been farther outside Louisiana than Arkansas and Texas. I remember being asked: *are you a Yankee or are you a Rebel?* I was neither.

We never spent Christmas in Natchitoches. To see grandparents, aunts, uncles, cousins, we drove hundreds of miles every holiday. One of the less humane features of life on the land-grant university circuit is that you rarely get a job in the community you come from, so you have to move to a small town with your family and live there as an outsider. Then, if you change jobs, your family has to pull up stakes. College brats don't have the luxury of roots.

A consequence of that academic system was that, throughout the small college towns of the United States, faculty members tended not to take much of a role in local politics or civic direction but remained bystanders, as befit outsiders. This meant that a town's better-educated citizenry was often not part of the town in any functional way. They were witnesses to the local political culture rather than participants. No one was more despised in a college town than the loudmouth professor from somewhere else who thought he knew better than the locals and might be moving along one of these days anyway. Certainly my parents stayed away from political activity. Challenging white supremacy was not their brief, nor would it have occurred to them to do so. Nor was it good for a professor's career to get a reputation as a kook.

I had just turned nine when we moved away from Natchitoches in August 1960. It was one of the worst days of my life, to this day. I was leaving the only home I knew: my town, my school, my nine-year-old girlfriends, the lushest green landscape there is, and the radio station that played Fats, Elvis, Johnny Horton, Brook Benton, Conway Twitty, Jim Reeves, and that song called "Mojo Workout," which I never heard again. I felt like I was leaving myself behind. I wept bitterly as we drove all the way across Texas to El Paso, where there is not a drop of water and nothing is green.

It did help that Marty Robbins's "El Paso" was #1 at the time, but only a little. One thing El Paso has is vistas, and as we drove around the scenic Rim Road at night with the twinkling city lights below, I kept looking for Falina's café. My birthplace of Texas had reclaimed me, and I was now a westerner, no longer a southerner. I didn't allow myself to think about Natchitoches after we moved away. I never corresponded with the kids I had known there and never heard from any of them again. I buried it. Did I ever really ride in a boat through a swamp? I knew I had, but in a place where spring meant sandstorms instead of a riot of flowers, it seemed like some other lifetime. The kids in my new town had no idea what I was talking about.

As I got older, the memory of the long-gone place faded into the memory of the long-gone time. The distant weirdness of Louisiana melted into the distant weirdness of the '50s, and I couldn't separate them out on the rare occasion when some childhood image crossed my mind. I was trying to hurtle forward, not look back.

Everywhere I've gone since then, I've always felt a little like a fly on the wall, watching the people who really live there. But that had its advantages. With it came a kind of freedom. I didn't feel much bound by the local pressures and I didn't have to believe the local lies. I knew that if you moved somewhere else it would all be different. Wherever I was, I was only passing through.

My dismay at moving to El Paso notwithstanding, 1960 was a good time to get the hell out of Louisiana, and not just because Dad got a better job. The South was in an uproar over school desegregation, and the next few years were going to be tense.

School is where the battle of the color line is fought. Louisiana didn't get a public school system at all until 1841, twenty-nine years after statehood, and then no black pupils were allowed to attend it, not even free people of color.[1] When schools were desegregated in 1871, whites immediately expanded the system of private schools from ten to over a hundred, generating a major pushback against the thoroughly rejected idea of Reconstruction. Five years later, Reconstruction was definitively overthown in the so-called Revolution of 1876 when the presidential election was stolen by Republican Rutherford B. Hayes, who lost the popular vote to Democrat Samuel Tilden by a margin of 47.9 percent to 51 percent. In the resulting Hayes-Tilden compromise, the South accepted Hayes as president in exchange for his agreement to withdraw federal troops from the South, ending Reconstruction.

With that compromise, the Ku Klux Klan achieved victory. The Republican party, which had been the open target of a sustained terrorist campaign throughout the South, split between "Black and Tan" Republicans and "Lily White" Republicans. (The Republican Party of the twentieth century was heir to the latter. Any reference to "the party of Lincoln" by the party of Bush is bogus; the ultra-reactionary Republican party of my adult lifetime shares a name with the radical Republican party of then, nothing more.) Schools in Louisiana were resegregated immediately, and the South entered the grim period of black peonage sardonically remembered by the minstrelic name of Jim Crow as successive court decisions whittled away the federal government's supervisory role over civil rights.

Plessy v. Ferguson, the 1896 Supreme Court decision that turned on the refusal of a not-visibly-black New Orleans man to ride in the colored section of a railroad car, established separate but equal—"the tag line that haunts American democracy," in Felipe Smith's words[2]—as law. It was a transparent lie: if society was to be divided into a superior and an inferior caste, each using separate public facilities, then the facility for the inferior caste was by definition inferior. As Keith Weldon Medley points out, by the time Louis Armstrong (b. 1901) was growing up, there was no public school at all for blacks in Louisiana past the fifth grade.[3]

A suit aimed at desegregating Louisiana schools, *Bush v. Orleans Parish*, was filed in 1952. It languished in the courts, subject to literally every delay and obstruction its opponents could imagine. At that time, school segregation was mandatory by state law in seventeen southern states and the District of Columbia and was permitted in four western states.[4] But despite the obstacles to African American education, there was a law school at Howard University, founded during Reconstruction; its 1933 graduate Thurgood Marshall, together with other black lawyers, mounted a successful challenge in the case remembered as *Brown v. Board of Education of Topeka*. On May 14, 1954, the Supreme Court's decision in that case finally made desegregation the law of the land.

A few years ago while visiting Buffalo, New York, I met a woman who had been going to high school in Tioga, Louisiana, an unincorporated town in Rapides Parish not all that far from Natchitoches, when the *Brown* decision was announced. Anne Bertholf remembers her civics teacher going around the room asking students what they thought about the decision. When it was her turn to answer, she said, "It seems to me to be only fair."

The teacher answered, "I always knew you was a nigger-lover."[5]

Those words burned into Anne's brain, complete with pronoun-verb disagreement. They brought her a kind of peace, in a perverse way. She recalled the episode to me, more than fifty years after the fact: "I said to myself, 'I'm out of here. I'm *so* out of here.'" And when she could be gone, she was.

The southern states not only refused to abide by the Supreme Court's decision requiring them to integrate their schools, but passed a forest of measures to thwart it. Schools in Little Rock were forcibly integrated in 1957 despite the efforts of Arkansas governor Orval Faubus, who made headlines worldwide by ordering the National Guard to keep black students out of Little Rock Central High, in defiance of President Eisenhower. It was the most open challenge to federal sovereignty since the so-called Battle of Liberty Place, the 1874 overthrow of the Louisiana government by mob action. I remember seeing "Faubus for President" bumper stickers in Natchitoches, but I was six, so I had him confused with a character in *Pogo*, my favorite comic strip, whose malapropisms seemed to me like daily reality.

At the start of the fall 1960 school term, six years after *Brown*, there were no integrated public schools at all in Alabama, Georgia, Louisiana, Mississippi, and South Carolina. Five other states had fewer than 1 percent of black pupils in public schools with whites.[6] Many southern schools proceeding with integration were going on a grade-a-year basis, which would have meant waiting until 1972 to graduate the first black student.

Judge Skelly V. Wright made it happen. Wright grew up in the Irish Channel of New Orleans—on a white block, next to a black block, in the characteristic checkerboard pattern of the city. For many Americans, to say nothing of southerners, a trip abroad is an eye-opener, and after serving in World War II and being posted to London he began to have a larger view. As Jack Bass tells it, after Wright returned to New Orleans he had an epiphany while attending a Christmas Eve party at the U.S. Attorney's office. Across the street, visible through the windows, he saw another Christmas party going on at the Lighthouse for the Blind. "He watched the blind people climb the steps to the second floor. There, someone met them. He watched a blind Negro led to a party for blacks at the rear of the building. A white blind person was led to a separate party."[7] It was real-life absurdist theater: blind people being segregated by color at a Christmas party. Skelly Wright couldn't get it out of his head. Named a federal judge by President Truman in 1949, in 1956 he ruled in *Bush*, ordering Louisiana schools to desegregate. When nothing had been done four years later, he ordered an end to the delays. The New Orleans school board was thus caught between a federal order to desegregate and a state government determined to prevent it. For political reasons—that is, to avoid embarrassing the Justice Department, which would have to back Judge Wright up—enforcement was delayed until after the presidential election of 1960.

I had never seen my mother so offended as that day in 1959 when she received a black plastic comb in the mail with Governor Earl Long's name on it in little gold letters. The sitting governor of Louisiana—"Uncle Earl," they called him—had apparently sent each of the state's women a comb so they could be reminded of him every time they combed their hair. My mother could buy her own comb, thank you.

Long's method of getting votes was to give largesse to the poor. It was the legacy of his assassinated brother Huey "Kingfish" Long, whose motto was "Share Our Wealth." Uncle Earl sent everyone over the age of sixty-five in the state a fifty-dollar monthly check. He counted on the black vote, so he was not in favor of disfranchising black people. "In Louisiana," A. J. Liebling wrote in the *New Yorker* in 1960, "there is a substantial Negro vote—about a hundred and fifty thousand—that no candidate can afford to discourage privately or to solicit publicly."[8]

Later that year, Uncle Earl was involuntarily committed to a mental institution. As Liebling memorably reported, he was hustled away to sedation on a National Guard plane after he shouted on the legislature floor at the hardcore racist state senator Willie Rainach, who was trying to curtail black voting, "You got to recognize that niggers is human beings!"[9] He had to be crazy, they thought, to say something like that. After Long managed to spring himself from the asylum, before embarking on a rest cure of Texas racetracks, he told voters, "I thought I owed it to you to come look you in the eye and let as many of you see me and see I'm livin' and I'm not nuts! If I'm nuts, I've been nuts all my life!"[10] There is something comical about all this in the telling of it, but it wasn't funny to live through, and especially not for African Americans.

Ineligible to succeed himself as governor, Long campaigned anyway ("For all the people / not just a handful" was his slogan), hoping to get around the term limit by resigning just before the end of his term and allowing the lieutenant governor to succeed him briefly. For a time it seemed as though it might work. The actual gubernatorial election in Louisiana was a formality, since there were barely enough Republicans in Louisiana in 1960 to fill federal positions for the Eisenhower/Nixon administration. The real election was the hotly contested Democratic primary, in which the specter of integration loomed large.

I watched the gubernatorial campaign in the *Shreveport Times*, and I remember the ad—I think it was Jimmie Davis's, but I'm not sure: "Every child deserves a hot school lunch . . . FREE." Free lunch, that clichéd bugaboo of neocon economists, is a longstanding Louisiana tradition—invented in New Orleans, so they say, when bars began serving lunch back in the nineteenth century.[11] Lunch was almost free at school already, anyway. Nobody brought a lunchbox to school in Natchitoches, because we were served a hot lunch that only cost a nickel.

My parents didn't think much of Jimmie Davis. They knew what I didn't, that the pious gospel singer, who had already been governor once back in the '40s, was running with the support of the racist White Citizens Council. Born in 1899, Davis had first become known in the late '30s, crooning on KWKH out of Shreveport. As a country-blues singer in the Jimmie Rodgers style, Davis recorded some raunchy, comic titles ("Tom Cat and Pussy Blues"), but he was best known as the composer of "You Are My Sunshine," which he did not actually compose but purchased, perhaps improved, copyrighted, and collected a king's ransom of royalties on.[12] His recording of it was a million-seller in 1940, and it did much to get him elected governor of Louisiana in 1944.

In that election, Davis campaigned up and down the state singing "You Are My Sunshine" backed by a ten-piece band. After he was elected, he put the band on the state payroll.[13] During his governorship he had a #1 country record, "There's a New Moon over My Shoulder," and he spent part of his gubernatorial term in Hollywood starring as himself in the Phil Karlson–directed Monogram Picture *Louisiana*, an autobiographical musical that had its gala 1947 premiere in Shreveport. After leaving office in 1948, Davis continued his musical career, largely switching over to religious music and releasing a plethora of sacred LPs on Decca.

In 1959, Jimmie Davis came back from the political dead to run for governor again. Following a vicious primary, the January 9, 1960, Democratic gubernatorial runoff was between Davis and deLesseps "Chep" Morrison, who was making his third run for governor. Davis was a Protestant from northern Louisiana; Morrison, a Catholic who had for fifteen years been mayor of New Orleans and was Long's longtime political enemy. Both promised to maintain segregation. Davis rode his Protestant credentials hard in the campaign, singing hymns in a wide variety of the state's churches with his own traveling male chorus for backup, and was supported by the *New Orleans Times-Picayune*.[14] Long ultimately threw his support to Davis, as did Willie Rainach, and Davis was elected.

Once in office, the Singing Governor convened an emergency meeting of the state legislature to respond to Judge Wright's desegregation order, and signed a twenty-nine-bill package of antidesegregation measures on November 8, the day of the presidential election. The strongest was an "interposition" law providing that "no federal judge, marshal or other officer of the federal government shall have the power to enforce school integration orders in Louisiana," with a mandatory penalty of six months in jail and a thousand-dollar fine.

These measures placed Louisiana one step short of secession. There was already a law on the books that allowed Davis to close the entire public school system of Louisiana if any one school was integrated.[15] Another law abolished compulsory school attendance in the event of desegregation. Judge Wright intervened five times to keep the state from taking over the New Orleans schools from the local school board or stripping the board members of their powers. He reinstated the superintendent of schools and the school system's legal counsel after the legislature passed a bill to discharge them. In short, he called Jimmie Davis's bluff, issuing a restraining order against him, the entire legislature, and several state officials.

On November 14, 1960, six days after the Kennedy/Johnson ticket carried Louisiana, four black first-graders in New Orleans's Ninth Ward started attending previously white-only public schools. One hundred thirty-seven children had applied to transfer, but only five of them met the school board's seventeen-point criteria, and one of the five had second thoughts about going through with it.[16] Hoping to minimize the potential for trouble, the board selected no boys. That put the girls on the front lines, leaving Leona Tate, Gail Etienne, and Tessie Prevost to be escorted to the McDonogh 19 Elementary School and back by U.S. marshals while Ruby Bridges was escorted to and from the William Frantz Elementary School. From the noise and the chanting (*Two! Four! Six! Eight! We don't want to integrate!*), "I thought it was Mardi Gras," Bridges recalled in 1995.[17]

The next day, at a Citizens Council rally in the New Orleans Municipal Auditorium, the oil-rich, arch-segregationist St. Bernard Parish district attorney Leander Perez told an audience of five thousand: "Don't wait for your daughters to be raped by these Congolese. Don't wait until the burrheads are forced into your schools. Do something about it now!"[18] A skit showing white children in blackface kissing other white children dramatized the stakes. The day after that, on November 16, a mob of whites variously estimated at between one thousand and three thousand, mostly teenage truants, tried to stage a mass march to the school board's building, broke up into small groups, and ran through the business district of New Orleans trashing cars, throwing bricks at buses, and assaulting blacks. They were unhindered by New Orleans police, though Mayor Morrison had cracked down on black demonstrations. That night, gangs of black people beat up whites.

At the schoolhouse door, a group of white mothers maintained a vigil. They spat, cursed, and threw eggs at the little black girls on their way into school and again coming out. They held up black dolls in coffins, and acquired a nickname: the Cheerleaders. Several hundred people, mostly women and children, gathered daily to watch the spectacle, oxygenated by the presence of TV cameras. The mothers stayed at their posts all year. After witnessing the scene, John Steinbeck used it to give a dark ending to *Travels with Charley*, his valedictory to the United States, in which he described them as "crazy actors playing to a crazy audience."[19]

Norman Rockwell, the magazine-cover illustrator whose stock-in-trade was heartwarming images of apple-cheeked families at home and hearth in a benign, loving America, created his most distinguished picture by painting the image of tiny Ruby Bridges in profile, in her starched white dress with her ribbon in her hair, walking upright with dignity, schoolbooks in hand, preceded and followed by the torsos of four tall white men escorting her. Bridges was the only student in her class all year long. Her teacher, Barbara Henry, was from Massachusetts, the very kind of person the rednecks had been complaining about since Reconstruction. The legislature froze the funds for the two schools so that their faculty and staff—still employed, though without pupils—wouldn't get paid.

Not the least pathetic thing about all this was that it was a struggle to get into the public schools of Louisiana, which had been inadequate all along. Supporting them had never been popular with taxpayers. The rich paid for their children to go to private schools, and they let the politicians know they didn't want to pay for public ones. With resources hard to get, the expense of maintaining a double public school system worked to the detriment of both. For that matter, all public facilities had to be duplicated, at double expense. There were two of everything in the South, even two delivery rooms in the hospitals, so that "black" and "white" southerners were literally separated at birth. But most hospitals didn't admit African Americans, period.

Legislatures around the South considered shutting down their public school systems entirely; Prince Edward County in Virginia did, and in Louisiana, St. Helena Parish residents voted to close theirs in 1961. "Attorney General Kennedy has finally revealed the real purpose of forced racial integration," explained Armand Duvio, president of New Orleans's Ninth Ward Private School Association, in September of that year, "the complete control over the lives of our children as in Russia. Because the parents . . . refused to submit them to the Communistic plan of forced integration, the federal government has finally shown its ugly hand by attempting to force our children to comply with its plan for their lives. Mr. Kennedy says, in effect, that our children are no longer ours, but now become property of the federal government. How much further can a tyrannical federal government go?"[20]

Ironically, that was the same message the Central Intelligence Agency was at that moment saturating Cuba with, across the Gulf of Mexico from New Orleans. Its new fifty-thousand-watt Radio Swan, broadcasting at 1160 from an island off the coast of Honduras and audible in much of the United States (in Spanish, and I used to tune it in), warned: The Communist government of Fidel Castro wants to take your children away from you! They want to make them the property of the state! To send them to Russia for indoctrination! They'll be fornicating with *Negroes* and you'll have colored grandchildren! They might not have actually said that last one, but it was implicit. In Cuba, where the school system was almost entirely private and Catholic, those propaganda broadcasts triggered what is remembered as "Peter Pan": the panicked flight of some thirteen thousand white children to Miami and points beyond without their parents, as wards of the Catholic church.

Of course, in Cuba there actually *were* Communists running things. But even they weren't taking children away from their parents, nor did Che Guevara have designs on Louisiana. It was true that in the dark years of Jim Crow the Communists had been the only ones in the United States to insist on full "racial" equality. And it was true that the need to convince the newly independent nations of Africa not to go Communist played no small role in convincing the Kennedys to back civil rights, because the South was receiving such bad press internationally. But Leander Perez would have explained to you that the Communists—make that Jewish Communists—used the gullible Negroes as dupes, because Negroes didn't have the resourcefulness to come up with something like a movement for equality themselves. The white citizens, however, were so resourceful that they convinced the legislature to give the Ninth Ward Private Schools Association $103,343 to build a whites-only private school with, while cutting $120,363 from the two integrated public schools.[21]

By 1962, Faubus was reduced to warning: "Some day some of you pseudo-intellectuals here in Little Rock will . . . find your white daughter being fondled by a black man. You will not like it."[22] Jimmie Davis, meanwhile, was releasing gospel albums like Judgment Day was coming—eight titles for Decca between 1960 and 1964. He had a top-20 country hit in 1964 with "Where the Old Red River Flows." And African Americans had a new enemy, this one infrastructural.

My first view of a "ghetto"—I didn't know the word yet—was on a summer car trip to the East Coast with my parents in 1963. Before the interstate, people on cross-country trips had to drive right through cities, so my hillbilly dad wound up negotiating his way through unfamiliar urban cores that were like nothing I'd ever seen. I sat in the back of the station wagon as we drove through East St. Louis in 1965, tuning my radio with great intensity, learning that the Four Tops' "I Can't Help Myself" had gone to #1.

But my dad wouldn't be driving through black neighborhoods much longer. General Eisenhower had seen the autobahn in Germany, and as president he brought it to America. The Dwight D. Eisenhower National System of Interstate and Defense Highways, an initiative that began in 1956 and built 42,500 miles of highways by 1973, was the largest highway system in the world and possibly the largest infrastructural program in history. With 90 percent of it paid for by federal funds, it was the ultimate peacetime big-government project by the richest nation in history. It made the heavy construction, trucking, automobile, and oil industries happy—socialism in action!—placating what Eisenhower would later term the "military-industrial complex" during the fallow period between Korea and Vietnam, even as it devastated central-city economies around the country. "In Miami," writes Raymond A. Mohl, "a single massive interstate interchange of Interstate-95 took up forty square blocks and demolished the black business district and the homes of some 10,000 people."[23] Overtown, the black neighborhood of Miami that was home to Betty Wright and Sam and Dave, went in forty years from being a thriving black nightclub scene with forty thousand residents to a blighted poverty island of nine thousand.[24] In city after city it isolated, rode roughshod through, or bulldozed black neighborhoods, which were now being called *ghettoes*.

It was an all-fronts assault on urban culture: historic districts were destroyed in city after city, business owners lost their places of business, and neighborhoods were cordoned off by the concrete barrier or razed entirely. Black people, huddled in the cities and discriminated against by mortgage lenders so that they could not move to the suburbs, were disproportionately affected.

In what is remembered as the Freeway Revolt, citizen resistance appeared around the country to this massive exercise of eminent domain and urban disfigurement. In New Orleans, where Robert Moses began trying to build a Mississippi Riverfront expressway running alongside the French Quarter in 1946, antifreeway activism had a long history, and New Orleans became the single most contentious battleground of the Freeway Revolt. Expressway opponents were helped in 1965 when Stewart Udall, secretary of the interior, designated the French Quarter as a historic district.[25] After an extended clash between builders and citizens that attracted national attention, during which the National Historic Preservation Act of 1966 was passed, the New Orleans riverfront superhighway was officially declared dead in June 1969, twenty-three years after it was first proposed.

Unfortunately, Udall did not also designate the Tremé, adjacent to the French Quarter on the other side of Rampart Street, as a historic district. And that's where they built I-10, over the oldest African American residential district in the country, an architectural and cultural treasure-house. They tore up the part of Claiborne Avenue that was its main boulevard, pulling out as they did so the longest stand of live oaks in existence anywhere. A long elevated stretch of interstate overpass was constructed directly overhead where it had been, taking out a major African American business district and reconfiguring the Tremé's most important parade route. "That strip was really our living room and our playground and everything when I was coming up," recalled Jerome Smith. "That was where the real Mardi Gras was—the intense, intense Mardi Gras." Coming at the same time as the school desegregation struggle, ripping out the main artery of the Tremé smelled of payback.

Since then, people passing through New Orleans on I-10 have been literally driving over the Tremé, which goes about its business while trucks speed overhead, spewing out exhaust for the children below to breathe. The massive columns that hold up the elevated concrete highway have been decorated with mural painting, but the former thoroughfare down below is dark and dank.

The interstates facilitated the abandonment of urban areas across the country by whites decamping to new suburbs. White flight out of New Orleans was already underway in the '50s, but in the '60s and '70s it accelerated dramatically, to suburban homes built in previously uninhabited parts of Jefferson Parish and other nearby areas. Even as most of the South continued to drag its feet on integration, the public schools were resegregated by other means. New Orleans and other "inner cities"—a new phrase in the national vocabulary—were abandoned to the [N-word]s and the [N-word]-lovers.

In 1961, Senator Russell Long of Louisiana (son of Huey, nephew of Earl) suggested that the only way to preserve segregation was to move to a system of private schools, a vision that largely came true in succeeding decades as *Brown v. Board of Education* was effectively circumvented. Long before I got to New Orleans in 2004, its public schools were almost entirely made up of black students—something like 93 percent—while white children were privately educated. Despite the presence of some dedicated teachers and supervisors (I met a number of them), their resources were scant and their facilities deplorable. To be sure, some distinguished students came out of those schools, but others were more like the young cashier who checked me out at the Winn-Dixie on Tchoupitoulas who, when she had to write something down, gripped the pencil in the crook between her third and fourth fingers and braced her wrist and hand sideways on the checkout conveyor belt while she wrote.

Integration brought a shift of political power. Between the exodus of white voters and a newly politicized black electorate, urban city governments changed hands. In 1973, African American mayors were elected in Los Angeles, Detroit, and Atlanta. Meanwhile, the allegiance of the Southern white electorate had abruptly flipped. For over a century the Democrats had been the party of white supremacy, though Strom Thurmond had bolted in 1948 to form his "Dixiecrat" ticket. But now the South became the new power base of the Republican party. Leander Perez became a "Democrat for Goldwater," and his fourteen-year-old acolyte David Duke went to work for the 1964 campaign of Republican Barry Goldwater, who carried only six states: his home state of Arizona plus five states in the Deep South, including Louisiana.

New Orleans, which continued to vote Democratic, remained an electoral anomaly in the state. Black people in New Orleans had previously been an important part of the electoral calculus, but in the forty years after 1960 the percentage of black people in the city more than doubled, from 37.2 percent to 67 percent. The change was almost entirely due to white flight; during that time the city's population dropped, registering its first-ever decline as it fell from its peak population of 627,525 in 1960 to 484,674 forty years later. Meanwhile, the greater metropolitan area's population increased, reaching 1.3 million by 2000.

New Orleans became a black-majority town ringed by unfriendly white-majority suburbs. Beyond them was the rest of Louisiana, where, as I can testify, there was a great deal of neo-Confederate sentiment.

3

THE GOOD DARKEY

It was a menace to society itself that the negroes should thus of a sudden be set free and left without tutelage or restraint. Some stayed very quietly by their old masters and gave no trouble . . .

—Woodrow Wilson, *A History of the American People*[1]

There were two bridges across the Cane River Lake, at different parts of town. One was concrete and hissed as you drove across it, and the other was an old wooden bridge that shook and rattled with every passing car.

Natchitoches is split in two by that skinny, thirty-nine-mile-long lake. It used to be part of the main channel of the Red River, but the river changed course long before my time. In the 1830s the snagboats of Henry Shreve performed the heroic engineering feat of dismantling the Great Raft, a giant logjam upriver that had been accumulating for four hundred years or more. Apparently as a result of Shreve's opening up of the watercourse, the Red shifted its channel four miles to the north, taking with it Natchitoches's raison d'être as the farthest navigable point upriver. Shreve's Port, later Shreveport, became the regional commercial power. By my time, that blind oxbow segment of what had once been the Red River had been dammed up and renamed the Cane River Lake. It looked like a river, but it didn't flow.

The business district of Natchitoches (population in 1960: 13,924) stretched along a few blocks of the west bank of the Cane River Lake. Front

Street, the old town's picturesque, brick-paved main promenade, was topped with a little traffic circle, and on a pedestal in that circle, high up in the air, was the only statue in Natchitoches.

The Good Darkey.

I didn't know how long it had been there or who put it up. But I knew that life-sized sculpture of a humble old black man, because I saw him every day of my childhood. The statue was erected, we were told, to honor the slaves who didn't leave their masters at the end of the war. There was no need to ask which war, though in other parts of the country "the war" would have meant World War II.

Born in 1927, the same year as my mother, the Good Darkey was a gift to the city from Jackson L. Bryan, a cotton planter, mill owner, and banker born in 1868 in nearby Mansfield. Bryan paid a forty-three hundred dollar commission to Baltimore's German-born monument sculptor Hans Schuler for the life-sized figure, cast in bronze and solemnized with a plaque that read "dedicated to the arduous and faithful services of the Good Darkeys of Louisiana."

That year, sixteen black people were lynched in the South. That was calmer than the year of 1892, when 161 blacks and 69 whites were lynched. But that wasn't much comfort to the family of John Carter, who was lynched in Little Rock in 1927 by a mob of two hundred that afterward burned his body, a typical thing to do with the bodies of the victims. On occasion they were burned alive. On other occasions they were torn to pieces.

In the 1919 Tulsa "race riot," meaning a massacre of African Americans by whites, perhaps as many as three hundred or more black people were killed—a careful count was not a law enforcement priority—and over a thousand homes were destroyed. There were twenty-six "race riots" in the United States in 1919, many of them related to the return of overseas troops. A "race war" broke out in Washington, D.C., on July 21, 1919, in which, reported the *Washington Post*, "at midnight thousands of men in soldiers' and sailors' uniforms and in civilian clothes surged through the downtown district, seeking negroes. Every negro found in the street or in street cars was roughly handled."[2]

Mob violence against black people was essential to enforcing the two-caste system. The whole world knew about the lynchings that went on in the South, but nobody stopped it. Lynchings were extended sessions of public sadism involving prolonged torture and mutilation of almost unbelievable inhumanity—I'll spare you examples—indulged in by sizable mobs that could number sometimes a hundred people, sometimes ten, twelve, or fifteen thousand, including children, grannies, and photographers. Sometimes fomented by newspapers and even on occasion by radio, once radio existed, they were carnivals of human sacrifice, on occasion complete with formal processions, burnt offerings of a victim's body parts as souvenirs, and a barn dance and a commemorative postcard afterward.

That's what happened to Bad Darkeys. Indeed, the burden of proof of Goodness was on the individual Darkey, who otherwise could be presumed to share the stain. But lynching wasn't all that happened to African Americans during Jim Crow. Douglas A. Blackmon argues against using the term *Jim Crow* at all, referring to it instead as the period of "neoslavery," when black men, and occasionally women, were seized and sent to what was effectively slave labor via long prison sentences for petty or trumped-up charges. An innocent man could find himself charged with something as vague as vagrancy, loitering, or abusive language. He would be assessed court costs that he could not pay, so he would be put to hard labor to work it off—two years, say, for a forty-dollar debt—then at the end of his sentence reconvicted on some imagined infraction. The right to use his forced labor was sold by the prison system, sometimes at auction, to businesses ranging from individual farmers to steel manufacturers, through a convict-leasing network that was the direct successor to a slave-leasing system previously in effect. The victim, who may have been guilty of nothing more than walking down the street, would find himself required to load eight tons of coal a day in underground mines with no safety or sanitation provisions whatsoever, or in chains in a remote turpentine camp in a dark forest, or on a cotton plantation, or on a road gang, or building a levee along the Mississippi River. Since the employer had no equity of ownership in the worker but was merely a lessor, the well-being or even the physical survival of the worker was not a priority. Arrests increased when more labor was needed. Blackmon writes that Alabama "supplied tens of thousands of men over five decades to a succession of prison mines ultimately purchased by U.S. Steel in 1907."[3]

Essential to this was the lack of federal supervision in "states' rights" and local affairs. A criminal justice system that barely existed in the South before the Civil War became a high-volume business that supplied the labor market. In southern towns, the sheriff was the law of the land.[4]

In Louisiana, the center of convict labor was West Feliciana Parish, north of Baton Rouge near the Mississippi border. That was where, in 1901, the State of Louisiana assumed control of the largest plantation in the state, one that used convict labor, converting it into the Angola State Prison even as it remained a working plantation. The inmates' agricultural work made the prison self-supporting. The name "Angola" expressed who the majority of its inmates were and are; expanded from its original eight thousand acres to eighteen thousand, it is still the Louisiana state lockup today, and is still notorious for its convict labor. Its agriculture is still unmechanized, done by hand, much the same way slave labor operated in the nineteenth century. As Afro-Louisianans are well aware, Angola inmates' hands still get cut up from picking cotton, the way slaves' hands once did.

In that same year of 1927, when the Good Darkey went up,

> an elderly gentleman of West Feliciana Parish responded amiably to a request for information from a graduate student in history who was studying the disputed election of 1876. He described the horrors of government by Negroes, scalawags, and carpetbaggers. He told of his activities as a "regulator," frightening some Negroes by shooting into their cabins, lynching a few, and waiting in ambush to assassinate carpetbagger leaders. It is possible that the passing of the years had magnified in his mind his role in the redemption of the state, but few students of the era would deny that he was truly reflecting the attitude of his parish and other rural areas of Louisiana toward Reconstruction.
>
> Part of his letter read as follows: "After the election, the negroes realizing that they were among their true friends became reconciled and West Feliciana now boasts of having the best class of negroes in the state. *You seldom meet one who doesn't touch his hat.*"[5] [emphasis added] [paragraphing added]

The Good Darkey was touching his hat. If you were black and wanted a job in the Natchitoches of my childhood, he beamed his benevolent bronze eyes at you—he was looking down, after all—to instruct you in deportment. The only jobs open to you were menial ones, since you wouldn't be considered, let alone trained, for anything else. Fuck up and you'd be in Angola, chopping cotton like your enslaved great-granddaddy—or worse, cutting cane.

New Orleans singer-guitarist "Deacon" John Moore, ten years older than me, recalled his high school years: "When I was coming up during segregation, the highest job you could aspire to was working in the post office, being a schoolteacher, a pullman porter. . . . You couldn't go to the medical schools, the dental colleges, the engineering schools. You couldn't even *dream* to be that." He became a musician.

If you were white, you encountered "colored people" only in service positions. You wouldn't want your child to suck on nickels *they* had handled, but *they* dished up your dinner in restaurants and cafeterias where *they* couldn't be seated. Not a few white people assumed "Negro" men to be sex maniacs, so businesses wouldn't hire *them* for jobs that required social interaction with

"Caucasian" women. *They* were also deemed likely to have (whisper it) venereal disease as a consequence of their presumed sexual depravity, and, since it was widely believed you could contract syphilis from a toilet seat, this was sometimes cited as the justification for not allowing *them* to use the same restrooms or drinking fountains as whites, although *they* were allowed to scrub the white folks' toilets. White undertakers wouldn't touch black corpses, which is why the black mortician was a prosperous figure in every African American community.

I'm not talking about some impossibly distant long ago. I'm talking about my childhood, when modernism ruled in arts, media, and design, and the filling stations had three restrooms, labeled Men, Women, and Colored, in the Esso or Mobil logotype. The nicer stations had restrooms for Colored Men and Colored Women both. "My parents wouldn't allow us to use them," an African American woman my age recalled to me in 2008. "They said, 'We'll go out in the *trees* before we'll use a restroom marked 'Colored.'"

But you couldn't go out in the trees when you went to the movies.

My parents, children of the golden age of movies (better known as the Depression), had the moviegoing habit. From the age of seven, when they let me go unaccompanied, I was a dedicated movie patron every Saturday and Sunday afternoon, and whenever else I could arrange it.

I was an obsessive fan, like only a manic, underchallenged little boy with a hobby can be. I cut out all the movie ads in the *Shreveport Times*, traced the display lettering styles, and knew the individual theaters' booking policies, though only rarely did I ever get to go to a movie in Shreveport. It wasn't just that I was a movie fanatic; the movies were the center of secular life in the American heartland.

Movie houses in other towns had names like the State or the Palace, but Natchitoches's two theaters were the Don and the Cane. The Don, on Front Street, was newer, and the Cane, a block back on Second Street, was bigger and a little dilapidated. The former name perhaps echoed Natchitoches's days as a Spanish colony in the late eighteenth century, when distinguished gentlemen were addressed as *Don*—or maybe Donald was the owner's name, I never knew—while the latter celebrated the fact that Natchitoches had been a far northern outpost of Louisiana Sugarland. The first show at each theater began every day at one o'clock, seven days a week, and ran continuously until closing at night. The theaters' booking schedule regulated the weekly rhythm of my imagination. In Natchitoches, both the Don and the Cane ran a first-run film that played Sunday through Tuesday, an older or less commercial one for Wednesday and Thursday, an even older one on Friday when the college students came to neck, and a double feature Saturday, heavy on westerns, for kids and country people coming into town. Out by a dark, tree-canopied subdivision called Pecan Park, the Chief Drive-In Theatre—its sign featured an Indian head, with headdress—had a similar booking policy to the indoor theaters, making for a total of fifteen different features a week on the town's three movie screens. I saw as many of them as I could.

At both the Don and the Cane, admission was fifty-five cents for adults and fifteen cents for children. Despite paying an equal ticket price, African Americans had to enter separately, through a side door. They were seated apart from whites, restricted to the balcony. Nor would I encounter them standing in line to buy popcorn and Dr. Pepper; they had to purchase concessions separately through a window outside. Moviegoing whites barely noticed them. At the Chief Drive-In, "colored" could only park in the back, and their children couldn't use the little playground up by the screen. But even that was a considerable improvement over the way things had been a hundred years earlier, when somebody's loved one might be raffled off as a prize to stimulate an otherwise dull auction of livestock and farm equipment, or impulsively bet and lost to a cardsharp.

Fictional visions of life outside Natchitoches came to me in my whites-only movie seat: Dean Martin and Jerry Lewis, the Blob, the Vikings, the seventh voyage of Sinbad, the Queen of Outer Space. It was left to me to untangle fantasy from history. The good Americans shot down the bad Japs over and over, and kept on defeating the Germans. No concentration camps, though; Americans didn't hear much about those until 1961, with the trial of Adolf Eichmann and the publication of William Shirer's *Rise and Fall of the Third Reich*. I saw gangster films, though only a few, because the gangster hadn't yet replaced the cowboy as the stereotypical movie American. But the transition was under way: I saw *Some Like It Hot* two days in a row, puzzled by a funny movie that began with an on-screen massacre.

It was the era of inexplicitly lurid adult-oriented films made from Tennessee Williams plays and Faulkner novels. There were no ratings then, and I saw them all. I loved everything modern, cynical, satirical, abstract. I couldn't wait to be an adult. I never missed a risqué (by 1958 standards) sex comedy set on Madison Avenue. When the downbeat *Some Came Running* came out—the first Rat Pack movie, though Frank Sinatra's circle of cronies wasn't known as that yet—I saw it three times. I even set its ad copy to music.

Thanks to the organist at the Presbyterian church, who was a friend of my parents, I was able to slip into the worship area once in a while when the church was empty to play the Hammond organ. It was exciting to touch a key and hear the sound fill up that big space. I had no idea how to play the thing, but I was used to fooling around on pianos. In that imposing space, I felt I had to play something appropriately dignified and somber. Under the big brass cross that dominated the altar, I composed a melody, feeling out a note at a time, in a somber white-key minor mode:

Some came running
Some turned away
Dave was ba-ack and the whole town knew
That trouble—and women—were close behind.

I thought perhaps the words could equally apply to Jesus. I never could come up with a second verse, though.

I saw *Song of the South*, a rerelease of the 1946 Walt Disney extravaganza that gave us a live-action Good Darkey singing "Zip-a-Dee-Doo-Dah" to an animated bluebird on his shoulder. And there was an age-inappropriate movie that made a great impression on me, though I couldn't have explained why, by eroticizing slavery. *Band of Angels* (1957), directed by Raoul Walsh from Robert Penn Warren's novel, was an edgy Civil War race romance, much of it set in New Orleans and rural plantation Louisiana. Clark Gable was the ex-slave trader turned kindly plantation owner, and Yvonne DeCarlo (*née* Peggy Middleton in Vancouver), by then well into the career trajectory that would later see her become Lily Munster, was his white-looking enslaved lover. Now *that* was a kinky movie. Anyone who was one-quarter black at the Cane Theater would have to sit upstairs to see that movie unless they were "passing."

Unusually for a Hollywood movie of the time, *Band of Angels* had a number of speaking parts for black actors. Of course, they played slaves. They drove to the Warner lot in Burbank, put on their colorful rags, and said things like "Yew ought to trah mah gris-gris luhv potion!" On a Wednesday to Thursday slot at the Don, I saw my first all-black movie: *St. Louis Blues*, a biopic about W. C. Handy, with Nat "King" Cole and sexy, purring young Eartha Kitt. The downstairs area was deserted. Except for the Bahaman-raised Sidney Poitier, who played the bastard slave-turned-Union soldier Rau-Ru in *Band of Angels* with the same remarkable dignity he demonstrated when handcuffed to Tony Curtis in *The Defiant Ones*, and except for a handful of other actors, black people rarely appeared in mainstream movies at all, let alone on television, so they didn't figure much in my movie-derived worldview.

The first director I became aware of (besides the self-promoting Alfred Hitchcock) was John Ford, who became famous in Natchitoches by making one of his lesser movies there while I was in second grade. *The Horse Soldiers* starred John Wayne and William Holden, who along with female lead Constance Towers were billeted in Alexandria during the shoot.

Ford was famous for his westerns, but *The Horse Soldiers* went back to the roots of the western, the Civil War movie. Despite its depiction of the Union soldiers as the good guys and the Confederates as suicidal fanatics, Natchitoches went gaga for *The Horse Soldiers*. Much of it was filmed just outside of town against a backdrop of live oaks and the Cane River Lake. There had to be slaves in a Civil War movie, so there was a part in it for Harlem-raised Althea Gibson, the first African American tennis champ. Her autobiography, published in 1958, was called *I Always Wanted to Be Somebody*. But in *The Horse Soldiers*, she was cast as a nobody: the faithful slave Lukey, who doted on her white mistress. Gibson didn't come to Natchitoches for the shoot, where she wouldn't have been able to stay in the same accommodations as the others, or eat in the same café in Alexandria that proudly displayed the white stars' autographed photos afterward. Her scenes were shot in Hollywood.

I was a seven-year-old film theorist, learning the grammar: some characters were more expendable than others. Someone has to die in a war movie, and of course it's going to be the Good Darkey. Lukey's death by gunshot occasioned a display of white grief that showed how much southerners loved their slaves.

She didn't bleed much, though. I never saw a movie in which anybody was shot on screen at close range with their brains blowing out. These were still the days of the Hayes Code, which reinforced the connection between explicit sex and violence by prohibiting them both as if they were the same forbidden thing. There was plenty of dramatic death in all those westerns and war movies, but it was curiously ungory. Dying seemed mostly a matter of gritting one's teeth and closing one's eyes. Sex, on the other hand—I learned the word from coming-attractions trailers—had something to do with a close-up kiss that was twenty feet high, and could be more than double that at a drive-in.

In a sense, every movie was an attack of the fifty-foot woman.

Perhaps because I can remember a time before there was a TV in the house, I've always considered it an optional appliance. I've never owned a television myself, and I'm known among my friends as a TV-hater. But for a few years after we got our first "TV set" in 1957, I was a child addicted. I bought *TV Guide* at the supermarket (fifteen cents) and obsessively memorized the schedules of the two stations from Shreveport as well as the one from Alexandria that didn't come in too well no matter how I twisted the antenna around. I watched game shows in the morning, cartoons in the afternoon, and westerns, sitcoms, and variety shows at night.

The cartoons were old theatrical shorts, many of them from the '30s, full of music. I saw the same ones over and over, but I didn't care. They were mostly of the funny-animal variety, but there was one character that I couldn't figure out what animal it was supposed to be. There was Donald Duck, Daffy Duck, Oswald the Rabbit. But what kind of animal was . . . Bosko? I asked my parents and got no definitive response. In this fantasy world of anthropomorphic creatures, I figured maybe he was a monkey. There was nothing else he could be. But they didn't call him Bosko the Monkey. I didn't get that he was supposed to be human. Sort of.

Bosko, it turns out, was a classic example of a simian racial caricature, copyrighted on January 3, 1928, as a "Negro boy."[6] In his first short, Bosko the Talk-Ink Kid (1929), he spoke with an adult man's voice in a strong southern black-stereotypical dialect and played piano, bursting alive off the vaudeville stage before being drawn back from off the page into the inkwell from whence he came. It was the first-ever cartoon with dialogue, and just as The Jazz Singer, the first feature film with talking sections, had Al Jolson in blackface, the first spoken cartoon dialogue was used to say, "Well, heah Ah is, an' Ah sho' feels good!"

Bosko became the first Looney Tunes cartoon character—he closed his cartoons by saying "That's all, folks!" before they gave that line to Porky Pig—but he had been transformed into something more vague, something that blurred the distinction between a black human and a funny animal. It was astoundingly, profoundly racist: he had a tail, but he kept it in his pants. With sound still a novelty, the cartoons were long on sight gags and music; the first ones were musicals entirely. Bosko's refried black-vaudeville routines inhabited a world that referenced African magic, not only animated but animist, in which trees and bathtubs might dance and everything was a musical instrument.

Bosko didn't appear in cartoons with humans, only in menageries with animated animals and others of his peculiar species. In Congo Jazz (1930), Bosko pacified wild animals by playing jazz to them, including a duet he played with an ape (they plucked their tongues), and he tapdanced. White people occasionally appeared as live action figures, literally as a master race; they were seen in the action of making the cartoon in which Bosko appeared.[7]

We haven't heard much about Bosko in recent decades. He's been put back in the inkwell, along with Song of the South and the Good Darkey, and so hasn't been part of our continually recycling selective memory, like his victorious competitor, another black funny animal with less obvious roots in greasepaint comedy: Mickey Mouse. But Bosko cartoons were on TV every day during my childhood. I didn't care for them much, though that didn't stop me from watching them.

I didn't much care for Ronald Reagan, either, but he appeared every week as the avuncular voice of authority introducing the GE *Theater*, where "progress is our most important product." When he ran for president two decades later, as much as I loathed him, his face and voice would almost subliminally bring back the memory of when I was innocent and the world seemed safe. Memories of being little alongside my big five-foot-two grandmother. Memories of when . . . Bosko cartoons were acceptable. Ugh.

Dad warned me not to get into conversations with adults about evolution, even if they were ignorant. He didn't quite explain, though, the reason so many people felt the need to proclaim indignantly that their granddaddy wasn't a monkey.

Monkeys were associated with "colored" people.

———

My parents must have made an appointment for the salesman to call, since no strangers were ever invited into our home, let alone at night. I watched in fascination as he pitched the *Encyclopaedia Britannica*. With two shelves' worth of large-format volumes, it required its own bookcase, which was included. To show us the glossy illustration pages, the salesman flipped to the "Motion Pictures" article. I was hooked.

Once the *Britannica* was ours, I looked at that article over and over, staring at the stills from *Potemkin* and *The Cabinet of Dr. Caligari*, movies I hadn't seen but that I understood on the *Britannica*'s authority to be founding classics of the art of cinema. And there was another one, whose aura of greatness shone resplendent down through the decades, though it was no longer being exhibited anywhere I could see it: *The Birth of a Nation*.

Made in 1914 by David Wark Griffith, a patrician Kentuckian who was not yet thirty, it was an innovative milestone in the infant art of cinema. After developing his skills by making hundreds of one-reelers in seven years, Griffith put dynamic editing, creative lighting, and a moving camera at the service of a complex narrative with a grand sweep at a time when films were short, flat, and didn't attempt much. He dazzled the public with the longest movie yet made—twelve reels, 187 minutes—filmed with a phenomenal budget of one hundred thousand dollars.

The American Film Institute webpage calls Griffith no less than "the father of American cinema" while noting that *The Birth of a Nation* was

THE GOOD DARKEY 37

"controversial." Which is a cowardly way of saying that it was outright white supremacist propaganda masquerading as a history lesson. An epic narrative of the Civil War and Reconstruction, it was based on the North Carolinian Thomas Dixon Jr.'s blockbuster 1905 novel *The Clansman, an Historical Romance of the Ku Klux Klan,* and to a lesser extent on his 1902 bestseller *The Leopard's Spots, a Romance of the White Man's Burden, 1865–1900.*

Dixon was an out-and-out race-hatred hustler. Prior to becoming a novelist he had been a Baptist minister. His rich, booming voice pulled a crowd, and for ten years he built up a large congregation in New York City. A self-promoting media figure in a way that is familiar today, he actively participated in the making and marketing of Griffith's film. The movie premiered in Los Angeles with the title *The Clansman,* but at Dixon's suggestion the name was changed before opening in New York to the more triumphal *The Birth of a Nation.* It came out in 1915, just in time to benefit from the hoopla surrounding the fiftieth anniversary of the Civil War.

The Birth of a Nation was two movies in one, cross-cutting back and forth. One was the definitive dystopian fantasy of the Reconstruction, believed to this day throughout the South, presenting a Confederate history book come to life on the screen, complete with *tableaux vivants.* The other was a sentimental melodrama with Lillian Gish, presenting a fevered vision of ignorant, vicious black satyrs and rapists who came to rule over whites and demand their daughters as though the reality of slavery hadn't been exactly the contrary: white men enjoying black daughters with impunity. In W. E. B. DuBois's words, the story "twisted the emancipation and enfranchisement of the slave in a great effort toward universal democracy, into an orgy of theft and degradation and wide rape of white women."[8]

The political villain in *The Birth of a Nation,* Austin Stoneman, was a caricature of Thaddeus Stevens, the powerful Radical Republican leader of the House of Representatives who, disregarding Lincoln's desire to treat the South as if it had never been gone, wanted the seceded states treated as conquered provinces. An ardent egalitarian who had pushed hard for emancipation as a wartime measure, Stevens was perhaps as revolutionary a politician as we have had in the United States. During Reconstruction, he disfranchised ex-Confederates—who had, after all, taken up arms against the U.S. government—while enfranchising black freedmen. The former Confederates took this as a humiliation to be avenged into all eternity, and some of their descendants are still trying to avenge it as I write these words.

Dixon described in the final paragraph of his preface to *The Clansman* "how the young South, led by the reincarnated souls of the Clansmen of Old Scotland, went forth under this cover and against overwhelming odds, daring exile, imprisonment, and a felon's death, and saved the life of a people, forms one of the most dramatic chapters in the history of the Aryan race." The Aryan race! This mythology, deeply rooted in the South, proceeded from the same philosophical and pseudoscientific sources as the Aryan-race stuff the Nazis were about to spout.

It's a critical cliché to say that *The Birth of a Nation* was actually the birth of cinema, the first movie as we know movies today. Shot with a single hand-cranked camera and without a written script, it was a spectacle beyond anything previously seen on screen, with scenes depicting Civil War battles (restaged in big-cast night shots with exploding flashes), Sherman's march, Lee's surrender to Grant, and the meticulously staged reenactment in Ford's Theater of the assassination of Lincoln (the still I saw in the *Britannica*). It was a massive box office success, and not only in the South. In New York it was accompanied by a forty-piece orchestra playing a score that cobbled together, among other sources, Negro spirituals, Wagner's "Ride of the Val-kyries," and Grieg's "In the Hall of the Mountain King." There were no scenes of slaves being sold at auction in *The Birth of a Nation*. The only sequence that depicted enslaved people doing field labor was accompanied by a title card explaining that slaves were treated well and got two hours off for lunch. The film characterized black people as a degenerate species, as in the tableau of a South Carolina House of Representatives full of black congressmen, one of whom takes off his shoes and puts his bare feet up on the desk while another gnaws grotesquely at a chicken leg on the debating floor. The picture's climac-tic scenes depicted the good guys—that is, the Ku Klux Klansmen—taking revenge, riding to battle with a flag baptized in the blood of a blond virgin who died fleeing a black would-be rapist. The story's payoff was a lynching, done off-camera but celebrated as a heroic deed, with the victim's body dumped on a doorstep. There was even a castration scene, though it was edited out after the film's premiere.

The objection to *Birth* was not merely that a person of tender sentiments might find it distasteful. The film had real-world consequences. "Without doubt," wrote W. E. B. DuBois, "the increase of lynching in 1915 and later was directly encouraged by this film." Dubois spearheaded the NAACP's effort to stop the film's exhibition, though he later concluded that their efforts "prob-ably succeeded in advertising it."[9]

The film inspired the rebirth of the moribund Ku Klux Klan. Founded in 1866, the Klan was a carnivalesque paramilitary cult that was effectively defunct after ten years or so, and but for Dixon and Griffith's propagandiz-ing it might have remained in the toxic past. But in the wake of the film's success, one William J. Simmons founded a new Klan, complete with hired public relations consultants, that became enough of a mass organization to field forty thousand hooded participants for a march on Washington in 1925 before it faded. It was revived again, a little before my time, to confront the civil rights movement.

At the age of seven I thought the phrase *Ku Klux Klan* was hysterically funny. I didn't know what it referred to. It sounded like something out of cartoons to me. When I made up a tongue twister about it, my horrified dad gave me an urgent, though somewhat vague, talking-to. The words never again escaped my lips.

For that matter, when I lived in Natchitoches I didn't know there had been lynchings of black people in the South. Miz My-yoo certainly hadn't mentioned it. I knew what lynching was, but from westerns. I thought it was what happened to horse thieves.

Griffith's film made exhibitors rich, empowering the new movie industry. It did much to wean movies off an implied theatrical stage and into an idiomatically filmic space. But as drama it was ludicrous. Dramatists back to the Greeks had given their characters complex inner lives, but Dixon and Griffith's characters were stick figures, literally stereotypes. Lacking any depth, their roles did nothing more than serve an agenda.

Infrequently noted in film-historical writing about *Birth* is its use of a theatrical device, left over from the stage version of *The Clansman*, that gave it a unique and perverse strangeness: cross-racial casting. There were a number of "colored" parts in the film, but, fat shuffling mammy and sniveling ravager alike, they were played by white people in blackface, who looked not at all like African-descended people. Griffith's white actors in blackface made what Felipe Smith describes as "exaggerated simian gestures, including an 'anthropoidal slouch' that practically has them dragging their knuckles across the floor . . . [in] clever stagings of the old ape libel." There was a lighter shading of greasepaint for the mulatto characters, who were archvillains. However, for bit parts that didn't require interaction with white actors, actual African Americans were used. In some shots both real and fake black people are seen. It's from Mars.

"Griffith's cinematography," writes Felipe Smith, "through improved technological 'authentication' of the past, and his staging of evolutionary regression simultaneously reinforced the belief that whites possessed a 'racial' monopoly on modernity."[10] That monopoly was still going on in my childhood: in the worlds that cinema opened windows into, black people were mostly absent.

As a historical pageant justifying the repression of African Americans, *The Birth of a Nation* had a tremendous impact on its audience. But its greatest impact may have been to call attention to the potency of moving images as propaganda. Dixon demonstrated a clear understanding of cinema's potential when he called the picture "the launching of the mightiest engine for moulding public opinion in the history of the world." In a 1915 interview with the Sunday *New York Times*, Griffith said:

> The time will come, and in less than ten years, when the children in the public schools will be taught practically everything by moving pictures. *Certainly they will never be obliged to read history again.*
>
> Imagine a public library of the near future, for instance. There will be long rows of boxes or pillars, properly classified and indexed, of course. At each box a push button and before each box a seat. Suppose you wish to "read up" on a certain episode in Napoleon's life. Instead of consulting all the authorities, wading laboriously through a host of books, and ending bewildered, without a clear idea of exactly what happened and confused at every point by conflicting opinions about what did happen, you will merely seat yourself at a properly adjusted window, in a scientifically prepared room, press the button, and actually see what happened.
>
> There will be no opinions expressed. You will merely be present at the making of history. All the work of writing, revising, collating, and reproducing will have been carefully attended to by a corps of recognized experts, and you will have received a vivid and complete expression.[11] [emphasis added]

With hindsight, one might be pardoned for thinking that Griffith's vision of a postliterate age has come true. In the century since his time, our population has received its attitudes about history from moving images instead of sorting out problematic facts from books.

Film historians, dazzled by Griffith's cinematic originality, have generally spoken of him with reverence while overlooking the appalling social vision his masterwork zealously imparted to an eager public. After Griffith's death in 1948, the heavyweight intellectual film critic of the time, James Agee, dismissed as "vicious nonsense" complaints that *Birth* was "anti-Negro," rhapsodizing in the pages of *The Nation*: "To watch [Griffith's] work is like being witness to the beginning of melody, or the first conscious use of the lever or the wheel; the emergence, coordination, and first eloquence of language; the birth of an art: and to realize that this is all the work of one man."[12]

Writing in 1966 in the first issue of *Rally*, a short-lived incubator magazine for young right-wing writers, Arlene Croce, then a thirty-one-year-old senior editor at William F. Buckley's *National Review*, called *The Birth of a Nation* "the first, the most stunning, and durably audacious of all American film masterpieces, and the most wonderful movie ever made," and even spoke of Griffith's "19th-century generosity of spirit" in depicting Reconstruction.[13] Croce later became an aesthetically conservative dance critic for the *New Yorker*, coming out of the closet as a neocon in 1994 with a notorious three-thousand-word screed denouncing "big government," the 1960s, and a show she hadn't seen by choreographer Bill T. Jones, a black man who wouldn't shut up and dance but insisted on speaking his mind while he had the floor.

In 1930, hoping to prolong the theatrical life of his now-obsolete silent film, Griffith made a six-minute sound prologue for *The Birth of a Nation* that consisted of a conversation between himself and Walter Huston, sitting and smoking in a comfortable den while adorable white children eavesdropped.[14] (This was our grandparents' generation talking; Huston's granddaughter Anjelica was born the same day and year I was.) In a staged moment of camaraderie, Huston presented the old Kentuckian with a saber that had belonged to a Confederate soldier. With the gravity and nobility of a great artist conscious of the weight of history on his shoulders, Griffith acted as if he were deeply moved. "My father wore one like that," he said quietly—and fuzzily, because soundstage microphone techniques had not yet been perfected.

Huston asked, "When you made *The Birth of a Nation*, did you tell your father's story?"

"That's natural enough," responded Griffith defensively, "when you've heard your father tell about fighting day after day, night after night, and having nothing to eat but parched corn, and about your mother, staying up night after night sewing robes for the Klan.

"The Klan at that time was needed," said Griffith, "and served a purpose."

That same year, *I'll Take My Stand* was published, a book whose credited author was "Twelve Southerners." These were first-tier intellectuals, men of literary repute who no doubt saw themselves as being of a higher order than Thomas Dixon, but who were nonetheless champions of the lofty, leisurely, agrarian ideal of the Old South over the crass modernism and industry of the North—while lesser beings did the hard labor, needless to say, and used separate restrooms. The book's keynote essay, "Reconstructed but Unregenerate," was by John Crowe Ransom, founder of the *Kenyon Review* and teacher of many southern writers—including the young Robert Penn Warren, whose essay in the book, "The Briar Patch," defended segregation.

Born in the Ku Klux Klan's home village of Pulaski, Tennessee, John Crowe Ransom was the father of the so-called New Criticism, which dominated university literature departments in the 1940s and '50s. I learned about New Criticism in freshman English in 1968, so it was still going around then. At its core was "close reading" of the text, which emphatically discarded as extraneous such paltry considerations as the author's biography or historical context. This seemingly daring modernism was a particularly convenient approach for someone who ran from history as hard as John Crowe Ransom.

"Slavery," wrote Ransom in *I'll Take My Stand*, "was a feature monstrous enough in theory, but more often than not, humane in practice; and it is impossible to believe that its abolition alone could have effected any great revolution in society."[15] He surely believed what he wrote. You have to believe your lies to keep telling them year in and year out. But it *was* a lie.

New Criticism was the best way anyone could have come up with to blunt the cutting edge of *The Adventures of Huckleberry Finn*. The past didn't matter, except as a literary device. What mattered was the use the author made of it. It was a perfect analytical tool for film courses once they began to appear: take the movie's Potemkin village on its own terms, and don't locate it in society. It was convenient for English teachers at small-town southern land-grant colleges, where actually confronting the *Birth of a Nation*–inspired consensual fantasy of history would have marked one as a dangerous radical if not an out-and-out [N-word]-lover.

That began to change when African Americans started becoming professors themselves. By now, in the post–Black Studies era, *The Birth of a Nation* is a blatant embarrassment. But historians still must deal with the film that helped establish cinema as spectacle and pretty much defined the concept of dramatic fiction features. It still has to be studied, but for different reasons.

What if the innovative filmic syntax is *not* so easily separable from the vileness of the content? In response to James Agee, we could say that to watch *The Birth of a Nation* is like being witness to the beginning of Fox News. Television's instant-response capability allows it to be a mesmerizing medium of disinformation for current events. But first there were movies, and they were from the beginning a medium of historical disinformation. In their century-plus of existence, movies have taught us a history that we know is false, sometimes ludicrously so, but that, to a greater or lesser degree, we believe anyway. Movies told me lies.

It seemed like two lifetimes for me since I had last seen Natchitoches. But it had only been seven years since 1960, when we moved away from Louisiana. When we stopped in Natchitoches for a couple of days while on a car trip to visit my father's colleagues in Florida, the Good Darkey was still gazing down from his pedestal.

I was a sixteen-year-old hippie, dragging my guitar along with me everywhere I went. We stopped for burgers in Shreveport, a visibly different city than the pre-interstate version I remembered. I played "Funky Broadway" (the Wilson Pickett version) on the jukebox. Black people were coming into the joint to eat, something they couldn't have done in 1960. In Natchitoches, I bought a copy of Jet—a magazine not available at the Greyhound terminal in Portales, New Mexico, where I then lived—and was horrified to see a photograph in it of Otis Redding still strapped into his airplane seat, grimacing in death after being fished out of the icy waters of Lake Michigan two weeks before.

Otis Redding went down before the Good Darkey did. They didn't remove the Good Darkey from Front Street until September 1968, so he didn't get to see downtown Natchitoches become a National Landmark Historic District and subsequently a tourist spot.

The next and last time I visited Natchitoches, it was 1977. I was driving cross-country with Constance, bringing her to live in glorious poverty with me in New York. Wanting to show her where I'd been a child, I detoured through my old hometown to spend a night. I saw a black cop and a white cop riding together in a police car, and I told myself, things have changed. As I was getting some ice from the machine at the motel, I asked the man at the front desk what had happened to that statue that used to be on Front Street.

He said, "Oh, they took it down when all that integration mess came th'ough."

The Good Darkey was mothballed, then resurrected. Today he's back on display, at the bucolic-sounding Rural Life Museum, maintained by Louisiana State University on the site of an old plantation outside of Baton Rouge, where various artifacts from the bad old days have found a home. There are a lot of bells at the Rural Life Museum, just as there were lots of bells on the old plantation to call the, shall we say, agricultural servants to work. It reminded me of my visit to the museum at Dachau, except that at Dachau they were less euphemistic.

They don't call him the Good Darkey at the Rural Life Museum. They call him "Uncle Jack." Which is almost as bad. Uncle and Auntie, of course, were standard ways to refer to slaves once they reached a certain age. After all, you couldn't call someone Mr. or Mrs. if they didn't have last names. If they had last names, that would mean they were people instead of property. That in turn would mean they could be married and not have one or the other of the pair sold away. Or have the right to keep their children instead of having them be sold off.

In Harriet Beecher Stowe's novel that galvanized the North against slavery in 1852, the saintly Uncle Tom came from Kentucky, was purchased in New Orleans, and was beaten to death somewhere that must have been fairly near Natchitoches by Simon Legree, a cotton planter on the Red River. Had the Good Darkey/Uncle Jack commemorated a real individual, that old man might well have been born in Virginia or Kentucky and sold down to a Red River plantation in his teens, never to see his family again, in what historians politely call the interstate slave trade.[16] That's what those sentimental lyrics of separation were about: Old folks at home. My old Kentucky home. Carry me back to old Virginny. They were the lamentations of the Good Darkey.

In 2004, in New Orleans, I kept intending to go to Natchitoches. Somehow I never made it. But I did drive to Baton Rouge to see Uncle Jack at the Rural Life Museum, just to reassure myself that I really did remember what I thought I remembered.

There he stood, high up in the air on a pedestal, surrounded by majestic live oaks at the front entrance to the plantation, submissively welcoming visitors like an exalted lawn jockey. The Good Darkey.

He had nothing to do with the running of a plantation, of course. He was a shameful piece of small-town municipal statuary from one of the darkest periods of American history, a monument to the repression of the rights of African Americans and the denial of black manhood in particular. The on-site signage spins the story as if putting up the statue were an act of liberalism: some of the townspeople were more conservative than Mr. Bryan, and they didn't want a statue to a Negro—even a thoroughly servile one—going up in their town.

I paced around, snapping pictures from every angle. I didn't make it up. I remembered it right all those years. Constance was my witness.

He really did have his head bowed, and his hat in his hand.

4

MADE OUT OF MUD

Racism has not left the building.

—Patricia Spears Jones

I t was one of those dramatic Louisiana afternoons that get black as night when the sky clouds up for rain. You go on about your business as the heavens open up onto your windshield, and when you get there you don't bother with an umbrella, you just run from your car to the front door.

I was five. I had convinced my parents to take me to the record store. I remember it as a big shack a little way out of town in the dense woods, where it was dark even when there wasn't a storm. The store's electric lights seemed like brave beacons of civilization as the thunder rolled and water dripped off the trees.

I looked in amazement at the stock of records: 78s (by then a dying configuration, as even I was aware) in plain brown sleeves that exposed the labels, seven-inch 45s with the big holes, and 33$\frac{1}{3}$-rpm LPs. Behind the counter was a rural Louisiana version of a hipster. I spoke up and told him the record I wanted, a song that delighted every five-year-old heart: "See You Later Alligator." But it was out of stock. No problem, I had a plan B. So my first single—which has sort of the same status as the person you lose your virginity to, only it stays with you longer and is a more pleasant memory—was, as the person you lost your virginity to may have been, a second choice. But it was a masterpiece: "Sixteen Tons" by "Tennessee" Ernie Ford.

I was already in the record-playing habit. My parents had bought me Little
Golden Records, a children's label of bright yellow small-hole seven-inch 78s
that always featured Mitch Miller and the Sandpipers, who must have spent
half their waking hours pumping those things out. But there was also a stack of
ten-inch 78s that had belonged to my mother's youngest sister in her teenage
years. It seemed strange to me that she wouldn't still want them. Aunt Nina
liked records with a beat, and so did I. I spent days playing those pre-rock 'n'
roll hits: the Clovers' "One Mint Julep," Nat "King" Cole's "You Don't Learn
That in School," Eileen Barton's "If I Knew You Were Coming I'd Have Baked
a Cake" (a 1950 record, smartly engineered by Tom Dowd, that was all hand-
clap backbeat, with New Orleans–style trad jazz for the break), Lefty Frizzell's
"If You've Got the Money (I've Got the Time)," and a rhythm-novelty number
I didn't realize was a white man singing about a black man, Red Foley's "Chat-
tanooga Shoe Shine Boy." My dad had a stack of Mexican 45s, so I listened
to "El Preso #9" and "Borracho de Ti," which is how I learned the words *preso*
(prisoner) and *borracho* (drunk). But "Sixteen Tons" was *my* record.

I took it home and played it, then I turned it over and played the other
side (originally planned as the A side, it was a version of Aubrey "Moon"
Mullican's "You Don't Have to Be a Baby to Cry"). Then I turned it back
over and played "Sixteen Tons" again. And again. And again, occasionally
alternating with the B side. If I had to, I could probably write out a pretty
good copy of the arrangement from memory.

Years later I learned a fundamental principle of orchestration: that two
instruments playing closely related pitches, at exactly the same moment, fuse
into a composite timbre that is no longer those two instruments but a single
sound all its own. I heard that happen when I was five, with the clarinet
and bass clarinet introduction of "Sixteen Tons." That sound seemed like a
swamp creature to me.

It's one of those records in which every element is perfect. The song. The
production. The orchestration. The interpretation. The fingersnaps, which
set up the entry of the deep baritone voice. The slinky feel of Cliffie Stone's
sparely deployed eight-piece band, with tense birth-of-the-cool chords. The
hillbilly-boogie balance of swing time and Latin tinge, with a strongly emphasized feeling of Cuban clave to the melody (SIX-TEEN TONS [rest], WHAD-
daya GET?) And then the grand pause and melisma at the end, for the final *I
ooooowe maaaaah soooooooooul*—so authoritatively sung that you would never
know, if you were a white child, that what Tennessee Ernie owed his soul to
was the black spiritual tradition. But it was such an obvious nod to black singing that only a segregated white child wouldn't be aware of it.

It was a live performance, with the
trating together in the same room to c
onds of eternity out of September 21, 1
captured with startling clarity by tube
Melrose Avenue in Los Angeles, so u
pioneers like Cosimo Matassa in Ne
Norman Petty in Clovis, or Bob Sulli\
I couldn't have explained any of that.

Hayride, broadcast befor
ride was the second m
more musically c
ating out acro
developme
rememb
J,
th

And above all, Merle Travis's wo
could only take all the images literall
stories in the Bible literally. Not coincidentally, I
started absorbing the bizarre tales of the Old and New Testaments with the
help of a Bible comic book. (I still imagine the story of Jacob and Esau as being
told in illustrated panels.) The first line of "Sixteen Tons" haunted me:

Soooooooome people say a man is made out of mud . . .

It wasn't hard to imagine a man made out of mud on those dark Louisiana
mornings.

IIIIIIIIII was born one mornin' it was drizzlin' rain
Fightin' and trouble are my middle name
I was raised in the canebrake by an ol' mama lion . . .

A canebrake was real to me, and I could see that ol' mama lion prowling
through it, raising Tennessee Ernie up from when he was my age. I didn't
know that Travis's song was a Kentucky miner's son's take on the Josh White
school of bluesy class-conscious folksong (Travis's guitar intro sounded a lot
like White's intro to "One Meatball," and Paul Robeson could have sung
"Sixteen Tons" without changing a word), and it would be years before I
would learn about the exploitation of mine workers. But from loving that
record I knew from the age of five what a company store was, how the labor-
ing poor were perpetually in debt to it, and what kind of job it was to load
coal all day. And what it meant to sing the hell out of a song that still sounded
just as great fifty years later. No wonder it was the fastest-selling record Capi-
tol had ever had.

Once I was tall enough to reach the radio dial, I lived in a world of lyrics.
The music that was going on in that place and time was so exciting that even
a little kid could feel it. The *Shreveport Times* ran big ads for the *Louisiana*

a live audience on Shreveport's KWKH. The *Hay-*
st important music show on southern radio, behind the
nservative *Grand Ole Opry* on WSM in Nashville. Radi-
a wide region at night, it played an important role in the
of both country music and rock 'n' roll. I'm just old enough to
when there wasn't that clear a line between the styles.

was on the *Hayride*, beginning in 1948, that Hank Williams attracted
attention that catapulted him to national stardom with "Lovesick Blues."
It was there that Elvis, who was too indelicate for the Opry, appeared in 1954
as "the Hillbilly Cat" in a pink sport coat and white bucks. He remained
there for over two years as a contract performer, gaining his first regular experience in front of a live, paying audience. At his final *Hayride* appearance on
December 15, 1956, female fans swarmed atop his Mercury as he left, leaving announcer Horace Logan to try to quiet the crowd with that twentieth-
century catchphrase, "Elvis has left the building."[1] In the two years that followed,
young male singers tried to look and sound like Elvis, creating the main corpus
of the style that would be called rockabilly. There was no need for that name in
Shreveport, where it was simply the way music sounded. That was my music. One
of my musics, anyway.

There was definitely a Shreveport sound, and it's been kind of overlooked
in rock 'n' roll history. A cousin of the Memphis sound, it was right there
when rock 'n' roll was being defined, and I heard it every day on the radio.
Creedence Clearwater Revival's first hit adapted it: "Suzie Q," originally
recorded at KWKH on February 14, 1957, by Dale Hawkins, a clerk at Stan's
Record Shop, for Stan Lewis's Jewel Records. The guitar player was James
Burton from nearby Dubberley, Louisiana, who at fourteen had become the
Hayride's house guitarist. That record in turn was based on one of Howlin'
Wolf's Memphis sides.[2] But one difference between the Shreveport and the
Memphis sounds was that all the Shreveport artists we heard of were white.
There were black musicians in Shreveport, sure, but they didn't get heard.

I would have died happy if I could have been in the *Hayride* audience,
though by then the show was in its decline, its bigger names having decamped
to Nashville—or in Elvis's case Hollywood, or in Hank's case hillbilly heaven.
I did, however, get my parents to take me to my second choice of all the places
in the world I wanted to go: Stan's, on Texas Street in Shreveport, where one
day in 1959 I bought Stan's Plug Platter, the weekly special hit single that
sold for sixty-nine cents: "It's Late," by Ricky Nelson (with James Burton on
guitar) on the Imperial label. Sixty-nine cents was also the price of a pound
of coffee, my first notion of money providing equivalence in commodities. I

knew the price of coffee because I was already a coffee drinker, having begun, like many southern children, at the age of seven. That jumpy music seemed just right to me.

———————

I was eight—impressively old, it seemed to me—swaggering up to the big brass cash register in the Piggly Wiggly, a supermarket name seemingly invented to mesmerize a child. The register transfixed me as it literally rang up each purchase, dinging a bell and popping up metal number tabs that made a grinding sound as they displayed the price. As Mom bought her groceries, I clutched the object of my desire: my first record album, stickered at $2.99. I'd marshalled the price up in quarters, mowing lawns at twenty-five cents a pop. That was twelve lawns I'd had to mow. Those Louisiana lawns were big, and it wasn't just that I was so little.

My first album had to be Elvis, even though the cover of *A Date with Elvis* was stupid: Elvis was in his Army uniform at the wheel of a car, presumably showing up at his date's house to pick her up. They would go for an evening at the soda shop and a movie, and then they would go parking and Elvis would do something with her (I wasn't sure what that consisted of), and he'd have her home by ten thirty. The idea of the cover was that Elvis was inviting you into his car. But I didn't want to get into the goddamn car with Elvis, I wanted to *be* Elvis and have that fifty-foot woman get into *my* car. But mostly I just had to hear that crazy music, at my command, in my own home.

I don't have many souvenirs of those days, but I still have that copy of *A Date with Elvis*. The back of the double-gatefold package is taken up with a full year's calendar headlined ELVIS 1960, with March 5—the day he was to get out of the army—circled in red. There's no discographic information. It was a repackage of Elvis's Sun sessions, interspersed with hokier tunes from his movies. (In case you forgot, Elvis made four movies before he was drafted: *Love Me Tender, Loving You, Jailhouse Rock,* and *King Creole.* The last of those, in this writer's opinion Elvis's best, was set in the French Quarter of New Orleans. "Crawfish," the movie's funky minor-key opening duet and the only duet of Elvis with a black singer that I know of, is rife with sexual double entendre as Elvis sings from up on a balcony down to Kitty White, who plays a peddler coming up Royal Street on her wagon. The band locks into a mechanical Latinoid rhythm that sounds like it's twenty years later.)

The tunes on *A Date with Elvis* were already oldies—the best ones predated "Sixteen Tons"—but that was cool. Elvis's white-man boogie didn't come out of nowhere, not when Tennessee Ernie was already singing "Shotgun Boogie" in 1951. But the Sun sessions changed record-making, and in my simplified way, I knew that even then. The first cut was "Blue Moon of Kentucky," a drastically repurposed 1954 cover of a bluegrass tune by Bill Monroe. It's easy to forget that the band consisted of only two instrumentalists. With Scotty Moore on guitar and Bill Black's percussively slapped upright bass, a tape-slapback echo, and no drum set, those Sun tracks rock harder than any multitrack kick-snare-hat soundscape.

I appalled my father by telling him, "I can't wait to be a teenager. So I can rock." Indeed, when I was a teenager, my generation would dedicate itself to rocking, having learned in childhood that teenagers were supposed to do that. What I wanted to do, to the extent I could even imagine what it was, had little to do with what *rock* meant later, when it had become, as one group's name had it, a Cheap Trick.

But I knew rocking when I heard it. It was perfectly defined by Elvis on "Good Rockin' Tonight." The song had first come out in a swinging, horn-driven version by its composer, Roy Brown, in the jump blues style made massively popular by Louis Jordan. Recorded at Cosimo Matassa's J&M studio in the French Quarter (just across from the site of Congo Square) in 1947, Brown's tune first became a local hit in New Orleans, a direct result of the locally new phenomenon of black radio. Bullet point: music started to rock when black radio started to happen. That is, black music programmed for black listeners; the "black" DJ in New Orleans, Poppa Stoppa, was white (actually, a succession of white announcers who used the name). Poppa Stoppa's character and patter were scripted for him by a black man, Vernon Winslow, who wasn't himself allowed to speak on the air until he debuted in 1949 as Doctor Daddy-O.[3] "Good Rockin' Tonight" kicked off a fad for "rockin'" songs, a wave that included Louis Jordan's "Saturday Night Fish Fry," which told the story of a party getting busted in New Orleans and which might qualify as either an early rock 'n' roll or a proto-rap record.

Roy Brown had written "Good Rockin' Tonight" hoping to get Wynonie Harris to sing it, and soon Harris recorded it too, scoring a #1 hit with a handclap-backbeat powered version recorded at Syd Nathan's vertically integrated recording-mastering-and-pressing setup in Cincinnati and released in February 1948. Harris followed it up in 1949 with "All She Wants to Do Is Rock," which retained the handclap and repeated: *All she wants to do is rock / Rock and roll all night long.* "Rock and roll" wasn't a new phrase even then, but Alan Freed, who popularized the phrase *rock 'n' roll* as an industry label to describe what had formerly been known as rhythm and blues, didn't begin calling it that until 1955.

Recorded by Sam Phillips in Memphis in 1954, "Good Rockin' Tonight" was Elvis's second Sun single and was only a regional hit at the time, but five years later they included it on *A Date with Elvis*. I played it over and over, torturing out the meaning of the lyrics. The song took place in a setting I could easily visualize: *Meet me in a hurry, behind the barn . . .* When you heard the news that everybody was rockin' tonight, you needed to be ready with your special rockin' shoes. It was clearly a magical pursuit.

Elvis's version, which dispensed with the horns and included a rave-up coda that hung out on the word *rock*, was more exciting than either of the previous records of the song. Roy Brown and Wynonie Harris were relaxed in their uptempo groove; Elvis was tense. That hillbilly rhythm singer had something else going on.

"Good Rockin' Tonight" was a cover of a song by a black singer, and Elvis has been much criticized for being a white guy singing black music. Certainly Elvis's records owe considerably to black music, but Elvis wasn't *copying* "Good Rockin' Tonight." He *became* it, the way Ray Charles became "Georgia on My Mind" six years later.

I don't buy the idea of Elvis as blackface minstrelsy. Elvis never pretended to take on supposedly racial characteristics or made fun of black people. He didn't shuck and jive. He was no coonshow. Elvis was being himself. And that *that* was who he was, was far more frightening to a white South that had done everything to keep the white "race" pure, to the point of separating two castes of people off into two separate, unequal worlds. Without realizing he was doing it, Elvis served notice that the days of segregation were numbered. As were my days of watching cartoons and reading comic books. I quit that kid stuff. It was rock 'n' roll for me.

I listened to black music every day. Elvis didn't sound like that to me. Partly that's because the black music Elvis copied came mostly from another generation that his black contemporaries had moved past. On his first hit, "That's All Right, Mama," he sounded a *lot* like Arthur "Big Boy" Crudup, a singer few people had otherwise heard of. Elvis freely admitted his debt; I knew about Arthur Crudup's influence on Elvis back when I lived in Natchitoches, because I was a fan and read everything I could find about Elvis. But to my ear, Elvis was a better singer than Arthur Crudup—which was, it should be noted, rarely the case when white singers covered black songs.

Elvis synthesized a whole bunch of stuff that was in the air in the early 1950s, from Tony Curtis's haircut and Dean Martin's croon to a hillbilly singer's storytelling, a gospel singer's intensity, a blues singer's sense of pitch, and a Latin singer's sense of time. There was some very hip stuff going on in those early Elvis recordings; specifically, his rhythmic phrasing was cutting edge for 1954. He was a ballad crooner *and* a rhythm singer.

But Elvis did bring something to his singing, over and above anything strictly musical, that he might well have learned from African American men. I don't mean the pelvis stuff. I mean his confidence in his own powers of performance, the sense of authority with which he sang a rhythm number.

The race romances from the age of Thomas Dixon sometimes featured as a bugaboo a seemingly white creature whose one drop of "black blood" would assert itself in the form of bestial African behavior—the "revenant."[4] Elvis was precisely what racists feared would happen. Even though the two castes had been kept as far apart as possible, here was a white man acting like a black man, like he had that one drop in him and it was coming out.

We had segregated society but integrated radio. For segregated whites, being forbidden to have personal contact with the possessors of those African American voices gave the radio listening experience the lure of the forbidden. It was a thrill not available at the movies. The title of Ralph Ellison's *Invisible Man*—published in 1952, just as what would be called rock 'n' roll was getting under way—points to the way black people were unseen in the media, as well as in society at large. Gregory Tate has suggested—this is my paraphrase of what I heard him say, anyway—that because black people had been excluded for so long from the visual media, they took to the audio-only space with extra intensity. Makes sense to me.

During the years I began tuning in—specifically 1956 through 1958—black musicians dominated rock 'n' roll, with Fats Domino at the top of the list. Rhythm and blues didn't "fuse" with rockabilly in becoming rock 'n' roll, it kicked it out of the way. Black musicians did the hard work of desegregation, playing color-line dances up and down the South, in places where the black and white audiences were separated by a rope down the middle of the dance floor, or one or another caste was exiled to the balcony. And after the gig it could be a long drive to a place that would let the bone-tired musicians have beds.

Writing in 1903 about an incident in which a black man and a white woman were arrested in Atlanta for talking together on the street, W. E. B. DuBois observed: "between the two worlds, despite much physical contact and daily intermingling, there is almost no community of intellectual life or point of transference where the thoughts and feelings of one race can come into direct contact and sympathy with the thoughts and feelings of the other."[5] But he was writing before radio existed. Radio let me listen to Dinah Washington, the elegant, sophisticated singer who spent her too-short life running from Tuscaloosa, Alabama. To this day, when I hear her voice, I stop being wherever I am and I go where she is.

Movies told me lies, but music told me the truth. I'm still trying to untangle the lies; it's why I read history. And I'm still trying to understand the truths. Music taught me about being human.

The relationship between the reality of songs and the reality of life is a riddle that I've puzzled over as a songwriter ever since. Perhaps the number one truth music told me was that love is the most important thing in life. I've always believed it, and I'm sure I took some of my notions of love from songs. But there was a lot of other music besides love songs, and it told me all kinds of stories—not only through lyrics, but also through timbre, harmony, rhythm, style, attitude, and the kineticism that spoke directly to the body even when the lyrics were corny.

When the world I lived in systematically denied me any contact with African Americans, songs reached across the barrier to me. I tried to imagine the worlds their songs projected: Dinah Washington, Fats Domino, Sam Cooke, Clyde McPhatter, Ray Charles, Jackie Wilson, Brook Benton, Etta James, LaVerne Baker, Little Richard, Lloyd Price, Hank Ballard and the Midnighters. And then came Ike and Tina Turner, Curtis Mayfield with the Impressions, Jerry Butler, James Brown, and on and on. I still listen to those records. I'll never get to the bottom of them.

We never visited New Orleans the whole time I was growing up in Natchitoches. It had the aura of something too impossibly grand for a kid like me. Before 2004, I'd only been there once. But it was a hell of a once—ten days spent hanging out there in 1992, producing an episode for the public radio program *Afropop Worldwide* with my friend and inadvertent mentor, the late Robert Palmer, who took me around. I'd already driven across Cuba and back with Bob (and Constance, who had to listen to us talk the whole way), so we were comfortable with each other. Bob, originally from Little Rock, was six years older than me, and those were six crucial years in American music history. He had a clear vision of it: a monograph he published was subtitled *Memphis Rock and New Orleans Roll.*[6] He totally got what I was about, maybe before I did, and he gave it back to me amplified.

Bob loved living in the Tremé. Despite its 1960s disfigurement by the I-10 trestles that run smack through it, you could still see an unbroken continuity— social, architectural, and in almost every other way—back to the birth of jazz, and beyond. Bob gave me the correct introduction to New Orleans. After that, I was on the right foot. He took me to Russell's Cool Spot to hear the Tremé Brass Band. He introduced me to Kermit Ruffins, and sent me to Rock 'n' Bowl to check out Boozoo Chavis. We interviewed pianist/composer/producer Allen

Toussaint together. I went to Greater St. Stephen's Full Gospel Baptist Church on Liberty Street and got permission to record the Sunday morning service, when they praised God with a mighty choir and a funky organ combo.

The town was bursting with music, but it was raw. On the way back from St. Stephen's, driving through Central City back to the downtown rooming house where I was staying, I saw a big, well-dressed young black man in an expensive car go into a rage, reach over, and smack his woman passenger upside the head while he was driving. I can still hear his shout, the slap, her scream and sob.

Driving through the Ninth Ward that week, I found myself between adjacent parallel streets named Piety and Desire that ran one-way in contrary directions. A lyric appeared in my mind:

> I live between Piety and Desire
> On my one hand a blessing, on the other hot hellfire
> By day I sweat, by night I perspire
> At home between Piety and Desire.

I couldn't come up with a second verse, though.

A record-biz buddy who had worked on a reissue project with Fats Domino had given me Fats's number and said, hey, call him up. I screwed up my courage and dialed the number from Bob's phone. Fats answered the phone himself. Friendly and gracious as could be, he wasn't the least bit perturbed that I'd interrupted whatever he was doing, and we conversed very politely for maybe three minutes before I excused myself.

I have no memory of what the conversation was about, but what I remember is that he talked like he sang. Anything he said to me, my brain was like, my God, it's *that voice*. I had nothing to discuss with him. I didn't propose to interview him, or do business, or anything. He would have been well within his rights to tell me to go fuck myself, but he was nice to me. I've met plenty of stars in my time, but I've never done anything like that, call up a celebrity because I was such a fan, like a thirteen-year-old, much less at the age of forty and presumably knowing better. I'm very respectful of other peoples' privacy. I couldn't believe I had done it. But this was *Fats Domino*. You would have done it too.

Antoine "Fats" Domino was born in 1928, the same year as my dad. He was delivered at home by his midwife grandmother, who had been born enslaved in 1857. Let me underscore that: the first rock 'n' roll star was pulled from the womb by an ex-slave.[7]

Domino was born to a French- and English-speaking Creole family in what was newly being called the Lower Ninth Ward, because it had been separated off from the rest of the bustling Ninth Ward in the 1910s by the digging of the Inner Harbor Navigation Canal, also known as the Industrial Canal. Most of the families in the Lower Ninth were recent arrivals from the sugar and cotton plantations, including Domino's family. It was like being in the country, but with the great city of New Orleans right there across the bridge.

Nobody had as many hits in the '50s as Fats Domino except Elvis. OK, Pat Boone, but forget Pat Boone. In 1957, the year the white boys started to come up, Fats and Elvis dueled out the #1 spot. Fats Domino remains the most widely loved New Orleanian since Louis Armstrong to this day. His first hit, "The Fat Man," was his take on a straight-up boogie-woogie piano style. Just as there was no recording artist more likable than Fats Domino, there was no music more likable than boogie-woogie. "The Fat Man" was an adaptation of "The Junker's Blues," sung by Champion Jack Dupree:

> *They call, they call me a junko*
> *'Cause I'm loaded all the time . . .*

That double entendre of a dope fiend talking as if he were a loaded-down junkman driving a wagon became in Fats's cleaned-up pop version:

> *They ca-all me the fat man*
> *'Cause I weigh two hundred pounds . . .*

That was in 1949, at the beginning of New Orleans's rhythm and blues explosion, before they called it rock 'n' roll. Fats Domino was the first rock 'n' roll star, and while his first record, "The Fat Man," might not sound like rock 'n' roll as it was later defined, it was rock 'n' roll *avant la lettre*: boogie-woogie simplified and locked down by Domino's right-hand pounding and insistent bass throb. Behind it was Earl Palmer's snare on 2 and 4, snapping out that shuffling backbeat and also providing a decisive last note on the record, as if to nail it shut.

With "The Fat Man," a line had been crossed. This stripped-down way of playing boogie-woogie, whapping out triplets in the right hand and thumping left-hand power chords instead of walking basses, was less flexible, and more driving, than what had gone before. Domino followed it with a string of piano-triplet-and-snare-backbeat hits. He didn't exactly swing. Boogie-woogie players called their grooves "rocks," and Fats rocked, literalizing the triplet feel implicit in the swing and shuffle of rhythm and blues.

Most of his hits were produced, arranged, and directed by Dave Bartholomew, whose band was the first professional R & B recording studio group, an important precedent for the great achievement of Motown's Funk Brothers many years later. Their style relied on each player taking a rhythmic part and repeating it, implying a polyrhythm that was only starting to assert itself in African American music (as opposed to its more polyrhythmic cousins in Cuba and Latin New York) and would continue to develop through the era of funk. Bartholomew had played on passenger-cruise riverboats up and down the Mississippi, which had their golden age between the two world wars; he recalled having to play the music more square as the boat went farther north.[8]

Besides Fats Domino's hits, Bartholomew's band cut a number of the early classics of rock 'n' roll, notably "Lawdy Miss Clawdy" by the teenaged Lloyd Price, with Earl Palmer on drums and Domino sitting in, pounding triplets on the piano. They did Guitar Slim's "The Things I Used to Do," arranged by Ray Charles, still on his way up; the raucous hits by "Little" Richard Penniman, who definitively made screaming part of rock 'n' roll vocal style; and plenty of others. In the '50s, the group's sound was a frequent presence on the pop charts, and Bartholomew retained a library of copyrights that would pay him handsomely through the years.

Though some non-New Orleanians will disagree, I am convinced that the general consensus is correct: New Orleans was the place where the transformative step was taken from ragged time, rural blues, marching band, spiritual church, and various other styles of music into what became called jazz—the birthplace of jazz, as the shorthand goes, though that oversimplifies the complexity of the process. I am also convinced that key elements of rock 'n' roll came out of New Orleans, in an open circuit with Memphis, just up the river.

Fats Domino's music doesn't sound anything like the music that was known as "rock" forty years later—a joyless, formulaic texture of electric guitars, overly miked trap drums, and white males howling into a hurricane of sound—but in 1956, Fats Domino was what rock 'n' roll was.

Earl Palmer, the drummer on "The Fat Man," probably did more than any other single person to invent rock 'n' roll drumming, starting back when the music was called rhythm and blues. He changed the way people thought about a drum kit. The way he played his bass drum and combined it with the snare, informed by the New Orleans parade band style, became such a commonplace sound that we don't recognize it as anything unusual. Palmer, who liked to joke that New Orleans was the town where even the white people clapped on 2 and 4, defined both basic versions of the rock 'n' roll backbeat, shuffled and straight, and laced them with outrageously tasty fills that no one could duplicate.

Earl Palmer controlled the tempo during a great period of New Orleans music, playing on years' worth of hits for various artists with Bartholomew. He was even the one who popularized the centuries-old word *funk*, meaning a bad smell, in relation to musical style—at least according to John Broven's pathbreaking 1978 *Rhythm and Blues in New Orleans*, which quotes Earl King as saying: "Earl Palmer the drummer was really responsible for that word 'funk.' . . . At the recording sessions, he would say, 'Look, man, let's play a little funkier,' and the word would start going around." [9]

Born in 1924, Palmer started tap dancing in the French Quarter for tips when he was "four, five years old," he told Tad Jones in a 1994 interview. "The Dog House on Rampart, the Silver Slipper down on St. Claude and St. Bernard, other clubs around town that had floor shows, we'd do three different shows in three different clubs on Friday and Saturday." In *Backbeat*, his autobiography/oral history with Tony Scherman, he recalled how he and his pint-sized friends would work their way along Bourbon Street, where a club manager would announce to the white tourists, "And now for a special treat, we're going to bring on some little nigger boys to dance for you all." [10]

In the classic Tremé manner, Palmer started to play drums while still a tap-dancing child, with a bass drum made from an orange crate (complete with a homemade version of that New Orleans innovation of the 1890s, the bass-drum foot pedal) and a lard-can cymbal. He traveled all around on the vaudeville circuit, getting to know the country while working with his mother in Ida Cox's Darktown Scandals revue. As a child, he once sat on Bessie Smith's lap, and he did a brief stint in the Rabbit's Foot Minstrels. When he was sixteen, in 1941, he stowed away on a United Fruit Company steamer for a three-day vacation on the down low in Havana. Again, from *Backbeat*: "Do you realize Havana, Cuba, in 1941 was one of the wildest places on earth?—gambling and prostitution and dope all over, and music hipper than anything I'd heard to that day." [11] That there was somewhere with hipper music than New Orleans was quite something for a New Orleanian to admit, but then, he caught New Orleans's big-sister city of Havana at a peak musical moment.

Palmer learned to read music and studied piano and percussion using his GI bill scholarship at the new Grunewald School of Music on Camp Street, which accepted black students, albeit in separate divisions. According to Bruce Boyd Raeburn, curator of the Hogan Jazz Archive at Tulane, "Guys I talked to said they had a white floor and a black floor, 'but everyone spent all their time on the stairs.'" He joined Dave Bartholomew's band in 1947, and, at least by his own account, he gave the young Antoine Domino what turned out to be an important break, inviting the poorly dressed Domino, over Bartholomew's objection, to come up and play between sets of Bartholomew's suit-and-tie band at Al's Starlight Inn on North Dorgenois Street.[12] Later, Bartholomew would lead Imperial Records head Lew Chudd down a dirt road in the Lower Ninth Ward to Domino's gig at the Hideaway, to sign up the youngster.

Pretty much all of the dozens of hits cut in New Orleans until the late 1960s were done at Cosimo Matassa's J & M studio, the only full-time music recording studio in town. Until 1956, the studio was at Rampart and Dumaine, in the back room of Matassa's record shop, a business he had branched into from selling appliances. When "Little" Richard Penniman came from Macon, Georgia, to record at J & M, Palmer played a shuffling backbeat behind him, and they started making hits. But one day in 1956, Penniman brought a number where the shuffle wouldn't work. Recalling the July 30 recording of "Lucille," Palmer said in *Backbeat*, "with Richard pounding the piano with all ten fingers, you couldn't so very well go against that."[13] So he played straight time, not shuffle time, in which the eighth notes were equal in length to each other, with a hard-hit snare on the 2 and 4. The rock beat was born.

This distinction between swing (or shuffle) time and straight (or Latin) time is crucial to understanding the music of this period, and to appreciating Earl Palmer's achievement. Alas, the difference is easy to hear but hard to describe. Let me try:

In swing time, each beat is subdivided into two unequal parts. The first part, or downbeat, is longer than second and is de-emphasized, while the shorter second part of the beat, the upbeat, has an accent, a kind of "push." African American music from the 1920s through the '50s was almost all swing time. If it's swinging in a steady, pulsing rhythm while the bass plays four or eight beats to the bar, that's a shuffle. Sing "Work With Me Annie" to yourself and you're shuffling. In straight time, on the other hand, each beat is subdivided into two equal parts. It could easily be called Latin time, because it has the feel of Afro-Cuban music, which never swings, and the rhythmic flavor comes not from a regular upbeat push but from where in the two-bar period the accents fall. (That two-bar period is what Cubans call *clave*).

Of these two feels, straight time is better suited for layering multiple rhythms on top of each other. The negotiation between the two was the major rhythmic drama of the late 1940s and '50s, as perfectly exemplified by the Dizzy Gillespie and Chano Pozo collaboration "Manteca"—a Latin number played by African Americans in swing time.

It was a great period of rhythic experimentation. Chuck Berry played straight time on his guitar while his drummer shuffled. Bo Diddley played the clave rhythm in swing time. First-generation white rockers played both shuffles and straight time, often resorting to the Latin book of tricks for the latter. Buddy Holly played in shuffle time for "That'll Be the Day" and straight time for the rumba-rocker "Peggy Sue." But that ended with the 1950s, and the second-generation British rockers of the '60s hardly played shuffles at all, because their drummers didn't swing. The shuffle wasn't Charlie Watts's forte, let alone Ringo Starr's. The Brit drummers went for that straight-8ths rock beat, simplifying and institutionalizing it in the rush of their popularity. By the mid-'60s, what Earl Palmer instigated had become the main style.

By then, Palmer was established in Los Angeles, having moved out of New Orleans in 1957. When he got to L.A., he was known as the rock 'n' roll drummer, which wasn't a compliment: he was the only professional drummer who would *accept* rock 'n' roll dates. Palmer didn't mind; asking him to play rock 'n' roll was asking him to play like himself, because, as he once put it, "I invented this shit." Producers in Los Angeles loved to hire him, because he could play all by himself what they were in the habit of hiring two, or even three, players to do. He became one of the most recorded drummers in history. That was Earl Palmer in 1958, powering the barely musically competent Ritchie Valens on "La Bamba," playing drums and *1-2-cha-cha-chá* woodblock both (the latter using the then-uncommon technique of overdubbing). With "La Bamba," Palmer created a cha-cha-chá rock template that future rock bands would recycle throughout the '60s (e.g., the Rolling Stones' "Satisfaction"). On Valens's "Come On Let's Go," he created a prototype for garage-rock drumming as we would know it in the '60s. If rock 'n' roll was boogie-woogie meets cha-cha-chá—and I argue that rhythmically it pretty much was—then Earl Palmer was the musician who, between "The Fat Man" and "La Bamba," played a key role in both ends of that rhythmic handoff.

Palmer explained his reasons for leaving New Orleans at least two different ways on different occasions, but they boil down to the same thing. The first explanation was that he was involved in an "interracial" relationship, at a time when such cohabitations were criminalized by anti-"miscegenation" statutes and could moreover be hazardous to one's health. He put a different perspective on it in a 1973 interview with the late Tad Jones, conducted by phone between New Orleans and Los Angeles at a time when few people were interested in the history of rhythm and blues or rock 'n' roll, and when Jones was just starting out on what would be his life's work. (Jones had to terminate the interview, now in the Hogan Jazz Archive, after fourteen minutes, because his telephone money had run out.)

TJ: What made all the musicians leave? What was it that we had the studio scene here and you used to play, and Harold Battiste played, and Lee Allen, and then everybody . . .

EP: The reason most black guys leave the South! Better opportunities! I was the best drummer in New Orleans, but I still didn't make enough to support my family, while the guys down on Bourbon Street were able to get the better jobs and we couldn't work those places. The same reason that a black guy would leave Atlanta, or Nashville, or Jackson, Mississippi, the same reason. 'Cause it doesn't matter how good he is, he can only do so much there.

TJ: So you'd say that New Orleans couldn't support its musicians?

EP: Well, I'm afraid . . . [pause]. How old are you?

TJ: I'm twenty.

EP: Well then, perhaps you don't remember New Orleans when it wasn't a matter of support. It was a matter of New Orleans would only support the white musicians because they got the better jobs.

There was another wrinkle to that. Sidemen were hired help, and the musicians' union in New Orleans was weak. Actually, it was unions, plural: there were two musicians' unions, Local 174 for "white" musicians and Local 496 for "black" ones. (The number of the New Orleans local today, 174-496, reflects the fact that the two merged, over resistance from both sides, in 1971.) The division made a mockery of the idea of a union. In Los Angeles, the two color-caste locals had already merged, in 1953, into Local 47, and in Hollywood, standing alongside the other performers' unions (SAG and AFTRA), the musicians' union had clout. Palmer's union card was his ticket to getting well paid to spread his beats through all streams of pop music, and he remained a passionate union man all his life. Doing residual-paying TV and movie dates as a union man—*Hawaiian Eye, The Flintstones, Mission Impossible,* and years' worth of other TV and movie themes—he was part of the first generation of black musicians to be well compensated.

And so were Dave Bartholomew and Fats Domino, for all the money Domino's business people made off with. At the beginning of 2005, when many of the stars of '60s rock excess had died, much of the first generation of rock 'n' roll was still out there gigging: Chuck Berry, Bo Diddley, Little Richard, Jerry Lee Lewis. But Fats Domino didn't really need to perform, and didn't like to. He wrote many of his own hits, and he kept his publishing, which is how you get paid in the music business. While some of his con-temporaries—Bo Diddley, for one—lived out their days wishing they hadn't taken the chump change and signed that piece of paper, Fats Domino had a nice big house in the Lower Ninth Ward, on Caffin Avenue, the street he'd lived on since 1950, when it was a dirt road. He told interviewer Michael Hurtt that he spent over two hundred dollars a day cooking.[14]

Two years before we moved away from Natchitoches, my parents ascended to home ownership, and we moved into a brand-new house with ultra-modern conveniences. Not only did it have an all-electric stove, it had trebly little speakers recessed into the walls, with push-button intercoms between the rooms and a radio tuner located over the stove. The future had arrived: we had a house with music coming out of the walls! I also had a Gridiron Football novelty radio, manufactured to look like a football, though it was considerably heavier. It was the most interested in football I ever got.

During our last summer in Natchitoches, as we prepared to move to El Paso, "Walking to New Orleans" was bopping out of my wall and my ceramic football. I listened to it on KEEL, the #1 station in Shreveport, and when I spun the dial to KOKA, the black station, it was there too. It would be Fats Domino's last top ten hit.

The record's rhythm described not dancing, but walking. The damped gui-tars set the pace: clip, clop, clip, clop—a purposeful cross-country walk. Nor was it a march. This wasn't a slave coffle where everyone's feet had to be synchronized so the leg irons wouldn't tear them up. This was a man walking by himself, set-ting his own tempo. I'm gonna need two pair of shoes . . . I tried to figure how many days it would take to walk the 282 miles from Natchitoches to New Orleans.

Part of Fats Domino's charm was his unique delivery, stemming from his black French Creole country way of talking. When he sang "Walking to New Orleans," written for him by Bobby Charles (Robert Charles Guidry), the white Cajun who also composed "See You Later Alligator," he was wrapping one French Louisiana linguistic heritage around another—not inappropri-ately, given how many blacks and whites (that is, people on different sides of that arbitrarily policed line) were cousins in south Louisiana. Part of the fun of the song is its permissive sense of rhyme. Even Fats couldn't quite manage to rhyme "hand" with "shame": I got my suitcase in my hand / Now ain't that a shame? And when he sings Noo Awlins is ma home / Thass the reason while I'm gone, it's not why I'm gone. Fats says, the reason while I'm gone. Kids can think about this stuff for days.

Meanwhile, Fats's biggest competitor had a hot new record out.

It was the year Elvis was discharged from the army, in what we would now call a media event. Elvis had something to prove, and as far as I was concerned, his comeback single proved it. I still have my scratched-up 45 of "Stuck on You," though I haven't had a machine to play it on for twenty-five years.

Not that it wasn't a little disturbing. The lyrics of "Stuck on You" seem to be told from the point of view of a jovial stalker bent on rape, part of the caricature of Elvis as an affable, thick-headed satyr that his post-army film career increasingly began to depict. The bridge goes:

> Hide in the kitchen, hide in the hall
> Ain't gonna do you no good at all
> 'Cause once I catch ya and the kissin' starts
> A team of wild horses couldn't tear us apart

Black men in the South had been lynched for saying less. Though women were lynched on occasion, and though pretexts varied, the victim of lynching was typically male and the classic allegation rape. The justification for vigilante action was the need to spare the victim the shame of having to testify in open court. Indeed, Reconstruction itself was often represented as black rape of the female South. A 1909 history of South Carolina put it succinctly: "The negro rapist, the black brute, fear of whom hangs like a dark cloud over all the south land—who is in latter days found and lynched—is a direct product of the teachings and practices of the days of reconstruction."[15]

The pace of lynching had abated by Elvis's day, but it hadn't entirely stopped. In 1955, when Elvis was a regular on the Louisiana Hayride, a fourteen-year-old Chicago boy named Emmett Till, on vacation to visit his country relatives in the tiny town of Money in Elvis's home state of Mississippi, was dragged from his bed at two in the morning, tortured, and killed for allegedly having been disrespectful to a white woman. Some fifty thousand people filed past his coffin in Chicago, which was kept open at Till's mother's insistence so the extent of his injuries could be seen by the world. Two white men were later acquitted of the crime in the face of overwhelming evidence against them. The following year they admitted their guilt and sold their story to Look magazine.

Apparently stimulated by Chuck D's dis of him in "Fight the Power," it seems to have become a common belief in recent years that Elvis was a racist. I didn't know Elvis myself, but I go with Peter Guralnick on that one: he wasn't.[16] At least not in the blunt way that we in the South associated with the KKK, George Lincoln Rockwell, and George Wallace, and leaving aside the question of the spiders we all have in our heads from growing up in a racist society. But that Elvis's success was a phenomenon of a racist society there is no doubt. He could literally walk through doors that were closed to the competition, especially when it came to flaunting his masculinity, something black male singers weren't allowed to do, at least in a mainstream context. There was one mainstream black sex symbol, a tasteful one—Harry Belafonte, whose *Calypso* was the first million-selling LP, and who would become the first big postwar pop music star to be strongly identified as an activist. But the nonsouthern, Manhattan-born, Jamaica-rooted Belafonte didn't come across as African American. Elvis stood in for black sexuality in the segregated marketplace. He benefited not only from the repression of his black musical competition but even from the repression of that competition's sex appeal, at a moment when that repression was being definitively repudiated and was about to burst open.

His bad-boy sex appeal was threatening to parents, but by 1960 something had changed. I remember the exact words my dad said: that he thought differently about Elvis "after he went into the army with such good graces." Even Elvis's sexuality had been legitimized by his stint in the Army. Priapism was normal for soldiers.

The post–World War II years saw a surge of fiction, written and filmed, about army life, often focusing on the sexual opportunities it offered. Much of it was based on real-life experiences of American everymen while serving overseas in World War II and afterward. Soldiers were in effect granted a license for promiscuity, or even predatory sexual behavior, in thanks for service to their country and in consideration of their remote posting. The thrill of screwing the entire world animated Elvis's first post-Army movie, *G.I. Blues*, a peacetime military musical comedy (there's a genre that didn't last long) set in occupied Germany. The plot hinges around a bet between a G.I. named Tulsa (Elvis) and his buddies as to whether he could nail cabaret dancer Juliet Prowse. From then on, Elvis made two movies a year or more, one for Thanksgiving release and one for Easter. Each one was a worse joke than the one before. I know, because I saw them all, until *Harum Scarum*, which was the last straw.

"Stuck on You" wasn't in any of those awful movies. I heard it on the radio in 2004 in New Orleans. It had lost none of its excitement. It's a real performance, everybody playing and singing together at one time, the way records haven't been made for decades now, and it's sharp as a shoeshine. It's a shuffle, which isn't as easy to play as it might seem, with a strong Cuban-clave feeling to the vocal: *ah-you can SHAKE an AP-ple off an / ap-ple TREE* . . . Shuffles were gradually disappearing from pop music as the straight-8ths Latin-style beat took over, but Elvis's drummer, D. J. Fontana, knew how to shuffle. He was from Shreveport, where he'd been the house drummer on the *Hayride* as well as punctuating tassel twirls at strip joints in Shreveport's sleazier neighbor, Bossier City. He's not on Elvis's earliest records, but once he joined the band in 1956 he became indispensable. Elvis always knew where his time was at.

The record's drama was built in by the songwriters (Aaron Schroder and J. Leslie MacFarland), who constructed the dynamics of their song around their knowledge of Elvis's voice. Elvis, who pretty much defined what a rock 'n' roll star would be, was one of the few baritones in a genre mostly dominated by screaming tenors. The whole tune sits in his full, round, lower register. Elvis could imply more with vowels than most singers could say with words: *aa-aa-ha / No, siree, aa-aa-ha*. When the release comes—the "team of wild horses" line—the melody jumps up to a higher degree of the scale than you think it's going to. He switches into head voice (which really means he sings louder and higher), and opens up his lungs full for "tear us apart."

Talk about a climax. The whole song is a life support for that moment. But the test is not how out can you go, it's how perfectly can you come back in. He drops back down into chest voice and goes back into the verse as if nothing had happened, and then does it all again—partly in case you didn't believe it the first time, and partly because it's a pop song and can only repeat, instead of breaking into an evolving call-and-response jam like a Latin tune or a gospel tune might do.

By the time "Stuck on You" was released, Elvis and I were old friends. "Stuck on You" helped me get out of the '50s and into the '60s. Which is to say, out of Natchitoches and into El Paso. When we got to our new home in August 1960, "Stuck on You" was still on the radio, though it was fading. I turned it up every time it came on, and I owned the single. I could play it on my most prized possession, my portable record player, whenever I wanted to remind myself who I was in that weird new town. And it wasn't my imagination—El Paso *was* weird.

But Elvis's best days were behind him, and meanwhile there was new music on the radio. There was increasingly more room for black music in the pop world, and they played a lot of it in El Paso. The age of Pat Boone covering Little Richard was over. As I watched lizards run around the dusty expanse of what was supposed to be a backyard, I heard "Hit the Road, Jack," its road-tight horn section speaking together like an organ, by Ray Charles, who had just started his own big band. On the heels of that came the Drift-ers' "Save the Last Dance for Me," with its emotionally complex lyrics writ-ten by a man in a wheelchair—Doc Pomus, a Jew from Brooklyn writing for Ben E. King, the black vocalist who would incarnate his emotions—one of the maximum expressions of the Cuban-pop feel of the Brill Building sound that dominated the charts in the interval between Buddy Holly's death and the Beatles.[17] One reason "Save the Last Dance for Me" was a hit was that it *sounded* so great, with clear percussion and a distinct bass. Engineered by Tom Dowd, it was the first hit to be produced using a new kind of tape recorder that only Atlantic Records had, with eight separate tracks, ushering in a new era of sound definition and gradually polyrhythmicizing American music.

Sam Cooke's "Chain Gang" chilled me, even when I heard it on the jukebox in the Thunderbird Lanes bowling alley in El Paso. And there was a funny, irresistibly catchy one—what people called a "novelty record"—that went to #1 in 1961, by an artist from New Orleans with the odd, memo-rable name of Ernie K-Doe, though the hook was Benny Spellman's deep bass voice. It was composed and produced by Dave Bartholomew's heir apparent in New Orleans hitdom, the twenty-one-year-old Allen Toussaint:

Mooother-in-law / Mother-in-law!

Without having a vocabulary for any of this, I knew every echo, every hidden sound in the wind-off grooves. As I listened to my slowly but steadily growing record collection, and to my transistor radio, I memorized every nuance.

I tuned in Mexican stations, trying to figure out what the words meant. For the rest of my school years, I was in a bilingual environment.

5

TELL IT LIKE IT IS

W e only stayed in El Paso a year. Dad changed jobs again, and by August 1961 we were living in the little town of Portales, New Mexico. You probably never heard of it. I never had.

Between my earliest memories and the eighth grade, we'd lived in eight different houses in three states. Between May 1960 and August 1961 I'd been in four different schools. But this time we stayed put, so I finished growing up out where the far western edge of the great High Plains gives way to the eastern edge of the great American desert. Despite the town's Castilian name, the Spanish had never colonized the area. Portales (pronounced by most of its residents as "Pertallis") was not even a hundred years old, probably because it wasn't fit for human habitation. The Indians camped in the region but had no permanent settlements there. The area had been pretty much uninhabited until deep water wells were drilled in the 1890s, and since the good people of Pertallis were gradually drawing down the underground water table to irrigate crops, grow lawns, and take showers, it was pretty much guaranteed that the town would at some point dry up and blow away, like Lubbock will.

Our local recreation area consisted of a formation of sand dunes. Clovis, the bigger town eighteen miles to the north, had the stockyards, but Portales had Eastern New Mexico University, which smelled better, had 1,680 students, and was growing fast. Beyond that, Roosevelt County (named for Theodore, not Franklin) raised peanuts and yams—the classic West African crops, because they'll grow in sandy soil. In the '40s, when Portales still had two movie theaters, one of them was called the Yam. By the time I got there, the town had one indoor movie theater, the Tower, and one drive-in, the Varsity, named in honor of the town's number-one employer.

One of the big attractions for Dad to take the job at ENMU was so we could be near my maternal grandmother in Lubbock, a hundred miles east. Every other weekend or so, we piled into the station wagon and drove to Lubbock for the weekend. It took me years to see the beauty of that part of the country, but once I did, perhaps aided by the last, elegiacal era of Cinema-Scope westerns, I came to feel personal about it. The drive from Portales to Lubbock was an endless two-hour trip on two-lane state roads through mostly pure flatness, punctuated by a couple of gentle rises and falls that seemed breathtaking, especially if there had been a little rain in June and everything had briefly turned from its normal yellow-brown to a glorious green.

Though we lived in Portales, I always felt like I was going home when we went to Lubbock, though I never spent more than a summer there at a stretch. We had always visited that house at 4408 19th in Lubbock, where my grandmother's phone number was POrter 9-7647, a number that had announced Lubbock's urbanity at a time when our phone number in Natchitoches was 5244.

Lubbock is usually talked about by non-Lubbockites as some kind of ultimate cultural backwater, but it was the big city to me. In Portales, we had the *Lubbock Avalanche-Journal* tossed onto our driveway every morning. We watched Lubbock TV stations. We went to Lubbock to go to the hospital, and if we had taken planes, we would have gone to Lubbock to do it. If you were interested, you could hear Julian Bream, Dave Brubeck, or Ravi Shankar when they played a concert at Texas Tech, and you could get Dylan Thomas in the campus bookstore. The Tejas Theater played foreign films, which at the time had a risqué connotation since there tended to be occasional nudity in them; the drive-in theater on the Levelland highway that showed Russ Meyer–type soft-core porn changed its name in the '60s from the Westerner to the Fine Arts Drive-In. Major recording artists came through on package tours—white artists, mostly—the high point for me being Eric Burdon with the Animals in 1966, opening for Herman's Hermits at the Lubbock Municipal Coliseum. "We Gotta Get Out of This Place" was practically my theme song.

My middle-class privilege opened a wider world of music to me. In spring 1966, I saw a flyer posted in the Portales High School band room about a one-week summer jazz workshop, run by Berklee School of Music, at Indiana University. The cost was negligible, and we were going to the Midwest that summer, so my parents were happy to drop their malcontent fifteen-year-old off in Bloomington for a week. I can't imagine how different my life would have been if that week hadn't happened.

It was the summer of "Reach Out I'll Be There" and *Revolver*. I had a horrible hand-me-down Holton saxophone on which I wasn't very good, and a cheap electric guitar on which I was worse. The serious seventeen-year-old cats, the ones who were going to be out there gigging in another couple of years, tried not to laugh at me. The faculty that week included Ron Carter, who was still in the Miles Davis Quintet. I had never imagined a bass solo could hold a theater motionless for minutes on end until I saw Ron Carter stop a concert dead with his combination of a conservatory-trained classical player's focus, precision, and technical vocabulary with a jazz player's self-directed sense of what note to play, which way to turn, and how to compose on the fly. And there was Oliver Nelson, five years after he recorded *Blues and the Abstract Truth*. I pondered the meaning of the title. He was all of thirty-four, which made him an elder. I remember standing one day, eavesdropping awestruck with other students, as he practiced his soprano sax, an instrument I'd never before heard in real life. (Like too many musicians, he died young, of a heart attack at the age of forty-three, in 1975.)

For a guitar teacher I had Attila Zoller, the Hungarian bebopper who played with a cold, bassy tone on his hollow-body Framus. When I went in for my first lesson with him, he said, "let's play a 12-bar blues." I didn't know what he was talking about. He had to show me, barely concealing his impatience. I'd been in school band for six years and I'd never heard of a 12-bar blues.

I didn't know what jazz was before I went to that workshop. After that week I did. Simple as that. Portales didn't have a jazz scene, or any other scene for that matter, and I never became a jazz player, though I tried for a while. But a door had opened. I quit the school band and started my own. I loved playing music but I hated the saxophone, which smells bad and makes your teeth vibrate up into your skull, and I really hated marching. Being in step with others was never my strong suit. It was time to play guitar.

———

When I was a junior in high school, at the end of 1966, the radio was playing a sublime record that my wide-open ears told me on first hearing was New Orleans to the bone.

If Aaron Neville had been run over by a truck the week "Tell It Like It Is" came out, we'd still remember him for that one perfect record. With more ornamentation than an aria by the Duc d'Orléans[1]—and if you want to get the right sound to New Orleans R & B, you need a touch of rococo—it's as fine an example of American melismatic singing as you could ask for, with a melodic Creole voice that couldn't have been more unlike the then-dominant shouting style of soul music, set against languid Fats Domino–style triplets.

Aaron Neville's "Tell It Like It Is" was a local New Orleans production. The impresarios (composer-guitarist George Davis, tenor player Alvin "Red" Tyler, schoolteacher Warren Parker) pressed up two thousand copies themselves and formed Parlo Records.[2] Their publicity photo showed Aaron Neville wearing a nice suit, in three-quarters profile so you couldn't see the dagger prison-tattooed on his cheek. Today the shot would be set up so you could see the tattoo bigger than anything else. The contrast between his angelic, confident, precisely tuned voice and the tense lyrics (in which Neville warns a woman that she's making him furious) gave the song power, to say nothing of the currency of the title catchphrase in the soul-brother era.

Their first release, catalog-numbered Parlo 101, was "Tell It Like It Is." It was a big hit for the brand-new small label, reaching #2 on the *Billboard* pop chart and #1 for five weeks on the R & B chart. Business-wise it was a small enough triumph, compared with the dozens of classics being churned out by Berry Gordy's assembly line in Detroit. It was small even compared with the string of hits from the Stax-Volt powerhouse up in Memphis. But it might have been a beginning. Unfortunately, the worst thing that can happen to a small label is to have one sudden big hit. You have to lay out a lot of cash, the distributor will find it cheaper to force you into bankruptcy than pay you, and your cash flow will seize up and take you out.

They only got up to Parlo 106 before they crumbled. The debts came due quicker than the revenue came in. In the ensuing fiasco, Cosimo Matassa wound up having his studio liquidated at a sheriff's auction to pay the IRS, with depressing consequences for the whole New Orleans scene, since it was, and for twenty years had been, pretty much the only functional recording studio in town.[3] The result was that New Orleans disappeared from the pop charts because the town's recording studio was gone. After "Tell It Like It Is," there weren't any more hits from New Orleans on the radio in Clovis.

Red Tyler, one of New Orleans's best-known beboppers as well as a core member of the R & B sideman clique, became a liquor salesman, which paid better than driving from store to store with records. Aaron Neville—who to my teenage ears, and to fans all over the world, was already one of the immortals—never saw any money from the bankrupt label for his hit. He went on to be a longshoreman, a ditch digger, a steel mill laborer, and, as he had previously been, a junkie before making a spectacular comeback in a group with his brothers. You saw the movie *Ray*, where Jamie Foxx as Ray Charles bravely foregoes methadone while kicking his habit in a fancy rehab clinic? Aaron Neville did it by getting on a cross-country Greyhound, where he went through cold turkey sitting in the back row. Maybe you sat next to him.

Sometimes a piece of music seems like it's talking to you in your secret language. Whenever I heard that augmented-7th piano arpeggio that meant "Tell It Like It Is" was starting up on the radio, I time-traveled back to Louisiana. When I tried to explain this feeling to a couple of my closest friends, it felt like I was confessing something.

After two years of high school in Portales, getting to spend the Summer of Love in southern California was like going to Paris in the '20s.

I lived for seven weeks of summer 1967 in a dorm room at San Diego State College, attending a National Science Foundation–sponsored workshop—socialism in action, once again—of advanced math courses for high school students. I dutifully studied Euclidean geometry, number theory, and computer science on a mainframe that took up much of the basement of the math building and had a tiny fraction of the power of your handheld. Learning about derivatives and DO loops was interesting, but it had more to do with my college-teacher father's ambitions for me than with my own inclinations. I wasn't the sharpest knife in the math-nerd drawer, and I was more interested in finding out about life than in theorems. I spent most of my time playing my guitar (a Stella, from Sears and Roebuck) and slipping off campus to hear music.

Thinking it might be about to merge with jazz, I was a fan of the new loud psychedelia, but what I was really into was soul. My idols were Otis Redding, Wilson Pickett, and James Brown. *Dis is da Wolfman, baby!* I listened to Bob Smith, better known as Wolfman Jack, every night. With a shtick ripped from Howlin' Wolf, Wolfman Jack was a white guy who played soul music on XERB, the Mighty 1090, one of those "blowtorch" border radio stations that transmitted at bird-frying levels of power. The signal came from Mexico, but the program came from a studio in the United States—Los Angeles, in XERB's case.

And holy shit, the Wolfman was advertising his own live shows, so the first week I was in San Diego, I took a city bus downtown to Convention Hall for the Wolfman Jack Caravan of Stars (that's how I remember the name of the show, anyway), featuring Mitch Ryder. I got there four hours early so I could be in the front row. It was the high period of groovy psychedelic soul, and black go-go girls with peroxide-blond hair gyrated on either side of the stage. The Wolfman sang—more like, croaked—his way through a version of New Orleanian Chris Kenner's "Something You Got," at the time a hit for Solomon Burke. After a series of black L.A. cover bands playing soul hits, the second-banana announcer ("Lou Rydah! From Cheetah!" in what I remember as a powder-blue suit, with a slick process and a very long see-gar in his mouth) took over from Wolfman Jack, announcing, "Wolfman grabbed one of the dancin' girls, so he might not be back." Indeed, the most bodacious of the dancing girls was gone, and Wolfman never came back.

This was way more fun than number systems.

Mitch Ryder, the only white act on the bill, had traded in his rock-combo Detroit Wheels for a sharp, professional, horn-driven band. But good as he was, Mr. Sock-It-to-Me was outdone that night by the second-billed act: the duo of Larry Williams and Johnny "Guitar" Watson. It was pure beginner's luck on my part that I caught them. Williams came from New Orleans, and Watson came from Houston, but they were both based in Los Angeles by then. Watson was the proto-funk guitarist who in 1954, long before Jimi Hendrix and even a year before Bo Diddley, recorded the effects-laden "Space Guitar" and in 1958 did "Gangster of Love." Larry Williams had been promoted in the '50s by Art Rupe's Specialty label as the follow-up to Little Richard, who had decamped from the roster, and he made several first-generation rock 'n' roll classics, three of which—"Slow Down," "Bad Boy," and "Dizzy Miss Lizzie"—received the ultimate certification: they were covered by the Beatles, in versions nowhere near as good as Larry Williams's. But even so, Williams was getting paid better, and presumably finding more personal fulfillment, in his alternative career as a full-time thief and pimp. Aaron Neville remembered him with a "baby-blue Rolls convertible the size of a boat, wide-brimmed white fur fedora on his head, gold-plated shades hiding his eyes, glitter-gold suit brighter than the California sun."[4]

Some people say that the street term *mack*, for pimp, comes from the French *mec* (meaning precisely, pimp), via New Orleans. Larry Williams, a *mec* gone Hollywood, was the first singer I ever saw throw the mike stand around like he really didn't give a fuck whose teeth it might knock out. Since I was sitting directly under him, that was a matter of some concern. But it was theater, supported by professionalism and timing. Even when he threw it away from him, and spun around with his back to it while it was falling in the opposite direction, the mike stand never actually left his control for a second. It was old-school stagecraft, something performers had to know in order to get over in those 1950s revues at the Dew Drop Inn, New Orleans's premier black nightclub, across the street from the Magnolia projects. Ernie K-Doe recalled:

> Now those tricks I do with the mike stand, I learned to do them by practicing with a broom. . . . See, to get good, working that mike like that, it

has to be part of you. . . . I can turn around and do my splits and I know the microphone will come right back up to me.[5]

What I saw that night doesn't come through on Williams and Watson's recordings. I didn't know I was seeing pure pimp style, but I knew it was the essence of rock 'n' roll. When I think of rock 'n' roll attitude, to this day I think first not of Jagger or Iggy, much less the latter-day white boys, but of Larry Williams, who in 1980 was found shot under mysterious circumstances, a true hustler's death.

"Stomp that out, boy!" Redd Foxx said to me, tossing a cigarette butt at my feet in front of a few thousand black people. If there were any other pink people in attendance, I didn't see them. It was Friday, July 21, 1967, and, owing to my teenage ability to wait in line longer than anyone else, I was back in that same front-row seat in the same hall. The veteran dirty-joke chitlin-circuit comedian, not yet a household name from a future network sitcom, chain-smoked while he did his standup act. As he finished each cigarette, he would toss the butt down maybe an eight-foot drop off the front of the stage. I was sitting right below. The cigarette butts would barely hit the floor when several of the women in the front row dived, each trying to beat the competition to snatch the butt up, wrap it in a Kleenex, and carry it away as a relic.

Foxx was preceded by several L.A. soul bands playing covers and by his female colleague Jackie "Moms" Mabley, who told raunchy jokes about old men's lack of potency and said, "They say Abraham Lincoln freed the slaves. Well, John F. Kennedy freed me!" She paused for applause while I asked myself, "Did she really say that?" She really did.

But the headliner, and the reason we were there, was Aretha Franklin. "Respect," her second single for Atlantic and her maximum achievement, had hit #1 pop the month before and was still hot. When they opened the house that evening and I ran to my front-row seat, I could hear Aretha singing, because they were still rehearsing on stage behind the closed curtain. She was working with a pickup band, presumably union guys under the baton of her music director. It's hard enough traveling from town to town, but when you gotta teach the band the charts that afternoon, now *that's* earning your money.

Aretha Franklin was still thin in 1967. I had never seen a woman drip sweat like that. I was conscious that her sweat was part of her power. She did her new single, "Baby I Love You." When they closed with "Respect" and hit the *sock-it-to-me* part, the audience began not rushing the stage but dancing up the aisle toward it, doing steps. I had never seen such a thing.

The next night, from yet again the same front-row seat, I saw a double bill of Quicksilver Messenger Service and Big Brother and the Holding Company. Quicksilver, which was what we would now call a jam band, was the headliner. This was a month after the Monterey Pop Festival, and though Big Brother didn't have a record out yet, its chick singer (to use period terminology) Janis Joplin was blowing up. She came out screaming "Down on Me," which I knew as an a cappella song crooned by Eric von Schmidt. Each band did two sets.

You couldn't ask for a better point of comparison. The hottest young female singers in their respective spheres, both on the fast track up, in the same hall, from the same seat, on consecutive nights. The difference was painfully obvious. Janis Joplin was ripping out her throat while trying to be somebody. Aretha Franklin opened up and let it flow from deep inside. I saw it. I heard it.

The comparison was lost on the local daily, the *San Diego Union*, which reviewed the hippie show but did not cover African American popular music.[6] As far as a reasonably diligent researcher would be able to tell forty-one years later, the Aretha Franklin concert I attended in San Diego—one of the great singers of the American century, arguably at her peak—simply did not happen, nor did the Lou Rawls show I saw in the same hall the week before. There was an issue of R-E-S-P-E-C-T.

As there was in Aretha's hometown, where someone forgot to tell them it was the Summer of Love. "Negroes Loot, Burn Vast Areas in Detroit" was the front-page headline of the Monday issue of the *San Diego Union* that carried the review of the Quicksilver/Big Brother concert. In the early hours of Sunday morning, rioting exploded when Detroit police tried to arrest all eighty-two people attending a party for two returning Vietnam vets in an illegal bar in a black neighborhood. Five days of disturbances ensued, during which forty-three people were killed and over seven thousand arrested.

I returned to Clovis from San Diego on the Greyhound bus at the end of the summer, back to my senior year of high school in Portales, but it couldn't touch me. My cool went unrecognized by anyone else in school, but no matter. I was a freak and proud, and, of course, in a garage band. We rehearsed for months, and in the grand manner broke up after one gig. I played bass, and by common consent of the rest of the band, I wasn't allowed to sing. But there was one night when we rehearsed at my house, in the built-on room my parents called the den. After the regular rehearsal was over, I got on the mike and screamed out a twenty-minute version of "In the Midnight Hour," the first time I ever sang over a rhythm section. I'm glad there's no recording of it. After my friends left, my mother, horrified at the noise we were making, said, "My lord, Ned, that sounds like Negro music!"

I flushed with pride.

But I didn't kid myself. Despite the examples of Eric Burdon, Mitch Ryder, Paul Butterfield, and other white guys, I never tried to be a bluesman. Which in the '60s took some doing. I would have sounded ridiculous, and I knew it. I had to find my own voice.

Which is easier if you've only ever been one place and only known one thing. It's not so easy when you've already got a lot of voices going on.

One of those voices I had going on was in Spanish.

———

Our county was "dry," meaning no liquor could be sold; the next county over, whose seat was Clovis, was "wet" and had an air force base. That's where I played my first gigs, at the Officers' Club on the base and in Clovis honky-tonks with names like the Cattle-Lac and the Prince Lounge. The band's repertoire included "The Girl From Ipanema," "Can't Buy Me Love," and "Harper Valley P.T.A." Then I moved to the big city, which in New Mexico was Albuquerque.

You know those guys who spent their college years playing guitar instead of going to class? I did something even more vocationally useless. I *majored* in guitar. Yep, I have a bachelor's degree in guitar from the University of New Mexico, where they only taught classical music. I wanted to go to Berklee and learn jazz, but my parents wouldn't hear of it because it wasn't an accredited school, and I've often kicked myself for not going there on my own anyway. Instead, I got a degree in classical guitar, not that I didn't enjoy it. That entailed traveling to Spain for summer master classes several times, something that in those days was ridiculously cheap to do if you were spending dollars. I went on to get a master's degree in music composition from the University of California at—once again—San Diego, in the postmodern Euro-American-Asian style that was then called "new music." After almost seven years in college, I chose not to piss away any more years of my youth, and I left school without getting a doctorate. My Master of Arts is not considered a "terminal" degree (though a Master of Fine Arts, which is what art students got for the same number of years, is), so I was uncredentialed to get the only job my course of study could possibly have qualified me for, which was to teach in a college. That was fine. It was the one thing I knew I didn't want to do.

I graduated into the post-Vietnam, post–gold standard, oil-shock malaise that definitively ended the economic expansion that had been going on since before I was born and began a problematic new phrase of American history. I went back to Albuquerque, wondering what to do now, where I met Constance. I wanted to play music, something you couldn't make a living doing there unless you played rancheras in a Mexican band or covers of country hits, both of which I respected but which weren't what I wanted to do. I wound up in Manhattan.

I resisted going there, and I felt like a bumpkin for a long time, but I never regretted it. I arrived on my twenty-fifth birthday, July 8, 1976, when New York was dangerous and you had to watch your back at night. The city was bankrupt, but an explosion of creativity was going on. My rent was low and I could make it picking up temp work, which I could drop again when a gig came up. My best survival skill turned out to be basic literacy, plus I was a hell of a typist at a time when executives prided themselves on not knowing how to use a keyboard. I became a virtuoso on a new kind of typewriter that was now being called a "word processor." My first job was at a Wall Street insiders' newspaper, transcribing recorded interviews with captains of capitalism for $3.50 an hour. I played less music than I'd hoped, but I played.

The program had been accomplished. The South had been desegregated. The Vietnam War had ended. Nixon had fallen in disgrace. And the bill for it all had come due. People stopped being activists, got jobs, went to the disco, and wore some of the ugliest clothes in history, while the Republicans prepared their devastating long-term counterattack.

Constance and I tied the knot in 1980. In the years that followed, I played at little downtown places: the Kitchen, CBGB, the Pyramid Cocktail Lounge, Danceteria, the Mudd Club, the Lone Star, Tramps. I sucked in as much music as I could find, which in New York is more than anyone can deal with. The downtown scene ended for all intents and purposes in 1982–83, when AIDS began to devastate my generation. Ronald Reagan ignored the problem, pooh-poohed scientific evidence for the existence of global warming while something might have been done about it, invited the far right and religious fanatics into the inner circles of power, started a war in Central America, and began dismantling the New Deal with a not-so-subtly racist program. For all of this he was hailed as a great communicator. We had a bad recession, another one. I started a band.

I insisted on complying with my childhood fascination for singing in spite of the lack of any natural ability for it on my part. It was an era of ridiculously loud music, so my singing was more like bellowing. Plus I was so scared to sing that I sang in an old-man voice as a character I imagined to be some disreputable uncle I never had, in a real but exaggerated version of the Texas side of my own dialect, emphasizing the westerner in me and ignoring the southerner. It was perverse to take country music as my model, I guess, but my love for it was real. The city was so loud no one could even *hear* my nylon-string guitar, and I wasn't a punk rocker, a rapper, a jazz virtuoso, or, for that matter, a New Yorker. The band was intended to be a showcase for my songwriting, and I performed maybe a couple hundred of my songs between 1982 and 2001. I still enjoy playing most of them now, but I can't listen to the recordings of how I sang them in the '80s.

But then, in the mid-1980s, I became an obsessive salsa fan. It helped that I understood the lyrics, but I also heard in the Monday night Salsa Meets Jazz jams at the Village Gate something I had liked about rock 'n' roll twenty years before, but that rock 'n' roll had long since stopped giving me. It spoke to my head, heart, and hips all at once in a way that no other music did. My Puerto Rican friends began to feel like family, and I began to feel at last like I was a New Yorker. My music had always been Latinoid. Most of my tunes were already in clave anyway, and, gig by gig, my band transformed from a loud-guitar dissonant country band into a salsa band. By 1987 I had congas and bongó in the band. I had become a rhythm fiend. I had to find out more. Beginning in 1990, I traveled to Cuba twenty-five times, where during the severe austerities of the Special Period in Time of Peace I witnessed up close the eruption of a volcanic, complex style of dance music that later came to be called *timba*. Cuban music became my specialty. I was spending all my time with music, but less time playing it.

I tried entrepreneurship in the go-go '90s. Naturally, I tanked, starting a record company to release music from Cuba a few years before record companies became obsolete. For seven years I was a producer for the public radio program *Afropop Worldwide*, making well over a hundred radio documentaries about the music of Africa and the African diaspora. *Afropop* opened doors of all sorts to me like nothing before or since, including an international network of friends who liked the same music I did. I went to Brazil, the Dominican Republic, Puerto Rico, Venezuela, and Colombia, multiple times. I became the person I am. It was the closest thing to a steady job I ever had, but the show's budget got cut, and my position, which I would gladly have continued, disappeared in 1997. Since then, I've been what is called "self-employed."

I recorded an album called *Cowboy Rumba*, and to my delight the single, a merengue version of "Ghost Riders in the Sky," went into rotation on the radio in the Dominican Republic. But the record didn't make any money, and there was no follow-up possible. I stopped bandleading, wrote a book about Cuban music, and got a fellowship to spend a year reading and writing at the New York Public Library, possibly the happiest year of my life, in 2003–04. I was taking groups of travelers on mind-blowing Afro-Cuban cultural trips when the George W. Bush administration shot yet another line of work out from under me by cutting down drastically on legal travel to Cuba at the end of 2003. As we go to press, I haven't been to Cuba in six years.

But in 2004, I found myself unexpectedly living back in Louisiana.

It was an unusual thing for a university to award a fellowship to a no-doctorate non-professor like me. But there I was, in a top-floor corner office, no less, with wraparound windows that looked down on the perpetually green canopy of live oaks below. Ravens swooped and cawed outside the glass. The panoramic vision intensified the mood of the weather, whether sunny or stormy.

I was on the fourth floor of the Howard-Tilton Library, at the private university endowed in 1882 by New Jersey millionaire Paul Tulane for "the promotion and encouragement of intellectual, moral and industrial education among the white young persons in the City of New Orleans." When he died in 1887, an editorial in a short-lived African American newspaper named the *New Orleans Weekly Pelican* said: "Mr. Tulane while giving large sums for educational purposes was no philanthropist. His charity was of that order which discriminates between white and black; which would elevate one portion of humanity and enslave the other. Over the demise of such seemingly benevolent personages we shed no tears."[7] Others did shed tears, but for a different reason: Paul Tulane's gift up until that point had proved disappointingly small—about $1.1 million—and he died without a will, in effect cutting the university out of his three-million-dollar estate.

It had been necessary to create a private university because the Louisiana legislature was uninterested in funding education. In founding Tulane University, the poorly supported University of Louisiana was folded into it, so for most of the twentieth century there was no University of Louisiana. (The present-day system of that name was founded in 1974.) The result was a weird hybrid of a private university and a public institution that, it would be argued in court, did not have to desegregate.

Tulane admitted its first black students pursuant to a March 28, 1962, decision in *Guillory v. Administrators of Tulane University*. The ruling, again by Judge Skelly Wright, held that Tulane was indeed bound by the equal protection clause of the Reconstruction-era Fourteenth Amendment. By then,

Judge Wright was "used to being spat upon in public for his unpopular decisions," as an article in the Tulane *Hullabaloo* put it. Tulane appealed, but the superior court refused to hear the case, and the university was desegregated in the spring 1963 semester, without the mob scene that had earlier attended the desegregation of the University of Mississippi.

Eleven years later, in 1974, the desegregating suit's plaintiff, Barbara Marie Guillory, turned in a sociology dissertation called *Black Family: A Case for Change and Survival in White America*.[8] It has the ring of something experienced firsthand:

> Blacks have only had about 110 years to have accomplished the American "ideal" family since their Emancipation. They have striven to accomplish this ideal with little or no help from any of America's institutions—governmental, economic, religious, educational—which are designed to support and help the family. Actually, in most instances these institutions have constituted formidable barriers to Black progress.

I read this at the university archives in Joseph Merrick Jones Hall, named in 1968 for a deceased university official, a member of the New Orleans business elite and a former Rex of Mardi Gras, who had been part of the process of integration and to whom it fell to announce the desegregation of Tulane.

A month after Guillory started her classes, on March 11, 1963, Jones and his wife Eugenia Elizabeth died when an unexplained fire broke out on the second floor of their home in Metairie, engulfing the roof in flames while they were sleeping. She was asphyxiated, and he died in the hospital of an apparent heart attack after learning of her death. Arson was suspected, but never proved.

During my ten months in New Orleans, I had what all us bookish types dream of—time to sit, read, take notes, and burrow in archives both paper and cyber. Howard-Tilton had open stacks, and their renowned Latin American Library was on the fourth floor with me.

The music collection (though not the Hogan Jazz Archive) was down in the basement, as was the microfilm room that smelled of vinegar, a by-product of the film slowly decomposing. With two semesters to roam the library and anywhere else I needed to, I had the luxury of following my curiosity wherever it led. The picture I drew was a long way from the child's version of American history, which glides over the horrifying parts and in particular does a very poor job with slavery. Perhaps at bottom I was still trying to break through the lies I'd been told in grade school and at the movies. My residency at Tulane led to the writing of *The World That Made New Orleans: From Spanish Silver to Congo Square* (2008), in which I focused on the making of the city's unique culture during its first century of existence. I would gladly have spent another year reading in that library.

My lifelong passion for playing music had been relegated to an after-dinner pastime, but my guitar sounded wonderful in our rented house. Built in 1886–87, the house was basically a box of wood, with a high ceiling and a hardwood floor that was raised up off the ground on stilts, leaving an air pocket underneath. It seemed like the room was another guitar wrapped around me.

I didn't pick the songs, they picked me. If it popped into my mind, I would sing it. Most of what came out of my mouth was rhythm ballads from between about 1958 and 1962, songs I had known since childhood but had never played. They slipped out of my fingers and my larynx of their own accord every night after dinner. "Kiddio." "Snap Your Fingers." "Long Lonely Nights." "Goodnight My Love."

That last song—not an easy one to nail, I might add—was by Jesse Belvin, who also wrote the doo-wop anthem "Earth Angel" in 1954. Originally from San Antonio, Belvin was the hottest black artist in Los Angeles. Signed to RCA, who hoped to promote him into being a superstar, he cut two albums, including the pop-jazz classic *Mr. Easy*. His recording of "Goodnight My Love" is a model of just about everything: how to compose a sentimental ballad with a heartfelt lyric and a good melody, how to keep it moving with a gentle shuffle in the bridge section, how to sing it in an understated if Nat Cole–ish way, how to write simply and effectively for strings, and what a baritone sax can do to put some jelly on a final chord. It was an R & B lullaby, the perfect closer for a radio show, and that's how Alan Freed used it, but its dreamy melancholy could as easily send a loved one off to the next life.

On February 6, 1960, about two months after the sessions for his second album, Belvin played a bill in Little Rock with Jackie Wilson and Arthur Prysock. They were supposed to play two sets, one for a black audience and the other for whites. After playing the first set, Jackie Wilson refused to do the whites-only show, and there was trouble. Not four hours later, Jesse Belvin, his wife, his guitarist, and his driver died in a horrific fiery car accident in the northern end of the Ark-La-Tex at what a future U.S. president would brand as "a place called Hope," Arkansas. Apparently someone had sabotaged Belvin's tires. RCA wound up spending its promotional dollars on Sam Cooke instead.

As I sat with my guitar in New Orleans in 2004, in that lovely room that wouldn't be mine for very long, 1960 came back to me in all kinds of ways. The song I found myself singing most was one I didn't learn till I was grown, but it was the biggest hit of 1960 in Cuba: "Sabor a Mí." The wistful lyric was told from the point of view of someone feeling nostalgic for the moment he was living right then, imagining himself looking back from the future at the beauty of the present. I worked out a version in English:

A thousand years could pass by, maybe more
I don't know if there's love in eternity
But even then there'll be on the tip of your tongue
The taste of me.

"Taste" isn't a good translation for *sabor*, but there is no good translation. I think of it as essence: your music must have *sabor* or it has nothing. But as a cognate of *savor*, the word has an unshakeable culinary connotation, implying that music and food are a continuum, and the metaphor can easily extend to love.

Recorded by Rolando Laserie—a scratchy-voiced *rumbero* singing a romantic bolero, to the disdain of the old guard of Cuban song—and backed by the orchestra of Bebo Valdés, "Sabor a Mí" was still a hit when Laserie and Valdés boarded a plane for a gig in Mexico on October 26, 1960, knowing they weren't returning to Havana but not realizing they would never return. Hundreds of thousands of Cubans left the island around the time they did. This won't last long, they told their families. The Americans won't permit this. Forever after, in Miami or Union City or Albuquerque, "Sabor a Mí" has been a standard. Cubans have played it to do exactly what I was doing, something beyond nostalgia, something that transported you back to the other side of the rupture, to a gone time in a lost world.

For years, working with Cuban music and with Cubans, I've been encountering people who could take you on an imaginary walk through Havana in 1960, every street, every building, even though they hadn't been there since then.

Like I could walk you around Natchitoches.

PART II

THE YEAR BEFORE THE FLOOD

6

CONSTANCE STREET

The party kept Constance on her feet for hours, and she wore those nice stiletto sandals.

Big mistake. Next day the pain set in. Days later, she still couldn't walk. We were supposed to move to New Orleans in six weeks.

We're not kids anymore. That's good and bad. The ongoing conversation we've been having for thirty years is only getting more interesting. But she can't stand for very long at a time because of back problems that do not seem to be correctible, at least not on our budget. She can sit, she can walk, she can even dance. But she can't stand still in one place without excruciating pain, so, for several years now, whenever we go somewhere I have to look for a chair for her first thing. It's a cruel trick of fate, because she's always worked out and taken care of herself so as not to wind up in this condition, but she makes the best of it. I try to do everything for her that involves logistics or lifting, and she'd do it for me if it were the other way around. It makes us closer, in an odd way. We ran up bills for a minimal program of physical therapy using credit cards, the poor man's medical insurance. She did her exercises, and slowly started walking again.

Moving to New Orleans from Manhattan for ten months was more complicated than moving there permanently would have been. It took me two full months to get us there. I did all the physical work of moving our household because she was simply unable, though since she was raised Lutheran she always pitched in anyway, just enough to cause herself some pain. I didn't mind doing it all, but it took a lot longer with one person than two.

I made a preliminary trip down there by myself, arriving the night John Kerry was nominated for president.

I stayed at the house of my friend Chris Dunn, the young department chair of Spanish and Portuguese at Tulane. I had worked with Chris in Brazil in the '90s, back when I was producing *Afropop Worldwide* and he was a grad student. He's a specialist in the Tropicália movement—Caetano Veloso, Gilberto Gil, Maria Bethânia, Gal Costa, Tom Zé, Os Mutantes, and the rest. In his living room in New Orleans, we watched the Democratic convention on TV, a ceremony in praise of militarism. The clueless, uncharismatic, now-forgotten rich-man candidate was nominated because he was "electable," because he was a "war hero." Little of Kerry's support was for him, it was for Anyone But Bush. He was running on the glory of the Vietnam War, an experience he apparently couldn't bear to think about. He was in favor of continuing the war in Iraq. Something was terribly wrong with all this.

Chris and his fiancée, Ladee (pronounced Lady), were going off to Florida to get married, with Ladee's four-year-old daughter, Isa, in tow, so for the next two weeks I house-sat for them. Ladee lent me her car so I could drive around the city, looking for a home I could bring Constance to.

I'd gotten us cell phones, which we'd never needed in New York. I had to get a driver's license—I'd let mine lapse—so I wound up taking the driver's test in Louisiana. As I was driving along the lakeshore with a driving examiner in the passenger seat, my brand-new cell phone rang. "You can answer it if you want to," shrugged the examiner. "It's legal in Louisiana."

Forget the compass. Learning your way around New Orleans entails developing a crescent-shaped sense of direction.

North, south, east, and west: those are for other towns. In New Orleans you have lakeside, riverside, upriver (or uptown), and downriver (downtown). New Orleans sits between the Mississippi River and Lake Pontchartrain. The old city was built along a bend of the Mississippi—ergo the nickname Crescent City—and with the invention of electric pumps it expanded in the late nineteenth and early twentieth centuries away from the river in the direction of Lake Pontchartrain (which, despite the name, is not really a lake but a saline estuary that connects via the water links of the Rigolets and "Lake" Borgne with the Gulf of Mexico).

The streets that run more or less parallel to the river curve along with the river's crescent, so the same long U-shaped street may take you south, then west, then northwest. Intersecting with them are the streets that extend from the river in the direction of the lake, which do not run parallel but in a radial fan pattern. Every major intersection in this nonrectangular lattice is at a different angle from the next.

Let me see if I can explain this: the main streets that run from the river toward the lake were the successors to plantation boundaries that existed before the area was urbanized, boundaries that were determined by points along the crescent-shaped riverfront. These plantation boundaries extended in theory from the river to the lake, and as they got closer to the narrower lakeside, they converged. But in the plantation days, the back end of those plantations was swamp all the way up to the lake, so there were no actual surveyed points of termination for the property radii, just a series of nego-tiated approximations, so it's not consistent. You can't really learn it as a system along which you can predict your course. You have to learn how each individual thoroughfare goes, along with the various paving idiosyn-crasies, like the steep gutter on Jefferson that you don't want your wheel to go into.

But it's even worse than that. The cardinal directions as used in New Orleans place names can easily mean their opposites. When you hear some-one speak of the "East Bank" or the "West Bank," you have to understand that those terms refer to *some other part* of the Mississippi River. Because, you see, as the mighty Mississip flows southward down the continent, it has an east bank and a west bank, right? But by the time the river has meandered to the bottom of the map, it's turned eastward, and New Orleans is located where the river takes the famous U-turn. The river's banks, however, keep the same names. So the "west bank" is not west at all, but south, of much of New Orleans. In fact, if you get on the Crescent City Connection—which, despite its drug-deal-sounding name, is a bridge—and drive from the East Bank to the West Bank, you are headed not west but pretty much due east. So forget about checking with the sun to see where you are. Now you're getting a sense of what the house-hunting newcomer has to deal with.

If you were so foolish as not to have lived in New Orleans all your life, you kept a folding map tucked in the crevice by the driver's seat. After two weeks of map study on location, I got pretty good at navigating the city's web, but house-hunting wasn't going well. I'd been living in the same place in Manhattan for twenty-five years, so my house-hunting skills were rusty.

The places I looked at were small and depressing, plus they were unfur-nished, and I wasn't going to be bringing any furniture. And then there were security issues to consider. I checked out a neighborhood festooned with ban-ners promoting a "Night Out Against Crime." I couldn't decide if that was a good indicator or a bad one. I came to the conclusion that you were never more than a few blocks from a crack dealer in New Orleans. There were tough spots and less tough spots, but what counted was how well an individual block watched itself. I didn't see a lot of police on patrol anywhere.

Driving around, I got a preview of a problem I'd have in New Orleans when I stopped at a little place to grab some lunch, having skipped the place that offered a prime rib with bacon sandwich. Instead, I ordered what looked to be the lightest item on the menu. It turned out to be roast turkey (fine) but topped with melted cheese (hmm) with fried green tomatoes (oops) and mayonnaise (oh boy). Served on a croissant. Well, it is the *ville croissant* (Crescent City), but how many calories were in that thing?

Amateur anthropologist that I am, I even checked out a "gated community" on the West Bank—that is, on the other side of the Mississippi River from New Orleans. With a storybook name and a nice webpage, it was the living definition of nowhere. A company had slapped up some buildings on a nondescript patch upside the levee. The identical apartments came in a few standard sizes, all had the same horrible carpet and, if you wanted it furnished, the same cheap assembly-line furniture in each one for an extra charge. Most of the tenants seemed to be military families in flux, so the rootlessness was total. No one quite knew where they were, let alone where they were going. They were temporarily warehousing themselves in generic America. It was, however, a secure-looking compound, with an armed guard at the entrance gate. If you went out walking, there was only one direction to go since you were slapped up against the levee, and once you turned left or right out the front gate—to try to walk to a store in the ninety-degree heat, say—you would go a long time before you came to anything but highway shoulder. If I were a kid I would never forgive whatever parent, stepparent, guardian, or mom's boyfriend forced me to move in there.

Already getting into the New Orleans swing of things, I interrupted my task of house-hunting to go to a festival. I had arrived in time for Satchmo Summerfest, a three-day celebration in the name of Louis Armstrong that takes place at the U.S. Mint, on the downriver edge of the French Quarter. There were free outdoor concerts by some of the many New Orleans jazz groups, and seminars featuring early-jazz specialists, for whom the festival is a mini-convention. Eighty-five-year-old George Avakian was there, who produced recordings by Armstrong and encouraged Columbia Records to adopt the LP format. So was S. Frederick Starr, author of that great biography of Louis Moreau Gottschalk. I sat for a fascinating afternoon, quietly taking notes in the back before returning to house-hunting, stopping to hear a traditional-jazz band on the Mint grounds as I left.

I live in an overly touristed neighborhood in New York, so I knew I didn't want to live in the noise and tourism of the French Quarter. Friends who had lived in the Bywater, down in the Ninth Ward, said it was a long way to grocery stores, so not good for Constance, who doesn't drive. I looked extra hard in the uptown neighborhood Chris Dunn lived in, the Irish Channel, located more or less midway between the Quarter and Tulane. Chris liked living there, and I figured it was a good idea to start out with a friend nearby. Camping out at Chris's house, I was already getting to know the nabe. Most important, it seemed like a place where Constance could get to essential services by walking.

Because of the large number of students in New Orleans, a lot of rentals go empty in the summer. So landlords try to get a twelve-month lease, which would have meant paying for two months I didn't need since I would only be there ten months. It's not like New York City, where the lease is the residential tenant's protection against the landlord. It's the other way around: Louisiana rental law is written to protect the landlord.

I looked at one place that was lovely, but the owner had done some questionable remodeling, including a cramped spiral staircase leading up to a claustrophobia-inducing attic, which had been tricked out with an extra bedroom and a bath. No way in hell could Constance get up and down that staircase with her bad back, and the rent was fifteen hundred dollars, which was five hundred over my budget. On the other hand, it was a pretty place, and I could rent it furnished. There were two bedrooms on the ground floor, and we hoped people would be coming down to visit us while we were here. I looked at a few other places, and wasn't enthusiastic about anything, when the Spiral Staircase Landlord, who had kept my cell number, called me back, offering to rent me just the four rooms on the ground floor and knock the rent down to a grand, and agreeing to a ten-month lease.

I put down a deposit on the place. The house was between Magazine Street, named for the warehouse further downtown at the street's point of origin where gunpowder was once stored, and Constance Street, named for the wife of early nineteenth-century property owner Robin Delogny. My new landlord was a Cajun computer jock who worked in Washington, D.C., and commuted back on the weekends to see his wife and their new baby, who lived upstairs in the back of the house.

I liked the idea of a street named Constance.

———

I had never bought a car before, nor had I driven anything but an occasional rental in over twenty years, but we were going to need a car to get around. In Long Island City I signed a commitment to make seventy-two monthly payments on a Saturn SL2 (four years old, forty-four thousand miles). Not that I had previously known what a Saturn was. Nor did I quite realize that in effect you have to buy a car twice, the second time in payments to the insurance racket. I was going to receive all of ten monthly paychecks from Tulane, but I figured I'd sell the car at year's end.

I spent an unbelievable number of hours putting stuff in boxes, padding the boxes out with bubble wrap, taping them shut, numbering them, keeping an inventory of what they were, and stacking them up. I shipped more than half my CDs, all the books I might need to refer to in a year of writing and researching, all my negatives and slides, and a lot of other things I might as well have left at home.

We drove in our newly acquired Saturn from Manhattan to New Orleans, spending two nights en route. It was a good car, but I really screwed up by not noticing that it had no radio antenna. It could pick up FM signals in town OK, but once we got out in the country, we could go for miles at a stretch without hearing anything at all. To me, a car is a radio on wheels. Highway driving without radio? Unthinkable. A car radio is your best way of understanding what you're driving through.

Alas, my Saturn was radio-impaired. I would put it on "scan," which sent it stepping through the frequencies until it locked in on a signal. Often it would be silent for twenty minutes or more until, passing a town, it found something. Suddenly out of nowhere a loud voice would snap on, startling us with the proclamation that Jesus had our backs as we waged spiritual warfare in the crusade against secular humanism. I left it on as a kind of early warning system that we were near a town.

I had booked us a room for the night in Birmingham. Founded in 1871 to make steel from local deposits of coal and iron, named for Britain's war matériel–producing hellhole, Birmingham became the industrial capital of the South through the massive use of forced black labor in the decades after the overthrow of Reconstruction. No one ever mentioned that to me in school. It's possible that my dad didn't know it either when he used to sing that verse of "Down in the Valley":

> *Write me a letter, send it by mail*
> *Send it in care of the Birmingham jail.*

In his 1963 "Letter from the Birmingham Jail," Martin Luther King Jr. wrote, "Racial injustice engulfs this community. Birmingham is probably the most segregated city in the United States." It's the home town of Angela Davis and Condoleezza Rice, each of whom knew one of the four girls killed in the 1964 church bombing, and of Odetta, who moved away to Los Angeles when she was six. Birmingham has become a stop on the civil rights tourism circuit, and they've got a tight little jazz scene there, but it's hard to build a thriving hospitality industry when your town's brand includes neoslavery, the KKK, murdered little girls, and Bull Connor's dogs and firehoses.

Coming into Birmingham, the radio locked into a welcome funky-music signal. As I blearily followed the directions to the historic-Tutwiler-Hotel-where-Tallulah-Bankhead-had-once-stayed-now-owned-by-Hampton-Inns, I heard for the first time the song that would mark our year in New Orleans. I could tell from the way the DJ hit it that it was the new jam in power rotation. It expressed the inner torment of a man trying to decide whether to obey the no-hands rule in a lap-dance club:

Unngh! I like it like that
She workin' that back
I don't know how to act
Slow motion for me, slow motion for me . . .

Every aspect of the vocalist's diction had a musical function. *That, back,* and *act* rhymed, with *act* snapping on the upbeat. The words "I like it like that" recalled the 1961 record of that title by New Orleans R & B genius and fuckup Chris Kenner, later a big hit for the Dave Clark Five. Its *L*s were juicy both-sides-of-your tongue laminal American *L*s, not tip-of-your-tongue frontal British *L*s, and the vocalist milked them for all they were worth. The *M*s outlined a subrhythm all their own. There was a funky Latinesque guitar loop behind it; the producer, I later found out, was Danny Kartel (Daniel Castillo), a guitar-playing Honduran-Nicaraguan kid in New Orleans with an appropriately hip-hop capitalist *nom du disque*. It was scientifically calculated to move at the same velocity as a slow-grinding stripper's big ass. It sparkled. I know a great radio record when I hear one. "Slow Motion" was the new release by New Orleans's Juvenile, but that part I just quoted—which was the whole appeal of the record—was by Soulja Slim, who had been murdered in New Orleans ten months previously and didn't get to see his hit happen.

Unngh, I like it like that. Our temporary new home was coming into focus, via a dead man's horniness.

The next morning, the last leg of our drive was through 150 miles of thunderstorms. I drove most of it at eighty miles an hour. I had told myself I wouldn't drive that fast, but everyone else was going at autobahn speed, even in the rain. Like religion, politics, and music, driving in the United States has become more belligerent in recent years. Despite the increased probability of carnage if you crash at a higher speed, it's easier to flow with the traffic than to have Hummers and semis whipping around you constantly, hurling blinding sheets of water onto your windshield, while a suicide-jockey motorcyclist darts around between you. A small truck passes with FEAR THIS painted on its back, and a verse citation from Revelation. A giant chemical tank roars past with the cautionary MOLTEN SULFUR painted on its side. Isn't that the stuff that spews out of volcanoes?

I-10 runs mostly through forest from Jacksonville to San Antonio, but to get in and out of New Orleans you have to cross water. Coming in from the east, we drove on a thin ribbon of concrete set atop thousands of pilings, a viaduct called the Twin Span that bridges a five-mile segment of the 630 square miles of Lake Pontchartrain. It didn't rise way high above the lake but sat right on the water, giving you the dreamlike sensation of driving on the surface of the lake. I don't know if there's a psychological term for the fear of being trapped on preposterous structures, but the only thing I can compare the feeling to is when I was working temp on one of the higher floors of the World Trade Center on a windy day, when the building swayed and the water sloshed in the toilets. Once in a while a vehicle will go out of control on the Twin Span and careen off the lane through the barrier, sinking horribly down into Lake Pontchartrain and drowning the occupants.

As we crossed the lake there was sunshine and blue August sky all around, but directly overhead a tiny squall was shooting lightning and pounding hard rain down on us, making for highly localized weather drama. I had forgotten that the radio was scanning, but suddenly, blam! It locked in on a frequency, making us jump with the sudden blast of sound. Welcoming us to our new temporary hometown as we drove through our personal mini-storm was the musical smirk of B. Gizzle:

> I want it, you got it
> Don't make me have to go in your pockets

It went on:

> It's game time, and I'm ready to play
> Gimme my remote and my remote is my K, I spray with it . . .

My K. Meaning, my AK-47. It seemed to say: welcome to New Orleans, Ned and Constance. Keep your hands where I can see them.

When we arrived at our new home, I called Chris Dunn, who, it turned out, was having a backyard barbecue around the corner from us. Four hours after pulling into town, we went to our first party.

As I cracked open a beer, I got to talking to a guy in the English department with a familiar-sounding accent. Turned out T. R. Johnson was from Louisville; my grandfather Sublette was from western Kentucky. We got to talking about jazz, and books, and then we got to talking shit. He could cuss as good as me. Five hours in town and I had a new running partner.

I'd sent Constance pictures of the house, but this was the first time she had seen it for real. She loved it. I felt like it was something I was giving her. We put up our beaded *dwapo*, ceremonial vodou flags made by a Haitian artist of some importance in the world of the spirit.

Built in 1886–87, the house had a hardwood floor, with windows that went up from that floor almost to the fourteen-foot ceiling, which made for lots of light in the daytime and a feeling of exposure to the street at night. It was a double shotgun camelback, which means that it was a shotgun house—that is, with a front and a back door, and no hallway—only it was double-wide, and with a second floor camel-humping up over the house in back. But to carve it into separate apartments it had been partitioned off laterally, dropping a wall into it parallel to the front of the house. Not having the New Orleans eye or architectural smarts, I didn't quite get when I first looked at it that it's contrary to the sense of this kind of building to partition the front off from the back.

In the corner of the dining room (the room where the front door was) was the spiral staircase that went from floor to ceiling. Until the month before, it had connected directly to the apartment upstairs, but since I wasn't renting it, the landlord had filled in the hole in the ceiling at the top of the stairs with a circular plug.

The neighborhood acquired the name of the Irish Channel sometime after the Civil War. There were Irish in New Orleans from Spanish colonial times, but they arrived in New Orleans in droves after the potato famine that began in 1845—a crisis that became a disaster of historical proportions through the British government's *laissez-faire* determination to let private, rather than government, resources deal with the problem of the starving masses. Many of the arrivals stayed right in the neighborhood where their boat landed, too poor to make it any further. That's kind of why I was there too: the first place you land looks like home. I had landed there first, because Chris Dunn lived nearby.

The Irish Channel was part of what was sometimes hopefully referred to as the Lower Garden District. The real Garden District—the largest extant stretch of nineteenth-century mansions in the country, Jefferson Davis died in one of them in 1889—began one block up from us, on the other side of the commercial corridor of Magazine, and extended up a few blocks to the grand boulevard of St. Charles. At our back, from Constance Street down to the Mississippi River, were six blocks of a tough black neighborhood. From Constance, across Magazine, up to St. Charles, it was white. But then, a couple of blocks beyond that, you were in Central City (not to be confused with Mid-City), also known as the 'hood.

The swank part of town was right next to hardcore ghetto, in a juxtaposition that went back to slavery days. As the grand houses of the wealthy whites extended upriver along the boulevards, most spectacularly along St. Charles, the interior streets between those arteries became home to much humbler housing stock for black servants and poor whites both. It took a lot of staff to maintain those mansions, so the rich of New Orleans had to have their cheap black labor close at hand; Joe "King" Oliver, Louis Armstrong's trumpet mentor, worked part time as a butler in an uptown home. "'Super-blocks' about one-half mile square, with white perimeters and black cores, developed along such boundaries as St. Charles, Jefferson, and Napoleon Avenues," writes Daphne Spain.[1] With white flight, some of this checkerboarding collapsed and black superghettoes formed. The main uptown avenues represented arteries of white affluence (median white income in New Orleans in 2000: $31,971), like St. Charles and Magazine, coursing through a body of black poverty (median black income: $11,332), like Central City and . . . the Irish Channel.

Our block was lined with live oaks, those big, witchy trees whose armlike branches reach all the way across the street. At least as much as the architecture, they define the look of New Orleans.

Live oaks can live a long time. There is a Live Oak Society, founded in 1934, whose members are trees (nominated by humans) that are over one hundred years old. The "president" of the society, the Seven Sisters Oak on the north shore of Lake Pontchartrain, is over twelve hundred years old, according to the humans of the Society. If so, that tree would not be much younger than the land itself, built up by sedimentary deposits from the Mississippi on the last leg of its way out to sea.

The live oaks in my neighborhood were landscaped, not wild. As live oaks grow, they extend their root system out even farther than their branches reach overhead, so they form a considerable part of the solidity of the ever-sinking ground. They keep their leaves through the seasons, constantly shooting out new ones and dumping the old ones, so New Orleans stays green all year. On our block, the cars that lived in the street below their canopy always had leaves and twigs all over the windshields and creeping into the trunks.

The overhead network of the trees was also home to the unruly patchwork of cables that supplied electricity and communications to the houses. You can't have underground cabling in most of New Orleans, for the same reason the dead are buried in aboveground tombs—a high water table—so everything goes overhead. That canopy was alive with squirrels, who, as you know if you've observed them, are all insane. They freeze, then run, then freeze, then run. I would open our front door in the morning and a squirrel in the big tree would suddenly freeze, its tail bushed up, staring straight at me. Then screech at me—*skrrriiiiii!*—and!—go chase another squirrel! Having hundreds of thousands of them running through the live oaks and across the overhead cables made it all seem that much madder.

Our street dead-ended at the river. More precisely, at Tchoupitoulas Street, pronounced Chop-a-TOO-less, the name coming from *tchoupic*, mudfish, and *tout lá*, there they all are, or something like that, maybe.

When the Irish Channel got its name, Tchoupitoulas was a rough strip of slaughterhouses, blacksmith shops, cotton presses, and even a sugar mill. By the time we moved in, it had been a long time since they did heavy port work down by the French Quarter, and we were near the busy part of the Port of New Orleans. New wharf facilities had been constructed in our part of uptown in recent years. A little farther uptown, where Tchoupitoulas intersects Napoleon, across from the entrance to the huge Napoleon St. Wharf, was Tipitina's, perhaps New Orleans's most famous music club. Named for Professor Longhair's 1953 song "Tipitina," it opened in January 1978 in a building that had formerly been a longshoremen's tavern.

Tchoupitoulas was home to Sav-A-Center, Walgreen's, and, as you got toward the fancier part of uptown, Pier One Imports, because, running along the side of the natural levee, Tchoupitoulas had space for parking lots, something lacking in much of the city. Tchoupitoulas was also home to the Behind the 8 Ball Lounge and the Rock Bottom Lounge, whose pessimistic-ironic names tell you something about New Orleans's "black space," a term I borrow from Felipe Smith.[2]

In Manhattan, we also live about six blocks from the river, the Hudson, and we've always had a feeling of openness from having the river so close by. But in New Orleans we could never see the river, because a high wall separated Tchoupitoulas from it. On the other side of the wall, a truck road connected the uptown wharves to the interstate entrance further downtown. That truck road was as invisible to us as the river was. Beyond the truck road, holding back the river, was the levee. It felt a little like living in a cave.

In the six blocks between Constance Street and Tchoupitoulas, there were no live oaks. In another era, not very recently, the people who lived there were poor and white. Now they were poor and black.

When I talk about the poor, I don't do it from Mount Olympus. I'm talking about my own terror.

I never wanted to be poor, and I've tried not to be, but neither did I devote my life to getting paid. Back when I was a kid, deciding what my life would be, I knew I'd have to risk winding up poor to live the life I wanted to live and hey, maybe I'd have a hit or something. We're not in the situation of the people in the projects, Constance and I, but we've been poor our whole life together, and we're getting poorer as we get older. I'm a freelancer with no pension and a shitload of debt, including to the IRS. We haven't had, and don't expect to have, adequate medical care. It's not just us either. A number of my friends—artists, intellectuals, free spirits, square pegs in round holes, and straight arrows who've played by the rules and gotten fucked—are destitute, getting old without a safety net.

I take responsibility for my choices, but we had help getting this broke. You'd have to be dumb and blind not to notice the massive transfer of wealth that's gone on since Reagan, and accelerating since George W. Bush came in; through a host of policies including regressive taxation, rationing health care by price, and a general starving of the arts, humanities, culture, and education spheres where so many non-Republicans lurk, resources have been systematically channeled away from our sectors and toward usurious banks, weapons and war, neocon media, and a generally better deal for what Mr. Bush memorably called the "haves and the have-mores." Class war? We've been on the receiving end. But in New Orleans, we were surrounded by people who were far worse off than we were.

Meanwhile, I'm an eternal optimist. I have my health and my skills, and I have some things going on. I was coming off a similar fellowship at the New York Public Library, so this was my second year in a row with money coming in—my best two years ever. My first book was out (*Cuba and Its Music*), and the reviews were raves. I was excited about my work. Maybe things were improving.

The Tulane appointment looked to be a net money loser, in that by the time we relocated to New Orleans and back, maintaining duplicate residences, we would probably be further in debt than we started with. But I can never resist a caper, and spending a year in New Orleans was the ultimate caper. Meanwhile, there would be some cash flowing. For ten months I wouldn't have to fend off bill collectors or have to figure out some hustle just to scrape next month's rent together. When I wanted a beer or needed a new pair of jeans I would have the money in my pocket. I could buy the books I needed. I could wear shirts with buttons, and drop them off at a laundry for someone else to starch and iron them way better than I could, paying a dollar and a half every day to wear a professionally prepared shirt and look like I was somebody. I could make my minimum monthly credit card payments (though not chip away at the principal). And in the library I would be getting my history on, every day.

I had lost my edge after twenty-five years of living in laid-back Manhattan. You want a stressed-out town? Come to New Orleans. The Big Easy was a thoroughly ironic nickname. In spite of the pervasive slackness, nothing was easy.

I had been warned not to walk on the streets at night. And I had been warned about places where the projects had been ripped out but the criminal element still stayed in the area. I didn't know what to make of all this. I'd lived in high-crime areas before, but it had been a long time ago, back in the '70s when everything was skivey.

A friend at Tulane told me about being held up at gunpoint at her front door two days after moving into her new place. They still talked in low tones about a student who had been murdered in his home. Well, you always hear stories, but the odds of such a thing actually happening to you are slight, no? Stay out of the drug trade and you'll be all right. You may hear people cite a not very comforting statistic about the vast preponderance of homicides being black-on-black, as if by your skin color exempting you from the bloodbath it's somehow acceptable. I don't care who's shooting at who, I don't want gunfights around.

When I rented the place, not knowing the town, I didn't realize that it was an area tour guides had considered too dangerous to go into fifteen years before. I didn't know that the St. Thomas projects nearby, on the other side of Jackson, had recently been torn out. I didn't know that our Constance Street corner had formerly been a crack spot, or that one of our neighbor's tenants had been murdered while trying to buy crack. What I did know was that crime in New Orleans is off the scale, and of course I was concerned with finding a "safe" block, whatever that might mean.

I'm hardly unaware that American society is still segregated and unequal, but even so, New Orleans was a shock. I was coming from twenty-eight years in New York City, where "white" and "black" Americans are both minorities. Something like a third of New Yorkers were born outside the United States. Much of my hang time is with Latinos, of various skin tones, of whom there were only a trace in New Orleans. Now I suddenly found myself back in binaryland, where there were only two kinds of people, a place where you could still hear people talk about "passing" for white. Indeed, the most famous case of passing for white in recent years was a New Orleans–born Creole, Anatole Broyard, the *New York Times* book reviewer whose family moved to Bed-Stuy when he was a child.

I was back in Louisiana, and I was a . . . White Person. I hate it when that happens.

St. Charles runs more or less parallel to Magazine Street, following the Mississippi River's contour. On its neutral ground (the median, in New Orleans-ese) runs the streetcar line, which dates back to the early days of the railroad revolution.

When that line began running in 1835, it was called the New Orleans and Carrollton railroad. It ran parallel to the riverbend through what previously had been plantation land, from what is now Lee Circle to the then-separate town of Carrollton. The idea was to link New Orleans to a proposed line that would connect the distant city of Nashville to Carrollton. But like many proposed railroads, the Nashville-to-Carrollton line was never built.

The lack of a major intercity rail connection, together with the panic of 1837, sent New Orleans into a terrible economic slump, its greatest years of growth already behind it. Instead of connecting to intercity rail, the New Orleans and Carrollton railroad line facilitated expansion of the city uptown until it engulfed Carrollton, making New Orleans the first American city to be connected by rail to a suburb. The railroad did not follow St. Charles; St. Charles followed the railroad as the city expanded. If you look at a map of the city, you can see how St. Charles is the curled spine of Uptown, along which the rest of it grew.

In 2004, that 1830s railroad was still in use on the city's streetcar route, the oldest continually operating line in the United States. The tourists loved it because it was cute and quaint, an antique in daily operation, like the 1928 Model T working taxi, painted bright blue and blasting merengue, that I once flagged down in Havana. If a tourist should decide to leave the French Quarter, chances are he or she will get on the streetcar and ride up through the

Garden District. But for a working person needing public transportation, the 170-year-old railroad was not the greatest. If the weather was nice the street-car was packed with tourists, which made it hard to find a seat. If the weather was foul, as it frequently was, you had to wait for the streetcar outside, standing on the neutral ground of St. Charles, where there were not only no seats but no shelters from what could be a hard rain and blow. If you depended on the streetcar for your commute home you might—guaranteed, on some days you would—have to stand out in the wind and rain for some minutes, then walk the blocks from the streetcar back home in your wet work clothes.

It was impressive how many people in New Orleans depended on public transportation. According to census data, 134,000 New Orleanians, or over 25 percent of the town, had no car.[3] A constant procession of people walked past our house all day, in all kinds of weather, to and from the streetcar. I hadn't noticed this when I was staying at Chris's a few blocks around the corner, because Chris lived on Constance Street, which runs parallel to St. Charles and Magazine. But I lived on a perpendicular street that led up from Tchoupitoulas to the train at St. Charles.

The traingoers, almost all of them black, usually walked in the street, not on the unruly, jagged sidewalk. Some were families. Some were dressed for work. Some were students. Some were young men who, uh, didn't appear to be students. The commuters didn't usually make eye contact with the people on our block, and rarely did anyone on the block speak to them. At that moment, they were in "black space" and we were in "white space." Or rather, "we" defined the white space that "they" were passing through. But our white space was contained within the larger black space of New Orleans, which was in turn contained by the white space of the surrounding communities on one side and the blue-gray space of swamp and sea on the other. This was something everyone in New Orleans had internalized.

The young men wore a uniform: XXL, or maybe 3XL or 4XL, white T-shirts that hung down to their knees, a simple, poverty-compatible, neither-red-nor-blue style popularized in New Orleans by the Cash Money Millionaires before going national. The paranoid view of that uniform was expressed to me by a White Person: "It's like all the muggers in town got together and decided, if we all dress alike no one can make a positive ID. What are you going to tell the cops—I was robbed by a black kid in baggy jeans and a long white T-shirt? There are 100,000 people on the street at this minute that fit that description."

Most of the other houses on our block were set back behind yards, surrounded by fences with padlocks and big signs that say BEWARE OF THE DOG.

And there really were dogs. They didn't bark at me, but the Rottweiler across the street went crazy barking at the black boys and men that hiked up and down the street all day, every day.

Even the dogs were racist.

They vexed the black mailman and, though they stayed on the other side of a fence, they sometimes startled the black deliverymen who occasionally had to service those houses. I don't like dogs, possibly because my earliest memories of them, back in Natchitoches, are of this kind of dog. And if you know the history of the use of dogs to control the slave population, well . . .

Our house was the only house on the block with no front yard. The front door opened onto a shallow porch elevated a couple of feet above the sidewalk. I'm so used to the front door opening onto the sidewalk in New York that I hadn't taken into account what that meant, that our house was the most accessible from the street. It was an easy step up from the sidewalk to our front door. Sometimes people walking up the sidewalk would leave their empties on our skinny little porch. A sign planted in the narrow strip of earth between the porch and the sidewalk announced that our house was protected by an alarm system. There was indeed an alarm system, but it wasn't activated, and I didn't realize when I rented the place that it would be inoperable during our entire tenancy.

We'd been in New Orleans less than a week, so not everything was unpacked and some essential items were still lacking. But, wanting to get an early start on being sociable, we invited a friend over for dinner.

Idelber (i-DEL-ber) Avelar was a colleague of Chris's who taught Latin American literature at Tulane. *The Letter of Violence*, his book about violence in philosophy and literature, was about to be published. He was a heavy blogger, in Portuguese. You had to listen to him speak for a long time to realize he wasn't a native speaker of English. He'd learned English by teaching it back in Belo Horizonte, Brazil.

That afternoon, as I was picking up some groceries for dinner, I looked up my one Cuban buddy in town. Yolanda ran New Orleans's only Latin record store, Música Latina, on Magazine Street, where she did a brisk business in phone cards. I used to sell her records when I ran a label, and I'd visited her store in 1992. As we talked, I found out that Yolanda lived on the very block I'd just moved to. "Which house do you live in?" she asked. I told her the number. And she more or less said (we were speaking Spanish):

"Oh, that's the house where that boy got killed."

Where that *who* got *what?*

Friends, before you rent a home, Google the address first. It took 0.38 seconds to link to a picture of my front porch, transformed into an altar with flowers and handwritten prayers.

It happened less than two years before. On September 9, 2002, at one P.M. on a Monday, twenty-one-year-old Tulane senior Jonathan Lorino answered a knock at his door. One of Lorino's roommates, a young woman, was home, upstairs, and, according to the New Orleans *Times-Picayune's* report, "heard him politely tell the men he had no money." The two guys forced their way in. One grabbed Lorino by the neck and the other by the feet. The roommate ran back upstairs, locked herself in the bathroom, and called 911. The intruders ransacked the bedroom and went into the kitchen, where they grabbed a knife and stabbed him three times with it. With a knife they found in *my* kitchen. In the second drawer, that would have been.

The perps took off onto Laurel Street. When the EMS finally arrived, which took a long time, they took Lorino to Charity Hospital, but he was DOA, one of the relatively few New Orleans murder victims without a criminal record. A Crimestoppers reward was put up, and the next day someone tipped off the cops to where the suspects were hiding—ten blocks up, on the other side of the Garden District, in Central City. The paper published a picture of the two of them being taken away in handcuffs, wearing their oversized white tees.

Twenty-three-year-old Thatcher and eighteen-year-old Terry McElveen—black brothers with a Scots-Irish surname, in a black neighborhood called the Irish Channel—were Jonathan Lorino's neighbors—our neighbors, from three blocks down. Thatcher had just gotten out of prison for armed robbery and had a string of convictions. They were charged with murder, and a third brother was charged with harboring fugitives.

I stared at this on my laptop screen and called for Constance, who'd been cooking dinner, to come in. She read the story and we looked at each other open-mouthed.

All those rationalizations you construct, about why this can't happen to you, just fell away.

Chokehold apart, there would have been no chance to escape. There's a side door in the kitchen, but there's no back door to this place because it was partitioned off to create another apartment.

As we stared at each other, suddenly there was a sharp rap at the door. I practically jumped out of my skin. At the door stood two white guys I didn't know. I was conscious of them as white guys. The top half of the front door was basically a window consisting of a single pane of glass—how unthinkable is that to a New Yorker?—and we hadn't found a curtain to fit it yet, so anyone who came right up to the door could look in.

"Whaddaya want?" I shouted through the front door window in my most aggressive tone, without opening the door. I am normally the soul of politeness.

"You're expecting someone over for dinner?"

Puzzled. "Yes . . . ?"

"He was in a car accident on the corner and asked us to come tell you."

Why did they push into the house? What did they think they were going to find? Did they figure there'd be cash?

Jonathan Lorino was the son of Tony Lorino, the chief financial officer of Tulane. He was just back from a Junior Year Abroad in Paris, and had a job around the corner clerking at Hollywood Video. He was going to study law.

Probably the McElveens walked past the house all the time. People would spare-change their way up the block, and it seems that Jonathan occasionally gave. Maybe he didn't see why the people on the block and the passers-by shouldn't talk to each other. They in turn probably thought a rich kid like that had a lot of money and kept it at home, which is where they would keep it if they had it. They wouldn't have bank accounts.

I want it, you got it, don't make me have to go in your pocket.

But why kill him? It wasn't thought through. They didn't even have a gun; they used a knife they found on the scene. Was it because Thatcher McElveen didn't know how to live anywhere else but prison and needed to get back there? Was it because their nerves were raw from wanting a rock and they were pissed they hadn't come up with anything to score with? Or because once they got the adrenaline pumping they couldn't stop? Were they just plain sadistic nut jobs? Or all of the above?

Mr. Landlord kinda hadn't mentioned anything about this having happened when I rented the house. Well, why would he? And yeah, it would have affected my decision to rent or not. It turns out that this is a classic real estate problem, called "notorious addresses."

Mr. Landlord, who was younger than me, was a hard worker who was doing what I hadn't done—devoting himself to the accumulation of wealth. Besides his job in D.C., he owned this and another property, both of which he superintended himself. The next time I spoke to him, the next weekend he was in town, I brought up the uncomfortable subject of the killing and said, as politely as possible, it would have been better if we had learned about this from you than finding out about it on our own. His first response, which I thought odd, was: who told you about that?

Mr. Landlord told me he thought enough time had passed since then, but if I wanted to move he'd let me out of the lease. Of course there was no possibility of us moving, not after I'd spent all my money and maxed out my credit cards to get us there. It was a freak occurrence, he explained, he didn't think that it was dangerous on an ongoing basis, and the proof of that was that he had his family living here while he spent most of his time at an out-of-town job. True. But they lived upstairs in back, and we were exposed to the street on three sides.

And besides, Mr. Landlord said, he let them in.

He let them in? Or just opened the door and they pushed their way in? *So fucking what if he let them in?* That's blaming the victim. That's part of the chain of rationalization: it won't happen to me, not if I'm not stupid and don't open the door.

It won't happen to me if I don't open the door when someone comes knocking on a hot Monday afternoon because I should expect that they might be about to kill me?

They won't come knocking if I don't hand out money.

They won't come knocking if I don't acknowledge they exist when they walk up the street.

Where does this stop?

A grief-stricken friend of Lorino's wrote in the Tulane *Hullabaloo:* "He knew the Arabic alphabet. He knew the ins and outs of French history. He knew all the lyrics to Lil' Kim's *Hardcore* album." Lil' Kim was one thing the perps and victim had in common.

The *Hullabaloo* tried to point out the bright side: Tulane students hadn't been murdered nearly as much as the New Orleans population at large. It had been five years since the last student murder, when a woman was abducted from the French Quarter, raped, and murdered on Valentine's Day 1997.

The next day I sent out an e-mail to my list in which I told the story of finding out about the murder. Theresa Teague, a friend in Atlanta, replied:

> My boyfriend was murdered in a rather spectacular fashion last July while on a business trip to New Orleans. All of the perpetrators have been caught and the criminal proceeding is underway.
>
> My first trip ever to New Orleans was in March of this year for a pre-trial motion hearing. After that nearly overwhelming experience, I set out to see if I could create some positive associations with the city.

I came back down for a weekend of Jazz Fest in the company of supportive friends, indulged my music fanaticism, and worked that music for all
of its healing powers.

I still have a murder trial to get through, but I can honestly say that
I like New Orleans despite the awful tragic thing that happened there.
The place has flava and I find the people to be genuinely friendly and
down to earth. And the music . . . well, you already know.

I Googled it up: the so-called Goth murder. Her boyfriend—actually, her
ex-boyfriend, they had just broken up—was Shawn Johnson, a thirty-four-
year-old lighting director who liked to party. On his last day of a week in town
illuminating a Microsoft convention, he made the mistake of flashing a wad
of cash in a French Quarter dive called the Dungeon, and failed to be suf-
ficiently selective about whom he invited back to his suite at the Courtyard
Marriott, where, in the hot tub, his head was bashed in with a champagne
bottle and he was held underwater until he drowned.

Damn. This town will *fuck* with you.

When I move somewhere, I don't go for second best. New Orleans was
the number-one city in the nation for murders per capita. Jonathan Lorino's
murder was one of 256 officially committed in the city in 2002, out of a population of 486,157, resulting in a murder rate 7.3 times that of New York. Or,
to quantify it another way, a rate of 52.6 murders per 100,000 population.
That's higher than Colombia, which was in a state of civil war.

The New Orleans Police Department has a handy website that charts the
crime in your neighborhood for you. Black squares are murder. Yellow squares
with black centers are attempted murder. Pink squares are shootings, dark
green ones are cuttings. Yellow ones are aggravated battery. Light green ones,
armed robbery. Red, carjacking. Purple, simple robbery. Those are the square
crimes. They also have circle crimes.

So that's why there was such coldness on our block between residents
and pedestrians. The vibe changed after the murder. Fences went up and dogs
came in.

I could kick in that flimsy kitchen door myself. Hell, Constance could do
it. Wouldn't even need a crowbar.

———

Fully conscious and quite annoyed, Idelber was lying on the sidewalk on Magazine Street, bleeding from a long window-glass cut on the side of his head. It
looked dramatic, but he wasn't badly hurt.

You can easily get creamed driving across Magazine. You have to creep way out into the street until you can see around the parked cars. Then you have to look both ways and *go*! In the time it took Idelber to look left and right and turn onto the street, an SUV came barrelling down the road from behind the phalanx of parked cars, outside his field of vision. It was going at least fifty when it made impact over Idelber's left front tire. Had he started out from the intersection a half-second earlier, he would probably have been dead.

As I got there, Idelber was being strapped onto a stretcher, and was asking them not to immobilize his head until he could have a cigarette. He had asked bystanders to come tell us about the accident not because he needed help but because he was concerned we'd think he was a jerk for pulling a no-show at dinner. I went through his glove compartment and scooped up all his insurance and personal info and jammed it into a bag. I called Chris, who raced over. The police said that since Idelber had a head injury he had to go to [cue ominous music] . . .

Charity Hospital! [Sound of screams in the background.]

Founded in 1736 (though not at the same location) with a bequest of ten thousand francs from a French sailor, Charity was the oldest continuously operating hospital in the United States. In 2004, Charity was the only place a lot of people in New Orleans could go for medical attention, and it was famous for its combat-hardened medical staff. It got the head wounds and the Saturday night gang-war casualties. A couple of years before, there had been a gunfight in the emergency room.

Chris went in the ambulance while I stayed with Idelber's car until it was towed. About an hour later, they called to say they were bailing from Charity, and they'd be waiting outside for me to pick them up. No one at Charity had looked at Idelber, who was perfectly able to walk and had had it with waiting around in what he called, possibly being hyperbolic, the hip-hop version of Dante's *Inferno*. As Idelber waited, someone came in with an eye torn out. Then someone arrived who'd been shot in the stomach, and then someone who'd been shot in the leg. But the one that sent Idelber out of there was the man who came running in, covered in blood, holding his detached penis in his hand and shouting, "My woman just chopped it off!"

Idelber was basically fine, though his head needed stitching up. We went to another emergency room, Touro (named for Judah Touro, the Jewish merchant who gave New Orleans its first library). I sent Chris home and waited it out under the fluorescent glare in the orange plastic bucket seats while Idelber kept slipping out to smoke cigarettes, his head still bleeding somewhat.

Most of the people in the waiting room at Touro seemed to be there for emergency liposuction. They looked like eyes and mouths set in blobs of fat. I wasn't sure which ones were patients and which ones were waiting, though I figured the enormous teenage girl who went out and came back with a bucket of fried chicken was not a patient. Yet.

Idelber and I would have had plenty of time to go out for fried chicken. Since he wasn't bleeding to death, it took a couple of hours for the doctor at Touro to see him. When he did, he took a quick look and gave Idelber the choice of having the wound closed up with stitches or staples. But, he pointed out, the injection of anesthetic along such a long cut before the stitching would be about as painful as the staples. With the staples, no anesthetic, but it's quick.

"If it were me?" he said, "I'd choose the staples."

He was pretty much telling Idelber which to choose. Well, OK, said Idelber without realizing that what the doctor was really saying was that staples hurt like a motherfucker, but they were quicker and easier for him to do.

I had never seen this procedure. I thought, staples, well, that's some kind of technical term. No, the guy pulled out a stapler. Not a puny little office stapler, either. A big one.

If you are ever given this choice, don't choose the staples.

7

IVAN THE TERRIBLE

Marilyn took the social initiative and invited us over for a little party at her place.

That's Dr. Marilyn Miller of the Tulane Spanish and Portuguese department, a tango-loving professor with a big heart, an excellent command of Spanish grammar, and class A kitchen skills. There was an extensive beverage menu. We knocked back a couple of rounds—damn, these New Orleanians can *drink*—and met some of my new colleagues: Vicki Mayer (communications), Gayle Murchison (music), Garnette Cadogan (an independent scholar like me, a Bob Marley expert, and an all-around polymath from Jamaica). Then Marilyn informed us that it was time to go on the second line.

A second line? Tonight?

I'll forego the explanation of what a second line is for right now, and cut to the short version: it's an ambulatory block party. It's about shaking your butt down the street to a brass band.

Most second lines happen on Sunday afternoons. But the Krewe of O.A.K., up in Marilyn's neighborhood of Carrollton, up by the riverbend, has its annual midsummer second line at night. For that matter, most second lines are put on not by "krewes," which are Mardi Gras organizations that are historically (and overwhelmingly) white, but by Social Aid and Pleasure Clubs, which are not Mardi Gras organizations and are historically black. So this was an unorthodox second line, with an atypically heavy concentration of white second liners, but a second line it was.

The Krewe of O.A.K. operates out of the Maple Leaf Tavern, a music freaks' bar on Oak Street, up at the end of the streetcar line. Pianist Jon Cleary told me the story of how he came from London on a courier flight to live in New Orleans in 1980, at the age of seventeen, after being turned on to the city's music by his traveling, record-collecting British uncle. When he landed at the New Orleans airport, he showed the cab driver a Maple Leaf matchbook that had found its way to London and said, "Take me there." Arriving at the Maple Leaf with only a carry-on bag, he was greeted by the barmaid, who was a girlfriend of a brother of a girlfriend of Jon's uncle. "Welcome to New Orleans," she said, and bought him his first Dixie Beer. As he sat drinking it, Earl King got up on stage and began to play.

Every Tuesday at the Maple Leaf, the late James Booker (1939–1983), the dysfunctionally mad, bad-druggie piano genius of New Orleans, played the beat-up old upright, sometimes for an audience of five people. Some of them were doing their laundry; at that time, the Maple Leaf had washers and dryers in the back. People would get started on a bender during the spin cycle and listen to Booker while their jeans dried. I was told a story of Booker playing a flamboyant upward arpeggio, then stopping and refusing to play anymore until someone bought a copy of his record. A standoff ensued between him and the audience until someone finally went up and bought a cassette so that Booker would start playing again. He resumed with a downward arpeggio at the point in the tune where he'd left off.

At six P.M. we'd had no idea that we'd be dancing down the street at ten. But in New Orleans it all goes back to the parade—it's the number-one thing you have to understand about the town—and there we were, New Orleanians for less than a week, second-lining away in the dim light, dancing along the bad pavement. The Maple Leaf had a discerning crowd, so they had to have a good band for their second line, led by one of the best-known young players in town, eighteen-year-old Troy Andrews, aka Trombone Shorty, who'd come up as a child in the Tremé playing for tips in the French Quarter. As Shorty's band blasted, the bacchanal stretched out for several blocks. At one point I guessed that there were about six hundred people strutting along, then later I revised it up to twelve hundred, then I lost any sense of it. I felt right away that it was, in effect, a Night Out Against Crime, asserting a right to inhabit the street. Some people wore carnival costumes. One guy kept shouting, "Mardi Gras is comin', baby!" though it was August 21 and Mardi Gras wouldn't be until February 8. There was a man with a motorized Barcalounger who puttered down the street half-reclining with a drink in his hand. Women kept hopping on his lap to ride down the street with him. Ambulatory vendors dispensed sloppy wet cans of the cheapest brands of beer. We got plastered.

I worried about Constance's back, but dancing along on the concrete seemed to have a healing effect. Seven weeks ago she couldn't walk, and now she was dancing. After two and a half hours of second-lining, she felt great. "She's thriving here," I wrote to friends.

———

We would have gotten there sooner or later, but Valerie, our ex-neighbor from New York now living on Esplanade, wanted to be the first to take us to the Mother-in-Law Lounge.

A local landmark in the shadow of the I-10 trestles on Claiborne, the Mother-in-Law was presided over by Antoinette K-Doe. *Née* Antoinette Dorsey, she was a cousin of my all-time favorite New Orleans R & B singer, the late Lee Dorsey, but more importantly for our story, she was the widow of Ernest Kador, better known as Ernie K-Doe, the self-proclaimed Emperor of the Universe whose big hit was "Mother-in-Law." A Charity Hospital baby, a Baptist preacher's ranting son, and a former gospel quartet singer, Ernie K-Doe's life was a show. He lived in a parallel universe where "Mother-in-Law" was not merely the #1 record on May 22, 1961, but had continued to be #1 for the next forty years. He was a down-and-out alcoholic when Antoinette, who had known him since they were young, became his significant other, cleaned him up, and resuscitated him as a local hero. They got married in '94.

Everyone in town seemed to have one or another air check of Ernie K-Doe doing his utterly bonkers program on WWOZ, in which he would rant and rave into the mike in classic radio preacher style. I asked Walter Brock, who founded WWOZ, how Ernie K-Doe wound up on the station. "He walked in the door," Brock shrugged. K-Doe realized there was a radio station that would let him do his thing. "He was a visionary, and a hustler," said Brock. "Which, you know, he had to be to survive."

But what was K-Doe's vision, which seemed to consist of surreally inflated self-promotion? "He wanted to make things bigger than life," Brock said. "Not just himself, but the lives of the people who were entertained by him." Which maybe explained the vibe around the Mother-in-Law Lounge. You walked in and, even if the joint was empty, it was some grand theater of life, like New Orleans itself. Antoinette and everyone else had been made bigger by their participation in the spectacle of Ernie. New Orleans was bigger because it had the Mother-in-Law Lounge.

Housed in what had formerly been a bar called Memories before the K-Does took it over, next door to the former site of the black musicians' union Local 496, the Mother-in-Law Lounge became an institution in its own right.

While commemorating the record "Mother-in-Law" as if it were not merely a funny hit of forty-five years ago but a central pillar of western civilization (the truth may be somewhere in between), the Lounge was at least as important a contribution to New Orleans culture as the record it was named for.

Ernie K-Doe was there, sitting in his place of honor. Or rather, an almost life-sized mustachioed wax mannequin of Ernie K-Doe, dressed in one of Ernie's stage suits, since the flesh-and-blood Ernie had passed to the next realm in 2001 after cirrhosis led to liver and kidney failure. One thing I learned in Cuba: a doll is never just a doll. Antoinette was the priestess, but Ernie's grandiose spirit still presided over the house. Inside the mannequin, a low-power transmitter installed by the unclassifiable musician Mr. Quintron (né Robert Rolston, who together with Miss Pussycat ran the Spellcaster Lounge in the Ninth Ward) broadcast a loop of various of K-Doe's pronouncements on 1500 AM to cars driving by the Lounge at 1500 Claiborne: "I'm cocky, but I'm good!" "Burn, K-Doe, burn!"

That was also the name of the signature drink of the Mother-in-Law Lounge. A Burn, K-Doe, Burn—pronounced *booin, kaydo, booin*—was a short, intense shot from a giant jar of maraschino cherries embalmed in what I think was high-potency distilled grain alcohol, perhaps Everclear, decanted into a paper dose cup. "I asked Antoinette what was in a Burn, K-Doe, Burn," Dan Rose wrote to me later. "I didn't know it was a secret. She wasn't going to tell me. I said, 'Well let's see, you got cherries in there.' She said, 'You got that right,' and then she got mad when I asked if there was Everclear in them. Real mad. It remains a mystery." *Burn, K-Doe, Burn!* was also the title of a four-hour play about Ernie and Antoinette's life together, written and produced by Antoinette at the Rock 'n' Bowl, a 1941-vintage Mid-City bowling alley with a bandstand and a dance floor.

We drank K-Doe in, and it burned.

I'd found another place where I felt at home. There were some "black" bars in New Orleans where four "white" people might not feel so comfortable hanging out, to say nothing of vice versa, but Antoinette saw to it that everybody who behaved themselves was made to feel welcome, and those who didn't would not be tolerated. It was an important point of friendly contact between white and black communities—a relative rarity in New Orleans, as I was beginning to realize.

The jukebox had all Ernie's records on CD, as well as those of his more-or-less contemporaries: Percy Sledge, Jackie Wilson, Otis Redding, and many more. I could stay in there for hours, and, as the year passed, I did, at some point or other always playing my favorite K-Doe song, "Ta-Ta-Tee-Ta-Ta."

In spite of the murder that had happened in the house, Constance loved living there.

We lived a romantic life together, simulating a middle-class existence atop a mountain of momentarily chilled-out debt in the poverty-stricken, termite-chawed city of New Orleans. We had things we never had for twenty-five years in Manhattan—different rooms, furniture, hardwood floors that didn't leave splinters in your feet, a dishwasher, sunlight. We had a regular paycheck, a car, and a kitchen with countertops. It might not sound like much, but it was all new to us.

The most poignant moments you remember are sometimes the most ordinary: coffee in the morning, coordinating the grocery shopping, listening to the radio at dinner, drinking supermarket wine. At the end of every day in the library, I e-mailed Constance my notes. She read as much as I did, working at her computer most of the day. We talked it about it all, all the time. It was an experience we always hoped we'd have.

As I began to inhabit my Louisiana self, my dialect got stranger. We'd been there a couple of weeks when Constance said, uhh, Ned, no one here talks like that? I realized: I was talking the way I remembered people talking in Natchitoches fifty years before. To some people, it might have sounded like I was imitating black dialect. No, that's how the *white* people in Natchitoches talked, the ones who never interacted with black people.

Memory, says my friend Jaime Abello, is neither fiction nor nonfiction. There are all kinds of layers of remembering. There are the stories you've told over and over, to the point where you're remembering your retelling more than the original moment. But then there are those things that float up unbidden. Natchitoches wasn't New Orleans, but they were both old colonial towns with little quirks in common that triggered long-forgotten remembrances of that other long-ago Louisiana. I suddenly saw myself in the barber shop in Natchitoches where my hair was burr-cut against my wishes every two weeks, with the barber pole outside and the gumball machine, where the barber would ceremonially put a penny in and reward me with a gumball for having sat more or less still. I remembered the barber's name: Maroon Antoon.

But the New Orleans style was different, and I had some idioms to learn. One night I went out to a bar with Valerie and some of her friends, who dispatched a rider with me, a man about my age, to make sure I found the place. After I parked and we got out of the car, the man said to me:

"Yo' ass is stickin' out!"

I beg your pardon? I quickly touched the backside of my pants.

"Yo' *ass* is stickin' out!" He said it louder, so maybe I'd understand it better.

I'm sorry? Exasperated pause. "The ass end of yo' *cah* is stickin' out!"

I had parked with the back end of the Saturn too far from the curb.

My ass was stickin' out.

I didn't know it, but I had just learned a Yat idiom. Some people find the term *Yat* offensive, but others embrace it. Yats—a colloquial term deriving from the New Orleans way of asking "Where y'at?" for "How ya doin'?"—are the ethnic white working class of New Orleans, the people of Irish, Sicilian, or German heritage (as opposed to the Creole, Cajun, or Anglo-American lineage).

In the nineteenth century, the Irish Channel was in constant maritime communication with the other great Irish port cities of the United States, especially New York, and to this day many New Orleanians sound not particularly southern but more like Brooklynites. Which is to say that the Irish Channel was one of the home bases of Yatdom. Nick LaRocca, the Sicilian American cornetist-electrician who made the first jazz record in 1917 with the Original Dixieland Jazz Band (an Armstrong-influenced group that had become known in New York as a musical comedy act), and who in his later days unfortunately insisted that black people didn't invent jazz, was a Yat from the Channel.

Yats eat ersters and shwimps, which is how those items are spelled on the chalkboard at Parasol's, a block over from our house. And if you spend much time in New Orleans, you will start agreeing with people by using the classic Yat locution: "Yeah, you right."

There were only sheers covering the floor-to-ceiling windows. From the street at night, you could see into the house through them, so we had to buy curtains, which required more shopping than I could have imagined. We couldn't get curtains that were tall enough to cover the full height of the windows, but with the ones we got, the only way you could have seen in was to get up on a very tall ladder outside the window.

The fourteen-foot ceilings created a wonderful sense of space, but changing the light bulbs recessed into the ceiling required mastery of a long-pole tool with which you unscrew and remove the dead bulb, possibly dropping and shattering it in the process. When you'd done all that, the light seemed a long way away if you wanted to sit on the couch and read. I began retiring to the bedroom at night, where we had what lighting manufacturers call a torch, a freestanding floor lamp. Tulane let me take out a hundred items at a time from the library, and I'm macho about my reading. I had stacks of books to choose from, piled high on the floor in the living room, in front of the floor-to-ceiling windows.

As I came home from Tulane in the evening, I often stopped at Parasol's to pick up a couple of draft beers for me and a martini to go for Constance, then drove the last block home, taking care not to spill the open drinks. You can do this in New Orleans because every bar has plastic go-cups. If you want to leave and you haven't finished your drink, they pour it into a go-cup and you take it out of the bar with you, no big deal. The go-cup is one of New Orleans's great inventions. You can hang out outside and enjoy your drink, then go back in to replenish it. You can get a summons (and I have) for drinking beer on the street in Manhattan, but in New Orleans it's perfectly legal. It's a drunk city, the home of the three-for-one happy hour. The local-pride bumpersticker says *New Orleans / Proud to call it home*, but I saw the parody version more often, which looked exactly the same except for the text: *New Orleans / Proud to crawl home*.

One night, as I was relaxing into bed under the reading lamp in a comfortable state of undress with a full Parasol's go-cup and a book, Constance went out into the kitchen to get some water. The experience of going into another room of a dark house was something we hadn't had in our twenty-five years together in a small apartment. I heard her suddenly call in a strange voice, "Ned, could you come in here?"

I was in the kitchen in a heartbeat.

There, on the floor, was this *thing*.

I didn't know what the hell it was. It didn't look like anything, really. It appeared to be alive, but it wasn't moving. It was gray, about two to three inches long, and there was a thin wet trail behind it on the floor.

"Is that a . . . *slug?*" said Constance.

You know, I had never seen a slug. They're basically big snails without shells. Their moist, slimy bodies can only exist in wet climates. They live in the forest. A slug crawling across a hardwood floor is tragically lost, trudging across a desert. Prodding it with the broom, we shoved a piece of cardboard underneath the slug and tossed it outside.

This underscored the idea that once we had retired for the night, the rest of the house was off limits. Kind of like when you were five and there were bears in the closet. You might step on a slug in the darkness. At least it wasn't rats.

There was a separate apartment in the back of the house, rented out by our landlord to Jennifer (not her real name), a student who usually had her boyfriend Ray (ditto) with her. Houses in New Orleans are built close together, and the paths between them are tight. Jennifer's place, like Mr.

Landlord's apartment above us in back, was accessed by a path that led right past the bedroom window I slept next to. Jennifer and Ray, who were nice kids working hard to make their places in life, tended to come home at unpredictable hours, often after we were in bed. So at any time of night there might suddenly be voices inches away from my head from out in the walkway, coming through the window glass like they were in the room with us.

Opening the gate to enter the path to the back automatically triggered a floodlight, which came on suddenly, shining through the window and the curtain into my eyes. That was good, because if they were unfamiliar voices I could peep out in the space between the window frame and the blinds to see what was up, though possibly being seen by whoever I was peering at a foot or so away. If someone smashed through that window, they would have you in seconds. I learned to wake up, check it out, and go back to sleep.

Constance took to sleeping with a mask and earplugs.

As we felt out the Irish Channel, establishing our circuits and our routines, we decided to walk up to the Bulldog for a beer in the twilight of the end of August. Being New Yorkers, accustomed to getting our exercise by walking twenty minutes each way and back to go somewhere, it seemed absurd to drive somewhere that was a ten-minute walk up Magazine Street.

Me, I follow a basic rule: coffee in the daytime, beer after it gets dark. The Bulldog was, and wasn't, my kind of place: it had fifty kinds of beer on tap (my kind of place), but it bombarded you with sports on multiple huge TVs (not my kind of place), so I much preferred to sit outside with a go-cup. The Bulldog was graced with a small parking lot that doubled, as New Orleans parking lots do, as a party space, complete with benches. We sat at the Bulldog's outdoor picnic tables on the blacktop adjacent their building, across the street from the A&P. It was a fine, sticky night. For that matter, I had liked the heat of the day. Everyone complains about summer in New Orleans, but having been a child in Louisiana, that hot humidity has a time-transport effect on me that tricks me into feeling younger and more energetic. I didn't even mind that a large flying cockroach—palmetto bugs, they call them—did a Mohammed Atta right into the side of my head. I kicked back on the bench with a cold wheat beer, relaxing into Magazine Street. Ghostly advertisements for long-gone businesses of fifty or eighty years ago were still visible as palimpsests, painted in faded but still-legible lettering on the sides of the two-story brick storefront structures. We were in 1928. The movie-set effect was pronounced, especially at night with a couple of floodlights on.

Magazine Street is narrow and tight, with parallel curbside parking that squeezed the traffic down to two slow-moving lanes (though as Idelber found out, they don't always move slowly). Without much space for parking, it isn't a desirable location for high-volume national chains, so there aren't many of them on Magazine. Most of the businesses were idiosyncratic local operators—boutiques, a costume store, and, as you might imagine in such a neighborhood, lots of antique dealers. Further up Magazine was a store that sold home brewing equipment and bongs, a bookstore or two, a lot of bad restaurants and a few good ones, and plenty of bars.

With all the crowd gathered outside the Bulldog drinking beer, there wasn't much less cigarette smoke than inside. The crowd was pretty much all white. Most places we'd been in town, it was either pretty much all white or all black, Tulane parties and the Mother-in-Law excepted. As we sat there, some kids walked past us, black space trudging through white space, probably on their way to the streetcar at St. Charles, or maybe walking to Central City. It wasn't a rainy night, but one of the kids, maybe fourteen, was walking with—I'd never seen this one—plastic bags tied around his feet at the ankles. He had new sneakers on, and he was gonna keep them nice until he got to the party.

After we'd had our liquid refreshment, we headed home, walking in the direction of downtown. After seven blocks, we passed the corner of Magazine and Washington, just past the sinkhole that made all the cars dip and was never repaired the whole year we lived there. As we passed from commercial into residential territory, the street got darker.

Something skidded past my feet. It was an empty aerosol can. It didn't just fly to me by itself. It had been accurately thrown. At me.

Immediately I looked around. There was no gaggle of kids jeering at us. There was no one close by on the sidewalk in any direction. No passing vehicles. It didn't come from the side where the houses were. There was only one place it could have been thrown from: the not very new four-door sedan with the windows open, pulling in to get gas at the Spur station across the street. Or was I missing something? I didn't get a good look at the driver, but I could see he wasn't a teenager, though younger than me. He was alone, didn't have a posse, and he wasn't looking in my direction. It was over. Nothing further was coming. Unless of course I wanted to go over there and make something out of it, which some people would have felt obliged to do.

It all computed instantly. There was no mystery to it. He had a used-up spray can to get rid of, and it amused him to chunk it at the old white couple walking down the empty street.

I'm aware of the history of crimes being pinned on black suspects without evidence, and I don't want to accuse someone of something I can't prove. But I wasn't being paranoid. There was no one else around, no other explanation that I could see. It was a misdemeanor version of a hate crime. Assuming it wasn't a ghost who did it, there were a lot of messages coded in that:

1. First and foremost, fuck you. You have to be careful with fuck you. The only time I ever got into a for-real street fight in New York, it was after I yelled "fuck you" at a cranked-up guy who almost ran us down. He turned around and came back. The fight lasted one punch, and I didn't win.
2. The fuck-you missile could have been something besides an empty aerosol can. It could have been a bottle, smashing at my feet. I had that happen in Fort Greene one time, and heard the teenagers across the street laughing.
3. It could have been accurately aimed at my head instead of accurately aimed at my feet.
4. It could have been a bullet. But he wasn't trying to hurt me, just fuck with me a little.
5. It could have been aimed at Constance.
6. By pulling up into the gas station instead of continuing on out of sight, he was calling me down as a pussy. He wouldn't have issued that kind of challenge to someone who would come over and make something out of it. He knew I wasn't carrying a gun, though you shouldn't make that assumption, even about mild-mannered old white guys, especially in New Orleans. From the other end of it, it would have been foolish for me to assume he wasn't strapped. And he knew something else, whether he knew he knew it or not:
7. He knew my life was worth enough to me that I wouldn't jeopardize it in a meaningless confrontation. He couldn't say the same. That'll make a hater out of you.

Us throwing missiles at *them* is an old story in New Orleans. When the Channel was Irish, its residents used to chase blacks out, defending it as a white area. On that very corner, 115 years before, January 12, 1890, to be exact, according to the *Times-Picayune*:

About 3:30 o'clock Sunday afternoon in the fourth district a small-sized riot took place between a crowd of negroes and whites, during which rocks, bricks and clubs were freely used and several persons were slightly injured.

It appears that a colored procession headed by the Onward Brass Band was marching out Washington Street. They intended serenading a colored woman, Mrs. Johnson, mother of one of the members. The usual crowd of negroes who follow parades of this kind were on hand in force and took charge of the sidewalk as is their custom.

The procession reached the corner of Magazine and Washington . . . when the negroes on the sidewalk were attacked by a force of young white men, who pelted them with rocks, etc. This was a signal for a general battle on all sides. The entire neighborhood turned out and men, women and children were seen running from all directions to escape the flying rocks and brickbats. The greatest excitement prevailed and several people made their appearance with shotguns.

The paraders and the members of the band also took a hand in the row . . . [1]

The gas station wasn't there in 1890, but our house was. Our block, already the route to the streetcar, probably looked something like it did that night. Except that then Magazine Street wasn't paved, there were horses instead of cars, and black people were something like 27 percent of the city's population. Now they were 67 percent.

From that night on, if we went to the Bulldog, we drove. No more walking at night. We'd been warned. We wound up not going there much. If we were getting in the car, we might as well get out of the neighborhood and go to Frenchmen Street, where we could hear a good band for a few minutes. Mostly we stayed home at night, like most Americans.

When I did go downtown at night, I loved the careen home: up through the Quarter (or, alternatively, up Rampart to Canal), then take Tchoupitoulas through the CBD (Central Business District) and the Warehouse District, slaloming around Wal-Mart, then up Jackson and hang a left on Constance. I quickly learned how fast I could go at each point and where the stops, lane changes, and bumps were. Sometimes I took the more lakeside route, through Central City and down Jackson to Magazine, but it was tenser, setting off more alarms on the urban safety radar.

New Orleans has the worst pavement of any American city. Cars bob up and down on the buckled, pitted pavement, the same way pedestrians climb, descend, and trip in order to remain on a sidewalk whose concrete slabs have long since been pushed upward and broken into irregular sloping chunks by a live oak's root growth. It's not merely the fault of the service sector in a notoriously corrupt town in a notoriously corrupt state, but also of the peculiar terrain. The Louis Armstrong International Airport's longest runway had to be redone, at horrendous cost, because it was sinking. The good thing about the poor condition of the New Orleans streets is that it probably reduces traffic fatalities. The streets are in effect a continuous series of speed bumps, making it impossible to drive very fast. Since so many New Orleanians frequently drive half-drunk, or more, the potholed surfaces have the effect of limiting the potential damage a driver can do on the surface streets. But on the interstate, watch out.

I made a decision to keep library hours, not nightclub hours, so I lived by day and not by night. This would have been a very different book if I had dedicated myself to collecting five A.M. stories. Also, smoking was permitted in bars in New Orleans, so a few hours in the clubs tended to inflame my lungs. The smoke in Tipitina's in particular was almost intolerable, with the result that I didn't go there often. Not that I didn't go out at all: like many New Orleanians, and unlike most Americans, I went out to hear live music one or two nights a week. Constance rarely wanted to go. I was always a little concerned about leaving her in the house by herself.

Our block had an empty house at the corner of Magazine, and another right across Constance. It added to the ghostly feeling of the place. With some thirty-seven thousand vacant houses in New Orleans, blight was the city's biggest problem behind crime. Since the neighborhood dead-ended at Tchoupitoulas, down by the levee, there was no through traffic. When I would come home after a night out, there was no one at all on the street. It was deathly quiet, as in George Washington Cable's breathtakingly predictive description in *The Grandissimes*, written in 1880 and set in 1803: "Faintly audible . . . through that deserted stillness which is yet the marked peculiarity of New Orleans streets by night, came from a neighboring slave-yard the monotonous chant and machine-like tune-beat of an African dance."[2]

There were no slave-yards now, just the 'hood, but "deserted stillness" was yet the "marked peculiarity" of these streets by night. And there was still a "monotonous chant and machine-like tune-beat," though, emanating from the occasional passing crunkmobile, it was more than faintly audible. It was sometimes loud enough to wake up the landlord's baby daughter upstairs.

But then there was another sound that lulled me back to sleep: the whistles of the passing trains from the railroad on the other side of the Tchoupitoulas wall, only six blocks down. They sounded like the trains of my childhood, and my grandfather's childhood. And the most wonderful sound: the boats on the Mississippi blew their horns. I'm amazed they haven't replaced them with electronic bleeps yet, the way they got rid of real sirens on police cars.

But there's one sound that comforts me even more than the sound of the railroad, or the boats. That's the sound of Constance's sleep-breathing next to me. I rarely go to sleep until she's dropped off first. Then, if I can't go to sleep, I spoon up behind my girl, pressing up against her back with both of us facing the same direction, threading my left arm between her body and her curled-up left arm, hooking my hand around her wrist, locking in with her sleep-breathing. Hypnotized, I go under. Works like a charm. It *is* a charm. It's the high point of my day, the best moment of my life, when we sink into dreaming together. It's when I know I'm home.

Sometimes, of course, there are nightmares. Constance has them more frequently than I do. I've been shaking her awake from nightmares for thirty years. But I have them too, we all do. In one of them, The Menace—whatever The Menace in this particular dream is—is coming at me, and I attack it. I call for help sometimes, but more often I howl in the face of the Menace. But your muscles are paralyzed when you're in rapid eye movement, so as hard as you want to try, you can't really cry out. You make this kind of strangling sound, *auugh-aghhhh*, and then you wake up.

In my dreams, I fight back.

I was beginning to see how much New Orleans was ruled by the year-long cyclical rhythm of festivals, saints' days, parties, and holidays. To relax in between, and to pay for everything, you have a job. It's a relief to go back to work after a big weekend.

New Orleans celebrates every holiday there is, and they do Labor Day right. But Labor Day comes at a freakish time of year—high hurricane season—and 2004 had been an active one. Florida was in the process of getting creamed by four major hurricanes one after the other, presumably as a punishment from God for having Jeb Bush as governor. It had been three weeks since Hurricane Charley suddenly made a hard right turn with its 150-mph winds, flattening the Florida town of Punta Gorda, seventy miles from where it had been predicted to hit. People in the area were outraged that they hadn't been warned, but there was no way to know beforehand.

The Saturday night of Labor Day weekend, September 4, I went to Basin Street, catty-corner from the French Quarter, down by the Iberville Projects (population in 2004: 1,624), for a concert at the six-thousand-seat Morris F. X. Jeff Sr. Municipal Auditorium. It was the good kind of concert, the kind you find out about from posters with cursive script over a day-glo color spectrum, posted on the telephone poles in Central City. What a lineup: Bobby Womack, Tyrone Davis, Bobby "Blue" Bland, Betty Wright—a sort of chitlin-circuit Buena Vista Social Club coming to town. I'd never seen any of them live, which is kind of unusual. Nobody's seen everybody, but I've been at it a long time, and I haven't missed too many veterans.

As it turns out, I still haven't seen Betty Wright, the Clean-Up Woman. She couldn't get a flight out of Tampa, because Hurricane Frances was bearing down. When they announced the reason for her cancellation, I imagined I heard the crowd shudder. But the tour package was rolling on to Mobile the next day without her, driving toward the hurricane to make their gig.

Betty Wright had been my number-one reason for coming. But reasons two, three, and four were still in effect. Memphis's Bobby "Blue" Bland had a string of big R & B hits that I remember from 1960 on. In 1963, he shared headline billing with Sam Cooke right there in the same Memorial Auditorium at a show that the black *Louisiana Weekly* referred to as a "rock and rollarama."[3] It had been a long time since his last #1 record, but there he was, still on the road at the age of seventy-five, on the bottom of the bill. The phrasing was intact, but the power was gone. He sang sitting down. It was one more in the endless series of gigs that was his life. The sound man didn't manage to turn on his horn mikes, so you could hear the horn section acoustically but not through the P.A. in the ugly, boomy, multipurpose hall.

Next up was Tyrone Davis, the early '70s ladies' man who started out imitating Bobby Bland. Coming with a softer sound, Davis kept the soul torch burning after the genre's greatest records had already been made. By the time he came along, the music world had long since fragmented into stations that only played one kind of music, so that "The Turning Point" went #1 R & B in 1976 without ever cracking the Hot 100 pop chart. At sixty-six, he wasn't energetic but he sang well, he had a good little band with him, and of course he did "(If I Could) Turn Back the Hands of Time," which was enough to make me happy.

There would have been plenty of white people in New Orleans who would have wanted to hear this music. But it wasn't at the House of Blues in the French Quarter, and it wasn't promoted to that public, so there were very few white people at the concert. I've been the only white guy in the audience so many times it seems like my normal gig, but it's not often any more that I get to be one of the younger people. As we all had a few drinks, and the hours rolled by, seniors were hooking up left and right.

It was Bobby Womack's night, and he came not with a little road band but with a double-digit number of slick L.A. professionals who sounded like a highly produced late-'70s record. He looked twenty years younger than he was, stalking the stage and flaunting bare arms. The band led off with a solid version of "Across 110th Street," and blasted out the gospel-funk for as long as I needed them to. They never played "It's All Over Now," his tune that gave the Rolling Stones their first American top-30 hit, though they did do "Lookin' for a Lover" from the same period—a time when Bobby Womack was working with New Orleans musicians. But the song that most connected with the audience wasn't one of Womack's own hits; it was "A Change Is Gonna Come" by his old boss Sam Cooke, whose widow Bobby married. It was arguably the transcendent song of the civil rights era:

> I was born by the river, in a little tent
> And just like that river, I've been runnin' every since . . .

You can see that river, you can see that tent, you can see the whole story of being kidnapped in Africa, you can see the American spiritual music tradition summoned up in a single image, all of it with the forward motion that a change is gonna come, at a moment when it seemed that a change really was gonna come. But the change that came to Sam Cooke was that he got shot dead a few months after he recorded it. The song was released posthumously as a "B" side and worked its way up to being a standard.

It sounds great when anyone sings it. Remember Aretha's version? Otis Redding's? Al Green did it great. Or New Orleans's own Aaron Neville. I heard an old man singing for coins on Royal Street who did it just fine. It was even a show-stopper when Three Dog Night did it in Albuquerque—I know, I was there.

When Sam Cooke finished making "A Change Is Gonna Come," complete with tremolo strings, French horn, timpani, and Earl Palmer on drumset, Bobby Womack was the first person outside Cooke's production team to hear it.[4] As I listened to him sing it in the Municipal Auditorium of New Orleans—where forty-four years before, Judge Perez had exhorted the white Citizens Council after Thurgood Marshall had been denied the use of the facility—people who were old enough to remember it all sang along, quietly:

> There's been times that I thought I couldn't last for long
> But now I think I'm able to carry on . . .

Maybe some of them had seen Sam Cooke with Bobby "Blue" Bland right there in that hall, that night in '63. Maybe a few of them could remember when Sam Cooke, a stellar young gospel singer from the legendary Delta blues town of Clarksdale, Mississippi, first started to make noise as a pop artist. His first solo recording session was in New Orleans, in December 1956, with Earl Palmer on drums.[5] Maybe they had seen Bobby Bland sitting in at the Dew Drop Inn on La Salle Street in the segregated years.

A few days after that concert, Tyrone Davis had a stroke at his home in Chicago. He never regained consciousness and died on February 9, after a life on the road. What was it Count Basie is supposed to have said? They don't pay me to play, they pay me to ride the bus. I remember Ernest Tubb, ancient and near-blind, in a bizarre early-'80s booking (the caprice of owner Steve Maas) at the Mudd Club in New York, telling jokes left over from World War II and, so I was told, retiring to an oxygen tent on his Silver Eagle between sets. Hell, Conway Twitty died on his tour bus.

Not me. I'm not a working musician any more. I like living at home. When I was twenty, I heard myself say, "no place is home." But I do have a home. It's where Constance is. She was in New Orleans with me, and that meant I was home.

The next day we were in the Tremé by noon. The Sunday before Labor Day is the kickoff of the fall second line season. They're called "anniversary parades," because they're more or less on the date of the individual Social Aid and Pleasure Club's founding, so each club has its own Sunday marked on the calendar. The beginning of the season belongs to Black Men of Labor, who proudly demonstrate the civic value of second lines.

Fred Johnson, cofounder of the club, told me:

> Greg Stafford, Benny Jones, and myself sat down, and we came with the idea that we wanted to put a brass band on the street that played the music we were accustomed to when we grew up. . . .
>
> We named it the Black Men of Labor because we thought that history was writing black men as failures, black men as not being productive, black men as being deadbeat dads. So we put together a crew of men that worked for a living, that didn't sell drugs, wasn't out there deliberately breaking the law, and that was taking care of their responsibilities, and understood the need to also sustain and support their culture. . . .
>
> A second line is a means to having a relaxed Sunday evening, after you done worked and grind and hustled. When you get to this second line, you can walk, dance, meet friends, drink, hear music that you're accustomed to hearing. That gives you a sense of pride, a sense of who you are, a sense that your community has something that you can't get any other place.

Every conceivable parking spot was taken within blocks of Sweet Lorraine's, the jazz club on St. Claude Avenue where the parade was to kick off. The neutral ground was full of SUVs, and the crowd seemed overwhelming.

The Tremé Brass Band started up, led by Benny Jones, and the Black Men of Labor emerged, dressed in identical shiny gold suits. It was ninety-three degrees and seemed hotter, and this wasn't a stretch with live oaks for shade, so the sun bounced off the pavement in a way that threatened to microwave my face. We didn't have the energy to follow the parade that day, but we helped them kick it off, then got back in the car. I took the way home through the French Quarter.

As I nudged the Saturn through the sweltering congestion, three large bearded men in dresses walked past my car. I had forgotten about Southern Decadence. I was in a drag queen traffic jam. One New Orleans rhythm was bumping up against another. It happens every Labor Day weekend.

Southern Decadence is older than Black Men of Labor, having begun in 1972 as a small party in Tremé. It became massive in 1996 after a gay website began to promote it, and by 2004 it was drawing over a hundred thousand same-sex-loving revelers to be flagrant in public, with parties, parades, and— what else?—flamboyant costume. Over the years, it's become a magnet for religious fanatics who come to repudiate the sinners (and eyeball something that obviously fascinates them), to the point where some gay people might feel intimidated. The response, needless to say, is to be even more outrageous.

Two very different ideas of manhood were in counterpoint in New Orleans that Sunday, as they are every year the day before Labor Day. But the two had something in common: a concept, however different, of community.

I felt uncomfortable leaving Constance in New Orleans by herself. But I had to make a quick run back up to what was supposed to be my real life, in New York.

Our building in Manhattan was built about the same year as the house in New Orleans, and is just as typical a construction. We have a "railroad flat"—built in a railroad-car configuration, with no hallway and the entrance on the side—in a tenement built for immigrants, in what had been an African American neighborhood before Harlem was black, but now the area is expensive. The good thing about our apartment is that you can cook dinner while taking a bath, because the tub is in the kitchen. Our countertop is a plank that sits on top of the bathtub. The landlord does almost zero maintenance on the interior of our apartment, nor have we invested much in it. The sink is falling out of the wall, has been for years. The amount of rent they can charge us is capped by law, so we know better than even to bother asking for anything. If the landlords could get us out, which they could legally do if we stayed gone more than a year, they would redo the place completely and charge more than triple what we pay. Of course, they would have to do something about the approximately annual flood through the ceiling from the home-carpentry shower drain in the apartment above. The place hasn't been painted since I moved in in 1979. I've put my foot through the floorboards various times. I had fantasies of putting out some money to remodel the joint while we were away in New Orleans, or maybe subletting it (yes, I know, my name is Sublette, you're not the first to point this out). Neither happened. So I wound up having to carry the rent on the unoccupied apartment—being rent stabilized, it was just barely thinkable—and I figured that at least I'd have what a New Orleanian would call a pied-à-terre.

I tried to get Constance to come back to New York with me for a few days, but she said no. She was liking it in New Orleans, and the airport experience might throw her bad back out. But I had to go. I had unfinished business, and besides, my pal and Latin music mentor Harry Sepúlveda had an El Gran Combo/Spanish Harlem Orchestra concert going in the Bronx. You used to be able to hear shows like this all the time in New York, every Monday at the Village Gate, but by 2004 it was a special occasion, all the way up at the end of the 4 train. I needed to hear my Puerto Rican music. New Orleans was only about 3 percent Latino, and maybe half of that was Honduran, so an important part of my musical diet—heavy on the salsa—wasn't available down there at all. I guess that didn't make a trip to New York mandatory, but it did kind of influence when I scheduled the trip. I laid in supplies for Constance and flew the coop, telling myself she'd be fine.

Flying from New Orleans to JFK, I found myself feeling fear as the plane took off. The flight was a little bumpy, not too bad, but at every bump I was feeling a sense of fear. I often get a little nervous in turbulence, but I don't feel *fear*.

What was I so afraid of? Dying? No, I know planes don't just fall out of the sky. And besides, I had that conversation with myself when I was twenty-one, and sure, I'm scared to die, but not that scared. Because I made a vow to live first, and I've lived. So if I die, I die.

But then, I'm not only living for me. Most of the time, I disclaim that my songwriting is autobiography, because I hear my songs as fictional pieces for a diversity of voices. But there's a song I wrote in 1985, five years after we got married:

I never was fearful or timid
I never backed down from a fight
My things always fit in a suitcase
Now I don't travel so light

Lately I've gotten more careful
I'm learnin' to pick and to choose
Now that I've found you to love me
Now I have something to lose.

What I was so afraid of was that I'd left Constance in that house by herself.

———————

It was a relief to be back in New York. On a Saturday night, the kind of end-of-summer night that pulls you out onto the street, I *walked*, heading east across Houston Street. I hadn't tried walking anywhere at night in New Orleans since the aerosol can incident. New York seemed relaxed by comparison, even if they wouldn't let you take go-cups out of the bar. But the two cities were going in opposite directions, neither of them good for me. Manhattan, my home for thirty years, was in the process of becoming a bubble for people of our mayor Michael Bloomberg's income level, with the poor being shifted out to the periphery, while New Orleans was sinking, geologically and socially.

From my kitchen in Manhattan, I perused the *Times-Picayune* online. Three kids were arrested at Laurel Elementary, the public school a few blocks from our house:

> When officers arrived they learned that yesterday, September 9, 2004, an 8-year-old boy sold another student, a 10-year-old old boy a handgun for $2.00. The 10-year-old then gave the weapon to another 10-year-old boy. Today, the 10-year-old with the gun returned it to the student who purchased it. While on the schoolyard, the 10-year-old, who placed the weapon in his waistband, displayed it to an 11-year-old male student and said he was going to kill him.[6]

According to its website, Laurel Elementary had a "program focus" of "open space/self-contained learning environment, developmentally appropriate, French culture awareness." Did you get that last part? Laurel was 98.6 percent black. *French culture awareness?* Hello? Let's go over the part about Toussaint L'Ouverture and Napoleon again, shall we?

But that was nothing. There was a quadruple murder in Tremé. A little after midnight on September 9—the second anniversary of Jonathan Lorino's death, it registered in my mind—three men walked into the Black Pearl, also known as Roosevelt's Bar, a po'boy shop on Claiborne. Announcing a closing-time holdup, they made the employees open the register, which had only a couple hundred dollars in it. The small sum of money sent one of the men into a rage. Lead homicide detective DeCynda Barnes wrote, "The unarmed perpetrator ordered the two armed perpetrators to kill the victims. The two armed perpetrators complied and began firing their weapons," shooting four employees to death for no reason other than their anger at such a small haul.

The *Times-Picayune*'s account, which pointed out the robbers' sloppiness in letting a witness slip away alive, said: "By the time the blood bath ended, the victims had multiple bullet and knife wounds, a scene that even hardened coroner office employees found difficult to stomach."[7] Two of the perps were picked up quickly. One, thirty-one-year-old Guy Hayes, lived two blocks from Roosevelt's, worked at a barbershop two doors down from it, and was a regular lunch customer. Let it sink in: they *knew the people* they were casually killing. Also arrested was fifty-six-year-old Willie Jones, better known as "Old-Timer." It took until December to find thirty-three-year-old Michael "Poonie" Boykins, who had six cocaine arrests on his record, with one conviction. Police heard that he was hanging out in the neighborhood, shooting hoops and bullshitting on the corner, semi-disguised with a new beard, but in spite of, or perhaps because of, having murdered four people in the community, no one dared turn him in. The article didn't mention anything about a reward, unlike in the case of Jonathan Lorino. The cops caught Poonie as he was walking along the railroad track.

September 11 brought its customary anniversary depression, but by the morning of Monday, September 13, watching from New York, I was getting concerned about Hurricane Ivan. It had for the third time attained Category Five status, as though the complex forces of a hurricane could be represented by a simple one-through-five windspeed scale. A "classical long-lived Cape Verde hurricane," Ivan had damaged 90 percent of the houses on Grenada and passed just west of Cuba, up the Yucatán channel toward the Gulf Coast. Tropical storm-force winds extended outward 290 miles from its eye.

The prediction was that Ivan would make landfall seventy miles east of New Orleans, somewhere around Mobile, but no one knows what these monsters will do. Hurricanes have a way of turning unpredictably, and Ivan had consistently been moving farther west than predicted.

"It's only a matter of time," began the article, "before South Louisiana takes a direct hit from a major hurricane. Billions have been spent to protect us, but we grow more vulnerable every day."[8]

It seems hard to believe now, but I hadn't paid much attention to the vulnerability of New Orleans. It wasn't until I'd been there a couple of weeks that I drilled down into the *Times-Picayune* website and read with horror "Washing Away," Mark Schleifstein and John McQuaid's five-part special section that ran in June 2002, which laid out in precise detail what could happen and why.

At the Howard-Tilton Library, I looked up the 2001 *Scientific American* article—it's all over the web now, but it wasn't then—called "Drowning New Orleans," by Mark Fischetti. The article framed catastrophic flooding of New Orleans as inevitable and described in some detail what might be necessary to forestall it: rebuilding the wetlands that provide essential cushioning to a storm surge. "A year from now," Fischetti wrote, "another 25 to 30 square miles of delta marsh—an area the size of Manhattan—will have vanished."[9] Presumably that had happened three times by the time I read it, and then some.

Saving the wetlands may sound like some altruistic do-gooder thing you do on behalf of snails. No. The wetlands served as barriers against storm surge. It was crazy to rely solely on levees at the edge of the city. You need buffers farther out in the water to break up and absorb the surge before it can hit the city.

The barely-land of the freshwater swamps directly below New Orleans has been eaten away, so that driving downriver of town, you could see it: the Gulf of Mexico now practically reached right up to the backside of New Orleans. Our ass was stickin' out, to put it in Yatspeak. The major culprit in the disappearance of the wetlands was the oil companies, who cut thousands of little canals into the marshes to get their stuff in and out, thereby allowing salt water in. That in turn killed the ground cover, promoting erosion of what tenuous soil the wetlands had.

Wetlands reclamation would have cost an estimated fifteen billion dollars. It wasn't even a question: the Bush administration was not about to spend that kind of money, much less to protect a city full of poor black people who voted Democratic, much less make the oil companies pay for it. Nor did the oil companies care if New Orleans continued to exist. All they wanted was to get the energy out of the Gulf of Mexico. They needed a port facility, but the city itself was of no use. Every year the Bush administration cut the funds for levee maintenance further. This did not go unnoticed by the *Times-Picayune* and other New Orleans media. It didn't matter.

I learned about MR-GO, the Mississippi River Gulf Outlet (pronounced "Mister Go"), a lethal manmade water gun pointed at the head of the most downriver part of our city, which, shortly after it opened, was the culprit in the 1965 flooding of the Lower Ninth Ward. Fourteen feet of water poured in during Hurricane Betsy and took ten days to drain away, marking the beginning of that neighborhood's decline. I felt like I had discovered arcane information.

So far that hurricane season there had been Hurricane Alex, Tropical Storm Bonnie, Hurricanes Charley and Danielle, Tropical Storm Earl that crossed over into the Pacific to become Hurricane Frank—damn, that *does* sound like Southern Decadence—and there were Frances, Gaston (Gaston?), and Hermine. Names that make them seem like vengeful gods and goddesses, which is a much sexier hook for the media. You can make your TV weather map into a story about Hurricane Danielle's pressure zones.

If Ivan were to close down New Orleans, I wouldn't be able to get back as scheduled and Constance would have to go through the hurricane by herself. Unacceptable. So either I drop everything and go back to New Orleans right now and maybe then have to evacuate, or she comes up here. That was a no-brainer. It seemed incredible to me that Jet Blue still had a few seats available for the 10:40 A.M. flight the next morning from New Orleans to New York. I grabbed one for Constance before it melted away, then told her she was going to have to evacuate.

She thought I was being silly. None of our neighbors seemed concerned. Mr. Landlord, who happened to be in town, told her, "This house has been through more storms and hurricanes than we can count, and it's just fine." Well, of course he was thinking about the house, but I was thinking about my wife. And remembering Hurricane Audrey.

Nineteen fifty-seven was a wet year. A federal flood disaster had been declared in Louisiana by May, even before the start of hurricane season. One day after a heavy rain we went to the appliance shop in Natchitoches to buy our first TV, navigating our way through the puddles of standing water in the parking lot.

Not long after that, my parents enrolled me in summer school prior to my starting first grade in the fall. Three weeks or so into the summer term—June 27, to be exact, I was about to turn six—my parents came to school one day to pick me up early.

Audrey was coming.

I tried to comprehend the idea of a storm having a name like Audrey, which to me was a cartoon character, Little Audrey. Giving storms feminine names was a new convention, having begun only in 1953 (masculine names were added later), and this was one of the first named storms in the Gulf.

At home, I immediately turned on the TV. Reception was terrible. When it came time for the guy who dressed like a sailor and introduced Popeye cartoons, the picture was fritzing out as much as it was on. I watched anyway, but it was clear that, in spite of the fuzzier-than-usual normalcy of Woody Woodpecker, the world had gone out of control.

Out our sliding glass back door, in the descending darkness, I could see trees blowing over. Since Natchitoches is some three hundred miles inland, we were getting off with a stiff wind. Down in Cameron Parish, where the damage was the worst, twenty- to thirty-foot-high waves crashed down on people who wouldn't, or couldn't, or didn't realize they needed to evacuate—though the crawfish, who started swimming away from the marshes the night before, could have told them. The water covered twenty-five miles inland, the worst natural disaster in the United States in twenty years. Fast-moving Audrey was one of the first hurricanes to be tracked by radar, but the practice was still rudimentary, as were communications down in southwestern Louisiana. Over five hundred people were killed.

The old-timers, of whom I am now one, still talk about Hurricane Audrey in Louisiana. One night on a plane in 2008, I sat next to Rosie Shetler, a woman my age from Cameron Parish, and we got to talking about Hurricane Audrey. "I couldn't bring myself to talk about it until I was grown," she said, and proceeded to tell me a chilling story about her infant cousin, apparently claimed from a Red Cross tent by an unknown woman pretending to be a family member, and never seen again. Years later, her mother saw a young woman whom she mistook at first for the missing girl's sister and would have been the right age, and she wondered: could that be . . . Cheryl?

After Audrey, I've always taken hurricanes with the utmost seriousness.

Constance saw the mood of the town change dramatically by afternoon. The newscasters who had been cracking jokes on local TV that morning were the picture of solemnity by two P.M. People were walking down the street carrying freshly purchased plywood boards. She spent the rest of the day doing what she's not supposed to do, because of her back—lifting, putting everything up as high as possible so that even if the house got flooded, things might be high up enough not to get ruined. Mr. Landlord had to fix the storm shutters in place, because there was a trick to it Constance didn't know.

That night, September 13, from my berth in Manhattan, I nervously read the National Hurricane Center's eleven P.M. bulletin, in their peculiar Teletype-era all-caps shout:

MAXIMUM SUSTAINED WINDS ARE NEAR 160 MPH . . . 260
KM/HR . . . WITH HIGHER GUSTS. IVAN IS AN EXTREMELY
DANGEROUS CATEGORY 5 HURRICANE ON THE SAFFIR-
SIMPSON HURRICANE SCALE. NO SIGNIFICANT CHANGE IN
STRENGTH IS FORECAST DURING THE NEXT 24 HOURS. . . .
    HURRICANE FORCE WINDS EXTEND OUTWARD UP TO 100
MILES . . . 160 KM . . . FROM THE CENTER . . . AND TROPICAL
STORM FORCE WINDS EXTEND OUTWARD UP TO 200 MILES
. . . 325 KM.

Constance was out the door by seven the next morning. Her cab driver
had been out to the airport once already. The road was filling up, he said, and
in a little while no one would be able to get anywhere.

The longer everyone waits to evacuate, the worse the traffic tie-up getting out. Driving along in New Orleans, you would see signs announcing
that you were on an Evacuation Route. Sure you were. About like we had an
Emergency Broadcast System on 9/11 after all those disk-jockey man-years
spent running drills. "This. Is a test. For the next sixty seconds, this station
will conduct . . ." Yeah, right.

There was no plan at all to evacuate the people who walked past our
house to the streetcar every day. Maybe there was a plan on paper somewhere,
but a civil defense plan doesn't exist if it's a secret from the people it affects.
Mayor C. Ray Nagin gave a press conference, reluctantly announcing that
the Superdome would be available as a place to evacuate to. There were no
shelters, nor was there any kind of neighborhood-based civil defense program. For that matter, I can't recall hearing the words *civil defense*.

No buses were chartered to transport evacuees. Five railroads converge
in New Orleans, but no trains came in to take people out of danger. No boats
came down the Mississippi to take people upriver to safety. No extra flights
came into the airport. And there was no place prepared to take people to in
any case. Right wingers will sniff and say, well, what you're asking for is logis-
tically impossible, just can't be done. And certainly it couldn't be done if no
one even tried. No one seemed to have ever even considered the idea. Just
shut 'em up in the Superdome if we have to.

In the supposedly third-world nation of Jamaica, there were shelters all
over the country and people knew where the shelters were, but not in New
Orleans, a town repeatedly buffeted by hurricanes since its founding and full
of poor people. The Superdome is a football stadium, not a hurricane shelter.
Instead of taking manageable small groups of people into local, decentralized

facilities, everyone who had no other recourse would be crammed into one giant, central, unprepared space.

The last time the Superdome had been used that way, for Hurricane Georges in 1998, fourteen thousand people spent two nights there. There had been little or no preparation for that space to be occupied by so many people. But then, the point wasn't to help them. Sheltering the poor wasn't the objective. The point was to keep them in, in order to protect property from the conjectured rampages of the poor. In 1998, once they were concentrated into the single holding pen of the Superdome, the authorities locked them in.

Fourteen thousand people. Locked in. Effectively imprisoned. They had been told to bring their own food but many had not. They graffitied, they broke into the luxury boxes, they stole things. They did a lot of damage to the place. No one wanted to repeat that experience.

This time, people were still deciding whether or not to evacuate, and many had no idea where they might evacuate to. By afternoon the roads were blocked by the volume of traffic as people fled for higher ground. There are four main ways out of New Orleans: I-10 going east and west, the twenty-six-mile causeway across Lake Pontchartrain, and the Crescent City Connection across the Mississippi—all of them across long stretches of water, offering multiple opportunities to get caught in a death trap. There are secondary roads out, but for some reason most people don't think to take them. That's how poorly prepared it all was: people hadn't given much thought to their route out, or where to go.

Hundreds of thousands of people were simply not going to be able to evacuate. It had always been like that. They had routinely waited hurricanes out at home, calling the storm god's bluff, for decades. Most of the people walking past our house on the way to the streetcar had nowhere to evacuate to, no money to go on, and/or no vehicle. They laid in such extra supplies as they could—drinking water, Pop-Tarts, canned goods, diapers, batteries, candles, cigarettes, and large quantities of low-priced alcoholic beverages—and prepared to have a hurricane party.

The United States, and especially the South, has an ideology of not giving away anything free to, or making survival too easy for, the undeserving, problematic poor. There was only the basic southern laissez-faire, which effectively sets everyone competing against everyone else on their own timetable, according to their own resources. It was a Darwinian evacuation: if you have an SUV, get in it and drive more aggressively than the others, and the race belongs to the one with extra gasoline stashed in the back. Given the potential for traffic crunch, it's also a good idea to live uptown, because that way you're closer to getting out of the city. And you not only need a car to be able to evacuate, you need ready cash, and probably a functioning credit card. For many New Orleanians, having all that is not even a dream. If you don't—well, Mayor Nagin was reduced to advising something called "vertical evacuation," which consisted of taking refuge in a structure taller than two stories, which there weren't that many of. Historically in New Orleans, that's what the projects have been, the *de facto* storm shelters. That's what he was telling people, in effect: go visit your friends on the upper floors of the projects.

Some people vertically evacuated by checking into a local hotel. Maybe they thought the hotel staff would deal with the hurricane for them? While you might at least be above the water level in one of those tall buildings if there were a flood, you'd be trapped in a room with a sealed (or possibly shattered) window, the power would go out, and you'd have no air-conditioning, in south Louisiana, in the summer. The TV wouldn't work, the water would be shut off, the ice in the ice machine would melt, and you'd be negotiating your way down a pitch-black stairwell to try to get supplies, which would not be forthcoming.

"It's a great thrill to ride out a hurricane," a friend told me, "and unless you get a direct hit, it's probably OK to do. But the problem is that after the hurricane, there is this incredibly intense, humid heat that I can't even begin to describe to you, that if you're sitting in a house with no air-conditioning and no ice and no lights and no nothin', except just sitting in this unendurable humid heat—think of if you've ever been in a sauna, or a steam room, and it was time to leave, and you couldn't?"

Many people who routinely stay behind to ride it out take the route of simplistic fatalism: well, if we go, we go. But it wouldn't work like that. You wouldn't just be painlessly wiped off the map from one minute to the next. You'd be trapped on top of your house, as the wind tore the clothes off your body, with tree branches flying past you and slamming into you faster than trucks on the highway, and the water rising, rising, rising. And that water would be a toxic brew of cadavers, dead animals, sewage, caustic chemicals, thick mud, alligators, and balls of mad, poisonous, churned-up water snakes. You might watch a loved one die and then be stranded up there, baking in the sun for days with no food and no fresh water to drink. You might even survive, to be traumatized by the ordeal for the rest of your life.

But there's always prayer. When a hurricane comes, there are prayers to turn the storm the other way, with New Orleanians hoping to outpray the people in Mobile, who for their part logically are praying against New Orleans. Jesus usually rules in favor of New Orleans, and the hurricane usually curves away. But this was looking bad. Just to the east, in Mississippi, Republican apparatchik-turned-governor Haley Barbour said: "I beg people on the coast: Do not ride this storm out." Yeah, well, Haley, it's not like your fiscally conservative buddies who were so busy covering your coast with casinos are gonna help us evacuate. Oh, and keep denying global warming exists while you're at it, why doncha?

On Tuesday, September 14, as Ivan moved toward the Gulf Coast, the *Washington Post* ran a piece about New Orleans emergency manager Walter Maestri and his stock of ten thousand body bags, a fraction of what would be needed if the area took a major hit:

> If a strong Category 4 storm such as Ivan made a direct hit . . . 50,000 people could drown, and this city of Mardi Gras and jazz could cease to exist. "This could be The One," Maestri said in an interview in his underground bunker. "You're talking about the potential loss of a major metropolitan area."

If I didn't realize how vulnerable the city was before I moved to New Orleans, I knew now.

We could evacuate because I was on top of the situation, and we had the means. Suddenly I was on the survival side of the rich/poor divide. I had up-to-date information, an abused but still functional credit card, an Internet connection to grab Constance a plane ticket, and, most important, a place to go. But if I didn't have those things? You can't evacuate south Louisiana on regularly scheduled airline flights. People with no access to a car mostly just stayed home.

Something called contraflow went into effect, closing incoming traffic to make all lanes outbound. But it was miscoordinated at the statewide level, so different places had contraflow at different times. That created bottlenecks and snafu everywhere, making it worse than if they had done nothing. Maybe six hundred thousand people—the numbers vary widely with the reports, because we're trying to quantify chaos—crawled along in cars, moving a fraction of a mile in an hour, stuck on flood-prone patches of road. The evacuation jammed up and the cars sat there, motionless. It took thirteen hours to go the seventy miles to Baton Rouge. A hurricane moves faster than that. But fortunately, the hurricane turned away—once again. It had been a dress rehearsal for mass death. After that people said: I'm not evacuating, ever again.

Constance had about the easiest evacuation possible. But left behind, in an easily looted house, was my only prized possession—my 1969 Ramírez, the only guitar I ever want to play. The one I bought for $410 in Madrid when I was a young guitar student after visiting Andrés Segovia at his home in Granada and he made a phone call to José Ramírez in Madrid on my and other students' behalf. Its sound is my sound. Constance put it in the bed and covered it up like it was sleeping. And there were the tens of thousands of negatives and slides I've taken over the years, along with other of our meager possessions. That's pretty much the definition of exposed. But when your personal person is freshly delivered out of danger, that other stuff doesn't matter, not even the guitar. Manhattanites don't do this, but I went out to the airport to get her. I never hugged her so hard.

I called my friend Dan Rose, a filmmaker who spent fifteen years making *Wayne County Ramblin'*, a rock-'n'-roll-and-African-gods road movie. He was newly married to his longtime friend Peggy O'Neill; originally from Detroit, she was a musician who had lived twelve years in New Orleans. Dan, also originally from Detroit, had moved to town from New York about the same time we did, and they were also living in the Irish Channel, down on the other side of Jackson from us on a more problematic section of Constance Street.

Peggy didn't want to evacuate, and they wound up at the Mother-in-Law Lounge just before curfew time, where Antoinette invited them to ride it out with her. They decided to head home, but not before downing some beers and a couple of Burn, K-Doe, Burns. There was one other person at the Mother-in-Law with them, a man who sat down at the beat-up old upright piano and began to play and sing: *All because it's I-I-van time . . .* It was Al Johnson, reworking his 1960 hit "Carnival Time" in honor of the hurricane, for an audience of three.

I got a call from Chris, who had started driving north with his family, winding up at a B & B in Natchitoches. Felipe Smith, in the English department, evacuated from New Orleans East in two vehicles with his family. It was a total drag: they got separated in the traffic congestion, then one of the vehicles broke down and had to be abandoned.

T. R. Johnson stayed with his house in the Bywater, but it was spooky. Only a few people remained in the neighborhood, and he seemed to be the only unarmed one. A handful of local men went in and out of the little corner store, all of them with open-carry guns on their hips, ready for self-defense. T.R. vowed to evacuate next time.

One reason people don't evacuate is to defend their property against looting or worse. But if you do that, you need to be ready to sit sentry all night with your shotgun in your lap. In LaPlace, about thirty miles upriver (west and a little north) of New Orleans, thirty-one-year-old Natasha Baggett-Butler decided to remain in her house alone while the neighbors evacuated.

She heard a noise and surprised three men in her kitchen, in the process of robbing the house. They bound and gagged her, and set the place on fire to destroy the evidence. It took weeks to identify the body.[10]

After all that, the hurricane curved to the northeast, like it usually (but not always) does. The prevailing winds over most of the globe blow from west to east because of the rotation of the planet, but the hotter tropics have east-to-west winds. So as a tropical storm moves north while being pushed by those east-to-west winds, at some point it gets far enough up that the west-to-east winds kick in. Exactly where that point is depends on the conditions of the moment. Ivan curved, and slammed into the Florida Panhandle as a Category Three, with 130-mph winds. Pensacola got smacked again, but New Orleans barely got an inch of rain. The skeptics were right—this time. Like they were right with Andrew in '92, and Georges in '98, and Isidore and Lili in '02.

Once again, New Orleans got off with a warning. It hadn't been hit by a hurricane since Betsy, in '65.

In Cuba, though Ivan's eye passed right by the western edge of the island and dumped a lot of rain and wind on the western half, the Cubans had not one fatality, apparently not even any injuries. Not only were they prepared, they also took advantage of the situation to treat it as a full-scale drill—that is, they used it as a practice scenario for the evacuation they would perform in the not entirely unthinkable event that George W. Bush's administration should decide to attack them. They evacuated a reported 1.2 million people.

Cuba began developing its present system of hurricane response in 1964. In Cuba, when a hurricane approached, citizens knew exactly where they would evacuate to. They were kept informed about the storm's progress to the smallest detail. They didn't wait to evacuate. Fidel Castro would go on TV and reassure Cubans that it was the intention of the government that not one single Cuban life be lost and not one person unaccounted for.

Television in Cuba is tightly controlled by the government, which has the effect of stifling contrary opinions, to be sure, but which also makes it a potent medium for civil and military defense. Cubans have repeatedly told me, spontaneously, without being asked, of the sense of security it gave them to know that the Cuban state was capable of dealing with the emergency. Transportation was available. Cubans could take their animals when they evacuated, and doctors evacuated with them. In the shelters they knew who needed insulin and who didn't. Merely sticking thousands of people in a stadium was unthinkable. If, as a last resort, they evacuated to a country high school, they had dormitories there. They also took great care to escort their tourists to safety. Cuba, the most fiercely independent state in the hemisphere, was the best-prepared place to defend itself.

New Orleans un-evacuated, and Louisiana went back to business as usual. We didn't manage to get back to New Orleans in time for the September 18 election in which the state's voters approved the Defense of Marriage amendment to the state constitution, specifying that marriage shall be between one man and one woman, thereby prohibiting not merely same-sex marriage but MFMs, FFMs, groups, bestial unions, and people solemnizing bonds with their vibrators, plush toys, or the Eiffel Tower.

Nor did anyone pay all that much attention to Ivan's alphabetic successor, Hurricane Jeanne, which, without passing directly over Haiti, caused some three thousand deaths from flooding, mudslides, and other disasters in the town of Gonaïves on and around September 17. It was reported and forgotten. In New Orleans, you would have had to be a hardcore web surfer, like I am, or have Haitian friends, like I do, or be studying the Haitian Revolution, like I was, for it to have made much of an impression.

Three thousand people dead in the United States would have caused an impression, one would think. Three thousand dead Haitians was nothing. Just mass horror, unheard by the world, for those unlucky enough to have been born in Gonaïves and smothered in a wall of mud, knowing from birth that no one would rescue them from anything, ever.

In an action that was close to civil war, Gonaïves had been the site of an armed uprising earlier in the year. Haiti was in a state of near-anarchy after its elected leader, Jean-Bertrand Aristide, had been flown out of the country in March—he said he was kidnapped, and you can either believe him or the Bush State Department—on a U.S. plane that sent him to one of the most remote spots on the planet, the Central African Republic, without telling him where they were taking him. Aristide's party, the party of the poor, was called Lavalas, which means "The Flood" and could also mean "The Avalanche." Because the poor can wash over the rich like a flood. But a different kind of Lavalas washed into Gonaïves: swollen from the hurricane rains, the three rivers that lead into the city poured down the deforested mountainsides bringing mud and boulders, entombing people alive.

Haiti, a client state of the United States during all its recent history except the Aristide years, was the worst-prepared place for a hurricane. Such popular organizations as had existed had been destroyed in the U.S.-sponsored coups against the elected government and the more recent U.S.-sponsored mass murder of the Lavalas members who staffed them.[11] There was no functional government, no place to evacuate to, an uneducated populace, an ineffective communications system, no infrastructure for distribution of relief, and no resources to work with.

Cuba and Haiti showed the two extremes of how to deal with a hurricane. New Orleans was closer to the Haitian model. Much closer.

Having been initiated into the fundamental drama of the Gulf Coast, we flew back to New Orleans and tried once again to get started living there.

I wrote to a friend: "This whole thing was a drill for what a disaster a real hurricane hitting New Orleans will be. Imagine if, instead of no rain, the heavens had opened up and gale force winds had begun to blow while everyone was stuck in a highway that had turned into a parking lot, as the water poured into the city treetop high."

In New York, we live about a mile north of Ground Zero, formerly known as the World Trade Center, and we went through 9/11 at close range. But long before that, we were aware how easy it would be to take Manhattan out. It's an island that has to receive daily supplies from the outside. When there's no refrigeration, you and your densely packed neighbors run out of food very quickly. For a long time, and especially since 9/11, Constance had been feeling claustrophobic in New York. We'd had two power blackouts downtown since 9/11, which served as reminders of how from one moment to the next you can be sucked from what you think of as your life into Disaster World. Constance had been wanting to go somewhere less vulnerable. So naturally we had gone someplace more vulnerable than Manhattan. I hadn't quite realized that New Orleans was an island too.

By then I realized that moving to New Orleans was one of the stupidest things I had ever done.

Except for one thing. Despite the fact that we had to live in New Orleans, we were getting to live in New Orleans.

We hadn't been there a month yet.

8

ELYSIAN BLUES

Desire and fear by turns possess their hearts,
And grief, and joy; nor can the groveling mind,
In the dark dungeon of the limbs confin'd,
Assert the native skies, or own its heav'nly kind;
Nor death itself can wholly wash their stains;
But long-contracted filth ev'n in the soul remains.
The relics of inveterate vice they wear,
And spots of sin obscene in ev'ry face appear.
For this are various penances enjoin'd;
And some are hung to bleach upon the wind,
Some plung'd in waters, others purg'd in fires,
Till all the dregs are drain'd, and all the rust expires.
All have their manes, and those manes bear:
The few, so cleans'd, to these abodes repair,
And breathe, in ample fields, the soft Elysian air.
Then are they happy, when by length of time
The scurf is worn away of each committed crime;
No speck is left of their habitual stains,
But the pure ether of the soul remains.

—Virgil, *Aeneid*, VI, translated by John Dryden

Lamps. Drapes. Computer furniture for Constance.
    There's probably some reality comedy series about people like me,
an aging bohemian slum-dweller with no property and little in the
way of domestic skills, trying to cope with the complications of sudden, temporary middle-class status.

141

I went out with my one credit card that still had some headroom on it in search of housewares, but there was almost no place to go shopping. Major retailers were scarce in New Orleans, so to buy anything that came in a box, you had to go to Metairie (pronounced *Mettary*). Located in adjacent Jefferson Parish, the unincorporated town of Metairie was a place where veterans settled after WWII. Well served by the new interstate, it was a major recipient of 1960s and '70s white flight. Metairie was the anti–New Orleans, the place that sent Republican David Duke to the Louisiana House of Representatives in a low-turnout election in 1989. A former Grand Wizard of the Ku Klux Klan who at the age of twenty pulled a much-noticed stunt of appearing on the Tulane campus in a Nazi uniform, Duke received 671,009 votes statewide when he ran for governor in 1991, in an election that drew 78.9 percent of registered voters. He did not get the votes because he had become more centrist. His sole issue was race. Two-thirds of a million Louisianans voted for a man with Klan and Nazi associations to be their governor. Metairie was also the home of David Vitter, a far-right Republican congressman who was running for the U.S. Senate.

I was having a hard enough time learning New Orleans, and didn't feel ready to deal with Metairie too, not realizing that all the stores there are lined up along the town's one main drag, Veterans Boulevard. But I found a store with office furniture in New Orleans—an Office Depot on St. Charles. I dropped what for me was a fair amount of money on prefab made-in-China furnishings and put the desk and chair together with those goddamn little wrenches marked J, K, and L.

On top of the expense of carrying two places to live, New Orleans was not proving any cheaper than Manhattan. There was a 9 percent sales tax—more than Manhattan's—half of it state, half of it city, with the city half applying even to groceries. Talk about regressive. I made the mistake of saying something about that to a (white) cab driver, whose comment was, well, but this way the drug dealers have to pay in *something*.

Security had us rattled. I feel safe in our apartment in Manhattan, but we have a strong police lock on our thick door, and a locking gate on the one accessible window. To put iron around all the floor-to-ceiling windows in this house, the way every nice house in Latin American cities has, would be prohibitively expensive, though I would do it if I were going to stay longer than ten months. Despite the murder that had taken place in the house, the only security was a sign out front announcing an alarm system, which wasn't in fact connected.

When we got drapes, that meant we also had to get double curtain rods. What the hell are those? This might not seem like a big deal to you, but I turn into a nutcase when I have to deal with things like this.

Fortunately, the first Wal-Mart in the city of New Orleans was having a grand opening, and it was right around the corner from us.

Constance was born nearsighted. She's been a four-eyes all her life. She can't see a thing without her glasses, and has poor night vision. She can't drive; she'd be a menace on the highway. Because we had to drive to do anything in New Orleans, I did the daily shopping, establishing a rhythm of popping into the supermarket every evening on the way back from a day at the library, calling her on the cell to ask what she needed. Depending on the answer, I would pull myself out of the eighteenth century and into one of five super-markets on the way home. Beer? Cheapest at Winn-Dixie. Sausage? Best at Whole Foods, unless I wanted to stop at the marine-odiferous Big Fisherman on Magazine.

My life in the supermarket every evening, learning how to shop for food in New Orleans, became a big deal. I felt like Murray, the Elvis Studies pro-fessor in Don DeLillo's White Noise who loves the supermarket because it's pulsating with data.[1] Should I buy that jar of pork lips? My conversation with the inventory became profound. The produce was mostly not local, and noth-ing much was cheaper than in New York—except for booze, which was sub-stantially cheaper.

If you have to stop into an American megamarket to try to find seven things, you will be in there for an hour if you don't know where everything is. After using one small supermarket in Manhattan for twenty-five years, I had to spend a couple of months learning where everything was in the hangars of five supermarkets, three of which were wicked big. Each one had its own plastic discount card to keep straight. A&P on Magazine had the yellow card. Sav-A-Center, catty-corner from Tipitina's on Tchoupitoulas, was bought out by A&P, so the same card worked there. Winn-Dixie was the sleek black card. Whole Foods and Wal-Mart: the alpha and omega of New Orleans shopping, and I especially liked them because they didn't try to make you have cards. All of them were spiritual descendants of Memphis's King Piggly Wiggly, the first (1916) modern-style supermarket, whose founder took out a U.S. patent on the self-service store where customers picked their own groceries off the shelf rather than asking a clerk to get them.[2]

With the 2004 election closing in, Whole Foods had a lot of SUVs with Bush/Cheney stickers in its parking lot. More than Wal-Mart, it seemed. Well, of course, because Whole Foods is far more expensive. Meanwhile, I had never shopped at a Wal-Mart. There are none in Manhattan. The acreage of even an ordinary American supermarket is baffling to a Manhattanite, but Wal-Mart is another category up from that. Constance and I had to be sure to take our new cell phones in case we got separated.

I could recite to you all the reasons to boycott Wal-Mart: predatory practices, extortion of tax breaks out of communities, below-survival wages, union busting, hammering its suppliers, its disastrous impact on American manufacturing, its general promotion of a right-wing agenda. To say nothing of its effect on culture; it's no small part of why we have such huge concentration of radio stations, which wasn't only because of regulatory favors but was created by market conditions stemming from the lack of local merchants to buy time on local radio. Instead, there was a giant national retailer that wanted to buy a very big bloc of time on a very large number of stations, all at once. Wal-Mart and Clear Channel, joined at the hip.

The bigger the deal, the better the price. Some 70 percent of Wal-Mart's inventory came from China; it purchased about 1 percent of that country's industrial output. Located right by the most productive seafood beds in North America, the New Orleans Wal-Mart carried shrimp on ice from Asian seas.

They had my double curtain rods, for pennies. They had things we didn't think we could afford. And hey, the rice cooker they sold at Ace Hardware was made in China too. A wall mirror for five dollars! We were saved.

Most of the customers at Wal-Mart were black. Most of the employees were black, and most of them were women.

Later I found out the backstory.

A spate of new zoning laws in the 1920s occasioned the separation of commercial and residential properties around the country, forcing residential tenants out of newly zoned commercial areas and creating a homeless population, a problem subsequently exacerbated by the Depression, which was in part a mortgage crisis.

Over the protests of southern congressmen, who have traditionally defended the planterly ideal of low taxes, minimal government services, and keeping the "colored" people in their place, President Roosevelt's Second New Deal addressed the housing problem in 1937 by providing funds for slum clearance and low-income housing, creating the U.S. Housing Authority. The first loan made under the Wagner-Steagall Housing Act of 1937, signed by Roosevelt himself, was for the construction of the St. Thomas Housing Project in New Orleans, which opened in 1941. St. Thomas—or as New Orleanians said, "the St. Thomas"—had 970 units, with 540 more added in 1952.

The projects were a good deal, and for people of modest means they were a step up—especially for black people, most of whom had been renting ramshackle wooden housing stock. Solidly built brick barrack-type structures, mostly of three stories, on generous tracts of land, the projects held through every storm. Unfortunately, they required a continuing governmental effort to maintain, which was less than forthcoming by the Nixon-Ford years, both in terms of bricks and mortar and in terms of the equally necessary social services. Concentrating the poor so densely made it possible to cut off their air—by underfunding their schools, for example. But even in 1978, there was a waiting list of ten thousand names to get into the New Orleans projects.

When they were built, the projects were segregated. The St. Thomas, for whites only, was a hotbed of Yatness. Nearby, on Magazine Street, a lively scene of bars featured country music. Meanwhile, the Magnolia project, which opened the same year, was for blacks.

One of the legendary black American nightclubs began as a barbershop that sold sandwiches to construction workers building the Magnolia: the Dew Drop Inn, which became an anchor of the so-called chitlin circuit. New Orleans has always been a good town to leave, and it had a dip in its music in the 1920s and '30s, after many of its most famous players moved on to Chicago or New York. But in the era of the Dew Drop, the city was cranking up for its next great phase: the early days of rhythm and blues. It was no less important a musical movement than jazz, at least to my life. The Dew Drop's house band was second to none. Name your favorite 1940s or '50s black American perfomer and he or she likely did a stint there. Not just playing there, but living there for weeks at a time, drinking in the vibe and interacting deeply with the local cats. They couldn't stay in white hotels, but the Dew Drop was also a hotel, with cheap eats available. A lot of musicians lived right across the street in the Magnolia, and the jams went on till morning. There was a time when Charles Brown would take over after the all-night jam ended and play all day, taking requests from whoever was in there, until the band started up again at night, so the live music went 24-7. The floor show featured a troupe of drag queens—or, as they said then, female impersonators, and the biggest annual event in this great American music fountainhead was the Halloween Ball given by cross-dressing MC Patsy Valdes (also known as Patsy Vidalia, or Valdia.)[3]

A law forbade blacks and whites drinking together. The presence of white audience members in black clubs was tolerated, though it didn't work the other way around, while black bands entertained white audiences at places black patrons couldn't enter. But the two populations remained pretty much separate in their entertainment habits. This was unfortunate for lots of reasons, but it had the beneficial side effect of allowing black music to develop in New Orleans according to strictly black criteria, with a captive audience.

The third public housing development, the Iberville, also opened in 1941. Like the St. Thomas, it was originally for white residents only. The Iberville was built along South Basin Street on the former location of Storyville, the most famous red light district in the history of the United States, which at its peak had 2,200 registered working girls and an unknown number of semi-pros.[4] Storyville closed down in 1917 with the entry of the United States into World War I because of the danger it posed for syphilis contamination to troops. To build the Iberville, the buildings of the old bordello district were ripped out; furniture rescued from Miss Lulu White's sporting house graces the Hogan Jazz Archive at Tulane University today, on the third floor of Jones Hall.

Near the Iberville, the Lafitte projects, built in 1941 for blacks and insultingly named for the slave-dealing Louisiana pirate, had twice as much land as the Iberville for about the same number of apartments. Local artisans worked on building it, and it was generally considered the best built of the projects, with handsome roof tiles.

Beginning in the 1960s, the ghettoization of the St. Thomas projects accompanied a corresponding deterioration in the adjoining Irish Channel. New Orleans lost about 19 percent of its population after 1970, but between 1970 and 1990, the Irish Channel lost double that. The loss was almost all whites; it changed from a 62 percent white neighborhood to a 68 percent black neighborhood.

Nationwide, the reputation of housing projects became more and more lurid as crack took root. New Orleans is not an early adopter, so it didn't jump on crack right away, but by 1987 or so things were getting crazy. Once again, New Orleans was rocking, only now it was crack rocks. Crack was a new way of selling and using cocaine—the American genius for packaging and marketing at work. It revolutionized the drug trade. Sold in affordable mini-doses, the little baking-soda-and-coke rocks brought a potent high within reach of even the poorest, democratizing cocaine psychosis. The Channel became a crack neighborhood, complete with gunfire, dead seventeen-year-olds, the works. This coincided with the bottoming out of New Orleans's economy when oil prices collapsed, falling below ten dollars a barrel in 1986.

The low point for the Irish Channel was perhaps 1990; 25 percent of the houses sat vacant, and the neighborhood qualified as an "extreme poverty" zone. After that, and especially during the economic improvement of the Clinton years, the neighborhood started to regain population, and property values began to improve. If you could handle the maintenance on those quirky old houses and tough out the neighborhood, it was a good bet for buying a house, fixing it up, and either renting it to Tulane students or reselling. As I was learning, one of the major occupations in New Orleans was being a landlord. Which is why those acres and acres that the projects sprawled across, spread throughout the city, were the most desirable real estate piñata in town, if you could only get *those people* out of there.

By the time I moved to New Orleans, the city's housing projects were famous for their toughness, even within the hip-hop world. The projects weren't the only loci of crime in the city, but they were pressure cookers. That projects don't have to be that way is clear from the experience of New York City, where, though some of the projects were made world-famous by hip-hop as tough places (Jay-Z's Marcy, Nas and Mobb Deep's Queensbridge), I walk past others every day almost without noticing.

White New Orleanians tended to avoid driving by the projects, which sometimes took some doing, given the way they were woven into the city's fabric. It was a subtlety lost on many nonproject dwellers that not only predators, but victims, lived in them. Many were single mothers, the most powerless segment of the population any way you look at it. If the stereotype of the project chick was the gold-digging, soap opera–watching, baby-machine welfare ho, the realer image was someone working for minimum wage in an orange polyester uniform at a fast-food joint with no child care available for her unsupervised kid who went to a pathetically underequipped school, and for health insurance used the emergency room of Charity Hospital. Her home turf was infested with drug dealers, and if she had a problem, the police weren't going to solve it for her.

Every day on my way to Tulane, I drove past the Magnolia—what was left of it, since many of its buildings were decommissioned and boarded up pending demolition. Change was under way, though it didn't necessarily take the fate of the project residents into account. Some of the city's projects had already been torn out pursuant to the so-called Hope VI initiatives, a federal program from 1992, the last year of the administration of George Herbert Walker Bush, that sought to replace projects with "mixed-income" housing. In practice, that meant cutting sweet deals for private developers, with the aim of raising real-estate values in cities nationwide by systematically uprooting concentrations of urban poor. Desire, the city's largest project and the site of Black Panther confrontations with police in 1970, was demolished in 2001. Along with the disappearance of the adjacent Florida project, those razings facilitated a slow movement toward gentrification of the nearby Bywater.

It was a long, tortuous process to raze a housing project, even as many of the city's residents cheered the process on. The St. Thomas, home to a drug gang called the Cutthroat Posse, was bulldozed after years of dispute. The 2,957 St. Thomas residents counted by the 2000 census were evicted in 2001. Some relocated to the surrounding area immediately east of the projects, while others went to New Orleans East. Still others went to the St. Bernard projects near Bayou St. John, where they found themselves living next to old enemies in the drug trade. There were thirteen murders in St. Bernard in 2002, and twelve in 2003.

The St. Thomas's sea of identical housing units was demolished, save five buildings that "for historical purposes" were boarded up and mothballed. Up went a new "mixed-income" development called River Garden, in a sort of ersatz historical style, sitting right next to some serious ghetto, along Race Street (named many years ago when people went there to see races. There is a corner of Race and Religious). For old-time homeowners in the immediate area who'd suffered living next to the projects, it was a godsend, as their homes appreciated in value. For project residents who'd been promised they could stay in the area, it was a betrayal, as only a few of the promised low-income domiciles materialized.

The anchor of redeveloping the St. Thomas was the Wal-Mart. It wasn't easy to find enough space in crowded old New Orleans to put in a Wal-Mart, and it wasn't easy to find a business that would invest in the area. After years of argument, complete with an anti-Wal-Mart campaign by neighborhood activists, it was built on part of the St. Thomas site, at Tchoupitoulas between Felicity and Jackson.

Unwittingly, we had moved to the Irish Channel just in time for a major change in New Orleans lifestyle: the grand opening of the city's first Wal-Mart. In Cuba, where dissidents charge that the country is in a state of "underconsumption," and people get what one songwriter called *chopimanía*[5]—shopping mania—people would die of happiness to have a Wal-Mart. Sometimes when I walked through it, with the walls of the giant structure so far away I couldn't see them, I imagined myself there with my Havana friends, watching them lose their minds. Of course, it was actually socialism, of a weird sort, funneled through a corporate maw. Wal-Mart got a massive subsidy. The Tchoupitoulas location paid $20,000 in taxes instead of what would otherwise have been $750,000, on a twenty-eight-million-dollar facility.[6] So, yeah, they could afford to sell cheaply made things to the masses cheaper than the competition.

Wal-Mart's information system beat that of the state government, which couldn't get contraflow working for Hurricane Ivan. Its 2005 shareholders' report bragged that

> We have a remarkable level of visibility into our merchandise planning. So much so that when Hurricane Ivan was heading toward the Florida panhandle, we knew that there would be a rise in demand for Kellogg's® Strawberry Pop-Tart® toaster pastries.[7]

For people living in our vicinity, the new Wal-Mart meant shopping without taking three buses to Metairie and three buses back, and their sales tax stayed in the city. It was about the most integrated spot in New Orleans, and it empowered the consumer with an endless inventory and low prices. Our house filled up with things we could never have in Manhattan, things we would have had to search for piecemeal in boutique stores at much higher prices. Picture frames for two dollars, lots of them, allowed Constance's family to appear on our mantel. Some of the stuff we bought fell apart pretty quickly—the pepper mill stopped working almost immediately—but hey, it was cheap.

One day I brought up the subject of unions with a Wal-Mart employee I occasionally conversed with. She said, "Before we opened? They showed us this film about unions? With a creepy guy in a trenchcoat, who was, like, *the guy from the union*." Hammered by Wal-Mart all across their territory, the Winn-Dixie chain, whose supermarket was previously the lowest priced in the area, went into bankruptcy, shutting down 346 stores in the South. The Winn-Dixie on Tchoupitoulas didn't close down, but its inventory got strangely spotty—they always seemed to have a good deal on cabbage. When there's nothing left but Wal-Mart, they can charge anything they want. But when the only jobs are at Wal-Mart, who will be able to buy anything?

Then, as the year passed, I realized: I was *looking forward* to going to Wal-Mart. Little plastic Sterilite drawers! We could use those! Hell, we can *afford* them! They negotiate sweetheart deals and cut me in on it! So as a consumer I'm invested in buying from China and keeping their employees non-union. Argggh.

I know, Wal-Mart sucks. On the other hand, it's a little late to complain about chain stores, which have been been exercising an unfair advantage for a century now. Meanwhile, the 'hood votes with its dollars. If I believed buying stuff at another chain store would have saved the world, I'd have done it. But it wouldn't have. And Wal-Mart was closer. And cheaper. Forgive me, God. I went years without a wristwatch, but one day I got a nice little Casio there while I was looking for something else. And a DVD of David Byrne's *True Stories*, irresistibly priced as an impulse item by the cash register. Hi, David.

Out in the Wal-Mart parking lot, it was eighty-two humid degrees outside. I turned on the ignition and popped on the air-conditioning. Up on the Saturn radio came Fats Waller: *I'm gonna sit right down and write myself a letter*, he warbled.

I had WWOZ on. In Bob Dylan's autobiographical *Chronicles, Vol. 1*, he mentions only one radio station: WWOZ, which he listened to while recording an album in New Orleans.[8] It's one of the greatest radio stations in the United States. Their mandate is to support the large local music scene, and in this age of talk radio they still play mostly music, much of it local music, new and old. A New Orleans musician with a new record is going to be interviewed on Oh-Zee (as it is generally referred to). That's how I found out about the new album by Chris Thomas King, the blues guitarist and actor who played the role of Lowell Fulsom in the movie *Ray*, shot in New Orleans in 2003. That's how I got to know about pretty much all the active players on the scene, most of whom sooner or later dropped by the studio to hang out.

At the top of every odd-numbered hour, the "Live Wire Concert Calendar" ran down in alphabetical order all the clubs with live music and the bands that were playing that day or night, always ending with the tag line: "Now get out there and hear some *live* local music!" Hearing this feature a couple of times a day or more, every day, I began to be able to reel off the list of bars with live music, and I'd heard the names of all the local musicians more times than I could count. It was free advertising for all of them. 'OZ wasn't in the hitmaking biz, but certain records became popular from being played on the station. Driving to the bank at noon, my day would be brightened by Rebirth Brass Band. Bet you don't have a radio station in your town that does that. In the morning, they play '20s jazz and old blues. In an oldies town, Billy Dell's oldies show, "Records from the Crypt," was beyond compare.

The station's call letters were an acronym for Wonderful Wizard of Oz, a name stemming from a New Orleans underground DJ who called himself the Wizard. It was a latter-day remnant of a movement started by the Californian Lorenzo Milam, one of the alternative culture heroes of the United States. Sometimes described as the Johnny Appleseed of the do-it-yourself community radio movement, Milam, a former volunteer at Pacifica station KPFA in Berkeley, started Seattle's (now-defunct) KRAB in 1962. Ten years later he self-published a how-to book for aspiring community broadcasters with the gleeful bait-and-switch title *Sex and Broadcasting* (it had nothing to do with sex) that became a community radio bible.

Milam's circle kept tabs on which towns might have frequencies available to start new stations, and in 1978, the twenty-seven-year-old Walter Brock, who was working at the Milam-inspired KCHU in Dallas, came to New Orleans with the mission of starting a community radio station at 90.7 FM. Brock spent two years lining up community support for the station, doing the paperwork to make it happen, learning how to be a Texan in New Orleans, and delivering the Sunday *New York Times* and washing dishes to make ends meet. After two years of prep work, his brother Jerry joined him in New Orleans, getting a job at the Maple Street Bookstore. Walter was more the paper-pusher, Jerry the gregarious people person. Between them, they made it happen. The two of them and engineer Ken Devine lived together in an apartment in the Tremé, where they let James Booker crash with them for six months.

The right to use 90.7 was contested by the Archdiocese of New Orleans before the Federal Communications Commission, which dragged the proceedings out. Finally, to establish its claim to the frequency, WWOZ went on the air December 4, 1980, playing a tape loop of Ras Michael and the Sons of Negus's "Keep Cool Babylon" for about six hours while they tuned the antenna, putting into service the broadcasting equipment that the Brocks had stockpiled in their apartment. Their office space upstairs in the Tipitina's building at Napoleon and Tchoupitoulas became a studio, with a phone-line link to a transmitter on the side of a levee in the nearby town of Bridge City.

A community organized itself around the station. With their studio upstairs from Tipitina's, they were in a perfect position to do live broadcasts, using a board feed mixed with a live mike, if the bands would agree. Sometimes Walter or Jerry Brock would simply go up to the band at sound check and ask if they wanted to be on the radio that night. They'd usually say OK.

Walter Brock remembers a live Saturday afternoon broadcast with James Booker, the master of which is now at the Library of Congress along with a selection of other historic 'OZ recordings:

> Jerry set up a series of Saturday afternoon interviews, and one of them was James. They had a piano on the stage at Tipitina's, just a couple of mikes on it. James did his standard James Booker interview, sitting at a piano, live on the air, real time, for an hour.

We didn't have a tuner come in and prepare the piano for him. We had no money to do that. But as the time went on, the piano seemed to get in tune. Because he remembered which keys were not in tune, right? And worked around it, and kept playing his music. So the piano's becoming more in tune, so that by the end, it's like, you forget the fact that early on you heard all these clunkers. And he's still doing what he's doing, and talking, and going on and doing little medleys of songs, but he's remembering which keys weren't good.

New Orleans native David Freedman, another member of Lorenzo Milam's circle, was in California at the time. There, with an initial invest-ment of six hundred dollars and parts donated from other broadcasters, he started KUSP in Santa Cruz, a Milam-inspired initiative that today is a solid fifty-thousand-watt station. Freedman relocated back to New Orleans at a time when Walter Brock had left, and Jerry Brock was managing the station, but it was broke. "The problem," recalls Freedman, "was that it was extremely erratic, and it certainly did not have any financial underpinnings. There was some incredibly great radio, and there was some incredibly bad radio, and it was all mixed in. If you know community radio stations, this was probably the most community radio station that ever existed, because it was the worst and the best, and it was the most fun, and at the same time the least able to sustain itself."

The New Orleans Jazz and Heritage Foundation assumed responsibility for the operating license of 'OZ in 1986, and the station began receiving a portion of its operating income from the proceeds of Jazzfest (full title: the New Orleans Jazz and Heritage Festival), one of the largest music festivals in North America. Freedman became station manager.

'OZ was one of the first stations in the country to start streaming on the Internet, back in 1995, pursuant to a handshake deal Freedman made with broadcasting entrepreneur Mark Cuban. During their pledge drives, they got contributions from around the world, making them a global New Orleans community station. The station's listenership was small by comparison with the commercial blowtorches, but its impact on the live music scene was enor-mous. For me, life in New Orleans without WWOZ would have been grim.

As I drove the few blocks home from Wal-Mart, a flatbed truck came toward me, its open back packed with muscular black men wearing identical yellow T-shirts that said "OPP." *You down with O.P.P.? Yeah, you know me.* No, not the 1991 hit by Naughty by Nature. It stood for Orleans Parish Prison.

It was a work gang. I wondered where they were going, what project they were working on, and what money changed hands to make it happen. O.P.P. was a huge complex that held some 5,500 prisoners. It received no direct budgetary support from tax revenues, but it was paid per prisoner by the city, state, or federal governments. It jobbed labor out.

New Orleans is home to lots of people who wanted to live somewhere they could be stoners and drunks. I didn't party with those people much, though one night I did meet a man who claimed—I have not independently verified this—to have gone pharmacy-robbing with Chet Baker. The modus operandi, he said, was to drive a car into the front window of the drugstore while it was closed, plowing a hole in the front wall, then run in and scoop up the drugs in a big hurry, and go back out in reverse gear.

Mostly I met people who had moved to New Orleans for its culture, which is nowhere better expressed than through music. Throughout my year, I met musicologists, historians, anthropologists, record collectors, archivists, activists, administrators, attorneys, photographers, journalists, novelists, small entrepreneurs, DJs, recording engineers, fans, students, and more, who felt privileged to be part of the music community of New Orleans. Mostly they were great people. There's plenty of cynicism about it all—New Orleans musicians are notorious for wanting to charge for interviews or even for having their pictures taken. But it takes a lot of nonmusicians to keep music running.

'OZ, which doesn't try to compete with commercial stations, doesn't play any hip-hop at all. There are two very distinct worlds of New Orleans music: hip-hop, and everything else. The music comes out of the same black community—the same families, even—but it exists in mostly distinct structures. New Orleans hip-hop, which at its peak sold many millions of copies, is played on powerful corporate-owned stations. So I had to choose which soundtrack I wanted: Brass bands, funky combos, jazz, blues? Or banging hip-hop and schlocky R & B? That is, 'OZ or Q-93? In the car, I went about half and half. If I didn't feel like what either one was playing, I punched up the oldies station, which in New Orleans might be playing Sly and the Family Stone.

Rappers in New Orleans, who are well younger than hip-hop itself, have been listening to Q-93 for as long as they can remember. The station already had a hip-hop format before it was gobbled by the conglomerate Clear Channel Communications. Q-93 played the national rap hits, but they played New

Orleans records too. As you might imagine, when Uptown Angela or Wild Wayne played your track, it had enormous influence, not that that was easy to achieve. Q-93 was best enjoyed in the car at night, not only because the slinky menace of hip-hop is more appropriate to the dark hours, but because in the daytime they played more R & B. What, since when doesn't Ned like R & B? Since the market divided it up so that hip-hop is ruff tuff stuff for male listeners and R & B is goopy ballads meant for females. I could only take R. Kelly's "Sex in the Kitchen" so often. Ewwww. But if I got Da Blockburnaz' "Work That Thing," with its nasally intoned melody seemingly straight out of Senegal, it was pump-it-up time. Not that the wimpy little speakers in my Saturn could really pump.

At some point, I realized I was addressing Constance as "Boo."

New Orleans didn't only respect its wealthy, it conferred sainthood on them. St. Claude Avenue in the Tremé was named not for any early Christian martyr, but for the neighborhood's developer, planter Claude Tremé.

Appropriately for the man after whom the St. Bernard projects were named, Bernard Marigny, who was a saint only of real estate, is credited with having introduced crapshooting to the United States. In the Faubourg (literally, fake town, meaning suburb) Marigny (pronounced *Merrany*) that he built across Esplanade from what is now called the French Quarter, he named a thoroughfare Rue de Craps, though the name was changed in 1850 to Burgundy (pronounced Bur-GUN-dy). He named another street Bagatelle, for a game at which he had lost a fortune.[9] If I had it to do again, I might focus my house-hunting on the area around the old Rue de Craps, home of a marvelous collection of mid-nineteenth-century urban architecture, heavy on the shotgun houses.

When the Spanish governor Alejandro O'Reilly definitively established Bourbon Spanish rule in Louisiana by executing five seditious French speakers in 1769, the deed was done at the downriver edge of town, on Esplanade.[10] Marigny's suburb, when he created it, extended downriver from that spot. In 1805, he cut a diagonal street down through his subdivision and named it Rue des Français—Frenchmen Street—to memorialize the resistance against the Spanish by the French-speaking colonials, a gesture in the direction of the ideology of Frenchness that thrived in the city during its early years of American possession.

Today, when locals head to Frenchmen, the term is understood to refer not to the entire length of Frenchmen Street, but to the three blocks of it lined with live-music bars. The trendiest strip in New Orleans, it's something of a public nuisance, but unlike Bourbon Street, the music is good and locals patronize it. Farther down, in what is today the 'hood, Jelly Roll Morton lived for a time at 1441–3 Frenchmen. The house is still there.

Constance and I went to Frenchmen on a lovely Friday night, September 28, to catch a set by someone whose music I'd loved for more than forty years but had never seen live: Mose Allison. He was appearing in a trio with New Orleans bassist James Singleton and drummer Johnny Vidacovich at Snug Harbor, a club much beloved by New Orleans musicians because it has music seven nights a week and always pays players a guarantee.

Before going to Frenchmen, we stopped off in the Bywater at T.R.'s for a preconcert beer. I wouldn't know what to do with it, but I would be happy if I could live in a house like his—a handsome, comfortable Victorian two-story that he was lucky enough to put money down on before prices in the neighborhood went up. T.R.'s house was so well fixed up that you would never know that in the 1960s it served as a clubhouse for the New Orleans chapter of the Galloping Geese, one of the first-generation California motorcycle clubs. It's an old wooden structure, the kind that occasionally needs "a five-thousand-dollar Band-Aid," as T.R. put it. The building on the corner was what was left of a bar where the young Fats Domino would play.

The Bywater's a real-estate name for the whiter, riverside part of what used to be called by its political-division name, the Ninth Ward. Beginning at the railroad tracks on Press Street and ending at the parish line, the Ninth Ward is the largest of the city's wards, though it was divided in two by the building of the Industrial Canal, which created the Lower Ninth Ward. (The other part, logically, is the Upper Ninth Ward, but people usually just call that larger part the Ninth Ward.) At one time the Ninth Ward was a thriving area, but now it was pulled tight between gentrification and blight. T.R.'s part of it was a living museum with many splendid houses, the prices of which had climbed in recent years in spite of the slight but very real possibility that coming home some night you might get your brains splattered all over the sidewalk. The Ninth Ward offered real bohemianism, the dangerous kind.

The house next door had been empty for three years. There was a light on inside all the time, so walking past it at night you could see through the window that the ceiling had fallen in. It could easily become a campground for crackheads, who might not notice that it was full of rats. Which meant it was a fire hazard as well as a health hazard. I'm used to seeing rats dart across the sidewalk in my neighborhood in Manhattan, but I've seen rats in the Bywater run overhead, across the telephone wires. Nearby is a house where—talk about notorious addresses—Lee Harvey Oswald, poster child of New Orleans madness, lived as a boy.

As we sat out on T.R.'s back deck in the cool of the evening, I mentioned that we had cable TV in our rented house, and that I was unused to having a TV. "Watch the local news," said T.R. "They take the insanity of New Orleans and run with it. An eleven-year-old girl sees God? They'll take the story and run with it for three nights."

It was the last time we sat out on that back deck, since Constance, who is so sweet that the mosquitoes just love her, was attacked by a swarm of the little monsters, leaving welts on her legs the next day. Ah, yes, the former yellow fever capital of the United States, where people used to sleep in netting. It had been a century since the last yellow fever epidemic, in 1905, at the end of which President Theodore Roosevelt had to come to town to show the rest of the country it was safe to go to New Orleans.

Parking at Frenchmen on Friday night is a problem, so we had to leave the car a few blocks away, on the other side of the broad avenue called Elysian Fields, which was also named by Bernard Marigny, though in French: Champs Elysées. Perhaps he was thinking of the grand Parisian boulevard rather than its Greek mythical namesake, but not necessarily. Elysian Fields is the paradise at the end of the earth where the virtuous go after death. Of the two possibilities, Elysian Fields resembles the afterlife far more than it does Paris, or at least the version of afterlife my ilk is likely to see.

As the three of us walked toward this region where the pure ether of the soul remains, a young, deranged-looking man on the other side of the street started spewing curses loudly in our direction. T.R. leaned over and said quietly, with a serious look on his face, *walk faster*. Unfortunately, there's only so fast a woman in evening shoes can go. We speeded up the pace as best Constance could. Once we were across Elysian Fields, T.R.'s grin came back. As we walked past the senior affordable housing facility on Royal Street, he recalled how one day, walking past it, he saw two residents, octagenarians from the look of them, on the sidewalk out front of the building with knives drawn, threatening to cut each other over a woman who lived there. By now this seemed funny.

It seems that sooner or later something happens to everyone in New Orleans, and T.R. proceeded to tell what had happened to him. About a year before, he had been held up in front of his home by three guys. He's convinced he's still alive because he got his wallet out fast enough. "I hadn't buttoned the button on my back pocket where I keep my wallet," he said. "If I'd had to undo it, it might have taken too long." They grabbed the wallet and split down the street. A woman in her house as they passed by heard one of them say they should have shot him because the wallet only had six dollars in it.

When T.R. made a definite ID on the main assailant from a picture album the cops showed him, the detective said, that's who I thought you were going to pick. The guy had recently gotten out of prison for armed robbery and they were pretty sure he was the one who had killed a tourist the week before. T.R. testified at a preliminary hearing in open court, but it was the old revolving-door story of New Orleans criminal justice: it was going to be hard to get a conviction with only one witness, so the D.A. didn't bring charges. The thug, who knew perfectly well where T.R. lived, stayed on the street. Chances are he won't live very long, if he's even alive today. People like that, somebody shoots them.

It's a good idea, T.R. told me, to carry mugger money. Two or three twenties. It can make the difference between a happy pistol-wielding crackhead and an enraged one. I remember mugger money from back in the day when the Lower East Side of Manhattan was dangerous, but that's been a long time.

Mose Allison was a delight. An old-school hipster from the Mississippi Delta playing piano and singing in the most unforced, natural-sounding way, he sounded very much like he did on *Back Country Suite* in 1957. I realized that his voice has been in my mind ever since the mid-'60s.

I felt inspired. When I got back to our house, I pulled out my guitar and started to sing. Some kind of change was going on. I was singing and playing a little differently—more relaxed, more playful. In a word, jazzier.

I had found a new, better way to sing. I might even say, I was starting to sing for the first time.

I had found something new in my ragged old voice. I was letting something come out that had always been there, something I didn't realize I had.

From then on, I made sure I had a couple or three twenties with me when I went out. And I never buttoned my back pocket.

9

The Kalunga Line

Any foreigner attempting to understand Kongo statements about their own history must be prepared to recognize a logic totally unlike his own. It presents us with an opposition between this world, which is the ordinary, secular daylight world of Kongo experience, and another world, which is variously . . . the land of the dead . . . and Mputu, the home of white people. The opposition is mediated by traverses of Nzadi or Kalunga, large bodies of water; by specially initiated black people; and by certain classes of the dead.

—Wyatt MacGaffey[1]

When the Portuguese arrived at the Zaire River in oceangoing ships, the Bakongo thought they were visitors from the land of the dead.

In Kongo theology, when you died, you crossed over to the other side of the water and lost your color. The world of the living was divided from the world of the dead, on the other side of the water. Between them was the *kalunga* line, a concept that persisted in African American spirituals that spoke of death as a crossing of the water. The people who were kidnapped and carried across the *kalunga* line to Louisiana comprehended New Orleans perfectly, right down to its watery aspect—midway between life and death, the one an integral part of the other. The management of that transition is one of the most important things spiritual technicians, whose ranks definitely include musicians, can do.

159

No cultural tradition in New Orleans is more important than the jazz funeral, a ritual with cousins in Cuba, Haiti, Spain, and various parts of Africa. "All these bands [in the early days of jazz] had two functions," I heard Ellis Marsalis say. "One was sacred, the other was secular. The sacred aspect was playing funerals. . . . A lot of people who have problems with jazz don't understand that jazz is the secular side of the music that people listened to in religious services."[2] It would be hard to live in New Orleans and not know that.

You can't just come in from somewhere else and buy a jazz funeral for your departed loved one. You could hire a band to march down the street with you, but it wouldn't make any sense, because the funeral is about the community turning out for one of its own. A brass band leaves the church after the funeral service, playing dirges and hymns—"Flee as a Bird to the Mountain," or maybe "The Old Rugged Cross." Sometimes the band goes all the way to the cemetery, if it's close enough. Or maybe the procession pulls over, and as the band plays, a grand marshal, in hat and sash, performs a ritual. Sylvester Francis, proprietor of the Backstreet Cultural Museum, has shot video of some five hundred jazz funerals, and I'll defer to his explanation:

> The grand marshal is releasing the body as the spirit. [He's] carrying what we call a streamer. Now on the top of that streamer, they have a artificial white dove. That white dove is the spirit. So when the grand marshal [is] cutting the body loose, this dove [is] release[d] as the spirit. And once the grand marshall feels the spirit been released, [he] move[s] to the side. Then the procession—the people in the cars—go the rest of the way to the graveyard with the remains, and bury the remains. And many times, once everything pass, the band will strike up the music a little faster, and come on back. And when they come back, they'll go to a local bar, or a house, or the hall, or where the repast is gonna be at.

On the way back, the band kicks in with uptempo music, perhaps "Didn't He Ramble." Frequently hymns got ragged up; Dr. John traces "When the Saints Go Marching In" to a minor-key hymn called "When the Wicked Shall Cease to Roam." Everyone in the second line—that is, everybody who's behind the first line, which is the band—offers moral support by strutting back up the street on their way to a party. It's a civilized way to go out, celebrating a life at its end by stepping high in spite of grief.

In an earlier time, these funeral processions sometimes engaged in turf war. Jelly Roll Morton recalled:

[O]n the way home, everything was sad when they'd be playing the dead march. There would be no fights, no trouble. But on the way back, they had boundary lines. The boys had knives, baseball bats, pickaxes, shovel handles, axe handles—everything in the form that they was supposed to try to win a battle. When they got to a dividing line, which was not supposed to be their district, they'd better not cross. If they do, they would be beaten up. And sometimes they were beaten up so bad that they had to go to the hospital. That's the way it always ended in New Orleans.[3]

The up-tempo parading second line of the New Orleans funeral migrated into another kind of New Orleans tradition. Visiting New Orleans, Mark Twain noted in *Life on the Mississippi* (1883) that:

I have a colored acquaintance who earns his living by odd jobs and heavy manual labor. He never earns above four hundred dollars in a year, and as he has a wife and several young children, the closest scrimping is necessary to get him through to the end of the twelve months debt-less. To such a man a funeral is a colossal financial disaster. While I was writing one of the preceding chapters, this man lost a little child. He walked the town over with a friend, trying to find a coffin that was within his means.

Insurance companies didn't want "colored" customers, so African Americans provided for their burial expenses and medical expenses through benevolent societies. In New Orleans, these societies were not unaware of the marketing value of having a good band play at their parade. They had their own halls, where they gave dances, and thus, along with funeral directors, they were an important part of the employment circuit for the earliest generation of jazz musicians. Gradually, as insurance companies began to sell to black people, the societies—Social Aid and Pleasure Clubs—took on a largely social function. Some now just call themselves Social and Pleasure Clubs. But the aspect of social service never went entirely away, any more than the community's awareness of its precarious social position did. Social networks deriving from those earlier ones are still a basic survival tool, for individuals and for the community.

"Although [the Social and Pleasure Clubs are] no longer providing health insurance for their members," says anthropologist Helen Regis, "they're still providing a benevolent function in a more subtle way. [If] you lose your job and you want to find another job, who are you going to ask about where there are job openings? You're going to ask your club members. And I think that, again in a more subtle way, they continue to organize major events in people's lives, from birthday parties to funerals. Some clubs meet once a week. So they really provide a kind of solidarity and a kind of emotional and social connection for people."

One of the things the clubs do is create employment for brass bands. As in Cuba, where music is dynastic, many of the players are the sons, or grandsons, or great-grandsons (it's pretty much a male thing) of musicians. Others come up through school marching bands. Sometimes the younger brass bands almost seem like punk rock—a bunch of kids getting off on playing as loud as they can, only blowing horns instead of blasting electric guitars. There's actually a brass band called Stooges, who could face off that guitar band with a similar name, both in toughness and in metallic sonority, especially if the electricity went out.

There's a visible link to an older, even more street tradition: the bands of "rough music," or charivari, at one time called "spasm bands" in New Orleans, which could be all percussion or could have horn sections of homemade noisemakers or toy instruments. Kids imitating adult musicians was a normal part of life in black New Orleans. Jerome Smith recalled in the Tremé "the children that would come through the streets with boxes and pans and bottles, imitating the older musicians." I asked him if there was a name for that kind of ensemble. No, he said, "that was just kids. It was *integrated into their play*. That was the magic." Some of the kids in those street bands of kazoos, tubes, and bottles grew up to be brass-band musicians, including some of the Dirty Dozen. There's also a link to the *rara* tradition: the loud street parades of Haiti, which use *vaksins*, or bamboo trumpets that look like narrow tubes with funnels on the end, a tradition that goes back to Kongo, where elephant-tusk trumpets were used; some *raras* in Haiti will occasionally even use brass-band instruments, not excluding sousaphone. There's a video of the jazz funeral of Paul Barbarin in 1969, in which one of the musicians is playing a homemade instrument he called a "bazooka," which looks very much like a Haitian *vaksin*—a funnel at the end of a tube.[4]

Once your band is organized, you hang together and work as hard as you can, week in and week out, quite possibly for the rest of your life. Some brass bands play regular slots in clubs—Rebirth at the Maple Leaf on Tuesday, Soul Rebels at the Bon Ton on Thursday. If you're downtown, Thursday is ex-Rebirth trumpeter Kermit Ruffins and the Barbecue Swingers at Vaughan's in the Bywater. Ruffins not only plays for the crowd, he sometimes cooks too, making a real New Orleans statement about music and food: if you want to savor my flavor, you got to eat my meat. Or something like that. In New York a band is lucky to have a gig every couple of weeks, but in New Orleans you always have that horn in your mouth. When these bands play in bars, they don't need amplification. If there are vocals, a lot of the time everyone sings together. The crowd may sing it for them.

If you've never been on a second line, there's something about jazz you don't know. When you see these brass bands, you're as close as you're ever going to get to what it might have been like back when jazz was being invented. It's not the same music, not by a long shot, but it's the same young working-class black men, the odds still against them from birth, who maybe can't read music. They're still speaking in pretty much the same distinctive accent, eating the same crawfish, shrimp, and barbecue, swatting the same mosquitoes, playing in the same streets, and maybe even on the same horns, burying the dead to make a living.

Some of them deal with their own grief on their horns, calling on the spiritual powers of music when they play funerals within their own families. James and Troy Andrews played as children to cheering crowds at the funeral of their murdered seventeen-year-old big brother, while their father poured a libation of forties onto the pavement and their mother danced on her dead son's coffin as it was held aloft in the air above the parading crowd.[5]

Brass instruments are well-nigh indestructible, and it may well be that some of the horns that jazz was invented on are still being played on second lines. Kirk Joseph's sousaphone has almost a century of music in it, though he takes pains to point out that the horn's many dents were mostly put there by airlines.

Kirk Joseph is the most imitated sousaphone player in town, which anywhere else wouldn't mean much, but in New Orleans is right up there with being a good rapper. The sousaphone is a specialized tuba, developed especially for marching at the behest of the Portuguese-German-American bandleader and composer John Philip Sousa. Its twenty or so feet of metal tubing twists around the player's body like a brass boa constrictor, the weight resting on the player's left shoulder as he stands inside the instrument's coil. The first prototype was made in 1893, but in its definitive 1908 version the sousaphone bell points forward instead of up into the air like a concert tuba, and it's bigger and flared, making it more omnidirectional in its sound radiation—an important consideration out in the street.

Joseph got his horn as a salvage from the marching band at Foucher High School. "They had stopped using 'tin cans,'" he recalls—meaning they had retired the thirty-five-pound brass heirloom tubas in favor of twenty-five-pound fiberglass tubas—"and there was a row of them on the shelf, tarnished black because they hadn't been played in so long." The band director let him take one home. It had a gash in it, and it took a while to find someone to fix it, but a repairman known as Nose managed to put a brass patch on it. "The first day I picked it up from the repairman," Joseph recalls, "I went straight to Jazzfest, because if you showed up with a horn, they let you in."

With fewer valves than a concert tuba, the sousaphone is clumsier in fast scalar passages, but that's something marching band players rarely have to execute. The U.S. Army Band's handbook notes that, "because of intonation problems [i.e., the difficulty of playing in tune], the sousaphone should not be used in a concert band situation, unless this is unavoidable." But if you're punching out a bass line for a marching band, the tonality is simple enough that you'll stay in tune. Kirk Joseph's lines, however, can be elaborate. It took me a couple of listens to his *Backyard Groove* album to realize that all the bass lines on it were played by sousaphone.

Joseph is best known for his role in the Dirty Dozen, the brass band that changed musical life in New Orleans, playing with them from their beginning in 1977 through 1991. At a time when the old brass band tradition of the city had fallen into a predictable pattern, the Dozen came out of their rehearsal room on North Dorgenois Street with a new sound (partly due to the interplay between sousaphone and one of my favorite instruments, the baritone sax) and a souped-up repertoire with funk, R & B, and bop alongside the traditional funeral repertoire. They also developed their own work circuit. I'll let Sylvester Francis tell it:

> The old musicians was playing only for funerals and for bigger events— hotel events for white people, or out of town. Then when the Dozen came, they started doing local barrooms, local funerals. That opened up a whole new door, cause they went to playing—oh man, anything you could name. The old musicians, they didn't really want to play at penny parties, at wedding receptions, you know, cause they had they gigs to go out of town, Preservation Hall, stuff like that. So the Dozen, they come in there and took everything. If somebody asked them to play at a wedding, they play at their wedding. At the kids' penny party, at the kids' house party. Club owners started asking them to play in their bars, and they started playing in bars. Local bars that sit way back in the neigh-

borhood where nobody used to go. The Dozen went in there and started playing, boom! Before you knew it, this bar got a name. So they opened the doors, and after that, other bands started coming and growing.

The Dirty Dozen first came to New York to play in 1984, at Tramps. I was there, and I remember how the horn players in town talked about that tuba player. Today its members make decent coin (I heard a number, but it's nobody's business). They spend a lot of time on airplanes. They work hard for their money, but you don't see them out playing those grueling Sunday afternoon anniversary parades.

But you will see the Rebirth (also written ReBirth) Brass Band out there. If you had to pick just one band in New Orleans to represent the second line in 2004–05, it would be Rebirth, founded in 1983 when its members were just finishing school and even less traditional in musical orientation than the Dozen. On the other hand, they now *are* a tradition. There's Rebirth, marching past the projects on Sunday afternoon. That's them up on the balcony on Frenchmen during Satchmo Summerfest. There they are in New York, at B. B. King's, but wherever in the world their gigs might be, they're in New Orleans when the Lady Buck Jumpers have their second line, because the Lady Buck Jumpers *always* go out with Rebirth. The musicians make pretty good money when you add it all up, but music is a blue-collar job, and it's hard work that they do, earning their doubloons one hotfooting step at a time.

After the Dozen and Rebirth came the deluge. There are a bunch of younger bands that are already veterans: Hot 8, New Birth, Stooges, Little Rascals, lots more. As well as old-school bands like the Tremé Brass Band, or the Pinstripe. You can always hire one when you need to. They hustle up work everywhere, they make sure the band's name gets out there, and when they hit the pavement, they deliver. After playing together on a daily basis for years, the musical communication gets right tight.

Rebirth is a good name for a band that plays so many funerals. While the tourist economy of New Orleans is reponsible for employing a large number of musicians, so is the city's mortuary tradition. Imagine how much money would flow into the musical economy of New York if important funerals there hired a band of eight or ten musicians. It would subsidize hundreds of musicians' families.

One of Kirk Joseph's mentors was Anthony Lacen, better known as Tuba Fats, who started playing sousaphone in grade school, because school band directors pick out the biggest kid, the tall boy with the weight problem, and say, you're the tuba player. Fats played with most of the brass bands in town at one time or another, developing a style of tuba playing informed by the "walking" style of upright bass players and serving as a bridge between the old school of brass bands and the post-'70s generation.

It's a tremendous workout to play a second line, especially if you're the tuba player. You're going to be marching on buckled, pitted asphalt for four hours, carrying a tuba on your shoulder, at the hottest part of the day, and baby, that sun in New Orleans can make you sweat in February, let alone in July. The parades spend about as much time stopping at bars as they do moving along, so you'll get some rest, but the rest of the time you're huffing and puffing as hard as you can, marching down the street, blatting out the bass line that two thousand or more increasingly drunk people are second lining along to. You're gonna get dehydrated no matter what, as well as hyperventilated. There are hazards: not only the occasional fight or shooting but just the boisterousness of it that can cause someone to bang into you accidentally, which can mess up your chops. It's a workout for your mouth, pushing air through your tensed jaws, buzzing it through your lips, hard enough to make thirty-five pounds and twenty feet of brass vibrate.

And you're the big guy, the one with the barrel chest, the frame big enough to drape a sousaphone over. By 2000, besides having blown out his front teeth, Tuba Fats weighed over three hundred pounds and suffered from OHS, obesity hyperventilation syndrome—he would fall asleep at inappropriate times, sometimes while playing. Shortly after rejecting a doctor's advice to put in a pacemaker, he passed—it's not "passed away," it's "passed"—on January 11, 2004, at the age of fifty-three.

There was music in the street for Tuba Fats every night during the week between his death and burial, and then he had a tremendous jazz funeral. I wasn't in New Orleans yet when it happened, but in my time there it was the jazz funeral I heard the most about, for the importance of the man to the community, for the magnificent event it was, and also for the tragedy that came out of it.

The Dirty Dozen played the four-hour crawl to St. Louis Cemetery #1, where Tuba Fats was laid to rest. Thousands of second liners marched down St. Charles, all the way downtown. Afterward, a crowd gathered at the party corner in front of one of the Tremé's best-known jazz bars, Joe's Cozy Corner, at 1532 Ursulines, between North Robertson and North Villere.

It was a pleasant January evening, and a guy outside the bar sold beers to the swelling crowd. This was a chronic headache for the bar's owner, "Papa" Joe Glasper. He'd written his city council representative the year before, and he'd gone to City Hall, complaining about the unlicensed vendors. Nothing happened. Issues of competition aside, the street vendors caused security problems. They would sell beer to anybody, including kids. Papa Joe, who with police help had already shooed away other vendors that day, went outside and told the vendor to beat it. The vendor, who had two prosthetic legs, got physical. A scuffle ensued, which ended when sixty-three-year-old Papa Joe, who was getting the worst of it, pulled out a gun he'd never previously used. He'd bought it the day he opened his bar, and he had a license to carry it concealed. Scared, he pulled the trigger and blew fifty-two-year-old Richard Gullette's chest open.[6]

Papa Joe was charged with second-degree murder. It didn't look so good that someone had been murdered inside the bar a year previously, or that none of the dozens of people present that night could identify a perp. Nor did the various drug arrests in the vicinity of the bar help, or the occasional fights between bar patrons and police. At his trial, Papa Joe insisted he fired in self-defense in a downward direction, only meaning to shoot Gullette in the (prosthetic) leg. But in December 2004, the jury convicted him of manslaughter.

A few weeks before Tuba Fats was laid to rest, Rebirth played another funeral that brought out thousands: that of Soulja Slim (James Tapp). Slim's thug-rap might seem a long way from Rebirth's pavement jazz, but Slim had recorded with Rebirth. His mother, Linda Tapp, was a serious second liner, a twenty-year veteran of the Lady Buck Jumpers Social Aid and Pleasure Club, and he was the stepson of Philip Frazier, Rebirth's sousaphone player and leader.

Linda Tapp had worked in a hotel for twenty-five years, bringing Slim up in the Magnolia Projects. Slim moved her out of the 'Nolia and bought her a house in Gentilly, where he kept a room upstairs for himself. On Thanksgiving Eve, November 26, 2003, he stopped by on the way to a show in Monroe, then ran to the gas station to buy a new T-shirt and cap. Coming back to the house, as he was getting out of his truck, somebody ambushed him, shooting him in the face and chest. He died at his mother's front door.

Earlier that afternoon, Slim had been with B. Gizzle, his friend since elementary school, who told XXL, "Slim wasn't being himself . . . [he] had bought five new guns that week. . . . His guns were still in his truck. If they would've caught him in the streets, or caught him in Magnolia or caught him any other place, then I doubt they would've gotten him. . . . I know Slim ain't get out that car nowhere in the city or in the world without that gun in his hand. . . . [His mother's house was] the only place they could've caught him slipping at it."[7]

The funeral was postponed till the second weekend following the murder to accommodate people flying in. But the weekend after Slim's death coincided with the Lady Buck Jumpers' annual second line, and his mother second lined with her crew through the streets for four hours, dancing her grief in the New Orleanian way. At the funeral, the deceased wore a doo-rag with his name in rhinestones, and a camouflage leather suit with a matching green coffin. His mother made sure he was wearing a pair of throwback black Soldier Reeboks, the shoes he took his name from. The paraders pulled his casket off the horse-drawn carriage, hoisting it up on their shoulders. Tara Young's account in the *Times-Picayune* noted that Rebirth "kept the mood uptempo. Having played at more than 30 funerals of young murder victims already that year, the musicians well knew what their audience wanted: skip the traditional dirges and start right in with jubilant, rump-shaking second-line music."[8]

Memorial T-shirts, a New Orleans art form, had become commonplace at funerals. It's a way to help defray the costs. You didn't go anywhere in New Orleans—not Wal-Mart, not anywhere—without seeing somebody wearing a blotchy picture and vital dates captioned "Sunrise" and "Sunset." I saw a woman wearing one with the deceased's portrait on it that said, "You had to pop me to stop me." The T-shirts are walking tombstones, fading as they pass through the washing machine again and again. Linda Tapp authorized Slim's memorial T-shirt at It's Marvelous, a shop specializing in funeral tees located, appropriately enough, on Elysian Fields. Bootleg shirts were on the street too, and vendors swarmed outside the mortuary before Slim's funeral got started.[9]

Slim's business relations had sometimes not been cordial. Feeling stiffed on royalties by his label, No Limit—a not uncommon feeling among their artists, or, for that matter, among recording artists in general—he had called out his former label head Master P as a "bitch-ass nigga" in an interview, during which he articulated the code that makes negotiations with rappers such a delicate process: "I got some paperwork where I could try to go to war, but I ain't no nigga to go to court. I'd feel like a ol' pussy-ass nigga takin' him to court. You heard me? I get it in blood, nigga."[10]

It is entirely possible that some of his other interpersonal relations were even more acrimonious. Somebody sure as hell didn't like him. There was talk of a paid hit, with a figure of ten thousand dollars floating around. Police arrested twenty-two-year-old Garelle Smith, but released him for lack of evidence. No one was charged with the killing. No one would talk. The cops also announced that Slim was a suspect in a September murder of a man who was shot and tossed into City Park Reservoir, weighted down with cinder blocks, something indignantly denied by the family. Slim was certainly an easy figure to pin something on. You could hardly claim he was a pacifist. He sold his first crack rock at thirteen and had been arrested more than a dozen times, including for armed robbery and murder. Some rappers exaggerate their criminal careers, but Slim got respect on the street, because nobody thought he was pretending anything. He'd spent six of his twenty-six years in prison.

You would never have predicted from Slim's hardcore approach that he would have a mainstream pop single. But he had it in him, and besides, mainstream's not what it used to be. After he was killed, a track he'd given Juvenile to rap on went to #1 pop on *Billboard* for two weeks, spearheading a new wave of southern domination of hip-hop.

"Slow Motion" was released under Juvenile's name and was the last cut on his *Juve the Great* album, but the chorus (*Unngh! I like it like that*), which was the hook, was all Slim's. It was Juvenile's first hit without a Mannie Fresh track, and the biggest single he had ever had. It established that beyond a doubt Juvenile was the dirtiest trash-talker on bubblegum radio, continuing a long New Orleans tradition of what Jelly Roll Morton called "smutty" songs.

Everyone shouted out Slim on their next album. After "Slow Motion" blew up not only in New Orleans, not only in the Dirty South, but all over the world, he became sainted in the street. Oh, yeah, thugs need saints too. If he didn't quite join the international pantheon of T-shirt saints along with Che, Marley, Selena, and Tupac, at least in New Orleans 2005 you would see somebody wearing Slim's funeral T-shirt whenever you went to a second line uptown.

The video for "Slow Motion," made posthumously, combined lascivious slow-motion booty shaking and the sadness of a wake, expressing the tension between Eros and Thanatos that New Orleanians felt every time they heard the track on Q-93 or in a club. One of the first shots of the video is the classic hip-hop funeral gesture, as African as you need it to be: a libation poured on the ground. Multiple wardrobes are an essential element of music video, and in one of his changes, Juvenile is sitting on bleachers, wearing a bright yellow tee and headwrap à la Ochún while surrounded by a surly tableau of men in dark R.I.P. Soulja Slim T-shirts. Intercut is the landscape of the Magnolia Projects, with its dirt-and-grass courtyard—there is green grass in pretty much every New Orleans hip-hop video—and in the center of the action is a giant live oak tree that is surely sentient.

Small and very indie-oriented, the New Orleans Film Festival happens in October. Among the 2004 offerings at the Contemporary Arts Center on Camp Street was *The Hot 8*, a fine thirty-two-minute documentary, shot in super-16, about the young brass band of that name. The film pulled no punches about how the musicians' lack of musical training limited them even as they organized into a high-energy band. It had taken director Greg Samata some time to get the film out, and the footage was four years old. What with the black and white cinematography and the period architecture, it seemed to be from much longer ago.

The Hot 8 Brass Band, founded in 1995, had a memorial section for deceased members on their webpage. Three former members of the eight-piece band were dead, including trumpeter Jacob Johnson, murdered in a home-invasion robbery at the age of sixteen in 1996. Another silver halide ghost, dancing down the street in the film with the others, was trombonist "Shotgun" Joe Williams. Shotgun Joe had newly crossed over the *kalunga* line when I saw the film, shot down by the New Orleans police on August 3, 2004, at the age of twenty-two. The official version of events was contradicted by witnesses interviewed by Katy Reckdahl, whose account in the *Gambit Weekly* I am substantially following here.[11]

Joe was a member of one of the city's most distinguished musical families. His great-grandfather, Frank Lastie, a revered figure in New Orleans, pioneered the use of the drum set in the sanctified church. (Fort Worthian Ornette Coleman hung out in New Orleans for a year or so in 1949–50, living for a time in the Lower Ninth Ward with the Lasties.) Herlin Riley, Joe's uncle, plays in Dr. John's Lower 911 and is one of the most in-demand drummers in New York.

But when Joe was eight, his father shot his mother dead at the dinner table in front of the family. Joe had to testify against him, sending him to the pen. Growing up, Joe became a junkie. He kicked it New Orleans style, going cold turkey in Orleans Parish Prison for six weeks after being arrested in June 2003 on a burglary charge, subsequently dropped. The composer of much of the Hot 8's original material, he was back in the band when he was killed.

The cops were on the lookout for a stolen white truck. Joe, who was on the way to a church to play a funeral with the Hot 8, drove a white truck. He was unarmed. The cops tailed him, and after he let out a female passenger, they surrounded his vehicle in the Tremé, at the corner of North Robertson and St. Philip, where they shouted, "Freeze!"

He apparently put the truck in reverse to try to get away, then put his hands in the air, but it was too late.

The police said Joe hit a cop with the truck; witnesses denied it. He half-fell out of the truck, his hands still up, with fifteen bullet wounds in him out of some three hundred shots fired. No ambulance came. But his bandmates did, almost immediately, alerted by cell phones, and were greeted with the sight of his body hanging out of the truck. There was a six-foot-long trail of blood on the ground. A furious crowd gathered. The cops pushed them back a block from the scene. The body hung out of the truck for three hours in an excruciating ordeal for friends, bandmates, and family. According to a report for local TV station WDSU, one of Joe's relatives, an Orleans Parish civil sheriff's deputy, began screaming and "ripped off his civil sheriff's shirt and his gunbelt and threw them on the ground. 'Y'all shot that boy down like a dog,' said one witness."[12]

Following the custom, there was a second line every night until the funeral. The Hot 8 marched down the street, singing out the old Mardi Gras tune that goes "Shotgun Joe! . . . Shotgun Joe!" They sang those words at every gig I saw them at during the year after Joe's death.

On May 22, 2005, Joe's twenty-third birthday, some three to four hundred people gathered on the block where he used to live in the Lower Ninth, to throw a memorial block party. After eight hours or so of it, the neighbors called the cops, who were greeted with a hail of bottles. The crowd was dispersed, and eleven people were arrested.[13]

His death did not figure in the city's murder statistics.

If the police kill you, it's not murder.

The flyer said "ORIGINAL PRINCE OF WALES ORIGINAL LADY WALES 76TH ANNUAL SECOND LINE PARADE" up top, and then at the bottom: "Dedicated to the Memory of Joseph 'Shotgun Joe' Williams. Respect yourself and you [sic] culture. Leave your guns and troubles at home." The only second line that passed near our house all year, it started at the Rock Bottom Lounge on Tchoupitoulas and paraded for four hours, marching past the Sandpiper Lounge, where the sign said MUSIC in big letters. Stooges were the band.

I've photographed a lot of parades. The best way is to catch the parade coming toward you up the street, which means being out in front of it. You want to be a little beneath it, looking up. If you're my height, that means dropping down on one knee. However, the parade is moving, and if it's a second line that has to complete its circuit in four hours and not a minute more, it might almost be running. So you have just a second or two to drop down, frame, focus, and fire, maybe squeeze it off twice, and then you have to get up and, being careful not to fall in a pothole, run backward at least as fast as they're moving or they'll run over you.

I joined in just as they were getting to Juicey's Lounge, followed along to Li'l Bruh's Hot Spot, and finished up with them back where they started out, at the Rock Bottom Lounge. Walking the few blocks home was a little tense:

a group of kids were talking tough and throwing big chunks of cement, and I was a little concerned they might decide to throw them at me.

In his 1954 autobiography, Louis Armstrong recalled that in his youth, "The second liners were afraid to go into the Irish Channel which was that part of the city located uptown by the river front. It was a dangerous neighborhood. The Irish who lived out there were bad men, and the colored boys were tough too. If you followed a parade out there you might come home with your head in your hand."[14]

That was the only time all year I walked the six blocks from Tchoupitoulas to my house.

Cotten was coming to town. That's Cotten Seiler, originally from Louisville, who turned out to be a mutual friend of T.R.'s and mine. He was only going to be in New Orleans one night, and he wanted to hear some music, so we all went to Funky Butt, down on Rampart Street, where the Wild Magnolias were playing their regular Monday night gig.

I'll talk about the Mardi Gras Indians later in the book. Maybe you know about them already, though I've found that few people outside of New Orleans do. For that matter, even in New Orleans, a lot of people have only the vaguest idea of what they are. This wasn't a full-fledged Indian event in the street, of course. It was an electric band in a club, playing the funked-up arrangements of Indian repertoire made famous on the classic 1970s Wild Magnolias sides done for the French label Barclay.

Bo Dollis, Big Chief of the Wild Magnolias since 1964, wasn't appearing that night. It was the Wild Magnolias band, a combo with Japanese New Orleanian lead guitarist June Yamagishi, fronted by a suited-up Gerard Dollis, also known as Bo Dollis Jr., whose style is very different from that of his father. I was disappointed at first, but once I started to listen I liked what I heard just fine, because it was plenty funky, and because Bo Jr. is his own man.

They were throwing out beads, Mardi Gras style. That isn't something the Mardi Gras Indians do, it's something the uptown krewes do, but hey, we're at the edge of the French Quarter, it's a tourist area. So it was that Constance and I caught our first beads in New Orleans, and they were thrown by a Mardi Gras Indian. Looking back on it, this seems significant.

Watching the Magnolias play, I realized: the Mardi Gras Indians are the only African American musical tradition I'm aware of that uses the *campana*, the bell that in English is dismissively called the cowbell. Sure, modern African American music uses the *campana* (e.g., Kool and the Gang's "Jungle Boogie"), but that's mostly the influence of Cuba, where the bell is a basic element in Afro-Cuban ensembles, understood by religious people to be the power secret of iron. The Mardi Gras Indians, however, seem to have been using the *campana* all along. For that matter, the white folks' Mardi Gras has a curious historical association with the cowbell (see chapter 15). But however it got into his hands, Bo Dollis Jr. was an astute bell player.

As the rhythms started to tug at us, the band tried to get people on stage. Bo gave Constance a direct look and motioned for her to come up.

She did.

Constance doesn't get up on stage to dance, ever. But in Cuba I learned that one of the things the bell does is push the envelope of the trance, and I have seen her feel the bell in Cuba. To a superficial observer, it might have looked like a drunk middle-aged blond tourist letting off steam in a French Quarter bar. But she wasn't drunk, or a tourist, and there were some things about her dancing that might tell you something different was going on. It was the *campana* that did it. For a moment, she was *in it*, in the real place that the music inhabits, and she'd been there before. I think Bo Dollis Jr., a particularly wise young shaman, recognized that. That was how it seemed to me, anyway. He handed her a special Wild Magnolia medallion, which she treasures.

By the end of the set I was onstage too, on the mike, singing chorus: *the Wiiiiiiild Mag-no-lias*. That never happens in New York.

On Thursday, October 21, twenty-six-year-old Tyrone Lawrence was gunned down on Painters Street in the Ninth Ward, apparently by his best friend, Hasan Clay, who was raised with him by Lawrence's grandmother.[15]

That same day, in a freezer behind a trash bin at an apartment complex in Slidell, police found a body naked from the waist down. It was the remains of thirty-four-year-old Michael Gosserand, who had been stabbed eight times with a large blade two days previously. On Friday, they arrested the dead man's wife and her brother, who lived with the couple. A neighbor told *Times-Picayune* writers Paul Rioux and Walt Philbin: "'They were big on lights, Christmas, Halloween,' he said. 'They seemed sort of happy.'" According to police spokesman Marlon Defillo, the couple's two-year-old daughter slept through the fatal fight.[16]

I wished the *Times-Picayune* had as many music writers as they did crime reporters. There was a fantastic second line pretty much every Sunday, a giant community event with thousands of participants. But you had to find out about second lines via the grapevine and video them yourself if you wanted anyone else to know they existed. Between the fundraising events and the parades themselves, a newspaper could keep a second line critic busy.

The autumn passed painfully for T.R., who had a bicycle accident on October 24, breaking his right arm in sixteen places. His mother came down from Louisville for a time to help him out. We didn't see him again for a while. Among the many things he missed was the launch of the Neville Brothers album, their first in five years, and one of their best records ever.

The Nevilles were part of a family that took a step up by moving to the Calliope projects. That was before the giant high-rise interstate trestles cut the Calliope off into a desert island, making it possibly the most isolated of all the projects. Art Neville, the oldest of the brothers, sang "Mardi Gras Mambo" with the Hawketts, in a quickie 1954 recording just in time for Mardi Gras that year. The number had previously flopped in a country version by Jodie Levens, but the Hawketts' version became one of the enduring classics of Mardi Gras, because it was a compelling bit of flavor that modestly did something new. Though it seemed like a novelty record, the novelty was that it was in straight, or Latin time, instead of swing time, ahead of Little Richard's straight-time breakthrough "Lucille." Art Neville made fifteen dollars for singing behind Richard on "The Girl Can't Help It," the title song of a Hollywood movie. That was him singing the Allen Toussaint-composed New Orleans ballad standard "All These Things."

All four of the brothers—Art, Aaron, Charles, and Cyril—were addicted to hard drugs at one time or another. Charles did three and a half years in the penitentiary at Angola for two joints, where he cut cane in a work gang. The music the Nevilles make is spiritual, all the more because they're so unable to hide their anger. Ivan Neville, a central force in keeping the band so together and strong now, isn't a Neville brother, he's Aaron Neville's son, but he's a Neville Brother. Art's son Ian is there on guitar. (Ivan also leads the band Dumpstaphunk, in which Ian plays.)

Records like *Walkin' in the Shadow of Life* used to cost several hundred thousand dollars to make. Back in the day, making an album meant spending weeks and weeks in another city with a high-priced producer and a meter clicking hundreds of dollars an hour. It had to sell very large numbers to be profitable, something few records did. But this was recorded at Neville Neville Land, the Brothers' own studio on Canal Street. They promoted the CD in their hometown, where the largest number of their hardcore fans live, so we were feeling it nicely over WWOZ, but it doesn't seem to have been noticed much outside their fan base. When I asked my voracious-listening rock critic friends in New York, none of them had checked it out.

One day, pulling up through the tense blocks below our house, I heard "Kingdom Come" on 'OZ. It was about media and urban violence, sung from the point of view of what might be an HIV-positive ghetto couple watching a TV preacher, that broke into a rap on top of a thunderous rock track:

They got crack to keep us null and void
Hairon [heroin] *to keep us numb*
I got my ack [AK-47] *and my nine* [9-millimeter pistol] *to ease my mind*
Until the kingdom come.

It was one of those moments where the music is too strong for the moment. I was passing the house where the McElveen brothers lived before they were led away to prison for the murder of Jonathan Lorino. I was living in the landscape of the song. This was the architecture that went with it, this was the lacy decrepitude of the town, this was the temperature and the humidity of the air outside the recording studio, crackling with the potential for violence. The song's narrator might live on this block. The thunder of the track was what it felt like to be him. It was only four more blocks home. I was in tears when I parked, letting something out that the song released. It turns out to have been written by Cyril Neville, the most outspoken of the brothers, and, of all cowriters, Bono.

The album featured a tight remake of "Ball of Confusion" that creolized the Norman Whitfield sound, the funkiest stuff Motown ever did. Why would you bother to do that when you can just play the Temptations' version? So you could hear it sung by Aaron Neville, who ranks up there as one of the great soul voices. There are multiple voices on the album, but it frames around Aaron. The Nevilles still have something of the cover band about them, but that's very New Orleans—what was jazz but a bunch of guys playing songs everyone knew? I thought their cover of "By the Rivers of Babylon" was a little hokey, but as I later realized, I just didn't get it. Every cut on this record was telling you something. "Junkie Child" included a guest rap by B.G., whose style I was getting to like—Aaron Neville and B.G., sadder but wiser ex-junkies, vocalizing at each other across the generations.

When some of the Nevilles appeared on 'OZ to promote the album, and the DJ asked how they shared out the responsibilities of tracking an album, one of them, I don't remember who, compared it to the process of making gumbo. "We just take turns watching the roux," he said, referring to the flavor base of oil, flour, and spices that has to be slowly simmered for hours, watching carefully to see it doesn't burn. In other words, they shared out the responsibility collectively among the family as they simmered the Hohner clavinet together with the Hammond B-3 and the wah-wah guitar. Put those three together in unisons or octaves, and you have the timbral signature of funk. Living in New Orleans was making me see the Nevilles as the unique American band they are.

A second major New Orleans album dropped right about the same time, by Dr. John (Malcolm Rebennack), the Nevilles' contemporary who, like them, watched recording studio procedures and sonic standards change all the way from one-track recordings at Cosimo Matassa's through the psychedelic years and beyond, and who, like them, survived his romance with the white lady of heroin. Although *N'Awlins, Dis, Dat, and D'uddah* (try to remember that name, I dare you) had better promotion than the Nevilles' album, it came and went like a blip in the larger world of American media. Dr. John, one of the glories of American music and the most professionally New Orleanian New Orleanian since Louis Armstrong, was a tough white kid from Mid-City who was at home with black music all his life. He moved away from New Orleans in the '60s after district attorney Jim Garrison closed down the clubs, but he always kept the faith musically, and he kept a profile in town. This album was done in New Orleans with the some of the brilliantest elders still around, including arranger Wardell Quezergue (b. 1930, he produced "Trick Bag," "Barefootin'," "Groove Me," "Mr. Big Stuff," and many more) and Dave Bartholomew.

N'Awlins, Dis, Dat, and D'uddah contained, by my reckoning, at least two all-time classics, both firmly planted in the past. One was a version of Papa Celestin's "Marie Laveau" (1954), in which Dr. John recited (now they call it rapping) the story of the voodoo queen over Wardell Quezergue's string chart. The original, also a recitation, was a Cab Callowayish party number, but Dr. John's version was laid-back and eerie. Cyril Neville emotionally soul-sang the same verses Dr. John calmly spoke, but placed at the back of the mix, like an echo from the spirit world.

The album also contained a dirge-tempo, minor-key, spiritual-church version of "When the Saints Go Marching In," featuring a perfect, raspy vocal from Mavis Staples, reminding us that jazz is partly rooted in the dirge, which is to say in making sure the ancestors are put away right. Earl Palmer was coaxed out of retirement for the album. He had stopped playing on doctor's orders, but, greatly irritated at being old and infirm, he showed up at the studio full of spirit to lay down a deceptively simple, definitive, slow 12/8 backbeat. Smokey Johnson, who played drums for Professor Longhair and Fats Domino, just to name two, had had a leg amputated, but he shook the tambourine with easy authority. All the ghosts—call them ancestors, if you prefer—in New Orleans were there to sing along, rounded up by Davell Crawford in the spiritual-church manner. It's not jazz. It's not rhythm and blues. It might be the greatest number Dr. John recorded in his long career, definitively reclaiming from the tourist repertoire, and bringing back into the sacred space, the most familiar New Orleans number of all.

Outside New Orleans, the Nevilles and Dr. John may have seemed like relics of another time. But not when you caught them on WWOZ while driving along on a dark day in the rain, past the old houses of the Marigny or the Tremé, or past the projects, or running across Mid-City on Carrollton. You weren't sure what year it was, if it was 1912 or 1954 or what, because in New Orleans all the times are present at once. Goosebumps would rise up on my arm when I heard Dr. John's tortured Yat voice sing:

When the wicked cease to roam
I want to step up with all the saints and the angels
Cause this ole earth ain't no place I'm proud to call home.

Three great New Orleans drummers: Earl Palmer, Zigaboo Modeliste, Smokey Johnson, assembled for a Tipitina's Foundation event, January 15, 2005.

"Saints" went back to the days before jazz was jazz. Buddy Bolden brought it into his dancehall repertoire. You can time-travel in New Orleans through music, and also through architecture. Louis Armstrong's old nabe was gone, replaced by the city's traffic court in the 1960s, but there were still plenty of houses in town where the first generation of jazz lived.

The house is still standing, but like many old houses in New Orleans, it's in disrepair.

You could drive by this sloped-roof, double-wide shotgun house at 2309–2311 First Street and never notice it, except you probably wouldn't drive by it. It's in a poor, high-crime neighborhood, and most of the time, there's not much going on around there. The right half of the duplex is where Charles "Buddy" Bolden lived, from the time he was ten until he was locked away.

No recordings exist of Bolden, who was born in 1877. But there's evidence to support the frequent characterization of him as the first jazz musician, or at least the first one to make an impact, in the town where the transformative step into jazz began, the leader of the band that was the "ur-jazz prototype," in Bruce Boyd Raeburn's words.[17]

Oral histories and interviews testify to Bolden's importance. Louis Armstrong recalled hearing Bolden when Armstrong was five, and that Bolden was an influence on him is clear.[18] Clarence Williams, a key figure in '20s jazz in New York, moved from Plaquemine to New Orleans by himself at the age of fourteen after seeing Bolden play a whistle stop, a musical train excursion that ran from town to town for a quick party before moving on up the tracks. "His trumpet playin' excited me so that I said, 'I'm goin' to New Orleans,'" he recalled.[19] According to Jelly Roll Morton, Buddy Bolden was "the most powerful trumpet player I've ever heard, or ever was known."[20]

King Bolden, they called him. He was known for his loud sound and for playing the blues at dances—in New Orleans there was already something called the blues, and it came in from the country with the tens of thousands of English-speaking black people who moved to the city in the decades after emancipation. We know he could make his horn moan, the way the preacher moaned in the uptown spiritual church, or play it sweet like the downtown Creoles.

What we don't know about Buddy Bolden would fill a book, and has. He's been an irresistible focus of writerly imagination in that literary zone where it's always the turn of the century—that would be the twentieth century—in New Orleans. For years he was most remembered as a character in a song he liked to close his sets with, later recorded by Jelly Roll Morton as "Buddy Bolden's Blues" with the words "I thought I heard Buddy Bolden say . . ." Danny Barker gives unsanitized lyrics for it that provide the first known use of the word *funky* in American music, referring to body odor:

I thought I heer'd Mr. Bolden say,
"Funky butt, funky butt, take it away."[21]

The Union Sons Hall at 1319 Perdido Street, where Bolden played, became popularly known as Funky Butt Hall. Barker goes on about Bolden's life as a barber, including a story of how he shaved the corpses in the funeral home. But he wasn't a barber, says Bolden biographer Don Marquis, that's a myth. There was, however, a barbershop right by Bolden's house, at First and Liberty, and he hung out there. A photograph unearthed by Marquis shows a big sign on the shop: the "N. Joseph Shaving Parlor."[22] That barbershop was still there when Marquis published *In Search of Buddy Bolden* in 1978, but now it too is gone.

Buddy Bolden headed a revolution in trumpet playing that displaced the violin as the lead instrument at dances. No instrument has a more central role in jazz than the trumpet, and New Orleans is where that new, conversational, extemporaneous way of playing the former military instrument appeared, subsequently brought to perfection and made world famous by Louis Armstrong. To this day, New Orleans trumpeters don't sound like anybody else. (More precisely, Bolden, like Armstrong a generation later, played not the trumpet but the cornet, which uses the same fingerings and is in the same key, but is a little shorter and stubbier, has an airflow that opens out conically rather than straight across cylindrically, and is consequently a little less piercing in its tone. If you've never been in school band, you probably wouldn't notice the difference.)

Buddy Bolden was at his peak during a toxic period in "race" relations in which African Americans had been silenced politically. After emancipation, the chains had been put back on, link by link, culminating in the Supreme Court's infamous 1896 *Plessy v. Ferguson* decision. It was followed in 1900 by the trauma of the Robert Charles shootout, in which a barricaded black sniper who had killed a policeman and so was certain to die, and who had a large supply of homemade ammunition, shot twenty-seven people in New Orleans, killing seven and seriously wounding eight. In the aftermath, inflammatory newspaper articles (one was headlined "The Negro Problem and the Final Solution," predating the Nazis' use of the latter term) warned of race war to the death. A mob of perhaps two thousand whites attacked blacks, killing several, and burned a black schoolhouse.

In a climate of intense repression, with African Americans permanently, legally, restricted to a less-educated, lower-earning, lower-caste status, there was no way for black people to be heard in New Orleans. Except, perhaps, by playing a trumpet, which instrument became a symbol of black manhood. Bolden was the man who played it the loudest.

There were plenty of horns available in that music-loving, dance-mad, military depot town, and Buddy Bolden was the man the boys with pawnshop horns wanted to copy. "He got a lot of attention with the things he did," Sidney Bechet recalled. "You always heard how he had three or four women with him living in the same house. You'd walk down the street and one woman would have his cornet, [another would have] his watch, his handkerchief, etc."[23]

But we don't know how he sounded. The loudest trumpeter in New Orleans is today conspicuously silent. When he was blowing at Lincoln Park, the infant record business had yet to come to New Orleans. He would surely have recorded if he'd had a full-length career, but he flamed out early.

"Thinking that he was being drugged by his mother," began the story in the *New Orleans Item* of March 28, 1906,

> Charles Bolden, a negro, living at 2302 First Street, jumped out of bed yesterday afternoon while in a state of dementia and struck her over the head with a water pitcher.
>
> Bolden, who is a musician, has been sick for some time. His mother was by his bedside yesterday afternoon, giving him what succor she could, when suddenly his mind was carried away with the belief that she was administering some deadly drug to him. Grabbing the water pitcher, he broke it over his mother's head, inflicting a scalp wound, which was pronounced not serious.[24]

The paper got it wrong: it wasn't his mother he hit, though he was at his mother's house at 2302 First Street; it was his mother-in-law, who was visiting. This clipping, reproduced by Don Marquis, along with a similar story in the *Daily Picayune*, were the only articles that appeared in the newspapers about Buddy Bolden during his lifetime. (In much the same way, Louis Armstrong's name first appeared in the newspaper when he was arrested at the age of eleven, after firing a gun into the air on New Year's Eve.)

Bolden's madness, coming on at the height of his powers in 1906, has never been satisfactorily explained. Some have linked it with his heavy drinking. Jelly Roll Morton and other contemporaries of his suggested that he blew his brains out playing too loud. Latter-day commentators have linked his dementia to the pressure of racism, or suggested that he wasn't really mad at all.

But there's another possibility to consider, that Buddy Bolden was right: his family *was* administering a deadly drug to him.

This hypothesis has not, to my knowledge, previously come up in discussions of Bolden. I'd like to assemble some circumstantial evidence for it, presuming that it can never be proved or disproved. Here's how Marquis describes what happened to Bolden:

> He began having severe headaches in March 1906. His wife Nora mentioned these bad spells and said that he seemed to be afraid of his cornet. Her sister Dora recalled that Buddy's playing began to cause him anguish—seemed to tear him up—and his headaches gave him so much pain he would play wrong notes. She used to go to Adam's Drug Store on Howard Street to get medicine for him when he was suffering.[25]

What medicine was Dora getting him at Adam's Drug Store? If it was a headache remedy, it quite possibly was cocaine.

Three months after Bolden's flipout, on June 30, 1906, President Theodore Roosevelt signed the landmark Pure Food and Drug Act, which required for the first time disclosure of ingredients in drugstore remedies. Upton Sinclair's novel *The Jungle*, an exposé of filthy conditions in meatpacking plants, is usually cited as having provided the public outrage that pushed the bill through. But that was the "food" side. The "drug" side of the law was propelled both by popular outcry and by growing concern in the medical profession about the excessive, unlabeled use of cocaine in a wide range of over-the-counter patent medicines, tonics, and other products.

As an element of New Orleans culture, cocaine is slightly older than jazz. Cocaine—pure, powdered, pharmaceutical cocaine—was first marketed in Germany by Merck in 1879, and was introduced to the American market in 1885 by the Parke-Davis Company, which also marketed cocaine cigarettes, appearing just in time for the period of dizzying financial speculation that Mark Twain memorialized as "the Gilded Age."[26]

Doctors prescribed cocaine for patients. Ulysses Grant, dying a horrible slow death from oral cancer, completed his memoirs while being given a cocaine-and-morphine spray to take the pain away.[27] Parke-Davis supplied it to medicine manufacturers in industrial quantities, and cocaine became a *very* active ingredient in scads of drugstore remedies for asthma, rhinitis, headaches, all kinds of things. One product, Ryno's Hay Fever and Catarrh Remedy, "clocked in at well over 99 per cent pure pharmaceutical cocaine," writes Dominic Streatfeild.[28] People around the country got strung out, suffering hallucinations and delusions without even realizing they were cocaine users. Dentists, who used it for an anesthetic and sometimes got to taking it themselves, had a particularly high rate of cocaine psychosis.

The world Buddy Bolden rolled in was cocaine-mad. After the Robert Charles shooting, newspapers speculated that Charles had been high on cocaine. The thirteen-year-old Louis Armstrong got his first music job (playing cornet in a whorehouse) through an older friend whose street name was Cocaine Buddy.[29] Bolden was a heavy drinker, which has usually been what his troubles have been blamed on, but heavy drinking and cocaine enable each other very well. The stuff was sold in bars. Bartenders would make a hot shot of whiskey with some cocaine dissolved into it. When Buddy Bolden came around, people competed to buy the cornet king a drink. Of course they bought him a *good* drink.

People were getting high in all kinds of ways. As of 1889, New Orleans had a Chinese opium den, like the many that existed across the water in Havana. Heroin was used in New Orleans from the time of its introduction by the Bayer Company, which trademarked the name *heroin* in 1898, just in time for jazz. Jelly Roll Morton recalled a product called "crown," apparently one of the popular over-the-counter products, perhaps with the image of a crown on the package. Speaking of the sporting-house pianists of Bolden's era, he said:

Jelly Roll Morton: The higher class ones always used opium. And uh, the lower ones they resorted to cocaine, crown, heroin, morphine, and so forth and so on.

Alan Lomax: What's crown?

Morton: Crown is some kind of powder form, a drug that you can—that you could at that time buy in most all of the druggists in New Orleans. There wasn't, uh, nothing prohibitive about it. It was some sort of a thing like cocaine.[30]

According to the following article from the November 29, 1902, *British Medical Journal*, cocaine was a habit in Louisiana town and country:

THE COCAINE HABIT AMONG NEGROES.

THE cocaine habit appears to be extremely prevalent among negroes in the United States. It is said to have begun among negro labourers in New Orleans, who found that the drug enabled them to perform more easily the extraordinarily severe work of loading and unloading steamboats, at which, perhaps, for seventy hours at a stretch, they have to work without sleep or rest, in rain, in cold, and in heat. The pay is high—150 dollars a month; but the work is found to be impossible without a stimulant. Whisky did not answer, and cocaine appeared to be the thing needed. Under its influence the strength and vigour of the labourer are temporarily increased, and he becomes indifferent to the extremes of heat and cold.

The habit spread among negro workers till it reached the plantation hand. According to the New York Medical News, while the work on the cotton plantations is not so hard as levee building or loading steamboats, at the cotton picking season, it calls for extraordinarily long hours. As there is never enough labour to pick all the cotton it is to the interest of the planters that the negroes should work as much extra time as possible. The planters therefore hold out every encouragement to the negro hands to put in a big day's work. The negroes found that the drug enabled them to work longer and to make more money, and so they took to it. Its use has grown steadily. On many of the Yazoo plantations this year the negroes refused to work unless they could be assured that there was some place in the neighbourhood where they could get cocaine, and it is said that some planters kept the drug in stock among the plantation supplies, and issued regular rations of cocaine just as they used to issue rations of whisky.

Efforts have been made to prevent the spread of the habit in New Orleans and other cities of the South, and with considerable success. It has been found impossible to save those who have become victims of cocaine and who are fast drifting to the lunatic asylums. [paragraphing added]

It was "found impossible to save" Buddy Bolden, who could easily have been a cocaine addict without even knowing it, especially if he was a regular user of headache powders. The paranoia that alarmed Nora—afraid of his horn—sounds all too much like cocaine psychosis as we have known it ever since, with its delusions, hallucinations, and voices, continuing on down through the hip-hop era.

Bolden was committed to a "lunatic asylum" in 1907, and in those days, when a black man entered a madhouse, he didn't come back out. He died on November 4, 1931, still an inmate, and was buried at Holt Cemetery.

Unlike the more famous cemeteries of New Orleans, where the dead have to be entombed in above-ground, mausoleum-style vaults because the high water table makes subterranean burial impossible, the graves at Holt Cemetery's high-ground Metairie Ridge location are underground. It's a seven-acre potter's field of mostly untended, unmarked graves. Bits of human bones, little pieces of fingers, vertebrae, are everywhere underfoot. Holt Cemetery is the place you would go if you needed human remains or graveyard dirt for your spells.

Decorations large and small appear all over the place, placed there in private rituals of memory. There's a grave with ten female names, the earliest of them from 1918—a whores' grave?—and one male name, maybe an infant? An eerie-looking, weather-beaten, stuffed toy cat is mounted face up on the tombstone of a man who died in 1958. There's a marker for "Brother John," as in the old New Orleans song that goes "Brother John is gone." There's a stone to commemorate drummer and singer Jessie Hill (d. 1997), the grandfather of James and Troy Andrews, who had a hit in 1960 with "Ooh Poo Pah Doo." But the markers throughout the cemetery represent only a fraction of the layers of dead there.

A handsome monument was erected at Holt Cemetery in 1998 to commemorate Buddy Bolden, whose first-generation jazz happened out of history's earshot. But it doesn't mark the specific gravesite. Two years after Bolden's death, when his sister was unable to continue to pay for maintenance on the grave, his body was dug up and reburied deeper so that other bodies could be buried on top of his in the years that followed. There is no record of the location.

Charles "Buddy" Bolden is buried somewhere in that boneyard, among a century's worth of the anonymous poor of New Orleans. But no one knows where.

Cocaine's still a part of life in New Orleans.

10

CREATIVE DESTRUCTION

The fundamental impulse that sets and keeps the capitalist engine in motion comes from the new consumers, goods,
the new methods of production or transportation, the new
markets, the new forms of industrial organization that capitalist enterprise creates. . . . Every piece of business strategy
acquires its true significance only against the background of
that process and within the situation created by it. It must be
seen in its role in the perennial gale of creative destruction.

—Joseph Schumpeter, 1942[1]

In corporate America, you dealing with people who got
lawyers. You can't just do what you used to do: shoot up
everybody. Next thing you know, you on the front page of
a newspaper.

—Master P, 1998

I now ask: "Where is Ògún to be found?"
Ògún is found where there is a fight.
Ògún is found where there is vituperation.
Ògún is found where there are torrents of blood.
Torrents of blood, the sight of which nearly strangles one.

—Nigerian ìjálá song to Ògún[2]

The usual way of dealing with hip-hop when people write about New Orleans music is to ignore it. Or, alternatively, to focus only on hip-hop as if none of the rest of it existed. Either one is a mistake.

I can see why people who love the other forms of New Orleans music might not like hip-hop. But its corrosive glory is an essential part of the story. New Orleans hip-hop might at first listen seem more or less indistinguishable with a regional scene that includes Atlanta, Miami, and Houston as well as every other town black people live in, which includes pretty much all the cities of the South. That by itself is an achievement, that such a distinct place could integrate into that regional identity of the Dirty South. That's African American unity in action. But when you listen closer, New Orleans hip-hop has a flavor to it, and a past behind it, that's as distinctive from everywhere else as "Mother-in-Law" was different from "Save the Last Dance for Me." It's the youngest part of the New Orleans music family, but it's family.

Though hip-hop is more than thirty years old and has spent many years as the bestselling music in America, there are many people for whom it's a mystery. But I can't tell the New Orleans story without it. So allow me to backtrack a bit.

———

New York City's musical peak in the last forty years came when it was bankrupt and the nation was just pulling out of the worst recession between the Great Depression and whatever we wind up calling the financial crisis Barack Obama inherited from George W. Bush. I moved there on my twenty-fifth birthday (July 8, 1976), when the graffiti-covered trains screeched to a stop at heavy-metal volume and you had to watch your back at night. Public school budgets had been slashed, and music education was one casualty. Even Louis Armstrong had been able to get his hands on a cornet in the Colored Waifs' home, but for kids in the Bronx at the time of the nation's two hundredth birthday, getting a trumpet or a sax from school was an impossibility. Still, the creativity of the street will not be denied, and the kids figured out how to make music with what they had at hand, which was turntables and cutout records.

They threw parties, along the lines of the sound-system model that the teenage Clive Campbell, better known as DJ Kool Herc, knew from back home in Jamaica, but with a different attitude and feel. They invented a new syntax for turntables that in expert hands turned them into musical instruments. (This unfortunately caused less expert hands to believe themselves musicians when all they did was play records.)

Not only was Kool Herc Jamaican; a number of the participants of the first-generation hip-hop scene were not from what is typically thought of as

African American culture in the traditional sense. Coming after decades in which African America was depicted as the Southern-accented civil rights movement composed of people descended from cotton-plantation slaves, and southern regional music had yielded up international hits all the time, Bronx hip-hop was a new pop prototype that came from somewhere else. Many of the first hip-hoppers came from one or another of the Antillean islands or descended from those who did. Despite a number of features in common, as well as mutual influence, Afro-Antillean musical culture was quite distinct from African American.

Certainly early Bronx hip-hop was embedded in the matrix of African American culture, but New York City, though it was the recipient of considerable southern migration in the Jim Crow years, had its own distinct black culture from the beginning. New York was the second place to have slaves in what is now the United States, after Virginia. Many of them came from the West Indies already "seasoned," and not a few were Akan (they were called "Coromantees"), a root New York City shares with Jamaica, where Akans figured heavily in the African population. New York was not a place of large-plantation agriculture. Slavery there ended decades before the Civil War, in 1827, and by that time New York City had long had a significant population of free people of color. In every epoch, it was a pluralist, polylingual, ultra-urban area, with a different social dynamic than anywhere else. The pioneers of hip-hop were people of color, but they were New Yorkers, most of whom did not drawl or use southern expressions in their speech. Though funk was certainly popular in New York in the '70s—I remember well—the city wasn't a funk stronghold. There were other things going on. For one thing, it was the heyday of the salsa boom.

The United States opened up its immigration gates in 1965, after having kept them largely closed for decades. That had the effect of providing a new source of cheap labor in the face of a developed union movement and the granting of civil rights to African Americans. The ensuing flood of immigration from all over the world, which transformed American music and culture, included many black people from the Antilles, as well as the first African migration to be allowed into the United States since the official end of the transatlantic slave trade in 1808. In New York, people intermarried with people from just about anywhere, making for a bewildering variety of national origins crossed together. Jamaicans, Trinis, Dominicans, Haitians, Barbadians—New York became an even more cosmopolitan city. Puerto Ricans had been coming in all along because they had been U.S. citizens since 1917. If the salsa boom of the '70s signalled a coalescing of New York Puerto Rican identity in a pan-Latin context, the early hip-hop scene in the Bronx, which followed on its heels, was the first shout from a new mixed-up world, in the town that had always been the country's number-one destination for immigration. Breakdancing in particular had a number of Puerto Rican pioneers, and if it reminds you of the Cuban solo male showoff style of rumba dancing known as *columbia*, that's because rumba was sung and danced in the projects. Being New Yorkers, the hip-hop pioneers came with a modernist cutup esthetic that rendered every kind of sound, and every other genre of music, somehow usable within their thing. Turntable manipulation was a new art form, while rapping was old as the hills. DJs were the heart of hip-hop, the thing that made it new. But it wasn't very exciting watching hunched-over guys manipulating turntables with one shoulder scrunched up to their ear to hear the headphones, so they took the time-tested step of adding vocalists for animation: *and you don't stop . . . and you don't quit.* It didn't take long for the rappers to become the face of the music. To this day, hip-hop has a split personality: rappers, who are the stars and are necessarily extroverted, often to the point of hyper-assholery, and who can be brilliant poets as well as frustratingly thick and sometimes really have been the criminals they claim to be; and the beatmakers and other musicians, who work in seclusion and are sometimes shy. The glamour guys and the geeks.

Hip-hop from that period had a joy to it that vanished a few years later when crack came in ('85, in my awareness). It was about partying, and though there was aggression, it was about resolving beefs through musical rather than street combat. Listening to it now, it sounds so jovial that it might be hard to remember that the '70s were a time of crime and racial polarization in New York, and that many white people found this new sound threatening, hearing in it the violent aura of someone who might be about to push you under the train for fun, or beat you up after school.

In the early '80s, even in New York, hip-hop as a block of programming was only heard on commercial radio Friday and Saturday nights from nine to midnight. By 1983 there were two mix shows opposite each other: Mr. Magic and Marley Marl with the Juice Crew on WBLS, and Red Alert on WRKS, better known as KISS-FM. They were the best six hours a week on New York radio. I rarely missed them, toggling back and forth between the two stations according to which program was turning me on more at any given moment.

The first non–New York hip-hop record that I remember making an impact on New York radio was in 1985, by one of the earliest gangsta rappers (though the term *gangsta rap* was not yet in use) from less than a two-hour drive away, Philadelphia's Schoolly D. His one hit, "PSK (What Does It Mean?)" (it meant Park Street Killers, a Philly gang), featured a plate reverb turned up to eleven. It came pre-cut up, as if an active DJ were cutting and scratching it, repeating lines literally and mercilessly, as it asked the same question, the same way, over and over:

> *PSK was makin' that green*
> *People always say, what the hell does that mean?*

It became an obligatory drop-in on the hip-hop mix shows in New York. In Los Angeles, an AM outlet called KDAY started playing hip-hop as a format in 1983, giving a platform to a generation of Cali artists who started going platinum a few years later. When N.W.A. (Niggaz With Attitude) dropped *Straight Outta Compton* in 1988, featuring the in-your-face "Fuck Tha Police," it ushered in the era of gangsta rap. Compton, a town most Americans had never heard of, became famous for being divided into red (Bloods) and blue (Crips). By then, hip-hop was taking on more of the characteristics of traditional southern-rooted African American culture, with deep funk and a drawl. Most of the great African American migration to Los Angeles had come from Texas, Louisiana, or Mississippi, and most L.A. rappers were only one or two generations removed from the Deep South.

By 1990 or so, hip-hop had taken a dominant position in the music industry. The majors had been moving in on it since Columbia cut a deal to distribute Def Jam in 1985. The rise of BET (Black Entertainment Television) transformed the music business at least as much as MTV did. Along with that came the rise, and then the mainstreaming, of the gangsta image, which began a transition from sweatsuits to boardroom wear.

There are those who like to blame record companies for the violence of hip-hop. But if you were in the business you quickly realized consumers *wanted* violent, aggressive entertainment, the same way they want to vote for politicians who promise war. Speedmetal, gangsta rap, cut-up-the-cheerleader movies: there was a seemingly endless market that would consume all the product it could get. The guys turning out the extreme stuff in quantity became big powers among independent record companies. "The kids are fascinated with murder," said a puzzled label owner to me shortly after Scott LaRock ("Criminal Minded") was killed in 1987.

Hip-hop was black-identified and problack, while most of U.S. society was white-identified and antiblack. It gave the power of public address to people otherwise unheard from. From this it derived considerable force. But a few people getting fabulously wealthy while everyone else stays poor is anything but revolutionary. In the '90s, hip-hop didn't invent a better world; it tried to be a better predator. It was the converse of the civil rights movement, which moved forward when enough people opted for collective betterment over individual advancement.

The South was about the last place to appear on the rap map. It took ten years or so. The first southern rap group to make big noise nationally was not from the traditional south: it was from Miami, by 2 Live Crew, the brainchild of Luther Campbell (aka Luke Skyywalker, though George Lucas sued to make him quit using the name). Campbell's parents, like many of the black people in Miami, came from the Bahamas. 2 Live was a regional underground thing, specializing in dirty songs, or what used to be called "party records," latter-day successors to those Redd Foxx records on Dooto. Only this time around the comedian owned the label. Ten years later, it would be de rigueur for a rapper to profile himself as a CEO, but Luke was ahead of the curve. 2 Live's career-defining hit, in 1987, was "We Want Some Pussy."

The next big southern rap act, Geto Boys, weren't about having fun. They made Houston's Fifth Ward famous as the place you would least like to visit. Most rappers brag about their stellar qualities, but the three Geto Boys didn't bother with glamour. Everything about them was ugly and cartoon-ishly squalid. They had the murderous stare down far better than the sullen-est London punks. Scarface (Brad Jordan) was a manic depressive on meds. Jamaican-born Bushwick Bill was a dwarf who had lost one eye by forcefully insisting his girlfriend shoot him while in a suicidal mood during a binge of grain alcohol and formaldehyde-laced weed. (Those toxic-edge joints, popu-lar in New Orleans, were called clickums.) Recording on Houston indie Rap-A-Lot, the cover of their 1991 album *We Can't Be Stopped* spawned a national hit, "Mind Playin' Tricks on Me," which described cocaine psychosis from a first-person point of view, using horror-movie clichés with a curious echo of Afro-Caribbean folklore. People in New Orleans felt that one: there's a lot of connection between Houston and New Orleans, including that much of the cocaine sold in New Orleans comes there from H-Town.

Arrested Development, a humanist, antigangsta group from Atlanta, had a southern-sounding, nonurban hip-hop hit in 1992 with the likable "Ten-nessee," but couldn't follow it up. The first mega-successful rapper with a deep southern accent came up not out of the South but as part of the West Coast surge: the charismatic L.A. gangbanger Snoop Doggy Dogg (Calvin Broadus), who'd moved to California as a child from Mississippi. His infectious, laid-back drawl made him sound like a Saturday morning cartoon character brag-ging about a happy life of homicide, weed, and hoes. He first surfaced in early 1992 on producer Dr. Dre's (Andre Young) sleeper-hit title song for an urban crime movie called *Deep Cover* ("cuz it's one-eight-seven on an undercover cop"). Then he was featured vocalist on Dre's *The Chronic* (yet another slang name for marijuana), which went triple platinum. His *Doggystyle* (1993), one of the most eagerly awaited rap debuts ever, did more than four million.

But the South broke through. Nineteen ninety-five saw the emergence of two Atlanta artists: future megastars Outkast, and the less successful Goodie Mob, who contributed the phrase "Dirty South." That phrase is over ten years old now, so white people are allowed to use it.

By then, hip-hop had long since ceased to be party jams. It had turned into something else: a new form of auditory cinema that became more visual as video became cheaper to do. It still rhymed, but the rhymes served a first-person style of tough-guy black fiction that owed something to Donald Goines and Iceberg Slim, and perhaps taking as its point of departure something like the question W. E. B. DuBois posed in 1903, on the first page of *The Souls of Black Folk*:

How does it feel to be a problem?

Looking at the dark-yellow project buildings looming behind New Orleans rappers on album covers, you'd be hard pressed to say which project you're seeing. To an outsider, they all look very much alike. In a city of surpassing architectural beauty, these complexes were, to my eye at least, prison-ugly. But maybe if you grew up there you would see it differently, and in any case, they were not put up to be in *Architectural Digest*. They were put up to house the poor, and to that end they were solid works of masonry in a wooden city. Like prisons, they were also deep pockets of culture, whether you liked everything the culture stood for or not. If fifteen years is a generation, these projects were on their fifth generation. There were people who lived their whole lives in the projects and never left the immediate area. That's a culture.

Rock 'n' roll came out of these projects. By which I mean rhythm and blues players who were seminal to the style that would be called rock 'n' roll, many of whom lived in the projects in the late '40s and early '50s, when New Orleans's music scene began producing a steady stream of national hits.

They already had sex and drugs, so they invented rock 'n' roll. You could always find reefer, cocaine, and heroin in the projects. Dr. John recalled going to the Magnolia and St. Bernard "'jecks" to cop dope in 1953, when he was thirteen.[3] The hip-hop fortunes made in New Orleans, and there have been substantial ones, have their roots in the projects, to the point where two of them became musical brand names and spawned multimillion-dollar entertainment businesses: Calliope and Magnolia. Those fortunes were made by bragging about making money by selling crack.

Let's talk about Calliope first, which is offically called the B. W. Cooper Apartments. The name Calliope derives from one of nine streets named for the muses—so not only was it not named for the steam-driven keyboard instrument so popular on the Mississippi riverboats, but Calliope Street predated that instrument's being patented in 1855.[4] Since the nineteenth century, the name has been pronounced Cally-ope; on the street it's "the Callio," or sometimes "CP3," the three standing for Third Ward, as the Magnolia is "MP3." Appropriately for our story, Calliope was the muse of epic poetry.

Master P (Percy Miller) grew up in the Callio. He moved to Richmond, California (known for its high crime rate, it's twelve miles north of Oakland), in 1990, where he took business classes, and apparently he did his homework. With a ten-thousand-dollar wrongful-death settlement stemming from his gandfather's death, he started a record store called No Limit, and in 1994 he released his first solo record, *The Ghetto's Tryin' to Kill Me*. It wasn't very original, on the model of the Oakland pimp/gangster style, and sounded not a little like Too $hort or 2Pac (whose name from now on I will spell Tupac). He put it out on his own label, No Limit, and sold it out of his store and out of the trunk of his car (like Too $hort had done). Then he moved back to Louisiana, relocating to a compound in Baton Rouge, near where his mother's ancestors were slaves, buying a place in a gated community known as the Country Club.

Just as it was becoming practical to make garage movies—in 1997, two years before *The Blair Witch Project* proved that a microbudget shot-on-video feature could succeed in a theatrical release—Master P shot a straight-to-video feature-length action film, *I'm Bout It*, almost entirely on location in the Calliope. It cost less to make than a lot of one-song shot-on-film music videos. Besides, whereas those major-label videos were merely expensive moving-picture commercials for an audio-only product—a defective business model—*I'm Bout It* it was a viable piece of merchandise in its own right. The movie was purportedly autobiographical, with Percy Miller playing Master P, the same character he played as a recording artist. The cast consisted of No Limit artists playing themselves, including P's rapping brothers Silkk the Shocker (Zyshonn Miller) and C-Murder (Corey Miller), the best rapper of the three. The movie tells the story of the murder of their fourth brother, Kevin. The biggest set piece in the movie is Kevin's jazz funeral, complete with a brass band (unnamed in the credits, and not included on the soundtrack album) playing "Shall We Gather at the River?" and then second lining down the street.

The movie's title was from Master P's catchphrase, "I'm 'bout it 'bout it," which means, the movie explains, that you're "down to do whatever." Thump your heart with your fist twice as you say it. If you wanted to discourage people from moving to New Orleans, you would show them *I'm Bout It*, which depicts P getting started in business not with a legacy but by running a crackhouse. It was a movie nobody else wanted to make. The extras smoking crack look, like everything else in the movie, depressingly real. The DVD package calls it a "comedy-drama," though it has the unfunniest comedy scenes ever as well as possibly the most limited vocabulary of any feature film of the sound era.

The movie's power comes from its insider status. Despite being a terrible movie by any objective standard, it conveyed the claustrophobia of project life like only someone could have done who had lived it, left it, and come back to see it again with fresh eyes. In doing so, it built up the Calliope's brand by bragging about its murderousness.

Perhaps influenced by the fact that there were only two movie theaters, and not multiplexes either, in New Orleans (you had to go to the 'burbs), P released *I'm Bout It* straight to video at a time when videos cost thirty dollars. It sold by word of mouth, doing some two hundred thousand units in a short time, and I rented it in fall 2004 at Blockbuster, so no telling how much it did in the intervening years. P made the cheddar, because it was on No Limit.

Being down south, P wasn't involved in the East Coast/West Coast feud that preceded the deaths of hip-hop's two biggest stars: Tupac Shakur (one of the few rappers to use the name his mother gave him, originally from the Bronx, moved to Baltimore, became known in Oakland, wound up in L.A., died in Vegas) and Biggie Smalls aka The Notorious B.I.G. (born Christopher Wallace, from Brooklyn). Former friends who became enemies in full view of the mass public, they were gunned down six months apart. Subsequent killings during the days and months afterward left a trail of dead young black men. In case you've been on another planet all these years, Tupac was shot by a gunman while riding alongside Suge Knight in Las Vegas on September 7, 1996, and died six days later, on Friday the thirteenth. Biggie was taken out six months later, also in a drive-by, in L.A. on March 9, 1997. The slayings have never been officially solved, nor was there great official enthusiasm for investigating them.

The West Coast hip-hop scene never fully recovered from the destruction the Tupac-Biggie death spasm caused. With the biggest rappers on each coast suddenly out of the picture, Master P, coming from the underground, was perfectly positioned to fill the void—if not with talent, at least with a suitably criminal-minded product. By September '97, his *Ghetto D* was #1 on the *Billboard* album chart.

The original cover of *Ghetto D*, subsequently sanitized for mass merchandising, showed a crack fiend taking a hit off a pipe. "D" stood for dope, and the track was a fable about moving from street-level drug-dealing into the music business. The wit of it, such as it was, consisted of drawing an analogy between selling music and selling crack. The title track began with the sound of water bubbling and a voice saying "May-may-may-make crack like this," parodying Rakim's line "Make 'em make 'em make 'em clap to this" from "Eric B Is President"—which is to say, biting from the greatest. C-Murder gave helpful crack-cooking tips over the "Eric B" bass line, definitively endorsing the glass tube method as opposed to the open-pan method:

> *Get the triple beam and measure up yo' dope*
> *Mix one gram of soda every seven grams of coke*
> *And shake it up until it bubble up and get harder*
> *And sit the tube in some ready made cold water . . .*

You can easily find the lyrics on the Internet. I think I transcribed it right, though no two transcriptions I've seen agree exactly on the not always distinct words. "Ghetto D" pretty much picked up where Biggie's final recording, "Ten Crack Commandments," left off. That was a set of easy-to-memorize nursery rhymes about how to survive and prosper selling drugs, so that five-year-olds learned to chant "Never get high on your own supply" the way I learned "Some people say a man is made out of mud." But Biggie had psychotic wit and advanced rapping skills—as a teenager he took rap-diction lessons from a jazz musician, his New Orleanian Fort Greene neighbor, Donald Harrison Jr.—and whereas Biggie only warned you about problems of distribution, in New Orleans, city of chefs, the lyrical emphasis is on the cooking technique.

In a sense, Master P made his fortune selling crack. By which I mean selling the image of crack. Not the image of smoking it; no hip-hop record ever told you to smoke crack. He was selling the image of selling crack, which, is to say, capitalism. Ultimately, "Ghetto D" expressed one of hip-hop's central themes: the urgent necessity of accumulating wealth, ruthless though it might require the protagonist to be. Its punch line was the last couplet, which advised you to launder your money and make it legal. If they didn't know the specifics, these artists were very well aware, in a more general sense, how many fortunes had been started with illegal trade—in slaves, in opium, in bootleg whiskey, to say nothing of diamonds and petroleum. And, for that matter, in cocaine and heroin.

Education as a route to a good job? Public schools in New Orleans were the worst in the nation, and you might have grown up in a home without books to start with. You could join the army and maybe find yourself in a for-real war. Or you could get that job at Popeyes and go to church, which is a whole lot better ticket to survival because you can be part of a stable community that practices mutual aid. But you'll be a poor person in a high-crime city, and your kids will grow up poor.

As any poor kid in São Paulo, Santo Domingo, or New Orleans can tell you, there are only a few ways to get to be the opposite of poor. The most attainable, but most hazardous, way is a life of crime. There's the classic third-world fairytale possibility of marrying someone rich, but it's not so easy to achieve, and much less so for men. Potentially attainable for the talented are successful careers in sports and music, though since only the biggest stars make real money, your chances are minuscule. But even slighter yet is the last possibility—the cruel delusion of the lottery and other forms of gambling.

So, for young men: crime, sports, music, gambling. There is a certain amount of overlap among those categories.

It had been a long time since we were walkin' to New Orleans or shakin' an apple off an apple tree. The single from Ghetto D was "Make 'Em Say Unngh." Time has not been kind to it. The album went triple platinum (three million units) in short order, ultimately selling six million or so (supposedly, anyway; real sales figures are a closely guarded trade secret). And it was on Master P's own label, No Limit, which meant he made the money himself. Let's see, at eight dollars wholesale, six million units would be forty-eight million in cash just for that one title. You'd have to sell a lot of crack rocks to bring that in, plus it's not illegal. But when you're doing megavolume you can renegotiate your distribution deal, so No Limit might have been getting closer to ten dollars a unit. With that kind of dinero, your soldiers can wear diamond tank medallions around their necks, which they did. To wear a medallion like that is a statement that you have sufficient defensive firepower to repel anyone who might try to take it off you; the chain of events that led to Tupac's death seems to have involved a medallion snatching in Las Vegas. A murdered soulja might have his chain taken as a trophy.

Dental bling raises the ante further: if someone wants it, they have to take it out of your mouth. You can put a quarter million dollars' worth of jewelry on your teeth. New Orleans rappers aren't clotheshorses, but they like those fancy grills, a tradition that goes back locally at least to Jelly Roll Morton's diamond-studded tooth.

If you had never encountered hardcore gangsta-style hip-hop or the world it came from, you would perhaps be puzzled by the sheer grimness of the sound. As with heavy metal, the upbeat, listener-friendly mood generally thought to constitute commersh entertainment is nowhere in evidence on these market-dominating records. In lyrics and in brooding minor-key licks endlessly repeated, gunshot sound effects, strident timbres, and generally ominous soundscapes, they depict a nation under terrorism: the world of the projects, where crack dealers are in a perpetual, paranoid war with the police and with each other, where your child might catch a stray bullet through the wall while sitting at home. It all played itself out in your ride as you cruised down the street, creating a satisfying aura of menace as your big-ass speakers threatened the world.

Black and problack intellectuals found themselves in a paradoxical situation. Here was an art form of high creativity, based on time-honored principles of African music. It had changed the music of the world, achieved commercial dominance for black artists and black-owned companies, and, moreover, it defined their own nostalgic memories, if they were the generation that had grown up post–"Rapper's Delight." And yet they couldn't sign on to the debased image of themselves that hip-hop so often presented, especially at the time of its commercial apogee and spiritual crisis in the '90s, and especially if you were female, which the majority of black people in college were. Hip-hop spoke to a class divide within the black community, between those who spoke standard English and may not have necessarily sounded "black," and those whose English was diverging further and further from anything having to do with books. That's what blues did in the '20s, with a diction and a vocabulary that white people in England ultimately adopted as the lingua franca for the caricature of rock 'n' roll that they then sold back to the United States. And there was a gender divide between hip-hop and those who were uncomfortable with using the former slave-breeding term *bitch* as a synonym for "woman." Pro–hip-hop intellectuals, frustrated by the self-caricature of the gangsta rappers, found themselves cheering on the concept of a "conscious" hip-hop. But who were they kidding? That was commercially marginal and, with the arguable, anomalous exception of Public Enemy in the late '80s/early '90s, was not changing the music of the world. (When pressed, the same two or three or four names would always be cited, all worthy of respect, none with much power to move the street.) Nor was conscious hip-hop necessarily better music. It wasn't what the massive weight of hip-hop was about. If you say that hip-hop in the '90s wasn't about drug-dealing, you can only make your case by ignoring most of it and focusing on the slender thread of stuff you approve of.

One answer was to blame the negativity of hip-hop on the white media and record companies, who, it was charged, wanted to portray black people in demeaning stereotypes. OK, up to a point. But you can only go so far in blaming the white man for the state of hip-hop. The edge—the hardest-core stuff that went beyond what had previously been thought acceptable—always came from the independent sector, where many of the producers and entre-preneurs, to say nothing of pretty much all the lyricists, were black.

After 9/11, it may have seemed that suddenly Cristal-sipping rappers didn't seem so scary next to Muslim sleeper cells bent on martyrdom. But in Colombia, and in Mexico, where the contraband rolled through, the drug business and political terrorism merged into each other. In American cities, crack created terror—not so much from violence committed by crackheads, though that could happen, but from the violence occasioned by the business.

The "war on drugs," which spent billions in an impossible quest to stop drugs from coming across a wide border, was a template for the equally bogus "war on terror" declared after September 11, 2001, marked by increased police powers over not merely people in the ghetto but the population at large, for whom the ghetto's population had served as a sort of field test. The carefully cultivated aura of sonic menace in gangsta rap of the '90s provided a proto-type for what the music of the war on terror might sound like. For many New Orleanians, however, terror was the sound of hip-hop booming down the block late at night in an SUV with high-powered subwoofers.

Meanwhile, another crack-spawned industry was making white men rich: the prison-industrial complex. The scare stories about the horrors of crack—one puff will addict you for life (not true, though it is addictive), coupled with the century-old fear of the black cocaine fiend, gave politicians a way to score cheap points. Crack—a cheap high, used disproportionately by poor African Americans—was criminalized at far smaller quantities, and with mandatory sentences carrying far higher penalties, than for powder cocaine, used by the more affluent. Draconian sentences for possession of rock filled the nation's prisons with black people, who had to pay several dollars a minute for collect calls to their families from prison and whose enslaved labor was on occa-sion jobbed out to corporations, undercutting the wages of free workers and the bargaining position of unions. Nonviolent drug offenders were thrown into the same cells as murderers and rapists. By 2005 there were 2.1 million

Americans in prison.[5] Or, to put it another way, fewer poor people with the right to vote, since felons are barred from voting in most states (though not Louisiana). Moreover, in a bizarre echo of the three-fifths clause, by which disfranchised slaves were counted as three-fifths of a person in questions of electoral weighting, prison inmates are counted by the U.S. census as residing in the communities where they are imprisoned, thereby taking electoral weight away from their typically urban communities and reassigning it to the primarily rural ones that house the prisons, though the imprisoned people cannot themselves vote.

The experience of prison, writes Asatar Bair, "exposes inmates to entirely different political, social, and economic processes than those experienced by other Americans."[6] Those processes interpenetrate with ghetto culture. Show biz, which in America takes its stylistic cues from black people, was transformed by having so many of them incarcerated. Prison style became a mass media style in which echoes of slavery were always audible. The prison-industrial complex complemented, and connected directly to, the ghetto-industrial complex, in which Master P was an executive.[7]

No New Orleans artist had ever done Master P's kind of numbers. Not Fats Domino—nobody. It was an unprecedented success for a town that famously could never do its business right. With an intimidating military-style image heavy on camouflage, weaponry, and vehicles, a whole tankload of Master P's souljas—the three Miller brothers, both individually and recording together as TRU; the gravel-voiced screamer Mystikal (Michael Tyler); and the chunky, bellicose Mia X (Mia Young) from the Seventh Ward—each went platinum, a phenomenal hot streak for any label. Their minor figures went gold, like Fiend (Ricky Jones) or the identical twins Kane and Abel (David and Daniel Garcia, Puerto Ricans who had relocated to New Orleans from the Bronx to go to Xavier University). That's real mainstream gold, half a million units, more than all but a handful of musicians can ever dream of. (In the tropical Latin market, they used to give salsa singers plaques for fifty thousand units and call it "gold.") Soulja Slim's 1998 *Give It 2 'Em Raw* might have gone gold too, except he was caught up by the lakefront with three guns and a bulletproof vest while he was also wanted on charges in Jefferson Parish, and wound up going to prison two days before the album came out, so he couldn't promote it.[8]

One No Limit soulja had been a real soldier. Mystikal wrote his first rap while in military prison during the Gulf War, where he saw eight months in combat (though not on the front lines). "Seeing a man without his head and all that shit, it got to be like seeing roadkill," he told *Vibe* reporter Rob Marriott.[9] With his first album finished and ready for release on a New Orleans label called Big Boy, one night Mystikal discovered his sister, dead, in the family house, stabbed to death by her druggie boyfriend. If you want to hear something disturbing, listen to "Murder 2" on Mystikal's debut album *Unpredictable*, which begins "Mothafuckin' murderer! Murdered my sister!"

When No Limit started hitting big, Mystikal enlisted in Master P's army, where he attained the rank of platinum soldier, then disenlisted again. In anyone else's career, we wouldn't be talking about anything but the remarkable fact that he went platinum, but in this surreal world, it's, oh, and then Mystikal went platinum. No Limit always had another title ready to drop. Distributed by Priority, who made megabucks with N.W.A. when the majors wouldn't touch them, No Limit didn't sign hot artists so much as mint them. If I may be permitted the use of '70s clichés, when you're hot, you're hot, so when you have your fifteen minutes, you'd better be prepared to get while the gettin's good.

For about two years Master P was one of the most successful black businessmen in America. His tales of thug life were so gritty, it didn't seem to matter that he was a terrible rapper. Indeed, given the creativity that permeates even the sleaziest hip-hop, it was remarkable how unimaginative his records were. To me, it sounded like hack work through and through, grinding out images of drug dealing and armed rivalry on an industrial scale from the compound in Baton Rouge.

But if Master P's rhythm-and-rhyme skills left something to be desired, he acted his role with great credibility, and his comprehension of the game was convincing. He spent little on production (his in-house production team was named Beats by the Pound) and contracted out the uniform-looking Photoshop-on-crack covers in bulk.

Away with those high-priced photographers and their fashionista New York covers! Pen and Pixel was a Houston graphics firm cofounded by the former general manager of Rap-A-Lot records, specializing in virtual worlds of bad taste so ludicrously over the top as to define a genre. The assembly-line covers collaged a dozen or more images each into eye-assaulting, perspectiveless panoramas, tantalizing the poor with possessions, possessions, possessions: white-columned Greek Revival mansions, Bentleys, Lexes, Hummers, stacks of benjamins, big-booty B-words, snarling rappers with gold grills in their mouths, pit bulls, guns of all sorts, humongous flames, and gleaming, diamond-encrusted lettering—a visual vocabulary that references *Scarface* (Brian dePalma's 1983 film with Al Pacino, not Howard Hawks's much better 1932 film with Paul Muni).

The albums' artwork was virtually interchangeable, but then so was their content. Master P was cheap on production, but he spent a fuckwad of money on advertising and promotion, the latter of which can be understood as a euphemism for payola. Maybe his real art form was not even the music he released as much as it was the full-page magazine ads that were a good chunk of *The Source*'s revenue—the art of the business of an art about business. P raised the ante for advertising, and pretty soon every No Limit wannabe label everywhere took out full-page ads for every release from their stable of hopefuls (and try explaining to your armed-robber-turned-rapper why he didn't get a full-page ad in *The Source*). All the artwork looked like Pen and Pixel. New hip-hop magazines appeared with an enviable ad-page count; by 1999, you had to turn through twenty-two color ad pages to get to the table of contents of *Murder Dog*. The availability of so much advertising spawned a curious subgenre: the criminal lifestyle magazine—titles like *Don Diva* and *F.E.D.S.*—in which criminals and celebrities were more or less interchangeable, and which focused as much on gangs, crime, and prison as on music.

Even in a business dominated by thugs, Marion "Suge" Knight, CEO of Los Angeles–based Death Row Records, was over the top. People were flat-out afraid of him. Six foot three and 335 pounds, he came up in the business as a security guard. A Mob Piru Blood, he liked to flaunt his affiliation by flossing a red suit and hat. He was a felon on parole the night his bestselling artist Tupac Shakur was killed, shot through the passenger-side window while Knight was driving, in Vegas. He went to prison for an assault charge stemming from that night, interfering considerably with his ability to run Death Row, which had done hundreds of millions of dollars in business by that point. Producer Dr. Dre, founding member of N.W.A. and leading beatmaker of Los Angeles, had already jumped ship from the label in 1995, tired of feeling like a captive in a studio where he once saw an engineer get beaten for rewinding a tape too far. That left Snoop Doggy Dogg, one of the most successful rappers ever, who wanted to get off what was looking all too literally like Death Row.

In a coup of thug CEOmanship, Master P went to see Knight in jail and bought out Snoop Doggy Dogg's contract, bringing him over to No Limit in April 1998. Snoop became a No Limit soldier, even relocating briefly to Baton Rouge, where he developed a taste for New Orleans's contribution to franchise fast food, Popeyes Chicken & Biscuits. Changing his name to the more mature-sounding Snoop Dogg, he served out his recording deal with No Limit, for whom he recorded three inferior titles that offered up tasty fantasies of cash, inebriation, violence, and, of course, hoes, complete with Pen and Pixel covers. On Death Row, Snoop had had the support of Dr. Dre, perhaps the best producer to come out of the Los Angeles scene. But on his first No Limit album, the clunky tracks from Beats by the Pound were a big comedown. It was titled *Da Game Is to Be Sold, Not to Be Told*—a truly weird title in south Louisiana, which 150 years ago was slave auction headquarters. Three albums is a long time to coast, but Snoop Dogg's career survived his strange turn as a No Limit soldier.

Hip-hop is always conscious of, and angry about, the slave past—to say nothing of the thwarting of Reconstruction, Jim Crow, peonage, the abandonment of the inner cities, the prison-industrial complex, and all the rest—but in New Orleans, where the past is all around, the memories are front and center. Asked how he came up with the name "Master P," Percy Miller said, "I look at where we come from. We come from slaves, us calling them master. I look at my grandparents. I said, 'That master thing, I'm a take it to a whole new level. I wanna master whatever I do. Instead of us calling them that, they will call us that.'"

Who is *they?* Maybe you're supposed to think *they* means white people, enslaving white people being presumably an acceptable sentiment. But despite the white boys who come into town to cop dope, the people enslaved by crack dealers mostly aren't white. For that matter, most of them aren't men, since more women than men use crack. The other enduring crack stereotype, besides the Cristal-sipping crack dealer, is Crackhouse Annie, sucking dick for a rock—a slave, no matter how you look at it.

As if we needed to be reminded that sexual coercion was at the heart of American slavery, there's a creepy scene in *I'm Bout It* where Master P objects to the security risk entailed by two hoes (his word) brought in to cook crack in his kitchen. They might steal product if they had clothes to hide it in. So he orders them to strip naked as they work at the stove, except for surgical masks protecting their nose and mouth (to keep them from getting too high off the fumes to do their job). I love to work naked at a stove, don't you? It wasn't even original, since the naked-crack-cooks shtick had already appeared in *New Jack City*, the movie that chronicled the rise of a fictional drug dealer who introduces crack to the New York City market. But in that movie, the crack kitchen is owned by the villain, who ultimately perishes at the hands of good renegade cop Ice-T, whereas in P's movie the hero is the owner of the crack kitchen, who ultimately triumphs. The "hoes" meekly comply with Master's order, with the resignation of faceless slaves who don't even own their own bodies. Like much else in the movie, it doesn't lead anywhere, but watching it, I had the strangest feeling it was supposed to be funny.

It wasn't the image of New Orleans music the city wanted to promote when it renamed the airport for Louis Armstrong in 2001. But then the people behind the vibrating tinted windows who rolled up next to you at the stoplight weren't bumping Satchmo in their ride. No, they were more likely to be giving the street an earful of C-Murder threatening death in no uncertain terms, guesting on Snoop Dogg's *Top Dogg*, shouting something between a football cheer and a war cry, over a minimalist, or maybe merely minimal, track: a single note repeating BOM, BA-BA BOM BOM / BA-BA BOM BOM for two bars, then going up a half-step to repeat, then once more up another half-step, and then yet again, inexorably, ratcheting up the tension. After four bars and four notes, it started over again, in an endless repeat cycle. The chant was an exercise in adrenaline and hyperventilation, like puffing up before physical combat:

> *Fuck them other niggaz, 'cause I'm down for my niggaz!*
> *Fuck them other niggaz, 'cause I'm down for my niggaz!*
> *Fuck them other niggaz! I ride with my niggaz!*
> *I die for my niggaz! Fuck them other niggaz!*

The tune opened with the chant, which was built around the N-word not only lyrically but metrically, so that each *niggaz* fell square on the backbeat, on 2 and 4. That led to a rap by C-Murder vowing death to anyone who tried to fuck with Snoop Doggy Dogg. Then the chant came back:

> *Fuck them other niggaz, 'cause I'm down for my niggaz!*

It was followed in turn by an extended, apoplectically angry, double-time gravel-voiced bellow from a rapper named Magic, and back to the chant:

> *Fuck them other niggaz, 'cause I'm down for my niggaz!*

Then on to Snoop, with his characteristic laid-back behind-the-beat feel-good death threats. Then they took it home, repeating endlessly:

> *Fuck them other niggaz, 'cause I'm down for my niggaz . . .*

The track was rhythmically oppressive, with a rigid, blocky straight-8ths feel, like a caricature of Teutonic music. But there was a weird disjunct between the feel of the track and that of the vocals. C-Murder being an Afro-Orleanian, he chanted with a swing feel. Drummers call this the half-and-half groove: straight time crossed with swing time. It happened a lot in early rock 'n' roll, and it happens sometimes when African Americans sing over drum-machine tracks. The performance of the "fuck them other niggaz" chorus was not particularly consistent, since the swing of it got wider as the tune progressed; C-Murder seems to have gotten more comfortable with the track as it played. Hip-hop prides itself on nailing it as fast as possible in the studio, but this one sounds like they were in too much of a hurry to get it right. Another take and he might have started with the degree of swing he ended the first take with, and might have locked in better. But, hey, it's what it is, they made their point, which was:

Fuck them other niggaz,' cause I'm down for my niggaz!

It was that week's winner in the ongoing contest to embody the word *crude* as vividly as possible—a contest not limited to hip-hop, but which hip-hop can arguably claim to dominate. But it was undeniably catchy. I mean:

Fuck *them other niggaz!*
Cause *I'm* down *for my niggaz!*
I ride *for my niggaz!*
I die *for my niggaz!*

I almost always have a song or a rhythm or something going on in my head. One reason I don't listen to much recorded music is I never have enough time just to press the "play" button in my head and listen to the music that's there. Often I find myself verbalizing whatever song is playing on the Ned jukebox. It's part of being a songwriter.

Which was how I found myself one day singing audibly: *Fuck them other ni—*

Erk. Oops.

I was standing in line at the post office on Louisiana Street. The one near the TLC Car Wash, where those two people got shot the year before by three guys with AKs. I don't think anyone heard me before my conscious mind leaped in to shut me the fuck up. Sometimes self-censorship is a good thing.

There's a big difference between hearing a track like that in some secure place, where it can be taken as entertainment, and hearing it come at you on a street where you're not sure about the motivations of the guy in the next vehicle. Those gunshot sound effects sounded particularly real banging out of someone's ride, at a time when rides had become personal sound trucks.

The average income of the 1,477 households at the Calliope—not individual, but *household* income—was $13,263 according to the 2000 census, though the census doesn't pick up on the underground economy. There was, however, one curious anomaly: one household with a reported income of $208,478, single-handedly skewing the project average upward. That household is anonymous, but it might have been C-Murder, who liked living in his 'hood and somehow managed to keep an apartment in the housing complex where he had grown up, even though he was making lots of money.

The boom in New Orleans hip-hop occasioned an enormous amount of wealth descending quickly on a very poor-born group of people. There is no indication that they put it into long-term treasury bonds. I don't know specifically how it played out, but I know what usually happens, even aside from the Bentley, the Gucci helicopter (I'm not making this up), the mink sheets, the tank outside the corporate headquarters, the bloated payroll, and the extraordinary security expenses. Signing Snoop Dogg was a coup for No Limit, but the hot streak still went cold. The street giveth and the street taketh away, and it took away from No Limit.

A friend of mine at a big label once said to me, "When you have seven hundred thousand copies of something out there, it's scary. You have so much money tied up." I repeated that to a friend with a reasonably successful indie label, who shot back, "It's scary when you have sixty thousand copies out there." I wouldn't know, I never got there in my days of running a small label. But what I do know, firsthand, is that the record label had to pay stores to take product in, even hit product.

It's like supermarket slotting fees. Cap'n Crunch isn't in your face in the supermarket aisle because the store manager thinks it's a nice cereal that would be good for your kids. Placement, sold to manufacturers at what is ultimately the consumer's expense, was part of the retailer's revenue stream and was a way the retailer could capture a substantial chunk of the markup of that CD that cost a dollar to manufacture and sold to you for thirteen. It was pure profit for the stores, and it even functioned as insurance against taking in a poor-selling title since they got paid by the label whether anyone bought the records or not. If the record company didn't pay the "promotion," record chains, which overexpanded in the early '90s and wound up having lots of high rents to pay, wouldn't even order the title. (Something like this happens with books too, by the way, though they cost a lot more than a dollar to make and the margins are smaller.)

If you did buy the promotion and the product went into the store but didn't sell, you were still out the promotional money, even if you got the entire inventory returned unsold by the skidload. Even if the retailer forgot to actually ever take it out of the warehouse and put it on the shelves. The CDs came back with the stores' stickers on them, which you then had to scrape off so you could rewrap the product—that is, *if* you had any market

CREATIVE DESTRUCTION 205

for it, because most hip-hop titles had a shelf life about as long as bananas, so there was nothing to do with returns of would-be hits except trash them. Keeping them around wouldn't make them salable, ever. But unlike bananas, CDs don't decompose, they just sit there. What you have then is a landfill problem. Like every one of billions of empty plastic bottles of water that was ever emptied by a thirsty person, every compact disc and every jewel box ever made is sitting out there somewhere.

In terms of cash flow, every unsold record canceled out one that was sold. If you supported a brace of releases like they were all going to go platinum and they stiffed, you multiplatinum tanked. You were set to take warehouses full of returns, for full credit against your receivables on top of the hefty retail promotion chargebacks. When they didn't want to pay you, and they never want to pay you, they'd find some boxes of your deadest title, still kicking around from three years ago, and send it back to you for full credit instead. The fatal hemorrhage could easily occur at the beginning of the downside of your peak sales moment, when the way you found out you were no longer hot was that unsold records started coming back to you. Having hits covered for a lot of mistakes, but one big turkey could hurt you bad, and two or three or four could take you out.

As if the problems of the record business weren't enough, Master P decided to have a concurrent career as a basketball player, going into training and attempting to play for various minor league teams. In 1999 Beats by the Pound quit No Limit, renaming themselves Medicine Men; P brought in a new team and called them Beats by the Pound. P spent a lot of time dealing with lawsuits—from artists, production companies, the bank, a construction company, the IRS. He lost his unfinished recording studio in Baton Rouge, which he'd spent three million dollars building.

No Limit finally reached its limit, filing for bankruptcy in December 2003. Bankruptcy, as I can testify from having had a distributor go bankrupt on me, is a way of protecting you while fucking the people you used to do business with. Master P started New No Limit Records, based in Los Angeles, and in 2005, his fourteen-year-old son Li'l Romeo was on the charts, generating income that would more than cover my Saturn payments, while P, characteristically immodest, released an album called Ghetto Bill, as in Bill Gates. ("Bill Gates!" the black teenagers shouted at me on Canal Street—because I'm white and wear glasses, I guess. "Bill Gates!") It did less than Microsoft-level business. For one thing, the record business had gone into a serious decline. Nobody was selling like they used to. And rappers were largely dependent on record sales, because hip-hop touring is problematic at best: first, because of insurance and security costs, and second, because so much of it is canned to begin with. (There are also third and fourth reasons.) Hip-hop celebrities had long since diversified into movies, TV, and clothing lines; Sean "Puffy" Combs was making more money from his Sean John line than from records. But No Limit apparel didn't take off like Phat Farm.

After leaving No Limit, Fiend did well as a ghostwriter for other rappers. In summer 2000, Mystikal had the #1 pop record in the country, "Shake Ya Ass," produced by very expensive pop geniuses the Neptunes. He headlined at the 2001 edition of New Orleans's Jazzfest. But in January 2004 he was sentenced to six years in prison for sexually assaulting his hairdresser—assisted by his two bodyguards and recorded on video, no less, which made nailing him easy.

On September 12, 2001, Kane and Abel entered a guilty plea to charges of conspiring to possess cocaine with intent to distribute, filed as part of a prosecutorial campaign against Richard Peña, a Dominican-born large-scale cocaine trafficker and part-time hip-hop entrepreneur whose street name was "the Cuban." He had, it was alleged, financed Kane and Abel's early career and put them to work dealing to pay off their debts. When Peña received a life sentence in January 1999 for having ordered *eight* murders, he told the court at his sentencing: "It's hard to regret something from a job you love to do," meaning moving weight, though he expressed remorse for the murders.[10] The twins claimed that the feds had made Master P a target, and that when they refused to implicate him, they were the object of a "vindictive prosecution."[11] Though they had never lived apart they were shipped off to separate pens, where they served two years. But first they published a pair of novellas in one volume, the first of which told the story of a young man from the Bronx who moves to New Orleans and gets caught up in the underworld.[12]

In January 2005, a makeup artist filed a twenty-five-million-dollar lawsuit against former No Limit guest soldier Snoop Dogg, claiming she had been fed drugged champagne and raped by a coked-up Snoop and his posse. Snoop, who filed a preemptive charge of extortion against her, had by then become the first pop star to produce both his own animated cartoon show and his own porno features. A cut on Snoop's then-new album contained the following chorus with guest Soopafly:

> *Can you control your ho?*
> *You got to know what to do, and what to say*
> *You've got to put that bitch in her place, even if it's slapping her in*
>   *her face.*

It did not bode well for the treatment of eleven-year-old girls by eleven-year-old boys. But then again, it wasn't a single. The single, which went to #1 pop on *Billboard*, was "Drop It Like It's Hot" (a title previously used in 1999 by New Orleans rapper Lil' Wayne). Riding to the top on the strength of an ingenious track by the Neptunes that left as much space as possible for Snoop's voice, it affably reaffirmed Snoop's blue-rag Crip affiliation and his commitment to rolling the best weed, while threatening violent death in the most likeable way imaginable. It was on Q-93 all the time as I drove around.

Despite being a platinum-selling rapper—which is to say for a brief period of time standing in a firehose-pressure of cash flow, and on his brother's record company, no less—C-Murder was incarcerated in the Jefferson Parish Correctional Center in Gretna, Louisiana, on January 18, 2002. (Not only does Louisiana have the highest incarceration rate in the nation—Mississippi is second—it's the state with the largest percentage of prisoners housed in local jails; the sheriff gets paid per prisoner.) He was convicted of murder in the dance-floor shooting, while strobe lights were flashing and loud music thumping, of sixteen-year-old Steve Thomas at the Platinum Club in Harvey, Louisiana, on the West Bank. The prosecutor alleged that C-Murder's boys had him down on the ground beating him when C-Murder fired one shot to the chest. Well, somebody shot the kid, who sure enough died, but witnesses weren't exactly forthcoming and there wasn't much evidence. Were the witnesses intimidated, as the prosecution alleged, or was he a tempting prosecutorial target because of his notoriety and the ease of convincing a jury that he was living his lyrics? Ask any black family in New Orleans if black men ever get railroaded by the justice system. But then, he would never have been convicted in Orleans Parish. He was convicted in Jefferson Parish by an all-white jury.

To put it mildly, C-Murder's persona as an entertainer did not help his defense. If you boast you're a murderer, you're setting yourself up to be charged with murder. We might call it the C-Murder paradox: when a crucial element of your celebrity consists of persuading your audience that you're not merely an actor playing a criminal character but are keeping it real, who are you lying to, the public or the jury? Nor did it help that he was already out on a hundred-thousand-dollar bond while awaiting trial for two counts of second-degree attempted murder (a club owner and a bouncer in Baton Rouge claimed he pulled a gun on them) at the time of the Platinum Club shooting.[13]

The conviction was set aside in April 2004 because the defense hadn't been notified that the key prosecution witness had an expunged criminal record. In 2005, after C-Murder had spent three years in jail, a three-judge panel reaffirmed the conviction, denying him a new trial. While in jail, unbeknownst to Sheriff Harry Lee, he laid down *sotto voce* vocals into a minidisk recorder for a depressing but dramatic new album (*The Truest $#!@ I Ever Said*) during visits with his lawyer, Ron Rakosky. It had a unique presence because he had to speak his lyrics softly (though he did *not* whisper). The whole album has the feel of a man speaking surreptitiously in prison—quietly, so the guards wouldn't hear anything. It tapped into a deep lore of slave communication. The rhymes were dropped in over rhythms in the studio and padded out with guest stars. "Did U Hold It Down," an audio love letter, complete with strings, from a man in prison to his wife, begins with the collect-call robot recording that family members hear when a prisoner calls (occasioning an extortionate per-minute charge for the family; prison calling is a billion-dollar-a-year industry).[14] When you listen to it, the cliché of keeping it real falls away into a sense that something is at stake. Very little music makes you believe something is really at stake. But everything is at stake when the story you're telling is:

> I got the money order that you sent
> Even though it made you short with the rent

That's the saddest little couplet. Presumably it didn't describe C-Murder's reality, money-wise. But it was the kind of story you'd hear in the joint. That's what we do, we songwriters.

He even managed to get Sheriff Lee to approve a TV crew coming into the jail. Boy, did it piss off the sheriff when the footage was used in a music video ("Y'All Heard of Me"), with C-Murder quietly spitting lyrics in an orange prison jumpsuit, implying, without having to try, a continuity of style in American prisons from Jefferson Parish to Abu Ghraib. He seemed to be reassuring his listeners that he really has done dirty deeds, though not this one:

> I know y'all heard of me
> I'm C-Murder
> I done things y'all ain't never heard of . . .

The second verse belongs to B.G., who in the video delivers his lines on location in front of the projects, surrounded by an intimidating-looking crew. The message is clear: one soulja is locked up, but an army is still outside, throwing dice, for as long as the projects shall last.

Released on electronically monitored house arrest pending a new trial after posting a million-dollar bond once his conviction had been set aside again, C-Murder read hundreds of books; Dean Koontz was a favorite. He started writing a novel, a grim story of life and death in the 'hood.

11

WHIPS AND ICE

Well let me take you to my neck of the woods
To my hood, show you what we're livin' like
Walkin' like a man, finger on the trigga
Money in my pocket, I'm a uptown nigga.

—Baby aka Birdman aka #1 Stunna with Lil' Wayne aka
Weezy aka Tha Carter aka Birdman Jr., "Neck of the Woods"

Master P's souljas weren't the only hip-hop millionaires to come out of the New Orleans projects. Nor was P the only one to see *New Jack City*. In that 1991 film, the ruthless crack gang is called Cash Money. The same year, a label with that name appeared in New Orleans.

Not only did Cash Money get their label name from the bad guys in *New Jack*, they adopted the movie gang's dollar-sign medallion as their logo, encrusting it with diamonds and making it a motif on their albums' Pen and Pixel covers and on their rappers' chests. They celebrated the riches to be had, the hedonism to be enjoyed, the necessity of heavy armament, and the inescapability of bloodshed in selling drugs. Their lyrics celebrated the exhilaration and the rewards of making your own rules while living in a microenvironment confined to a few blocks of a city that was itself isolated from the world. In Cash Money's uptown, there was no president, no mayor, no news, no history. There was only the eternal, local present, in which the good guys were the bad guys, who always won. You were allowed to pay for the privilege of seeing them have fun flossing their panky rangs and tossing rhymes and strippers around.

No Limit represented for Calliope, Cash Money for Magnolia. But that wasn't the only difference. No Limit's records were grim, whereas Cash Money's were funny. And Cash Money's were way better. In fact, sleazy though they were, Cash Money records were great, largely thanks to their in-house producer, Mannie Fresh (Byron Thomas). Not from the 'Nolia, but from the Seventh Ward, downtown, he started out DJing, which meant he had the fundamental structural skills of hip-hop: cutting and scratching behind a rapper, knowing when to change up the rhythm and when to repeat it mercilessly. Knowing what to jump-cut it to, and what the relationship of the tempi should be. Sometimes there are complaints about hip-hop people having no legit musical skills, but it goes the other way too: a beatmaker who doesn't come out of DJing is ungrounded.

Mannie Fresh first produced a record in 1988 and joined up with Cash Money in 1992. He turned out to be a genius. The records he made with Slim and Baby's "four little niggaz" (Baby's phrase) were some of the swingin'-est records being made in New Orleans, despite the fact they were filthy from start to finish. But that too is in the New Orleans tradition.

I went to Odyssey Records on Canal Street when I visited New Orleans in '92, looking for local hip-hop records. There weren't many. I bought a 12-inch by Mia X on a local label called Peaches.

In those days, the local thing was a party-music style called bounce. It was largely built on a quotation from a single record, the basic breakbeat of bounce having been jacked from Show Boys' "Drag Rap," a 12-inch released in the mid-'80s on the New York label Profile. Produced by Cliff Hall, "Drag Rap" was apparently introduced to New Orleans during a visit by Profile superstars Run-DMC (who were in the second wave of rappers, but were the first to have a big hit record rapping over a DJ cutting and scratching instead of with a band).

"Drag Rap" featured the voices of Triggerman and Bugs Can Can; the DJ had the not overly ambitious name of Rent Money. Like their labelmates Run-DMC, they were from Hollis, Queens. Neither "Drag Rap" nor Show Boys' other single sold enough to generate an album. But though "Drag Rap" moved fewer than five thousand copies on its own, the B-side instrumental mix, with an electro-cowbell on the first and (swung) fourth 16ths of the "4," became the basis of a genre of music.

VARIETIES THEATRE

NEW ORLEANS.

FEBRUARY 13th, 1877.

The

Mystic Krewe of Comus

PRESENT THE

ARYAN RACE

In their idiosyncrasies of FASHION from the zenith of
civilization in Egypt, to the present day, with
our "Future Destiny" in the next
Centennial year of 1976.

IN FIVE TABLEAUX.

eft: Program cover from *The Aryan Race*, Comus's Mardi Gras presentation after the victory of the Hayes-
Tilden compromise. Among its other satirical tableaux, Comus imagined women being allowed to vote a
century in the future, in 1976.

op: Mozart rolls down St. Charles through the Garden District in a Mardi Gras krewe parade.

bottom: A bead tree. Strings of beads by the thousands catch in the trees along St. Charles and remain

left: Michael "Aldo" Andrews, of the Bayou Steppers Social and Pleasure Club, in front of the entrance to the Mother-in-Law Lounge in Tremé as their anniversary parade drew to a close on January 16, 2005. Moments after this picture was taken, the police turned on their sirens and ordered the area cleared.

top: Zulu member in the parade down St. Charles, Mardi Gras morning, February 8, 2005.

bottom: Big Chiefs Alfred Doucette and Donald Harrison Jr., with poet Ed Skoog in the background, on Mardi Gras 2005, in front of the Backstreet Cultural Museum, in Tremé.

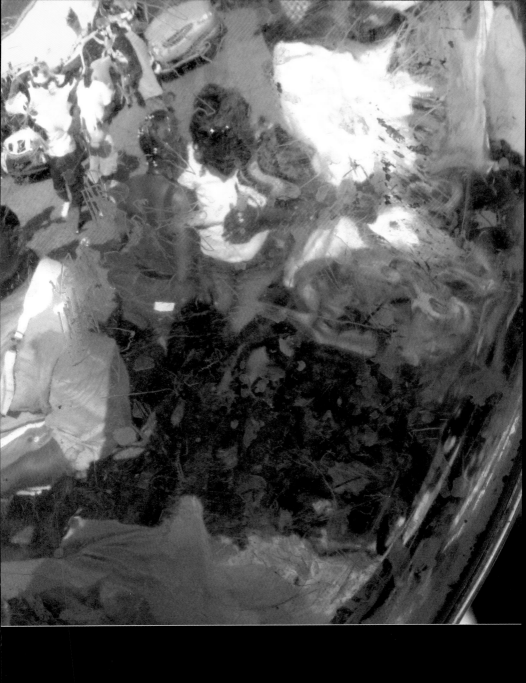

Central City as reflected in a sousaphone bell on September 28, 2008, during the anniversary parade of the Young Men Olympian Junior Benevolent Association.

top: Antoinette K-Doe at work on Mardi Gras day, February 5, 2007.

bottom: Partying on Frenchmen Street as Mardi Gras 2005 wound to a close.

right top: St. Patrick's celebration getting started, outside Parasol's on Constance Street in the Irish Channel.

right bottom: Mardi Gras Indian at uptown Super Sunday, April 3, 2005.

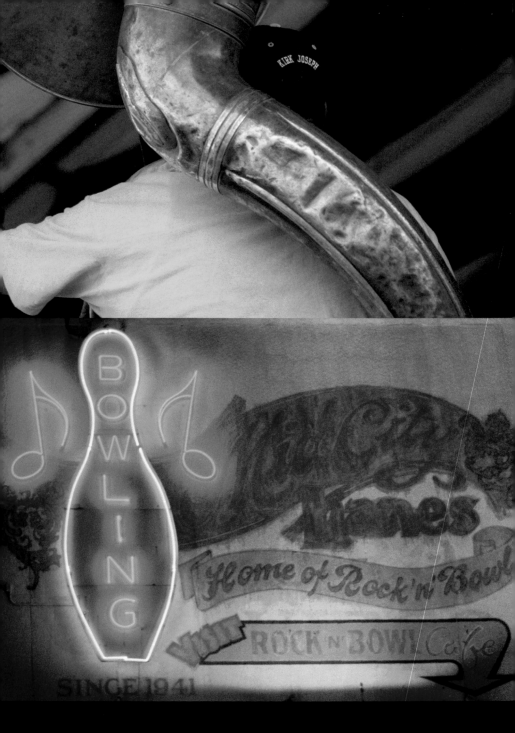

top: Kirk Joseph and his hard-traveling sousaphone at Jazzfest 2005.

bottom: Mid-City Rock 'n' Bowl on the first night of the Ponderosa Stomp, April 26, 2005.

right: Hard Head Hunters at Jazzfest 2005, upholding the name of Big Chief Otto.

right overleaf: Dave Bartholomew after a panel at Jazzfest, looking good at the age of eighty-five.

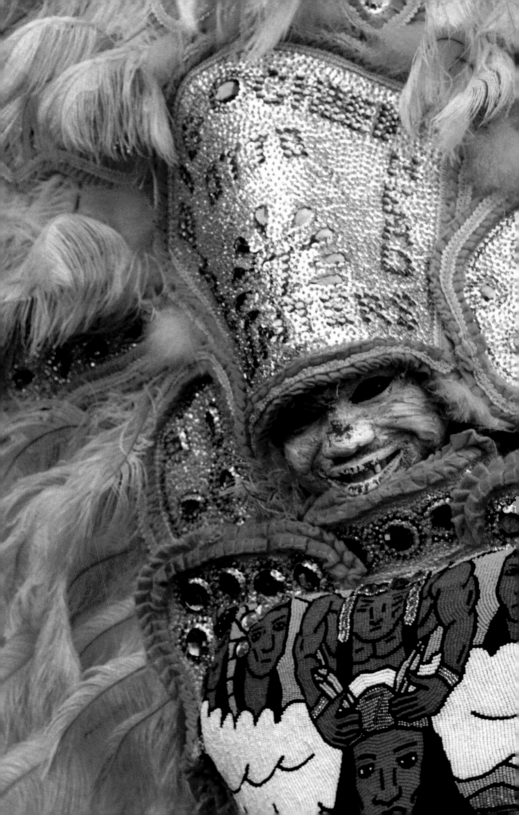

left overleaf, top: Tamborine and Fan parading down Orleans Avenue in the Tremé on downtown Super Sunday, May 8, 2005.

left overleaf, bottom: Later that same parade, along Claiborne below I-10. The crowd's attention was focused on the two men dancing high on the elevated roadway.

top: Desire Street in the Ninth Ward, Sunday, August 7, 2005, three weeks before the flood.

In New Orleans, they called it the Triggerman (sometimes written *Trig-gaman*) beat. It had no obvious connection to New Orleans, except perhaps that it was in swing time instead of straight 8ths, but its rhythm track became the New Orleans bounce beat, providing the framework for scores of releases that were mostly small sellers on local labels. The most famous early one was probably the heavily cut-up "Where Dey At" by T. T. Tucker (Tucker Ventry) with DJ Irv (Irv Phillips), a rudimentary chant with a long section of "Fuck David Duke, Fuck David Duuuke" as well as another that went "lemme hit it from the back 'cause I got a jimmy hat [condom]."

This phenomenon of an entire genre growing out of one recorded rhythm track strongly resembled, as has so much in hip-hop, the way they did it in Jamaica. Producers there worked with "riddims," or beats—a word that is understood to mean a simple multitrack rhythm bed recorded over by scads of different singers. The Dem Bow (or Pocoman) beat, which later morphed into reggaetón, is perhaps the best example, but there were many. Similarly, a lot of the early '90s Miami movement known as "bass music" was built around the beat from Afrika Bambaataa and Soul Sonic Force's "Planet Rock" (the track, by Arthur Baker and John Robie, was in turn based on two tunes by Kraftwerk, "Trans-Europe Express" and "Numbers").

"Drag Rap" came out in the early days of what would later be called gangsta rap (though that term didn't come into common use until NWA's "Gangsta Gangsta" became a hit in '89). Lyrically, "Drag Rap" fit perfectly with the New Orleans thang: it was a crime show on vinyl about gang war—including a river drowning, which resonated perfectly with time-honored New Orleans criminal methods.

A recurring motif in the Show Boys' record was the four-note minor-mode *Dragnet* theme, which to American ears is less a musical motif than an emblem of police procedural drama: DOMM, DA DOM DOM. The rhythm of that theme, also known as *habanera* or *tango*, has been part of New Orleans music probably since the late eighteenth century.[1] While that tango rhythm didn't itself serve as the basis of the Triggerman beat, the *Dragnet* motif was dropped in as a quote on many bounce records, in effect serving the rhythm up as an object with a lexical meaning: crime.

All the Triggerman bounce records were technically illegal, since the samples were never cleared with Profile. On the other hand, Profile never cleared the use of Walter Schumann's *Dragnet* theme either. Among the other things it did—also perhaps following the Jamaican model—hip-hop directly challenged notions of single-creator copyright, representing on behalf of a millennia-old poetic and musical tradition that relied on quoting the classics (the *Dragnet* theme, say), sustaining poetic dialogue through competitive displays of erudition. Of the various crimes committed in the 'hood, copyright violation was fairly low down on the list of police concerns.

Thugs often being too macho to dance, hip-hop is not often dance music. It tends to be ride music, head-nodding music. But early '90s New Orleans bounce was good for twerking, coochie-popping, titty-bopping, and all the rest of that nasty dancing they like to do in the clubs. Bounce, with its cheap, easily available, pinball-machine kind of sound, courtesy of the all-time classic beat box, the Roland TR 808 Rhythm Composer, was the precursor of both the No Limit and the Cash Money styles.

Mannie Fresh came up with a lucrative combination of hardcore thugging and bounce feel—which tended to mean ominous-sounding timbres in minor keys. By then, major-label rappers were paying out one to two hundred thousand dollars an album to buy tracks from big-name freelance beatmakers or to clear samples. But Mannie Fresh could build a track from scratch in forty-five minutes or less, working together with the rapper, putting it together in front of him and giving him a greater sense of involvement in the track. Having your own guy who could make you a no-clearance hit just by cranking up the 808 started you out much closer to profitability and left you freer to experiment. Mannie Fresh made every beat on every Cash Money album. His sound was their sound.

Since Cash Money literally raised their own in-house stars to guest on each other's records—necessary to relieve the monotony of a single voice over the course of a seventy-minute CD—they saved having to pay ten thousand dollars a pop for each of three or five or ten guest stars to drop by the studio for an hour. Whoever's name was on the record, it was the group—the gang, if you will. Mannie Fresh put in his time on the mike too, dropping in verses and appearing as a full participant in the Cash Money videos, becoming known for his dirty, funny, stentorian almost-singing. He was in some ways their most effective rapper, maybe because he didn't take it too seriously, and he definitely had the best sense of time and pacing. He talked shit for fun. He appeared with two of his Cash Money brethren in a fashion spread in *The Source* of November 2003, wearing a twenty-two-thousand-dollar white pimp-style mink coat that he looked like he was born to wear. He didn't look all that serious about it.

***

Cash Money was the creation of brothers Bryan "Baby" (aka "Birdman") and Ronald "Slim" Williams, from the Magnolia projects, who cultivated a well-researched image of being crime kingpins. Their first signing was Kilo G, may he rest in peace, who put out an album called *The Sleepwalker*. They put out Pimp Daddy (Edgar Givens), who had a local hit adapting Jamaican dance-hall style to his New Orleans accent (sample lyric: *Bi-itch, if you wanna get to heaven, then you gotta get down and suck my dick*). But Pimp Daddy was killed, after an argument with his girlfriend's brother, in 1994.

A posthumous Pimp Daddy album, *Pimpin' Ain't E-Z*, included a tribute cut to him in which Yella Boy of UNLV rapped: *Now how the fuck you figure that my boy was really dead / Each and every day I'm seein' him in my head.* UNLV—Uptown Niggas Livin' Violent—did well for Cash Money with their 1994 album *6th and Baronne* and had a hit on the 1996 album *Uptown 4 Life* with "Drag 'Em 'N tha River," a ferocious dis on Mystikal. Not only was the record built on the *Dragnet* melodic tag, but the title was taken from the lyrics of "Drag Rap." Yella Boy too was murdered, in 1997—by whom, I don't know.

The Williams brothers made their fortune by signing children to their label, acting as father figures to their investments. Their first durable sign-ing was Lil' Doogie (Christopher Dorsey), who came on board in Cash Money's inaugural year of 1991, at the age of eleven, after a neighborhood barber hipped Baby to a kid who could rap. In 1993 Lil' Doogie formed a duo called the B.G.'s, as in Baby Gangstas (the fact that there was already a group called the Bee Gees didn't seem to matter), with eleven-year-old Lil' Wayne (Dwayne Michael Carter Jr.) from Hollygrove. But Lil' Wayne had some trouble—he accidentally shot himself in the chest while playing with a nine-millimeter at home one Friday afternoon after school, which sidelined him for a time.[2] When he came back, he promised his mom he wouldn't curse on records until he was eighteen, though that apparently didn't apply to using the N-word.

By that time, Doogie had become known as B.G. He too contributed to the tribute album for Pimp Daddy: *My partner had to go over a ho, but it's cool / I can't be calmed down, when I see her I'm a use my tool / Act a fool, let her know how it feel to be underground / And when she get there I know Pimp gonna beat her down.*

A younger half-brother of the Williamses, Terrance "Gangsta" Williams, is doing life plus twenty in a federal pen in Florida. In a jailhouse interview, he claimed to have had a reputation for having killed more than forty peo-ple.[3] Gangsta's gang—all of them dead now but him—was "some ol' gangsta-ass killin-ass niggaz" called the Hot Boys.[4] By 1997, Cash Money had created a teenage thug rap quartet, which, borrowing the name Hot Boys, had the branding advantage of name recognition on the Uptown streets. Besides seventeen-year-old B.G. and fourteen-year-old Lil' Wayne, they were twenty-one-year-old Juvenile (Terius Gray) and fifteen-year-old Young Turk (Tab Virgil Jr.). They put out records as a group and as soloists, but they all appeared on each other's records and in each other's videos. They were rarely alone even when they flew solo, because most of their vocals were doubled, a forty-year-old pop procedure by which a vocalist records exactly the same track twice or more, cloning himself to sound like a one-man group. It's much easier to double your track when you're rapping than singing. The mixes were claustrophobic: the voices were always beneath the beat machine and inside the synth wraparound, as though the keyboards were the boundaries of their turf.

Cash Money was their family. B.G., whose father was murdered, had been in and out of group homes. Lil' Wayne's father was murdered two years before he joined Hot Boys; Cash Money people would go pick him up after school. Baby, the Fagin of the crew, got himself appointed legal guardian of both B.G. and Wayne. Got that? Record company *and* guardian. Wayne referred to him as his father.

Juvenile, the oldest and most experienced, had already made a name on his own, rapping on an early local bounce hit: "Bounce for the Juvenile," by DJ Jimi (Jimi Payton), which did *not* use the "Drag Rap" beat. His voice is practically unrecognizable on it, because he hadn't found his rich baritone register yet. Coming out in 1992, when dancehall was at a commercial peak in the United States, Juvenile's singing-chanting rap on "Bounce for the Juvenile" channeled the Jamaican style, right down to a put-on accent; despite there being no Yardies to speak of in New Orleans, imitating the double-time dancehall cadence was popular, and it became part of—forgive me—the New Orleans hip-hop gumbo.

The Hot Boys' first album, *Get It How U Live!*, was composed and recorded in three days. It was done in the spirit of New Orleans: stand and deliver. It was jazz, in the sense of getting up and blowing. It was pure ghetto. It sold four hundred thousand copies. These kids didn't know from having a job. They didn't go to school too hard. What they did do, every day, was rhyme with each other. How do I know? By listening. You don't get that good without a lot of practice. Nothing about their records encouraged you to take them seriously, so they were easily overlooked, except that they were funky as hell, swung effortlessly, and sold very well. As the violent passions of the time and place they represent become as distant as those of the jazz age, the records of the Cash Money crime-jam family will stand, the way thousands of once seemingly disposable R & B records have stood for half a century now.

The baby-faced Hot Boys were the same age as their audience. Baby, their mentor, looms as the center of gravity of the videos, and not only because he's bulkier. His image had great emotional power for children of single mothers: a violently protective, infinitely permissive, surreally wealthy, doting father, who was into the same things the kids were: whips (vehicles), ice (jewelry), and hoes (uh, women). He didn't have heavy-duty rhyme skills, but he was better than a lot of people rated him. And insofar as rapping is acting, he played the authority figure with conviction.

Baby and Mannie (who recorded as a duo called the Big Tymers), together with the Hot Boys, created a lucrative legal industry by bragging about the techniques and rewards of illegal industry. In doing so, they slapped their name on the Magnolia Projects, branding them worldwide. Women never appeared in Cash Money videos as actors or vocalists, but exclusively as gyrating possessions, and, as in many hip-hop videos, they tended to be noticeably lighter-skinned than the male protagonists—fancy girls, if you will. The only white men in the videos wore police uniforms; they chased the stars in video after video.

To outsiders, it was a dystopian image of armed, feral children, boasting of criminal deeds and empowered by unbelievable amounts of money. To the kids in the projects, it was just good nasty fun, with a laid-back drawling delivery:

> Juvenile: *What kinda nigga be drivin' these hoes crazy?*
> *Claimin' that they pregnant, wanna be his ol' lady?*
> Lil' Wayne: *What kinda nigga be sparklin' like silver?*
> *Lil bitty soldier thuggin', playin' with a million?*

The album covers sported not only hood wealth but also burning cities. It added up to a countercultural image, but countercultures don't have to be progressive. Young black men, uniformed and organized into armies, ready to die: it was resistance, all right, and it had a black consciousness, but it was thoroughly reactionary. To call it "politically incorrect" is to fall into the same euphemistic trap that requires corrupt Louisiana politicians to be referred to as "colorful"; it was overtly criminal-minded.

The only social program it contained was acquisition of money and power through ruthless elimination of obstacles, along with a kind of violent hedonism. It wasn't the minstrelsy that some critics see in gangsta rap, i.e., black people acting out whites' stereotypes of black people. It was something more subcultural. It was part of a different kind of world revolution, also reflected in the *narcorridos* of Mexico and the gangster funk of the *favelas* of Brazil: praise songs to warlordism, to the ascendance of criminal enterprises that fill the vacuum created by overwhelming poverty, governmental corruption, and a generally dysfunctional state. It was the music of the ever-enlarging worldwide slum, where the most brutal kind of capitalism holds sway. It was passionate, compelling, and even funny, because the sense of menace was constantly undercut by clowning. It exemplified perfectly hip-hop's perplexing combo of stupidity and brilliance. If you were a White Person, or even a middle-class Black Person from another part of the country, you very possibly could listen to an entire number and not make out a word.

But it was also entertainment, rooted in a longtime white folks' tradition: the gangster movie. Black folks didn't play cowboy in New Orleans, they played Indian. And when they played cops and robbers, they didn't play Eliot Ness, they played Al Capone. So how come it's OK for Frank Sinatra to play gangster but not B.G.?

In 1997, Juvenile sold two hundred thousand units of *Solja Rags* for Cash Money. The following year, his *400 Degrees* sold more than three million. Southern rap hadn't been big in New York, but Funkmaster Flex broke Juvenile's 1998 single, "Ha"—a singular combination of exuberant and sinister—at The Tunnel and on Hot 97. When Juvie came to New York and guested on Flex's show, he answered Flex's questions with "It's all gravy, big baby!" Though he snarled and held guns in the ads, he had no police record. The image projected in his hits was that of a happy young horndog with a potty mouth who just wanted to smoke weed and tell a [B-word] to, as his second single was titled, "Back That Ass Up" (spelled "Azz," but bowdlerized to "Thang" for radio; its backing track was described by Mannie Fresh as "some Johann Bach type shit.")[5]

It's a cliché that rap is made for white consumers, catering to their preconceptions about black people. But that's only true when you get to the bigger numbers: in the '90s, you could do a hundred thousand units on word of mouth alone without ever leaving the tastemaking subculture. However, when you're selling as many records as Juvenile was, you were selling records to white people, and your videos were on TV.

Lil' Wayne had a major hit in 1999, one of the great moments of New Orleans hip-hop: "Tha Block Is Hot," accompanied by a suitably hot video. It was one of Mannie Fresh's best tracks, showcasing his style: simple, spare, cheesy, and highly dramatic, with a DJ's sense of when to change the rhythm up before everyone got tired of it and an unerring sense of what to change it to next. Front and center was Lil' Wayne, who at fifteen had a major hit and was on his way to covering every square inch of his body with tattoos.

From about 1996 to 2000, the Cash Money crew worked with engineer Eric Fletcher at a studio called American Sector in New Orleans's Masonic Building, but that studio went out of business. Its SSL consoles wound up in a new studio being opened by Mark Bingham down on Piety Street, in a solid building that had first been a post office and subsequently been the Louisiana Center for Retarded Citizens ("and, yes, they actually called it that," said Bingham). Cash Money worked at Piety Street for a while.

Everybody who worked with Mannie Fresh says nice things about him. Engineer Wesley Fontenot, who as an intern did his first session assisting Fresh, recalls him as "gracious." "There was a certain amount of professionalism among the chaos," Fontenot recalled. "It wasn't that it was really disorganized. They just kinda went on their own time. It was just like a party. As soon as the beats started gettin' made, it was loud. These guys would come in and it was just a good time, and they'd listen to the music, they'd write the lyrics, they'd go in and cut up, and once they were puttin' the words down, if there was a mistake, it was a joke, and everybody'd kinda laugh it off and keep runnin' with it. It was basically just a listening and writing party, and then all of a sudden the microphones needed to be turned on." Which is to say, they did their job as record producers, which is above all to capture an experience.

"One thing that kinda always impressed me," said Fontenot, "was that whenever Lil' Wayne was on the session—even back then, when he was a young guy—he was always there early. And he always had his notebook. And he always just sat there and wrote and waited. If everybody was late, that means that he just had more lyrics written by the time the beats were ready to be done."

Camaraderie came easy enough in the studio. "Every now and then you'll kinda get a tough guy," recalled Fontenot, who also worked with a zillion unfamous rappers, "but as soon as you make him sound good, he's your friend. Some people feel like they have to prove that they're tough, you know, the alpha kind of thing. But you get their track sounding good and you get them sounding good, and everybody realizes, we're all here for the same common goal."

Doing business, however, was another story. "It was really not fun working with them," Bingham recalls about the Cash Money sessions at Piety Street. "They had a huge entourage and the neighbors were goin' crazy. 'Cause they'd have maybe four to six, depending on the time of day, Escalades parked outside, and they'd all be blasting a different track. So the whole neighborhood was like crunked out from our block, was just like blasting in every direction, and not just crunked out by a single car, but by many. All the posse would hang out on the street, so there'd be all these like, you know, ferocious-looking youngsters out there, hanging out being—acting *hard*, I don't know how else to describe it." If this was what Bingham's new studio was going to bring to the neighborhood, the neighbors weren't liking it, and they began organizing to shut it down.

Mannie Fresh was cool, says Bingham, and some of the guys were nicer than others, but "I've worked with musicians from all over the world, and this was the first time I ever got treated like I was Stepin Fetchit. They would just *look* at me like, everybody would look at me hard all the time. There was not one moment of, 'hi, I'm so and so, who are you?' It was all like, 'fuck you, you bitch.' That was the whole vibe, the whole time." They brought in a daily case of Cristal, the ridiculously expensive champagne of choice for brand-conscious rappers, which they drank mixed with red Kool-Aid to kill the taste of the champagne, which they didn't actually like.

The last straw was the crawfish incident.

"We had to sue them to get paid," Bingham remembers. "They were too big [to pay cash] by now, and they had accountants, and then the accountants in typical fashion don't like to pay, ever, so we had to get a collection agency. But the coup de grace was them goin' out and gettin' crawfish and puttin' newspaper on top of the grand piano and pouring the boiled crawfish out on the piano and everyone just eatin' crawfish off the grand piano. And then to object to this, I was told, 'Fuck off, I'll buy your motherfuckin' piano if you want.'"

The Williams brothers ultimately got their own studio, carpeted in dollar signs. Baby and Wayne appeared on *MTV Cribs*, in a September 2004 episode called "Cash Money Cars," showing their collection of whips, tricked out with rims and enormous sound systems. The Hot Boys Escalade limo, with monogrammed seats, had room for twenty-five to ride to an event in. The inside of the Lexus 2002 was all speakers, and had a full bar with champagne flutes. "Every whip that I own," Baby told the camera, "and I own fifty whips, right? So that mean two hundred pairs of rims. Every last one of 'em I could do this—" and he started the engine of one of his whips by remote control from the key ring.

How much did insurance on fifty whips cost, I wondered.

———

Ex-Hot Boy B.G., also known as B. Gizzle, or Geezy, never shouts; his words, which typically take the form of poetically elaborated threats, are more effective for being delivered softly. B.G.'s second solo album, *Chopper City* (1997),

sold one hundred thousand pretty quick. A chopper is a K, that is, an AK-47—
a Kalashnikov, or more generically, an assault rifle. The choice of urban guer-
rillas the world over, at top speed it fires something like six hundred bullets a minute, with notoriously poor accuracy. Chopper City is Uptown New
Orleans. One hundred thousand units meant approximately eight hundred
thousand dollars coming in to the Cash Money millionaires, not counting
that the fact that your cash, the blood that circulates oxygen through a business, is flowing healthily, which means you have all kinds of possibilities
open. But that was chicken feed to what came in when Cash Money signed a
distribution deal with Universal, on terms favorable to the Williams brothers.
Different numbers found their way into the press, and while the usually cited
figure of thirty million was likely a face-value number, not to be confused
with the real bottom line, the deal was certainly lucrative.

B.G.'s third and fourth releases, which came out simultaneously, did a
quarter million units each. His fifth, 1999's *Chopper City in the Ghetto*, notched
142,000 on Soundscan the first week, ultimately going platinum (a million
units) on the strength of "Bling Bling," a breakout hit that introduced the
world to the term—though the "bling bling" chorus was sung by Lil' Wayne,
and the tune, featuring the entire Cash Money family of millionaires, could
have been on any of their albums with equal appropriateness.

But B.G., who had Baby's name tattooed on one arm and Slim's on the
other, and Cash Money across his back, fell out with Baby—I wouldn't have
wanted to have been present when they aired their disputes—and was no longer Cash Money for life. "I Want It," the track Constance and I were hearing
as we drove across the bridge into New Orleans in August 2004, was from a
new album called *Life After Cash Money*, on B.G.'s own Chopper City label.

Part of the fire of New Orleans hip-hop was the group spirit—the sense
of how well everyone knew each other and how much everyone involved
depended on each other for their survival in a murderous world. Magnolia
and Calliope, the spawning grounds of the two big New Orleans rap labels,
were both uptown, though Magnolia was further uptown. In a 1999 interview
with *Murder Dog*, Juvenile was asked if he would work with No Limit rappers.
He said:

> If Ronald Williams tell me, you gotta rap on this with No Limit, I'll do.
> Until that happen, I can't say. . . . Truth is, I don't think it'll ever hap-
> pen. P from the Calliope and I'm from the Magnolia. It really means
> something. Even though muthafuckas actin like it don't mean nothing,
> it do mean something. . . . He ain't from where I'm from. Just like he
> cool with the niggaz where he from, I'm cool with the muthafuckas from

where I'm from. If I rap with him, muthafuckas where I'm from gonna be like, Maaan? I won't be able to go to where I'm from. I be lookin' over my muthafuckin shoulder.[6]

At least two of the four Hot Boys got into heroin. B.G. was a junkie for years, and has since devoted a number of rhymes to talking about having kicked. In January 2004, a SWAT team looking for heroin and an assault weapon raided twenty-two-year-old Turk's (he had dropped the "Young") apartment in Hickory Hill, Tennessee, a community annexed by Memphis in 1998. Though about thirty shots were fired in the ensuing gunfight, neither Turk nor his girlfriend (who hid under the bed) was hurt, but one of the six deputies was seriously wounded by a 9-millimeter bullet, which was not police ammunition. Turk was already wanted on a probation violation in New Orleans at the time.

As we went about our lives in New Orleans in 2004, Lil' Wayne had his biggest hit since "Tha Block Is Hot," with a hook jacked from UNLV's "Don't U Be Greedy": *Go DJ, that's my DJ, go DJ, that's my DJ* . . . And Mannie Fresh, reluctantly coaxed into doing a solo album—*The Mind of Mannie Fresh*, it was called—was on the radio with a goofy song that recycled lyrics that previously had appeared in Lil' Wayne's "Drop It Like It's Hot":

Put yo' hands on yo' knees and bend yo' rawmp
Put yo' back in, back out, do da hawmp

That one was a guaranteed turn-it-up in the Saturn whenever Q-93 hit it.

Like most hip-hop stations, Q-ninety-threezie in New Orleans plays radio edits—alternate mixes, made as a routine part of the production process—which mute out curse words. The blanking out of words is so common on hip-hop radio that it's built into the record from the start. It's a necessity, given the FCC regs, but it's become marketing: you have to buy the record in order to hear all the blank spaces filled in. Some records seem to consist of more gaps than words, often with a curse word at a rhythmically important spot in the phrase, so the resulting empty spot creates a tense vocal rest. You couldn't do that with a song because you would lose notes in the melody, but with rap it works very well. The other way of doing it is to record a second, "clean," vocal, substituting euphemisms. One or both of these bowdlerizing methods is necessary to get airplay, and also so you can sell the record at Wal-Mart, which won't sell records with obscenity on them.

Definitely buy your hip-hop at Wal-Mart, because the clean version is often better. I first noticed this in 1998, when Big Pun's (Christopher Rios) "Still Not a Player" was on Hot 97 in New York once an hour: "I'm not a player, I just crush a lot." A weird and memorable line. I bought the album, but instead the track went, "I'm not a player, I just fuck a lot." Which had no charm at all.

Or the hysterically funny bellowed lyric from Mannie Fresh, in heavy rotation on Q-93:

House real big! Cars real big!
Belly real big! Everything real big!
Rims real big! Pockets real big!
Rings real big! Lemme tell ya how I live!

I was disappointed to get the album and find out that "belly real big"—the line that gave it character—was an edit, and the album version was "dick real big." Yawn.

The radio edits mute out not only *fuck, shit, dick, pussy, muthafuckin'*, etc., but also *nigga* and *bitch*. Criticism of hip-hop within the larger black community pretty much breaks down along the lines of those who those who call each other *nigga* and those who think the word should never be used. White People are not allowed to use it, ever, in any context—except you can't make that rule, because, as William S. Burroughs put it, language is a virus. I can testify from personal experience that whether you are a White Person or not, if you are in an office all day with people calling each other "nigga" you will start to do it too. I knew the meaning of the word had changed beyond recognition when someone in the office said, of a family picture showing my Brooklyn white-boy colleagues Will and Ben Socolov in high school, "y'all look like them Brady Bunch niggaz." If we can speak of Brady Bunch niggaz, the word has definitely changed from the days when I was carefully instructed to say knee-grow.

Nigga, as you surely know, is the third-person masculine pronoun in hip-hop, and is not to be confused with *nigger*—as Tupac explained it, nig-*gers* were the ones hanging from ropes, but nig-*gaz* are the ones hanging out wearing gold ropes. *Nigga* is a power word. It's part of what I call the encryption. By making it an essential element of your music, every time you snarl it, you are inoculating your sound against its ever being taken over by white people, who aren't allowed to say it and thus can't be credible. No white person could get away with B.G.'s performative negritude: *Cash Money is a army, nigga / A navy, nigga / So if you ever try to harm me, nigga / It ain't gravy, nigga*.[7] If you do a bluegrass version of that, you don't sound clever, you just come off like a twerp.

Hip-hop is the contrary of rock 'n' roll, which was a black music that white people could appropriate and inhabit. Rock 'n' roll was assimilable as soon as it received its name, and it was dropped like a hot potato by black listeners. But, the achievements of a handful of white rappers notwithstanding, part of the ongoing evolutionary mutation of hip-hop is to be impenetrable if not downright unfriendly to white people except as consumers. Talk about a copy code: hip-hop is multiply encrypted in all kinds of ways so that unlicensed users will have as hard a time as possible hacking it and taking it over, both artistically and in simple terms of a protective shell of violence. And if a cultural hacker should get it right, the code can change next week. Which is not to say that there aren't plenty of white people involved in making hip-hop, sometimes uncredited, as musicians, beatmakers, and engineers.

If the hip-hop industry believes in anything besides money, it's the color line. Despite hip-hop's domination of the world pop music market, and despite the existence of Japanese and Norwegian rappers, it has remained a resolutely African American music, still essential on a daily basis, for thirty years—a very long time in the pop lifespan.

The first constructive use of the N-word on record, as far as I know, was in the proto-rap—and they were definitely *rapping*, as such term would have been understood in 1970—of The Last Poets, with the scorching, and still perfectly timely "Niggers Are Scared of Revolution." I guarantee you Black Panther baby Tupac Shakur knew that one backward and forward. The word *niggaz* was established for all time in hip-hop by the first gangsta rap supergroup, N.W.A. (for Niggaz With Attitude), who used it several hundred times on *Straight Outta Compton*. One place you will not hear the N-word much is reggae, though there are exceptions. Most Jamaicans don't use it, either in song or in daily parlance. Biggie Smalls's last gig before he was killed was at Reggae Sting '97 in Jamaica. He came with his usual nigga-this and nigga-that. Jamaican audiences, notoriously tough, don't like that word. They "bottled" him, as they call it in Jamaica. I can't resist reproducing a comment from an Internet forum, by one Chams Rocwelz: "Biggie Smalls came with that big poppa fuckry, an him get bokkle." Imagine having bottles fly at you from a crowd of thousands.

Nigga is never allowed to be heard on the radio, though it permeates the texts of the records that are on the air. Nor is *bitch* allowed, so that in B.G.'s line

One shot to the head is how we slank a bitch

the B-word is gone in the radio version, leaving an empty, accented rest, drawing attention to it all the more. (Lexical note: the B-word here does not refer to a woman, but to a bitch-ass nigga, that is, a punk or a snitch.) Dispatching someone with one shot to the head? Not offensive. But you can't say *bitch* on the air.

There was one other word Q-93 muted out, though in New York, Hot 97 played it unedited. In Yonkers rapper Jadakiss's "Why?," a brilliant if frustrating record that was a series of questions all beginning with *why?*:

> *Why do people push pounds and powders?*
> *Why did* [mute] *knock down the towers?*

It was a cleaned-up vocal to begin with, since the album version has *niggaz* in place of *people*. But the muted word was *Bush: Why did Bush knock down the towers?* A truly obscene word, and the election of 2004 was approaching. Hot 97 in New York wasn't owned by Bush-supporting, San Antonio–based Clear Channel Communications, but Q-93 and six other stations in New Orleans were.

Me, I don't think Bush knocked down the towers. His people wouldn't have been capable of accomplishing that precise an operation. But Bush sure as hell let the towers get knocked down. About the lack of response to pre-9/11 warnings, Thomas Powers wrote: "The President did nothing. It would be hard to find words adequate to describe the full range and amplitude of the nothing that he did. My own preliminary, working explanation is that for reasons of his own the President decided to do nothing. Why? Historians will be occupied for many years before they come to agreement on the answer to that question."[8]

So maybe Jadakiss's *Why?* isn't so far from Powers's *Why?* Though Thomas Powers probably wasn't as upset about Halle Berry's explicit scene with Billy Bob Thornton in *Monster's Ball*, another of Jadakiss's *Why?*'s: *Why did Halle have to let a white man pop her / to get an Oscar?*

———————

If you think the artist has a social responsibility, and if you think that the reality an artist creates, however dystopian, is a template for society, and that the artist ought to be responsible for that reality, hip-hop has a lot to answer for.

There was a definite programmatic narrative to the music played on Q-93: What is open to you is a life of crime. You can make a lot of money by selling drugs, which you will then spend in conspicuous consumption of branded goods, which is the ultimate good in life. Probably you will be killed or go to prison, and your way to escape that fate is to become a successful rapper or, better yet, take your launderable drug-hustle money and parlay that into becoming a music-business executive. If you're female, there's a version of this for you too, which turns on making sure you get paid when you give up the coochie.

On the other hand, if you think the artist's responsibility is to synthesize, describe, or embody his or her times, hip-hop has done a brilliant job. It gave a voice to people you didn't otherwise hear from. In my time in New Orleans it was omnipresent. It was the loudest, wealthiest, most mass-based part of the soundtrack. Its creativity continually surprises. And if you try to ignore it, it will still be thumping all around you. You might as well read the story it's telling you. Let me see if I can put it more succinctly:

Hip-hop is poetry, music, rhythm, visual language, gesture, drama, culture—a composite artistic movement. Just looking at hip-hop as poetry, without even considering its other aspects, it was the most significant poetic movement of the last half-century—and I don't only mean in the United States, but globally. Scholars haven't begun to parse the wealth of information it's given us. The only place you find adequate critical discussion of hip-hop is in the meta-criticism embedded directly in its rhymes.

The big New Orleans rappers had little to offer in the way of what some people like to call "conscious" rap. While there was an underground that didn't get heard on Q-93, and there was more to New Orleans rap than No Limit and Cash Money, there was no Rakim in New Orleans hip-hop, no "The Message," no Mos Def. There wasn't even a polemic—no angry Ice Cube calling for arson against Koreans and addressing white women as "cave bitches." (That was a sweet one: *You can be my fan, but don't expand / and try to get my dick in your hand.*) New Orleans can't be disregarded if you want to talk about what hip-hop is, instead of what you wish it were; its violent mind-set and lumpen avarice are an embarrassment to those who feel idealistic about hip-hop.

But.

Stepping back a moment from the hardcore world of hip-hop business and into the musical environment of black New Orleans, with its rich crosscurrents, it takes on a different perspective. The New Orleans tradition flowed into the local hip-hop, but it was an open circuit. If you want to talk about black music in New Orleans, MC means move the crowd. The most happening thing on Q-93 was at night, when they'd open up the phone lines for high school kids to rap on the air. It seemed like pretty much every schoolkid in New Orleans could come up with a compelling story in rhyme. Rapping fit so naturally into the New Orleans flow that everyone did it: second liners,

Mardi Gras Indians, zydeco accordionists, everybody. For that matter, they were rapping long before it was part of something called hip-hop.

Once rapping, an ancient tradition, had become hip-hop, a contemporary movement, why wouldn't New Orleans have contributed one of the most important versions of the art form? Other cities keep it ghetto, but when you keep it ghetto in New Orleans you're accessing a whole other flow of culture that nowhere else has. And why wouldn't they come on like murderers? New Orleans is the murder capital, a town where murder is not an imaginary transgressive thrill but a daily obstacle, and hip-hop, a masculinity cult, is very much about being the fastest gun, even if your weapon is lexical.

Business-wise, there was a firewall around hip-hop in New Orleans. It was off by itself, on its own radio station. I couldn't even figure out where people got the records. There weren't that many stores in New Orleans you could buy hip-hop CDs at in 2004, since most of the mom-and-pop record stores had long since closed. There was one store, Odyssey on Canal Street, that specialized in it. Wal-Mart only carried the clean versions. Louisiana Music Factory, the record store in the French Quarter that mostly stocked music by Louisiana artists and had frequent in-store performances, pointedly didn't carry hip-hop, perhaps because they didn't want thugged-out kids coming in. Tower and Virgin in the French Quarter had it, but, apparently because of shoplifting, they didn't display it in the racks—you had to ask for B.G. at the counter.

Meanwhile, rappers' relatives played in brass bands and second lined in Social and Pleasure Clubs. Because in New Orleans, people knew that styles weren't locked doors, so they all coexisted. It was all one community. Sometimes it was all one big genre. On the porous, sinking ground of New Orleans, styles and tunes coexisted in the same house, the same family, and even in the same body.

12

THE DAY OF THE DEAD

As he boarded a boat in New Orleans en route to Havana for his next concert, pianist Henri Herz saw an altercation develop between two men at dockside:

> Without any regard to the people all around them, and with the risk of wounding innocent people, each one took out a revolver from his pocket. They exchanged a dozen balls, and the street combat only stopped when one of the combatants fell with an injured shoulder.
>
> No one was astonished at this improvised duel. It was as if it were normal.
>
> . . . New Orleans has been in all eras the place mostly sadly renowned for its savage street fighting.[1]

That was in 1846. On Sunday, October 24, 2004, two teenaged gunmen opened fire in the crowded breezeway of Frenchmen's Wharf, a grandly named apartment complex with the unpoetic address of 6800 I-10 Service Road. They killed their target, an alleged motorcycle thief, but not before he squeezed off some shots. Miraculously, no bystanders were hurt. One of the gunmen was holding a baby the entire time he was firing, suggesting that the gunfight was unplanned. Tara Young's account in the *Times-Picayune* quoted a seventeen-year-old friend of the victim: "'Everybody said he went out like a soldier,' Jackson said. 'He had to shoot back. They were shooting at him.'"[2]

The next night, in Pontchartrain Park, a neighborhood generally thought safe though there is no such thing, three masked robbers confronted six youths who had returned from playing football, shooting nineteen-year-old Ryan Morgan to death in front of the house owned by the father of one of the youths. The father had just returned home from a citywide prayer meeting on crime.

On Tuesday night, October 26, four corpses—three men and a woman—were found in a house on Egania Street in the Lower Ninth Ward. A fifth survived the gundown and was taken to Charity Hospital.

And then it was time for Halloween, which lasted three days.

In a town where there's always fresh blood for vampires to feed on, Halloween is a natural state of mind that stretches out before and after the date itself.

October 31 fell on Sunday in 2004, so the fancy balls took place the night before. There's even a holiday industry term of art for October 30: "Halloween Eve." (But doesn't "Halloween" break down to "Hallow E'en," and thus is an eve itself? So it's the eve of the eve? Better not to ask.) Monday was the Day of the Dead, so it was a three-day party.

I'd acquired another running buddy, Joel Dinerstein. Joel, who was pals with T.R.—they'd met on a second line—was a jazz scholar who taught in the English department, and the author of *Swinging the Machine*, about the influence of machine rhythms on the swing era. He invited me to the Pussy Footers Ball, a costume event at the Country Club, on Louisa off Royal in the Bywater, around the corner from where T.R. lives. That it was called the Country Club shouldn't lead you to think I was hobnobbing with the business elite, though possibly there might have been a banker's queer son there. Occupying a spacious, gracious 1890 mansion, it's a social club with a largely gay clientele. But on Halloween Eve, there were Pussy Footers wiggling all over the place.

The Pussy Footers are yet another of New Orleans's many carnival societies: a group of maybe several dozen women who get together to dress up and do dance routines. And, I suspect, receive communications from the mothership. It's very much in the spirit of Mardi Gras, complete with the flavor of postmodern camp, which New Orleans could pretty well claim to have invented. I mean, *The Bad Seed* was written in the French Quarter. *A Streetcar Named Desire*, in a town that has a whole festival in honor of Tennessee Williams, the high priest of the high-strung. We won't even mention Anne Rice, a four-volume paperback set of whose works came with the house we rented. Even Lee Harvey Oswald's black-op Fair Play for Cuba committee was on Camp Street.

Joel's future ex-girlfriend Larisa was a Pussy Footer, and Joel had been cheerfully pressed into auxiliary service for the event. As a mark of office, he got to wear a sash, always a great honor in New Orleans. "Pussy Handler," it read.

"Is that a responsibility or a privilege?" I asked him.

"A little of both," he said pensively.

After the lovely Larisa barked out instructions for all the scattered per-formers to assemble (anyone who's done this can sympathize), the performance kicked off outside, in front of the clubhouse.

If you like chorus lines of exhibitionistic southern women, this was for you. Costumed Pussy Footers lined the full front porch up above the Country Club's front yard and down on the sidewalk in front of the house, doing dance routines as more and more partygoers arrived, all of them in costume. The routines weren't exactly well coordinated. The women on the sidewalk could barely hear the music and kept shouting to turn it up, but nobody seemed to mind. It wasn't supposed to be a professional group. By the end of the first number, you would have had to be a crank not to be having fun as the Pussy Footers shook their moneymakers.

In New Orleans, a Halloween costume can seem like a justifiable business expense. You can wear it at least five different times during the year. As a long-time veteran of New York Halloweens, I couldn't help but compare. The first thing I noticed was how different the costumes, and even the idea of costum-ing, were than in New York. Big difference: almost no one wore masks in New Orleans. You could see everyone's face. This, it turns out, is rooted in a long-term municipal prohibition on wearing masks in public during carnival, in turn rooted in crime prevention (which concept, until 1862, meant prevent-ing slave uprisings). No prefab plastic costumes. More mades than boughts. Much imagination. And, given the warmer weather, skimpier—it was a lovely night to be bare-shouldered. You can't make these costumes up at the last min-ute; you have to work on them on an ongoing basis, scoping out the numerous shops that can hook you up to participate in this venerable municipal costume tradition that helps underpin the city's economy year-round.

One thing I noticed immediately: in this black-majority city, attendance at this party was maybe (unscientific, impressionistic figure here) 90 percent or more white.

As far as I could see, this was not a party for people who cared what color you were or I wouldn't have wanted to be there, and many of the attendees would surely have been happy to have more black people there. But that's what happens in New Orleans. All across New Orleans that night, people were having parties, and I suspect that not many were proportional to the city's overall demographic.

The carnival organizations of New Orleans—the extravagant white krewes as well as the black counter-carnival of the Mardi Gras Indians—grew up around, and embody, the structures of class and caste in the city. This is made all the realer by the poverty, undereducation, corruption, crime, crack (still big in New Orleans), racism, rage—in short, drama. New Orleans is a drama queen, and drama queens can go from spectacularly beautiful to spectacularly ugly in the blink of an eye. White, black, or mixed, every successful party felt to me like an attempt to take the street back for peaceful purposes, and not a few were themed like that. A few weeks before, a nighttime "second line against crime" had paraded around from Congo Square through the Tremé for four hours.

After the Pussy Footers finished their routines—it seemed like a half-hour or so, but time had started to ooze, so I'm not sure—the DJ took over inside the house, and soon people were dancing to funk classics. The entire night I don't think I heard the DJ play one record that used a drum machine. Everything came from the live drums period, much of it using a full arsenal of other percussion, including congas. I couldn't have picked them better. "I Know You Got Soul" (Bobby Byrd), "Fire" (Ohio Players). Obscure James Brown sides. And the greatest of them all, "Flashlight" (Parliament).

Usually when the DJ comes on is when I want to get out, because it's always too loud and I rarely like the music. But this was enjoyable by ordinary human beings—the exact volume you'd want it to be for dancing, loud but not ridiculous, and not overdriving the system.

Beer in hand, I meandered out into the other party universe, something the Country Club is locally famous for: its spacious, very private patio around a big swimming pool. In sunny weather it's the sunbathing hang for the hung, where open-minded naked people of all genders take the rays. There's a bar at the back end of the yard, and the neighboring lots have tall tropical trees that ring the place around with privacy and atmosphere.

The temperature that night was a seductive warm-cool, ideal for being outside. To the side of the swimming pool was row upon row of wooden deck chairs. I lay down on one of them, far away from everyone else, and I began to moonbathe, fully clothed. A sense of peace fell upon me as I lay on my back, staring up at the sky. There was no one within about twenty feet of me. I listened to the party go on all around, staring at the moon and idly watching the party. Hmm, there's a girl stripping off her clothes and jumping in the pool. That's fine with me. More people went to skinny-dip. I'd been to four pool parties in the ten weeks I'd been in New Orleans, but this was the first nude one.

Inside the house, the band had started. Naiads or funky music? Funky music, definitely. The Pussy Footers didn't want half-assed music, so Joel had turned them on to Big Sam's Funky Nation. I would recommend Big Sam's Funky Nation for any party you might care to give. The music lives up to the promise of the band's name. Stylistically, the Funky Nation might remind

THE DAY OF THE DEAD   233

you a little of P-Funk, but that also reminds you how much P-Funk owes to New Orleans.

Big Sammie Williams, who was all of twenty-three in 2004, previously played trombone for the Dirty Dozen. He and his wife, Shaneka Peterson, owned Funky Butt, the Rampart Street club named after Buddy Bolden's famous song. The genealogy is not clear, but Sam's father was named Bolden, and so was his grandfather. There appears to be a possibility that Sam might be Buddy Bolden's great- or great-great-grandson. One thing is sure: Bolden was known for playing loud, and Big Sam's got to be the loudest trombone player in town. That instrument looks like a little bitty thing when he holds it, and he can set every molecule in the metal to vibrating.

The Funky Nation was playing in what used to be somebody's living room, with a five-piece over a simple P.A., and, marvel of marvels, they didn't play too loud. Very few party bands with electric rhythm section can resist the temptation to blow out a little room. They didn't, though by God, Big Sam can project. In fact—I think this was the first time I've ever seen this happen—there was an almost seamless transition from the DJ to the band, playing at approximately the same volume and the same style of music.

Daylight Savings Time ended at two A.M., and the party hit a one-hour time warp. Temporal lagniappe: we got to flow from one A.M. to two A.M. all over again.

The Pussy Footers Ball was the most fun I'd had at a party in a long time. Uh-oh. This was starting to seem normal.

The Bush/Cheney posters along Magazine Street were set way high in the air so that no one could vandalize them. Down at shin level, the neutral ground of Louisiana Avenue was dense with one-color posters depicting candidates for local offices, impaled in dizzying multiples on pickets into the fine, slimy silt.

As it turned out, the real Day of the Dead took place on November 2, the day of the presidential election of 2004. It was a rainy day in New Orleans, heavy at times. "It looks like New Orleans is becoming a major hotspot for voting problems," said an Electronic Frontier Foundation posting on election day, with over eighty incidents reported, including electronic machines that wouldn't boot up. The line to vote at historically black Xavier University was five hours long at one point.

Everything's a party in New Orleans, even funerals, so that night we went to a neighbor of Chris and Ladee's to watch the returns. As the results arrived, depression set in. Funerals in New Orleans were happier than this.

Ohio provided the margin of victory. You can read elsewhere how the Republicans rigged the election there.[3] Short version: for the second time, George W. Bush stole the presidency via chicanery in a swing state. It was as crooked as could be. In between, the Republicans stole the 2002 gubernatorial election in Alabama, throwing the election to Bob Riley by old-fashioned vote fraud and subsequently prosecuting and incarcerating his opponent, Don Siegelman, on a bullshit charge. In the South, where they were strongest, they went so far as to harass and selectively prosecute Democratic fundraisers, like Mississippi trial lawyer Paul Minor, investigated in 2002 and later incarcerated on a trumped-up charge. By 2004 the Republican Party had become a flat-out crime syndicate with the structure of a political party, a hard core of racist support, a theocratic ideology, and a powerful media operation that exulted in bullying and intimidation. That's not polemic on my part, that's a simple statement of fact.

In effect, the Karl Rovians said to the hapless John Kerry, who was running as Mr. Electable Warrior: how are you gonna be tough enough to deal with terrorists when you aren't even tough enough to deal with some torture-happy frat boys like *us*? They had such media firepower that, though they were running a draft-dodging ex–party animal against a decorated veteran, their goons could paint *Kerry* as the phony soldier. It didn't matter that everyone knew it was fake.

None of it mattered. It didn't matter that Iraq was a disaster from the beginning, or that Seymour Hersh had broken the Abu Ghraib scandal, with home-porno pictures of Hooded Man, Lynndie England, the Pyramid of Naked Muslims, and all the rest representing America to the world. Dick Cheney continued to receive money from Halliburton, which was raking in no-bid contracts. It didn't matter. The Bushists had cut the Army Corps of Engineers' request for funds to maintain the levees around New Orleans by 80 percent. It didn't matter. They had ditched the Clinton administration's standards for wetlands protection, allowing the oil companies to continue to cut channels, removing the buffer zone that was crucial for protection against storm surge. It didn't matter.

In what began to look like a red-vs.-blue civil war, with the major media owned by the reds, Kerry proved himself unfit to be a general. With a battery of lawyers at the ready to challenge the irregularities, he simply folded his cards and capitulated, essentially collaborating in the theft of the election, to his running mate John Edwards's muffled outrage. "Today," said Kerry, forgoing a recount, "I hope we can begin the healing." He couldn't possibly have believed that.

He took a dive. He rolled over.

Once again, the Democrats failed to provide a meaningful opposition and caved at the moment of truth. Dixiechicking was okay. Swiftboating was okay. Nobody was gonna say boo to the Bushists now. As he conceded the election, Kerry spoke of the "desperate need for unity, for finding common ground and coming together." He was answered by an editorial on November 4 at the cyberpolitical *Black Commentator*, to which I said amen: "The last thing America needs is unity with thieves, pirates and punks."

In his first postelection press conference, also on November 4, George W. Bush declared, "I earned capital in the campaign, political capital, and now I intend to spend it." He didn't say invest it, which is what capital is for. He said spend it, which is what a robber baron does with the capital of a company he's looting. The Republicans would have four more years to implement their vision of a society where people spend all their time and energy looking for work, trying to keep that work, struggling to make ends meet while paying through the nose for basic survival, and serving as sources of extractable cash for corporations to whom the citizens were increasingly indebted. Socialism for the rich, capitalism for the poor: the ideology came complete with party organs that repeated the central committee's message while masquerading as news media, in what was looking very much like a right-wing version of Soviet methods.

The crazies were in power and were seriously pursuing a vision of a one-party state, with the eventual goal of the withering away of the state—they called it "starving the beast"—in favor of a pure corporatist, rather than communist, paradise, where man exploits man instead of the other way around, as the old Soviet joke went. Soviet humor was starting to seem relevant. You know, jokes about censorship and torture. The Republicans were, and had been since Reagan, working to radically restructure the government so as to render it as ineffective as possible, memorably expressed in the unfortunate May 25, 2001, metaphor of Karl Rove associate Grover Norquist, who, speaking on National Public Radio, said he wanted to reduce government "to the size where I can drag it into the bathroom and drown it in the bathtub."[4]

It was getting harder to avoid using the F-word to describe the Republicans' burgeoning authoritarianism. *Fascism* was a word with little credibility in America, perhaps because of its frequent hyperbolic overuse. Was Bushism fascism or was it something new? I'd been wondering this for a while. At the Howard-Tilton Library, I had Mussolini's *The Corporate State* brought out of storage for me. I concluded that the corporate state is the corporate state, and yes, Bushism was fascism.

But we need to reevaluate the idea of fascism in light of American history, because we've had it before. That's what the slaveholding South was. *The Black Commentator*'s editorial about the electoral capitulation to Bush/Cheney continued with something that resonated with what I was thinking: "Black Americans do not need European models of fascism to understand the grave threat these people represent to life and liberty."

In Louisiana, Republicans gained a Senate seat. Replacing outgoing Democratic Senator-about-to-turn-lobbyist John Breaux, the future sex scandalee and defense-of-marriage stalwart David Vitter won election to the Senate with 51 percent, that Bush-era margin. But he got less than 23 percent of the vote in New Orleans.

For years, the formula for a statewide Democratic candidate in Louisiana had been to carry New Orleans and 30 percent of the rest of the state. The Crescent City was home to a major black voting bloc and was therefore a Democratic-voting stronghold as well as the political antagonist of the rest of the white-dominated state. Which is not to say that either side offered good government.

Almost sixty thousand more "black" people than "white" voted in New Orleans in the 2004 election. In New Orleans Parish, Marlin Gusman was elected sheriff, the first African American to hold that office. Blacks held a majority on the New Orleans City Council and the Orleans Parish School Board. The mayor, Ray Nagin, was an African American Democrat—specifically, a Creole, a member of the class who had dominated black New Orleans politics since before emancipation, descended as a group from the lighter-skinned, francophone free people of color.

Louisiana still had a Democratic governor and one Democratic senator. Bush/Cheney carried the state of Louisiana by a substantial margin, 56.7 to 42.2 percent statewide. But they lost Orleans Parish almost 4 to 1.

New Orleans was on their shit list.

What it meant to be on the Bush regime's shit list, and what political capital can buy, was demonstrated on November 8, six days after the election, when U.S. Marines assaulted the city of Fallujah, where four "contractors" from the United States mercenary force Blackwater USA had been dragged through the streets, set on fire, and their burned bodies hung high on March 31, 2004. Before the beginning of the Iraq war, Fallujah was about the size of New Orleans, and it was relatively undamaged in the initial blitzkrieg ("shock and awe," in English) that destroyed the infrastructure of Baghdad.

The Americans had been waiting until after the presidential election to unleash Operation Phantom Fury against Fallujah, prior to which they "softened" the city up with eight weeks of aerial bombardments and by cutting off the city's power, water, and food supplies.[5] Though maybe 75 to 90 percent of the city had evacuated before the Marines hit, those who didn't leave were slaughtered in "house-to-house clearing operations." The official death toll for Iraqis was 1,350 "insurgents." If you can bear to look at the unembedded Dahr Jamail's photos of the Fallujah dead, you can see that the "insurgents" whose bodies he encountered included many victims of collective punishment—a boy waving a white flag, various people killed in bed, an old man and his daughters, a disabled man with prosthetics. Their bodies were left to be eaten by dogs.[6] The U.S. military used as an offensive weapon a chemical called white phosphorus, which forms a cloud that melts the flesh of everyone unlucky enough to be caught within it. They deployed this in an urban area, burning the still-living bodies of women and children in the process, and then lied about having done it. Mike Marqusee reported in the *Guardian* that "36,000 of the city's 50,000 homes were destroyed, along with 60 schools and 65 mosques and shrines."[7]

After the United States devastated their city, the people of Fallujah began returning late the following month. By March 2005 only about a third of the people of Fallujah had returned. Two years after the attack, about two thirds of Fallujans were back. "Only a fraction of the promised reconstruction and compensation" ever materialized.[8]

The details about the destruction of Fallujah were slow to come out and didn't receive much coverage stateside. Needless to say, images of it did not receive much television play. And as far as I could tell, most people in New Orleans didn't pay much attention to news from beyond the swamp.

That's partly because bullets were flying at home, and partly because New Orleanians were thinking about that next meal.

Guns or butter. In New Orleans, either one can kill you.

People in New Orleans act like they invented the very idea of eating, but the city is pretty much synonymous with obesity and a proud tradition of arterial blockage. It's true that New Orleans has an original cuisine, which developed around a unique combination of available foodstuffs and which embraces strong smells and tastes, and heaviness in all its varieties. The city is near fantastically productive shrimp and oyster beds, and there are crawfish in season (if you like the way they smell when they're boiling, which I don't). Yeah, it tastes good. But it could be the unhealthiest diet this side of McDonald's.

It's not French cooking. It's, well, the dreaded gumbo metaphor again. Everything in New Orleans—music, history, you name it—ultimately turns into gumbo, which is as tasty as it is fattening. Restaurants featuring other cuisines are a curious experience in New Orleans, because there's a tendency for everything to tend toward the condition of gumbo, whether it's pad thai or steak au poivre. And then there's the southern tradition of deep-frying everything, alongside the American tradition of eating lots of sweets and highly processed food.

One thing I like about New Orleans is that it's the only place where I can pass for physically fit. People who aren't corpulent stand out. Here's a New Orleans food day:

Breakfast could be bacon and fried eggs. Or you could just have French toast, with butter and syrup. If you ate the thirty-five-dollar "Typical New Orleans Breakfast" at Brennan's in the French Quarter, you might have a baked apple with double cream, poached eggs, French bread, coffee, and bananas with ice cream.[9]

For lunch, why don't you drive over to Parasol's, serving up delicious Depression-level loads of saturated fat since 1932? Or have we decided saturated fat is OK again? I can't keep track. Parasol's was originally Passauer's; the family was German, from Passau, but New Orleans pronunciation being what it is, the sign says Parasol's now. They have three brands of beer on tap, video poker, overhead TVs tuned to different channels, a jukebox that only plays one side of the stereo pair, and a perpetual blue cloud of cigarette smoke. They specialize in po'boys, the New Orleans French-bread sandwich that became established as a tradition in the 1920s. You can make a po'boy out of almost anything. Parasol's is best known for oyster po'boys, for which, naturally, the oysters are breaded and deep fried. But if you already had an artery-pleasing oyster-and-bacon omelette for breakfast, you could get a French fry po'boy at Parasol's instead. To make a real po'boy, you have to "dress" it with shredded lettuce, tomato, and plenty of rich mayonnaise. Then have that after-lunch cigarette, ahhhhh. Like the one the lady at the next table was smoking the whole time you were eating. Then back to work. For an afternoon snack you could have that New Orleans specialty, a beignet—fried bread topped with powdered sugar. And wash it down with Coke—sorry, we don't have Diet Coke.

For dinner, let's start with a shrimp and corn cream soup, then maybe fried chicken, with mashed potatoes or french fries, cole slaw (with that good dressing of mayonnaise, buttermilk, and sugar), and buttered cornbread. Ready for another beer? For dessert, what'll it be, peanut butter pie or strawberry cheesecake? Or—I swear I am not making this up, though I won't say it was typical—bacon chocolate torte. The people I was having dinner with ordered it. I tasted it and spit it out.

Repeat 365 days a year.

No, not everyone in New Orleans eats like that. I even know a couple of vegans there. On the other hand, I seemed to see a lot of obits for people who'd had heart attacks at age fifty-eight. This part of the world has a frightful number of cases of extreme obesity, people who have to go around in carts because their legs don't work anymore. It's not surprising that New Orleans has one of the highest rates of Type II diabetes (associated with obesity) in this fat country. You could walk into a club and see a banging band with a four-hundred-pound musician who had to play sitting down and clearly wasn't going to live very long.

By tradition, Monday is red-beans-and-rice day, from back when Monday was laundry day, so Mama could leave the beans to simmer while she and the girls did the washing. Have a fat, juicy sausage with it. Mmmm. I enjoyed the taste of the red beans and rice I ate for lunch on Mondays at Tulane, but it always left me feeling kind of heavy and bloated. Then I found out what the deal was: if you want to get those beans nice and thick? Easy, just add a stick of butter for every pound of beans.

Lest you think I'm gratuitously trashing Louisiana cooking, let me hasten to add that my childhood in Louisiana left me with a lifelong taste for rice, and I do love sausage, of which Louisiana has many varieties, and okra, which Constance doesn't like. The other thing I love about Louisiana food is that they use lots and lots of hot sauce. I was happy to see Constance's cooking adapting to the local style and ingredients immediately—minus deep-frying, butter, sugar, and excessive salt—and I came home at night to a plate of rice with chicken, shrimp, and sausage, and sometimes even okra, moistened with Tabasco. Marilyn gave her a cooking tip: mountains of chopped onion, celery, and green pepper—the New Orleans trinity, she called it. I gained weight even though I restricted myself to one po'boy a month.

In the spirit of research, I took Constance out for a fancy dinner in late November. We drove the four blocks from our house so I could hand over my keys and a tip to the parking valet at the historic Commander's Palace, founded in 1880 by Emile Commander in a mansion at Washington Avenue and Coliseum Street.

The Commander's Palace experience wasn't really for me. I like to take my baby out to dinner, but I'm not a restaurant freak. I don't actually *like* restaurant food very much; it's mostly fake fine food that has too many calories, too much butter, too much salt. I enjoy a good meal as much as anyone else, but, perhaps after so much time in Cuba in the '90s, I'm usually just happy to eat and I don't want it to cost a whole lot. I don't want my food to be art. I want it to taste good and not kill me, be made from fresh local ingredients if possible, and I want to have enough of it. Constance feels pretty much the same way.

And I'm especially uncomfortable being treated like a pseudo-aristocrat by a liveried waitstaff playing servant. It makes the whole dining experience seem ghastly somehow. Trust New Orleans to put that in perspective: the Commander's Palace staff was mostly black, and the diners in the upstairs dining room were all white. The staff was conscious of their theatrical role and, I thought—not that I could possibly know what they were thinking— that they treaded the layers of irony nimbly. They were remarkably efficient and icily obsequious as they performed their jobs. The turtle soup was delicious, but once was enough.

Very near Commander's—four blocks lakeward and two blocks upriver—is a street corner known wherever hip-hoperati hang. UNLV made it famous as a murderous forty-swigging dope-selling hangout with "6th and Baronne" (1994). In Lil' Ya's words [transcription approximate], over a Mannie Fresh track:

> I was chillin' on the corner of 6th and Baronne
> With a forty in my hand and about to get stoned
> I got my dope stash and a tec [Tec 9] on my side
> For them jokin' mutherfuckers who be doin' drive-bys . . .

Leaving Commander's Palace, I wondered what the parking valets saw going down out there on Washington Avenue night after night.

Sixth and Baronne would have been a ten-minute walk from my house, if I had wanted to take that walk.

———

I had to go to New York to meet up with Elijah Wald so I could produce a radio companion to his book *Escaping the Delta* as an episode of *Afropop Worldwide Hip Deep*. Elijah, who is something of a gypsy, had lived in New Orleans, and as we were talking things down over the phone, me standing out on my Irish Channel porch, he asked me how I was liking the city. Without thinking, I immediately answered:

"I hate it."

There, I'd said it. He seemed surprised. As soon as I'd said it, I wanted to take it back.

Driving myself to Louis Armstrong International Airport for the trip to New York, I took a wrong turn—no, you can't go all the way up on Broad Street— and found myself at the intersection of Jefferson Davis Parkway and Martin Luther King Jr. Boulevard. Suddenly a verse appeared, the second verse of that song I had started in 1992:

I live between Piety and Desire
On my one hand a blessing, on the other hot hellfire
By day I sweat, by night I perspire
At home between Piety and Desire.

O Death, where is thy sting?
I've been here six months and I don't feel a thing.
I hit a detour somewhere in the land of bling
And wound up where Jefferson Davis meets Martin Luther King.

Constance stayed behind in New Orleans. Besides our phone calls, I had her send me an e-mail every night when she powered down her computer and every morning first thing when she got up, just so I knew she was OK.

Online in New York, I read of the killing a block up from Commander's Palace that sent valets scurrying and frightened the hell out of patrons. A 2004 Dodge Magnum with Florida plates pulled up alongside an identical vehicle with Texas plates and opened fire. One dead, one hurt. Tara Young's account in the *Times-Picayune*, filed under the neatly alliterative headline of "Motorized Mayhem," noted that:

The mother of the critically wounded driver said he was her second son to be shot in recent days. . . . The mother said the son who was wounded Monday night was aware that someone wanted him dead too.

"He knows," the mother said. "He owns a gun and keeps it with him."

The mother, who now fears for her own life, said she also has bought a gun and carries it for her own protection.[10]

I wondered if I shouldn't maybe get a gun. I mentioned it to a couple of my Tulane friends, who looked at me like, a *gun?* Hell yes, a gun. I grew up with guns, but I've never owned one. If you fired a gun in our building in New York, you could easily hit one of our neighbors on the other side of our flimsy walls, ceiling, or floor. Whether through an accident, a terrible mistake, a moment of passion, or the gun falling into the hands of your enemy, people can get killed with a gun. And then you've got problems. That's why my home defense weapon of choice in New York—I came close to using it once—is a skull-cracking nightstick from the police supply store.

I had always thought that if I got a firearm for home defense, it would be a shotgun. But now I was inclining toward a pistol. Maybe because I could carry it with me if I needed to.

13

THE BLIZZARD OF '04

Coping with the peculiarities of a nineteenth-century house had become part of life. So when one day in early November Mr. Landlord mentioned that he was going to have the outside of the house painted, I said, fine.

Ha ha fucking ha.

Silly me, I had no idea that the first thing repainting the house entailed would be sanding off all the old paint. Large vibrating sanding wheels would be carefully, deliberately applied to every inch of the outer walls, slatted storm shutters and all, producing a harmonically rich din that resonated throughout the wooden structure, turning the entire house into something like a buzzsaw, or maybe a Magic Fingers motel bed, all day long while Constance was trying to write. This phase went on for over a month, resulting in paint chips and fine dust piling up in the dirt outside, containing whatever toxic elements they contained, even if the painters did make an attempt to catch most of it on their tarpaulins and then shake the tarpaulins out I know not where. Needless to say, the chips and dust and gunk also migrated inside the house. Did I mention I have dust allergies?

The paint-crew labor was Central American, with maybe a Mexican or two. Which was OK for me since I could converse with them. When they put the radio on really loud at eight in the morning right outside the window my still-sleeping head lay next to, I could very politely and respectfully ask them in impeccable Spanish to please, sir (third person formal), if you would be so kind, *turn it the fuck off!*

Nor, being foreigners, did they know about Thanksgiving, so we were jolted awake at eight A.M. on Thanksgiving morning by the house shaking from multiple sanders attacking its various sides simultaneously. One neigh-bor was already outside berating the workmen before we could get dressed. They packed up their sanders and left, sorry to miss a day of getting paid.

Bang, we were awake. I'd drunk a little extra beer the night before, think-ing to get a couple more hours in the sack in the morning. Oh, well, clear your head with coffee, Ned, and get ready for hard work: on to Chris's at three for our first Thanksgiving dinner of the day, then to Marilyn's by seven. New Orleanians can entertain like nobody else, and at both places the food was wonderful. Marilyn had a spectrum of rums on hand, and five of the hand-ful of Puerto Ricans in New Orleans were there, which made me feel extra-special at home. We played pass-the-guitar, singing and drinking till we got too sleepy, then carried leftovers home. New Orleans Thanksgiving: eating to satiation, twice.

The next morning, the painters didn't show up and we slept in. When I got up, I started writing, both about the results of my historical research and about the year we were having. For a time it was one jumbled-up project, then it separated out into two books. I elected to finish the book about New Orleans's first century of existence first, which was published in 2008 as *The World That Made New Orleans: From Spanish Silver to Congo Square*. But on the same day I began that book, I also started writing the text you've been reading, which I continued to rewrite and tweak over the subsequent years until the publisher ripped it out of my hands.

Thanksgiving was a good time to spend writing because it was no weekend to go driving around. If you live in New Orleans, you know that Thanksgiv-ing weekend is the State Farm Bayou Classic, to give it its proper name that reminds us that the insurance companies own our asses. It's the annual nation-ally televised football game at the Superdome between two rival black col-lege teams, the Southern University Jaguars and the Grambling State Tigers. Almost as big an attraction as the game itself was the night before, when the Dome was used for the McDonald's Battle of the Bands (that's marching bands, son) and Greek Show, with a stepping competition. After the game, the New Orleans Arena hosted the Classic Crunk Fest Explosion, with Atlanta's sex-and-weed rapper Ludacris, at the time in ultra-high rotation on Q-93 with "Red Light District," and a group named Disturbing the Peace.

Me, I was born without the sports gene. Grown men sweating all over each other, shoving their hands up between each other's butt cheeks, tromp-ing each other into the dirt, falling all over each other in a big pile, for con-trol of a *ball*? I never could understand why anyone would care if the Giants beat the Cowboys, or whatever. I'm the Vietnam generation, and I saw sports as training us to be sent off to war, with athletes playing the role of soldiers and cheerleaders playing the press. Oh, well, if I say anything else, I'll just get myself into trouble.

The State Farm Bayou Classic occasioned an invasion from out of town by fans of black college football and people who wanted to party with same. Attendance in 2004 was 68,911, so the streets and highways were next to impassable all weekend, as I found out when we tried to go to the Bywater on Friday night. I had never *heard* of the Bayou Classic, and here I was ensnared in its traffic. I had learned what every New Orleanian knows: stay home during Bayou Classic weekend. It's a pain in the ass.

On Bourbon Street, someone fired a gun into the Sunday crowd and wounded three people, but nobody died, so it hardly counted.

One day when I wasn't home, Mrs. Landlord, baby in tow, accidentally locked herself out of the house and came knocking on the door. Would it be OK if she came in through our place?

How would she do that? Constance wondered, and let her in. She started up the spiral staircase toward the ceiling, where a circular partition had been dropped in when I didn't want to rent the top space. She popped open the ceiling plug and continued upward through the hole, into the vacant room on top, and on to her place in back.

We hadn't realized you could do that. I guess that meant someone could come down from the vacant room into our house too. Hmmm.

The painters arrived every day, except when they didn't. Usually they were already at work when I got up. You couldn't see in through our windows unless you climbed up on tall ladders, but that's exactly where they were, on tall ladders right outside our windows. As I sat in my informal wear at the antique bench table in the dining room after rising, sunlight flooding in from the upper part of the windows as I drank morning coffee and checked e-mail, there were faces peering down at me. I started making sure I wasn't indecently dressed when I stumbled into the kitchen to make coffee.

It wasn't that the painters wanted to be peepers, but they had no choice. Pretty much wherever they were positioned around the house, they faced into a window as they worked, staring in at us for hours at a stretch. They kept poker faces no matter what detail of our lives they happened to see. However, if one were not the trusting sort—if one lived in a high-crime area, say—one might also consider that the painters had a pretty good idea of whatever there was inside the house that might be worth anything. At night, the painters left their ladders on the premises, horizontally on the ground, so anyone who knew the ladders were there could easily have sneaked up and peeked in or gained access to the second-story windows of the vacant apartment upstairs. Further facilitating the possibility, the painters also tended to leave the gates to the backyard open and unlocked. We complained to the contractor about it.

The whole month of December they were there. I left the house every day for Tulane, but Constance stayed alone in the house, working on her computer. She was more than a little creeped out to have a group of men surrounding the house, peering in, all day long, every day. Nor does she speak Spanish. Not that any of the crew was in any way disrespectful, ever; they were always polite, and even deferential, as people working illegally in a foreign country must be. They used the space outside the kitchen door (which had a window in it) for their sawhorse, and as Constance chopped and cooked, there they all were, their gaze facing into the house, unable to avoid watching her as she worked in the kitchen within their field of vision. She wasn't about to get down on the floor and exercise with men looking in. When she wanted to get to the washing machines out back to do laundry, the front door was blocked by ladders.

There was a gang of men—not a crime gang, a work gang, but a gang nonetheless—surrounding the house, looking in at us, intermittently, for pretty close to the rest of the time we stayed in New Orleans.

Constance no longer loved living in the house. In a way I was relieved, because I'd been afraid she'd want to stay in New Orleans and I knew I didn't. I was only passing through.

On December 22, the painters didn't appear. Instead, the termite treatment guy woke me up, knocking on the door. I had no idea the termite guy was coming. It wasn't termite season yet. Termite season is in late May, when the winged beasts swarm in dense black clouds under streetlights, in vacant fields, wherever. Formosan termites are thought to have come to the port of New Orleans after World War II in wooden packing crates from Asia. In a city of wooden houses, they have a banquet. They cost New Orleans property owners something like three hundred million dollars a year in damage control. The termite treatment guy wanted to know a whole bunch of things that I had no answers for.

When we next saw Mr. Landlord, who flew in from D.C. to spend the weekend in New Orleans with his family every couple or three weeks, he was excited about his new job—repairing printers, I think it was, though I'm not sure. It was in the . . .

White House.

That would be the Bush White House. The Karl Rove White House. Which was about to begin a merry stolen second term.

It was a good job, indeed. We were happy for him.

Maybe it was my imagination, but after that, his personality seemed to change.

In spite of having a regular income, I was screwing up on the bills.

Since I was only going to be in New Orleans ten months, I had opted not to change my addresses with all the companies I pay money out to and then have to change them back. Instead, I stupidly had my mail forwarded. I don't know what's up with the U.S. Post Office and New Orleans, but forwarded mail took so long to arrive—and sometimes didn't arrive—that by the time I got my credit card statements my payments were already late. I know, I know, it's my responsibility to make the payments on time. I got confused, or maybe distracted, and pretty soon I had made late payments at some point to all four of my credit cards. The interest rates shot up into the stratosphere. I'm just glad they can't put you in prison for debt, the way they could in old London or in Dubai now, and I wondered if that might not be in the offing.

I was broker now with a salary than when I was a freelancer, and further in debt. I had maxed out my checking account overdraft capacity in New York in the process of moving to New Orleans—my bank account in New York was thirty-five hundred dollars in the hole, at 18 percent—to say nothing of my four credit cards. I was paying out a ridiculous amount of interest every month, and continuing to accrue it. Now I was *really* living the middle-class life: I was a cash cow for finance profiteers.

I had medical insurance for the year, which I was required by Tulane to carry at my own expense—it didn't come with the fellowship—but we couldn't afford it for Constance, who was the one who really needed it, given that she was in constant pain from her back and really should have been seeing a physical therapist. Forget it. Insurance is a protection racket and the insurance companies are organized crime. Pay or die. We couldn't pay the protection. I was starting to wonder what would happen after that last check in June.

But I had enough cash on hand to buy po'boys and beer. *Cuba and Its Music* was getting rave reviews from people I admired. It took me three years to write, with no job and basically no income, for which I received an advance representing about two months' living expenses from the small publisher for whom even that advance was a lot to pay out. It was no bestseller, but the publisher's gamble—and, I felt, my editor's faith in me—had paid off. *Cuba and Its Music* had just been listed the number-two music book of 2004 in the year-end *Rolling Stone*, behind Bob Dylan's *Chronicles, Vol. 1*.

Maybe I would see some royalties.

The two facing mansions on St. Charles that had been the Kerry and Bush headquarters, respectively, were now competitively decked out for Christmas. We drove slowly up and down the beautiful avenue one chilly evening, admiring the rich folks' displays.

We weren't alone for Christmas. Tom Andre, a resourceful young New Orleanian from uptown who had been helpful to me getting oriented, invited us to his mother's house for dinner on Christmas Eve. He had produced what was by all accounts a fabulous New Orleans–Brazil festival, involving travel to both places by collaborating musicians, the kind of thing we need more of. We were happy to be part of something familial, feeling something a little like at home, enjoying the Christmas spirit in Tom's mother's lovely home off St. Charles.

Christmas Day was dreary and wet, but it was a day of good feelings. We began it as we had celebrated Thanksgiving, at Marilyn's house. As we left Marilyn's in the overcast late afternoon, it was snowing lightly, flakes dancing in the gray. It doesn't snow in New Orleans at all most years, but on Christmas Day 2004 it did.

Everyone in town was changing shifts right then to go to the next Christmas hang. Ours was out to New Orleans East, where Felipe Smith's family was holding their annual Christmas open house. Felipe is an associate professor of English and director of the Africa and African Diaspora Studies program. He's an Afro-Orleanian exactly my age, born in New Orleans and shaped by the experience of the school desegregation battle and the changes wrought pursuant to white flight. But his parents came from Honduras, so growing up in the Seventh Ward, he had the status of an outsider.[1] Well, intellectuals are outsiders in the United States anyway. If there was a more incisive scholar at Tulane, I didn't meet him or her all year. Felipe's work emphasizes race and ethnicity in modernist American literature, but his thought is applicable way beyond that specialization. I was partway through his book, *American Body Politics: Race, Gender, and Black Literary Renaissance*, which became an important text for me, giving me historical information and a set of analytical tools with which to think about issues of race and racism I was groping at. My understanding of ideas from it resonates throughout this present volume. It isn't quick reading: after a couple of pages I would find myself stopping to think about what he'd said. It's academic in the best sense, where the uncommon vocabulary is at the service of precision. At its core is iron, as it projects a calm, reasonable expression of cold moral rage with scholarship and insight.

Felipe had the longest commute of anyone I knew at Tulane. Part of the Ninth Ward, New Orleans East sits on the patch of reclaimed swampland between the Lower Ninth Ward and Lake Pontchartrain, bounded by the Industrial Canal on the west, the lake on the north, and MR-GO on the south, with the Lower Ninth Ward on the other side of Mister Go. Developed in the 1970s, it has the reputation of being a middle-class black suburb, but it's home to a variety of classes, and it's not only black. There are plenty of Yats there. It's the principal base of one of New Orleans's few visible minorities, the Vietnamese community—a post–Vietnam War diaspora, mostly Catholic and obviously conservative, but with divergent attitudes among its younger generation.

To get to New Orleans East, we had to drive on I-10 over the Industrial Canal, on something called the High Rise, an alternative to a drawbridge: a bridge that curves sharply up into the air so as to be arched high enough to let boats pass beneath. It's a surreal moment, driving upward on a bridge toward a vanishing point in the sky. Let alone when it's snowing. In New Orleans.

It was getting dark at the end of the short winter afternoon. New Orleanians don't know how to drive on snow and ice, and cars spun out of control left and right. Not that there was any accumulation. To anyone from back east, this was nothing. But people *really* didn't know how to drive in it, and unfortunately, despite the slipperiness of the road, the congestion, and the poor visibility, slowing down didn't seem to occur to them. It didn't help that so many of them were on Christmas party shift change and were at least a little drunk. I negotiated the High Rise warily in nearly bumper-to-bumper traffic that was moving faster than it should have been, given how sloppy the roads were becoming and how flaky the drivers were. We passed one flipped-over SUV, then another.

Felipe is one of the few people I know in academia to manage the feat of having his career in the same town he grew up in. His wife, Roslyn, from the Ninth Ward, is an area superintendent of schools for Orleans Parish. She comes from a family of twelve, so holidays at their wonderfully spacious two-story home are high-traffic affairs. I met brothers and in-laws, nephews and nieces, everyone. The gumbo was as good as any I've ever had, and there was turkey, ham, tons of holiday food. But outside it kept continuing to spit snow. I stayed sober. We didn't know whether the snow would accumulate or how crazy the roads would get, but we figured they wouldn't be out spreading salt like they do in places where they plan for this. We excused ourselves and left to drive home on the unfamiliar wet roads in the dark, which was worse than coming out had been. Every twist and turn seemed dramatic under these peculiar, unstable conditions, but my Saturn obeyed me. I soldiered on, forging a manly bond with my car, thinking of my insurance payments. I turned up WWOZ as loud as it would go. Constance's passenger-seat confidence in my driving skills made me feel extra responsible.

It had snowed less than an inch, but that was enough to discombobulate the city.

We had survived the blizzard of '04.

Late on Christmas Day we heard news of a catastrophic tsunami in South Asia. By the twenty-seventh, television was filled with images of it.

I stopped by Parasol's that evening to get Constance her martini to go and me a couple of Guinness-Abita black-and-tans in go-cups. With draft beer available for less than what a can of beer costs at the deli in SoHo, I was losing the habit of drinking any other kind of beer. I ordered myself a bar-b-q beef po'boy to go, hold the mayo, giving myself permission to have my one po'boy for March a few months early. At this rate, I could be eating my 2007 allotment of po'boys by summer 2005.

The place was jammed, unusual at that time of the evening. I wondered if it was a seasonal rush or some big sports event and said something about it to the barmaid. She shrugged and said, "It's the tsunami."

People were looking up at the TV screen on high, as people in bars do.

I couldn't tell if she was making a joke or not. As I made my way out of Parasol's with my po'boy and our drinks, I passed a red-nosed man talking loudly to anyone who might be listening.

"Never evacuate!" he said. "Never evacuate!"

That night, I wrote a friend: "It is by no means unthinkable that the casualty levels of the Southeast Asia tsunami of December 26, 2004, when twenty thousand or more people were wiped out by a wall of water, could occur in New Orleans." Actually, that number was more like 230,000. A major factor in the fatalities in South Asia, not surprisingly, was the disappearance over the last three decades of mangrove forests from the river deltas, converted to shrimp and fish farms. Previously they had acted as barriers to block the surge from high water.

Tourists are sometimes warned that if they leave the French Quarter, they might be accosted and perhaps killed. True, there are predators. It's not a good idea to walk around exploring at night in New Orleans. If you venture into some places within walking distance of the Quarter without knowing what you're doing, you might find yourself in hostile territory. But, as the "Goth murder" made clear, you could get killed just as dead if you got crossed up with the wrong people in the French Quarter.

At about one A.M. on the morning of Friday, December 31, 2004, Levon Jones, a twenty-five-year-old African American senior at Georgia Southern University, was jumped by three bouncers in front of Razzoo's, a big, flashy Bourbon Street dive. It happened in the course of an argument that began when one of Jones's flag-football teammates was denied admission because of an alleged dress code whose implementation was not otherwise readily apparent. This is, needless to say, the most common excuse used to keep black men out of a club, on a street where the clubs were off limits to black people until well into the '60s, and Jones's friends weren't buying it. Then Levon Jones was down on the ground with three guys on him, and he didn't get up again. The bouncers said Jones sucker-punched one of them. But the incident was photographed and videoed, so it was hard to deny how it played out: the cops stood by while one bouncer held Jones's legs, another sat on his back, compressing his chest, and a third held him in a head vise-grip, strangling him. They kept him down like that for from twelve to fourteen minutes. Finally the cops cuffed him, then let him lie there for some minutes before they noticed he was motionless. Then they uncuffed his dead hands and called the paramedics.[2]

There was anger over the killing. The NAACP held a protest outside the bar. There was a protest from the Greater New Orleans Coalition of Ministers, a group of fifteen leading African American ministers.[3] The words *murder* and *lynching* were used. Jones's family filed a lawsuit, and a second suit was filed against Razzoo's that same week, by one Clayton Spears, which alleged that a year before, "two Razzoo bouncers pounced on him, twisted his arms behind his back and dragged him across the club floor to a side alley. . . . There the bouncers knocked his feet out from under him and slammed his face into a brick wall until he lost consciousness."[4]

The bad publicity made no visible dent in Razzoo's business, where the crowds kept howling for three-for-one drinks as fast as the barmaid's elbow could pump.

Q-93 was advertising a New Year's Eve show by B. Gizzle, but we went to visit Chris and a very pregnant Ladee, strolling out to their front porch for the midnight countdown. Down toward Tchoupitoulas, the air was full of smoke from firecrackers, pistols, small sticks of dynamite, and for all I know surface-to-air missiles, rolling like thunder or maybe the ultimate arena-rock drum solo. That's what Louis Armstrong got put in the Colored Waifs' Home for: shooting off a pistol in the exuberance of New Year's Eve on December 31, 1912.

I proposed a toast:

May we survive
2005
And have no more
2004.

And so I ended my fall semester at Tulane University, to the sound of jubilation in a war zone. At 12:39 A.M., New Orleans's first homicide of 2005 occurred in the Seventh Ward when twenty-eight-year-old Daniel Washington was "shot several times in the head and abdomen," said the *Times-Picayune*. The second homicide of 2005 was discovered later that day: a twenty-seven-year-old woman found dead at a home in Algiers along with a live child, who was covered in blood.

On January 2, at Galatoire's, the old-school French Quarter restaurant that still has the same nutritional concepts it had in 1905, a retired sixty-nine-year-old radiologist tossed an after-dinner mint onto a table where another party was dining. A twenty-eight-year-old diner from Dallas at the table, apparently unaware that this was a traditional greeting, took it as an insult. He followed the radiologist outside, slammed the elderly man's head down into the sidewalk in front of the restaurant, fracturing his skull, then calmly returned to his dinner.[5]

Down on the other side of Jackson, on Constance between Terpsichore and Euterpe, Dan Rose and Peggy O'Neill had a problem. They had moved to a nice block, with lovely old buildings. But there was some drug dealing going on, quite openly, a couple of blocks upriver from them, and sometime in December the police installed a surveillance camera on that block. In response, the thugs moved their operations to Dan and Peggy's block and began hanging out all day directly in front of their house, sitting on their car. When Dan and Peggy came home with groceries, the drug dealers had to get off their steps so they could pass to their front door. They weren't mean or threatening. They were polite. More or less. At first.

But then there were the occasional episodes of gunfire outside.

It was just about time for Mardi Gras.

14

KING KONG

Cultures unfold not in physical or global time but in local time—that is, in time as the natives constructed and interpret it.

Jan Assmann, *The Mind of Egypt*[1]

Thirty-three days is a cruelly short party season in New Orleans.

Mardi Gras—literally, Fat Tuesday—is not merely a day, it's the final day of carnival, and Mardi Gras is shorthand for the entire season of festivity that leads up to that day. It begins on January 6 (Epiphany or Twelfth Night for the English, Día de Reyes for the Spanish) and continues up to the actual day of Mardi Gras, or, as the Brits call it, Shrove Tuesday. The last twelve days are very busy.

Mardi Gras is a moveable feast, dated by the full moon. Which is to say that it's at heart a pagan holiday: lunar festivals trace back very far in human history, to Egypt at least, and on to the rest of Africa, where they have been part of life quite possibly since the dawn of consciousness. Fat Tuesday can fall anywhere between February 3 and March 9 in a given year, and in 2005 it fell on February 8. So the season would be short and dense with activity. Blame it on the moon.

In the weeks leading up to Mardi Gras, there are balls and parades of all sorts. There are church services, fancy-dress debutante balls, formal dinners, costume parties, fundraising events, orgies, a parade for dogs (the Krewe of Barkus), and one for cats (the Krewe of Endymeow). There's even more music in the bars than usual. There are Mardi Gras Indian practices on Sunday nights, if you know someone who knows where they are. The royal chromatic combo of purple, green, and gold that announces Mardi Gras is everywhere in the decor of New Orleans—front porches, doorsteps, signage, hats. The colors are even on the frosting of king cake, a high-calorie brioche ring with a miniature plastic baby hidden somewhere in it. La Boulangerie on Magazine does a brisk business in this obligatory French-derived Mardi Gras pastry during the weeks between Epiphany and Ash Wednesday. A king cake was the last thing we needed. I bought one anyway.

The season kicked off as usual on the chilly night of January 6 with the streetcar ride of the Phunny Phorty Phellows, a modern (1981) revival of a group founded in 1878. When the group was first founded, its great novelty was precisely that it was funny—OK, phunny. Post-Reconstruction Carnival had become a set of highly serious pageants of would-be civic royalty, and the PPPs were formed to poke fun and lighten it up. In 2005, as they did every year, the PPP's costumed maskers boarded the streetcar at the far uptown barn where the streetcars sleep on Carrollton Street and rode the whole distance to Canal, retrograding the city's historical expansion into uptown. Along the way they ate king cake, made champagne toasts, and second lined on board the streetcar, complete with a brass band.

But before the 2005 Mardi Gras season could really get under way, there was one more Sunday afternoon second line to go on, the only one that happens during Mardi Gras season: the Bayou Steppers. It's a unique Social Aid and Pleasure Club, founded in 2002 as a biracial organization with both a black president and a white president. Its anniversary parade is one of only a few second lines to take in both uptown and downtown.

Their four-hour march began at the Purple Rain at Washington and Saratoga, uptown, and ended at the Mother-in-Law Lounge on North Claiborne downtown in the Tremé, right under the trestles of I-10. In between, the Steppers made their customary rest stops. (In Louis Armstrong's day, when these stops were at members' houses, they were called "punches.")[2] They stopped at the New Look at La Salle and Washington; at Donna's, the music bar at St. Ann and Rampart, across from Congo Square, where I joined the parading party in progress; at Little Peoples Place on Barracks near Tremé; and at Dumaine St. Gang at N. Robertson and Dumaine. At each one, there was plenty of time to have a beer and a pork chop sandwich with my friends before rolling on again. There was Joel Dinerstein—he never misses a second line. There was Garnette, and Vicki.

The Bayou Steppers were decked out in purple from head to toe, with hats and sashes. Antoinette K-Doe was a queen up front riding in her pink Cadillac convertible. Al Johnson, whose song "Carnival Time" (1960) is a Mardi Gras perennial with oddly unpredictable numbers of measures, was an honoree as well. Elder drummer Lionel Batiste was there. It was a fine second line on a beautiful day, with lots of high stepping and no small amount of reefer smoke wafting through the air.

The good feeling stopped, however, when we reached the endpoint, under the dank shadow of I-10, at the door to the Mother-in-Law. The parade had run slightly overtime—like five minutes—against a very strict clock. I had just snapped a picture of Bayou Stepper Michael "Aldo" Andrews, as his nephew James ("Twelve") Andrews and the New Birth Brass Band tore into what was obviously their finale from the front doorstep of the Mother-in-Law.

It was overtime, and the cops were not inclined to let the band finish their last few bars. The law must be obeyed to the letter in New Orleans, at least if you're black. The cops turned a number, maybe seven, of their car sirens on at full blast, right in the assembled crowd's face, drowning out the band completely. It's the rudest thing you can do to a musician aside from physical assault. It was loud enough to be deafening, and the effect was intentional. Cherry tops were spinning like it was a drug bust or a terrorist swat. You must disperse!

Uh, I was supposed to hook up with my friends here who have a car, mine is back by Donna's, and it's too loud to use my cell phone, the Mother-in-Law's already full, where am I supposed to go around here?

The cops in New Orleans had been calling time on Sunday—that's enough outta you—all the way back to the Congo Square days, when they dispersed the dancers with cutlasses at the appointed hour. The people were used to it. Refusing to be baited by the provocation, they just took it—not only the physical insult to their hearing from the piercing, ultra-loud sirens, but the blatant disrespect to their culture. The same blatant disrespect that in 1968 put up those trestles we were all standing under, when North Claiborne was replaced with I-10 running overhead all down its length. Well, if I were to catalog the disrespect, it would be a long litany.

The police in New Orleans know very well that there's a thin line between a parade and a riot. They also know, or should know, that the most notorious riots in New Orleans history—and there have been a few—were by white people.

I never saw the police close down a white folks' parade like that.

The Krewe du Vieux (pronounced *kroo-doo-voo*, applying the New Orleans *oo* rule for all French vowel combinations) parades early in the season every year: a raunchy, satirical krewe that parades downtown, through the French Quarter, which the bigger krewes can't do. They make a point of hiring multiple brass bands, so it's a music fan's delight. Their parade is composed of different sub-krewes, one of which, the Krewe of Drips and Discharges, paraded with a float featuring a gigantic dripping penis. I saw it on their website but didn't see the real thing, because we had the flu, flat-out knocked out, on our backs, delirious with a fever, as sick as I've ever been. I was also unable to go to the Jazz Funeral for Democracy, scheduled to coincide with the second inaugural of George W. Bush. We missed the Martin Luther King Day parade, an enormous event in New Orleans. We had to wait to recuperate before we could go over and see Chris and Ladee, who had a new baby, Joaquín, born on January 21. Welcome to New Orleans, Joaquín.

Walking out to my car one morning in midwinter, I learned yet another accent in the New Orleans calendar rhythm, a messy one: the week the hackberries drop off the trees. Not all the trees in New Orleans are live oaks and magnolias. The hackberry tree, which looks something like an elm, is the pigeon of the tree world. The hackberries, also known as sugar berries, drop in clusters and splatter all over the place. Parked beneath the overhead canopy of trees, your car gets covered, and I mean covered, with gooey purple-black blobs that spread out in circles like high-impact bird shit. It happens one week, suddenly and decisively. At that point a visit to the car wash becomes mandatory, but you gotta wait in line.

Meanwhile, it was time for what most people think of as Mardi Gras: those giant parades that go along St. Charles with floats and marching bands and thick sprays of beads flying through the air. These uptown parades are formal processions that feature floats riding high up in the air, with a clear separation between participants and spectators. They're very different from second lines, which are not Mardi Gras–related events and which are street-level participatory parades that go through different neighborhoods in the city, picking up people as they strut along.

My graduate assistant, Stephanie Clark, was in a women's marching society called the Camel Toe Lady Steppers, in its second year of parading. Still recuperating, I crawled to their fine fundraising party at the King Bolden Bar on Rampart Street on January 28, where a roomful of pink-clad women pranced to New Orleans's #1 funky vinyl DJ, Soul Sister.

By then, the krewes were rolling. Pygmalion, Pontchartrain, Oshun, Shangri-La, Sparta, Pegasus, Carrollton, King Arthur and Merlin, Bards of Bohemia, Ancient Druids, Morpheus. . . . The time slots these krewes occupied were negotiated over a long history, the beginnings of which go back to before the war of southern rebellion. Since we lived only five blocks below St. Charles, it was an easy walk up to the krewe parades, so I took in as many of them as I could, playing amateur anthropologist once again.

All along St. Charles, people staked out their turf on the neutral ground with custom-made high viewing stools. There were two or three parades a day, rolling one after the other, on float after float, each filled with krewe members in uniform neutral masks that made them all faceless. (Being masked is historically a privilege accorded float riders but denied street particpants.) There was a facelessness to the parades as well. The large number of parades—they also have them in Jefferson and St. Bernard Parishes—and the economics of annual ritual have combined to make for standardized floats that are recycled and redecorated from year to year, most of them more or less similar to each other even as the krewes vie to make their parades seem distinctive. So while there's no central Mardi Gras organization to coordinate things, there's kind of an overall look to the parades, and I got bored with them pretty quickly.

A city law forbids advertising on Mardi Gras floats, so the numbing level of uniformity of corporate decor that goes with our larger public events doesn't disfigure Mardi Gras. But there were military recruitment vehicles, with people in uniform tossing out beads and trinkets soliciting you to join the Navy, Marines, Army, Air Force, or National Guard. Overhead, a chic orange-and-white Coast Guard HH-D65 Dolphin helicopter buzzed low over the parades the whole time, "in an effort to reduce crime during Mardi Gras," says the Coast Guard's webpage. I had previously thought of crime prevention as the responsibility of the police, not the military, but the Coast Guard is now part of Homeland Security, which can do any damn thing it wants.[3] In any case, we had gotten used to the sound of low-flying helicopters over the Irish Channel; it was part of the general at-war feel.

Mardi Gras parades rely heavily on school marching bands. With the money the bands earn, they can buy instruments, uniforms, etc. There are restrictions on how many days they can parade in a row because it's hard work for the kids, who often look tired. Most parades a school band might play are a mile and a half or so, but Mardi Gras parades can be six miles long. School bands from out of town that don't know how to pace themselves burn out a quarter of the way through. The repertoire leans heavily toward pop tunes, sometimes those with one-note melodies. I think I heard one old-school Sousa-type military march the whole season.

But what the parades are really about is beads—tons and tons of brightly colored, shiny, Chinese-made, acrylic beads on strings, thrown from double-decker floats that ride as high in the air as the tree canopy and overhead cabling will permit. This medieval *noblesse oblige* of the lordly on high tossing coins to the rabble below is commemorated in various versions throughout the hemisphere.[4] On January 6 in mid-nineteenth-century Havana, to take one example, the palace would be opened to the crowds outside for Kings' Day and the governor would throw out coins—the *aguinaldo*—to the multitude, a tradition also commemorated in Puerto Rican holiday celebrations.

Every krewe member buys his or her own throws. One person I know spent nine hundred dollars on them. Imagine how many strings of beads nine hundred dollars will buy and multiply that by all the people who ride on all the floats in all the parades—Endymion alone has a thousand members—and you understand why the city spends so much money street-sweeping literally thousands of tons of post-parade trash, in effect subsidizing this vision of carnival, and why so many New Orleanians wind up with bags full of beads at home, including me.

But knowing all that doesn't prepare you for the frenzy the bead-throwing inspires. It took control of me almost immediately. As the float passes, and the people on it toss out strings to the passers-by—well, first of all, you have to put your hands up in the air to protect your face, because if you're not careful a string of beads will catch you smack between the eyes, which is an extra drag if you wear glasses. But once your hands are up in the air? You *want* the prize. It's almost instinctual. You have become one of the multitude, shouting at the riders for beads, competing with others to grab them as they fly through the air, scooping them up off the ground when no one catches them. You put them around your neck—what else are you going to do with them?—and you notice that some of them are bigger and prettier than others. And you want more of the big, pretty ones to adorn yourself with. I can't explain it. I was astounded at how easily I was swept into it. I guess this is what sports fans experience, the rush of excitement over something ultimately meaningless. This was the magical moment of uptown carnival: bead lust. Gimme, gimme, gimme! It goes on along St. Charles day after day, in parade after parade.

It's a very American idea of carnival—compete with the greed-crazed mob to get yours, and never mind how many tons of trash you produce. It's only symbolic money, of course, because the beads are worthless. But they're shiny. Their ultimate mission is to beautify our landfills. Many of the beads tossed from on high never reach the crowd and spend eternity glinting in the branches of the trees.

The last week before Mardi Gras was dense. On Wednesday night at six, I was there when the Krewe of Saturn's parade rolled—I was attending on behalf of my car—then stayed for Muses, the whimsical ladies' krewe that parades with a float of giant high-heeled shoes, trimmed with lights that flash and blink in the dark. The year before, gunfire on the Muses parade route killed eighteen-year-old Latasha Bell, which resulted in the enactment of a law that added extra jail time for shooting anyone within one thousand feet of a parade.

I caught a pair of miniature pink squeeze-toy plastic pumps that Muses threw out along with their beads. The Camel Toe Steppers were there, flossing pink and black coochie-cutters and white go-go boots with black tassels, marching in the street between floats, shouting their womanist motto: *Hey! Ho! We got camel toe!* The Pussy Footers were there. So was another womens' marching society, the Bearded Oysters, who wore furry merkins. A theme emerged.

New Orleanians live with snarled traffic during Mardi Gras. The krewe people and the police have the logistics down to a science, but it causes blockups driving all those slow-moving floats to the stepoff point where the parade begins. They get there in a caravan, and if you run into one you might be sitting in your car for a few minutes. People improvise alternate routes to avoid them. Take extra time to get anywhere uptown that week.

And they rolled on: Krewe d'Etat, Hermes, Isis, Endymion. I was carrying pounds of beads around my neck. Then Sunday was a quadruple-header: Okeanos, Thoth (pronounced *toath*), Mid-City, and Bacchus.

Though most of the krewes in New Orleans go down St. Charles for much of their parade, they don't all take identical routes, and many of them had different routes historically. My favorite krewe, if I have one, is Thoth, named for the Egyptian god of hieroglyphic script, the scribe-deity who recorded the utterances of Ptah, the creator from Memphis; their route historically zigzagged because it paraded past hospitals and institutions for the benefit of shut-ins.

A friend who lives near the Bacchus parade route was hosting a party, and we trundled over to her house, parking in an illegal space and accepting as the parking fee the bright orange ticket. As if to compound the ceremonial importance of the event, it was also the night of yet another annual ritual, the Super Bowl. (Sometimes the Super Bowl has been held in the hopefully named Superdome, playing havoc with the Mardi Gras parade schedule, but not in 2005.) It was the year after Janet Jackson's nip-slip at the halftime show brought the phrase *wardrobe malfunction* into the American vocabulary, and the Super Bowl was taking no chances on having a sexually intriguing star this year. As we got into the Bacchic spirit with numerous libations, a sports-fan contingent of the party, glued to the TV in a back room, watched a grizzled Sir Paul McCartney pound out "Hey Jude."

Bacchus is one of three gargantuan "superkrewes," the others being Endymion and Orpheus. It's egalitarian in the American way: you don't have to be from an old family to join, you just have to be able to pay. Its parade, which began in 1969, represents the influence of the televised spectacle. King Bacchus is played by an imported media celebrity; the first King Bacchus was Danny Kaye, and in 2005 it was Sean Astin, whom I suppose I should Google so I can find out who he is. Needless to say, there has never been an African American King Bacchus.

Bacchus's floats were based on fantastical characters from what are deemed kids' movies. Beads and souvenir tchotchkes flew through the air by the palletload. Then a ride came along that wasn't tossing beads, but was being *hit* by beads thrown from the crowd. I didn't see this reverse-flow bead throw at any other carnival parade.

It was an eighteen-foot tall statue of King Kong, glowering fiercely, his arms upraised as he rolled along. People pelted him with beads. Mercilessly. It reminded me of stoning in the ancient world. There were no people on the float to hurt, so you could throw as hard as you wanted. The float was for that purpose, apparently, with a big container to catch the beads, and it was a tradition, since everyone already knew to do it.

Was I really seeing what I thought I was seeing?

The parade continued, and some floats later, there was a female version: Queen Kong. This effigy was more anthropomorphic than the first.

It looked like a giant caricature of a fat, scowling, ugly black woman, with a bow in her hair, a bikini top, a bulging bare midriff, and a short skirt.

I couldn't believe it. Well, yeah, I could. The ape libel. I'm looking at the photo of the Queen Kong float right now on the Krewe of Bacchus website. They're proud of it. Again the crowd gleefully vented its aggressions, pelting the giant lady ape with dense volleys of hurled beads.

And later: a giant Baby Kong, wearing a baby bonnet and holding a banana. Those monkey babies! Slam!

King Kong is one of Bacchus's signature floats, introduced in 1972 when the theme was "the Bacchus Book of Horrors." I can hear the objections now: lighten up, you Tulane eggheads are so politically correct, don't make trouble, it's just good fun, it was a great movie, my kids love it, it's a Mardi Gras tradition.

I'm not the first to find a racial allegory in the 1932 film *King Kong*. Nor am I suggesting that people who pelt King Kong with beads in the Bacchus parade are necessarily thinking racist thoughts. I have no idea what they're thinking.

But I saw what I saw.

It's one of those things white people and black people tend to interpret differently. Some white people Constance and I talked to thought we were kinda off the wall with this. Black people we talked to didn't.

Let's start by remembering that Mardi Gras is all about tradition and symbolism, as we unpack the image of the gorilla in Mardi Gras lore.

New Orleans was taken by the Union early in the Civil War, in 1862, and with it control of the Mississippi River. The city was to provide a model for Reconstruction and its discontents even as the Union Army struggled to subdue the rest of the South. To the horror of white Louisianans, once black people in Louisiana could vote (as of 1867, and over a number of dead bodies), they became legislators and rewrote the state's constitution in 1868— the so-called black and tan constitution—to desegregate schools and public accommodations.[5] As of 1871, African American children could go to public school. Their parents could serve on juries in judgment of whites. President Grant, whose reputation has never recovered from the southern smear campaign against him, saw implementing civil rights as necessary to redeem the bloodshed of the Civil War. A federal anti–Ku Klux law was passed in 1871, and he enforced it vigorously, obtaining the indictments of some three thousand KKK terrorists. The election of 1872 was "the fairest and most democratic presidential election in the South until 1968."[6] It was an extraordinary moment.

The per capita black population of New Orleans in 1860 was one of the lowest in the city's history—about 24,000 out of almost 170,000 total.[7] But ten years later it had more than doubled as newly emancipated people moved from the country to the city, swelling its population of color to over fifty thousand. Granting them civil rights was not merely benevolence on the part of northerners; there was an active campaign on the part of political leaders of color, who were by and large not ex-slaves but people who came from the antebellum families of free people of color. In Louisiana's three-tiered caste system, these prominent individuals were not "black" but "mulatto." Many of them came from the French Quarter, and many spoke French.[8] Some had been educated in France, and they generally looked to Europe for their models of culture. They saw no cultural continuity between themselves and the newly emancipated, darker-skinned, English-speaking masses. The stakes were high for this caste of people; if there were to be civil rights for black people, they could lose their privileged positions vis-à-vis the lower caste. But if there were not to be civil rights, they would remain disadvantaged with respect to whites.

The first nonwhite lieutenant governor of Louisiana was Oscar Dunn, a mulatto former house painter, steamboat barber, and music teacher. He took office in 1868 and died in 1871, under circumstances that strongly suggested arsenic poisoning.[9] His post was filled by the president pro tempore of the state senate, Pinckney Benton Stewart Pinchback. Educated in the North, Pinchback was the light-skinned son of a wealthy white plantation owner and a formerly enslaved mother, and was an associate of the corrupt carpetbag Republican governor Henry Clay Warmoth. When the state legislature impeached Warmoth on December 9, 1872, Pinchback became governor of Louisiana for thirty-four days. To the ex-Confederates, it was as though the Antichrist had taken over.

It was a high artistic period in New Orleans. Edgar Degas, the archetypal Parisian artist whose mother was a Saint-Domingan-descended New Orleanian, spent the winter of 1872–73 with the Louisiana branch of his family, during which he painted A Cotton Office in New Orleans, one of the best-known depictions of nineteenth-century American business. Reconstruction-era carnival was the fine-arts wing of the campaign for white supremacy and removal of black people from the political process, a campaign that achieved its goals through torture, murder, and the violent repression of the entire black population of the South. The most notorious Mardi Gras ever was that of 1873, at which the Mistick Krewe of Comus achieved the perfect artistic expression of their obsessive themes of miscegenation and misrule in the grand spectacle "The Missing Links to Darwin's Origin of the Species." It mocked both Darwin's theory of evolution and Reconstruction politicians, depicting recognizable figures of the day in beautifully rendered but uncomplimentary caricatures that merged animal and human—sometimes Negroid—features.

Comus's full-color program book, and the costumes for its Darwin parade and ball, set new standards for concept and design even as its racial and political antagonism set new standards of vitriol. The cigar-smoking President Grant was portrayed as a tobacco grub. Warmoth was a snake, and cross-eyed General Benjamin Butler (who received the popular nickname of "Beast" Butler after he hung a gambler who tore down the Union flag, to say nothing of Butler's having organized black regiments) was a hyena. The likenesses were impressively accurate. I have examined the one hundred leaves of this bestiary in Tulane's Louisiana Collection, and despite the obvious skill and misdirected charm of the artist the cumulative effect is depressing. An Indian with feathers on top is depicted as a coiled rattlesnake with a forked tongue, a monkey in a jockey's cap and coat plays tambourine, a black grasshopper plays a fiddle, an African American is depicted as a leech. There are many white figures as well, each apparently caricaturing some specific individual, but however each is caricatured, all of them are unremittingly ugly.

Comus's carnival was a cultural event with national reach, as written up in the *New York Times*:

> It was the finest display they have yet given, consisting of more than 200 [sic] figures, all in the most elaborate and artistic costumes. . . . The pageant began with the zoophytes sponge and ended with the gorilla. . . .
>
>   Both the carnival [i.e., Rex] and the Mistick Krewe people gave balls tonight. . . . The invitations were distributed mysteriously, as usual. . . . The attendance at both places was unusually large and brilliant. There are thousands of strangers in the city, and the hotels were overflowing.[10]

If the *Times* correspondent actually saw the event (the "mysteriously" distributed invitations to the ball were hard to come by), he chose to ignore completely the political allegory, which was inescapable to anyone who knew what President Grant looked like. Nor did he explain the punch line of Comus's evening.

The gorilla, the "missing link" of Comus's theme, was a clearly recognizable caricature of recent ex-Governor P. B. S. Pinchback.

In the tableau at the ball, the anthropomorphic gorilla was seated high on his throne as the lord of all creation, wearing a pink shirt and playing a banjo, with his primitive companions on either hand, the very image of evolution run amok and nature turned upside down. "Underneath, a staircase descended through the inferior species until Comus himself was discovered ruling humorously from the bottom of the evolutionary heap," writes James Gill.[11]

It is one of the most infamous images in Mardi Gras history. This was the first African American governor in the United States, and until 1990 the only one. Though he was undeniably corrupt, he attempted to establish voting rights and education for African Americans and would be instrumental in the 1880s in establishing Southern University for black students, a beacon in an age of black undereducation. Comus portrayed him as a gorilla,

Comus's gorilla in the likeness of P. B. S. Pinchback.
(*next page*) Other images from the Comus bestiary.

parading through the streets of uptown. Race hatred doesn't get any more blatant than that.

Bacchus in Greek mythology was the father of Comus; choosing that name for a krewe was a statement of alignment with the oldest uptown Mardi Gras tradition. Especially given the extent to which history, precedent, and genealogy are part of Mardi Gras, Bacchus's King Kong looked very much like the racial effigy critics have read into the *King Kong* movie. A fierce, grimacing gorilla paraded through the uptown streets for the white folks of New Orleans to smack with volleys of beads. Then his wife. Then his son. It gave me the creeps, somewhere deep down in my Good Darkeyed ex-Natchitoches bones.

In New Orleans, once something happens it continues to happen, and the lunar holiday of Mardi Gras in particular is a time machine. New Orleans presents a peculiar challenge for a writer, because it moves not only in linear time but also cyclical time, a notion I borrow from the Egyptologist Jan Assmann. Linear time, representing a progression of numbered years—2003, 2004, 2005—coordinates the world; it's the time history takes place in. It's the scale of Christian philosophy, where there is a beginning, middle, and end. But in cyclical time, each year is the same as the last—as in ancient Egypt, where the years weren't numbered. Cyclical time relies on an elaborate schedule of festivals associated with the calendar to reinforce its timelessness, creating a rhythm that propels the year.[12] Cyclical time is pagan, and local; it's the time myth takes place in.

The next two chapters take place in the nineteenth century—which in New Orleans is not exactly the past—as I lay the linear time of passing ages on top of the cyclical time of our passing year, in order to try to reconstitute some of the ghosts that parade through the city's streets still.

15

THE HEART OF THE PRANKS

COMUS enters, with a charming-rod in one hand, his glass in the other: with him a rout of monsters, headed like sundry sorts of wild beasts, but otherwise like men and women, their apparel glistering. They come in making a riotous and unruly noise, with torches in their hands.

—John Milton, *Comus*, stage direction

I affirm we possessed the elements in ourselves that needed only the occasion of a great revolution to develop them.

—P. B. S. Pinchback, 1873[1]

I t's common to hear people in New Orleans say: "New Orleans is the northernmost town of the Caribbean." I've even had it attributed to me, though I definitely *don't* say that. It sounds good, and it acknowledges an essential truth, that in many ways New Orleans faces south culturally. But there's one problem with it: it's not true.

News flash! New Orleans isn't on the Caribbean. It's on the Gulf of Mexico, which geographers have consistently classed as a different body of water since its discovery. Don't try to tell a sailor that the Gulf of Mexico and the Caribbean are the same thing.

New Orleans's most important tie was always with its great trading partner, Havana, although the 1962 embargo of Cuba has caused this relationship, central to New Orleans's history, to disappear into a memory hole. (I've said it before and I'll say it again: the embargo of Cuba is also an embargo of New Orleans, since it denies the city its natural and historic trading partner.) But neither is Havana a Caribbean city. It too is on the Gulf of Mexico.

I've been jokingly using the term *Caribbean imperialism* to talk about the idea that we have to apply the word Caribbean, freighted with romantic and mythological baggage, to everything that's cool. I propose that Gulf culture is its own thing—that Havana, New Orleans, and Vera Cruz define a different, albeit related, cultural circuit than the Caribbean conjunction of Santiago de Cuba, Port-au-Prince, Santo Domingo, Kingston, Mayagüez, Pointe-a-Pître, Cartagena, Panamá. Certainly one flows into the other: the Gulf of Mexico is penetrated by the Caribbean. But when one body is penetrated by another they remain distinct bodies, even though there may be some kind of ecstatic conjunction. And certainly Caribbean culture did have an effect on New Orleans, most specifically in a single intense jolt during 1809–10 when about ten thousand mostly French-speaking refugees from the Haitian Revolution fled eastern Cuba for New Orleans and transformed the city. But unlike, say, Brooklyn, the New Orleans of 2005 didn't have large or even detectable Haitian, Dominican, Jamaican, or Puerto Rican populations.

New Orleans is the northernmost edge of *something*. It's the northernmost city that shuts down entirely for pre-Lenten carnival. But that's not something specifically Caribbean. What New Orleans is the northernmost town of was well expressed in a letter written almost a century before the city's founding by two Dutchmen who had gone as emissaries to the English King Charles I, hoping to enlist him in the Dutch fight for independence against the Spanish. In 1623, they reported back to the States General in Amsterdam: "We cannot perceive that his majesty is indisposed towards us . . . Because we have neither saints nor festivals, wherein the Spanish nation is very superstitious."

Neither saints nor festivals. In other words, we're Protestant, they're Catholic.

What New Orleans is at the northern edge of is what I call the Saints and Festivals Belt. From New Orleans, across the Gulf, down the Antilles, and on to Brazil. Which is to say the historically Catholic part of the hemisphere, which had all kinds of different cultural practices than the Protestants, right down to very different laws regarding the treatment of slaves and their religions.

Not only was New Orleans the northernmost town of the Saints and Festivals Belt: the precise boundary was Canal Street, "practically a national boundary," as one writer called it, between French-speaking Catholic New Orleans and English-speaking Protestant New Orleans—between the part of the hemisphere colonized by Catholics and the part colonized by Protestants. (Most of rural South Louisiana was also Catholic.)

But Protestant New Orleans began to participate in the Catholic tradition of Carnival. What most people think of as Mardi Gras—those big, bead-throwing parades down St. Charles—was created by Protestants in the 1850s, and it arrived from Mobile. Nor was it a simple festive impulse. Parading in New Orleans is about taking control of the street. The English speakers uptown took over the French downtown tradition and anglicized it as part of consolidating their control of the city.

On March 8, 1836, the Anglo-Americans in New Orleans in effect seceded (though historians have generally refrained from using that term in speaking about it) from the city, separating themselves off from their French-speaking counterparts, whom they saw as receiving an excessive share of the public purse.

At the Anglo-Americans' instigation, the city was divided into three more or less antagonistic municipalities. The First Municipality, French-speaking and Catholic, was the French Quarter. The Second, English-speaking and Protestant, was the Faubourg Ste.-Marie (St. Mary), uptown above Canal Street, extending to Felicity. The Third Municipality, French-speaking and Catholic (and unpaved and unlighted), was the Faubourg Marigny, downriver from the French Quarter below Esplanade. Each municipality had its own tax base and its own police force, built its own levees, and made its own infrastructural improvements.

In seceding from New Orleans, the Second Municipality made off with the new railroad, the one that would later become the St. Charles street-car, which had just begun operations on September 22, 1835. Carrying both freight and passengers (it even had a ladies' car), it made the far-flung Carrollton Hotel a chic place for downtowners to repair to for supper and encouraged the development of the territory in between.[2] But the breakup of the city left the English speakers without the year's biggest fun. Mardi Gras was a French thing, done at that time in New Orleans more or less on the Parisian model. The pre-Lenten carnival season was celebrated with masked balls galore in the French Quarter, the masks being the main difference between carnival balls and the year-round schedule of dances. Street parades sprang up on an informal basis.

The first organized Mardi Gras parade that we know of took place in 1837, less than a month before the inauguration in Washington of President Martin Van Buren, the virtuoso professional politician who formed the alliances that created the modern Democratic party.[3] Unfortunately for him and for everyone else, within weeks of his inauguration the Panic of 1837 erupted, with New Orleans as its southern epicenter. It was the most severe economic slump in the history of the United States, with the (later) exceptions of the Great Depression of the 1930s and perhaps the one that reached crisis proportions in 2008, though that is still in its early stages as this book goes to press. More than a quarter of U.S. banks closed, and the banking system lost perhaps 45 percent of its value, resulting in a five-year depression that made a one-term president out of Van Buren.[4] The crisis came to a head in May, with a run on the Mechanics' Bank in New York, followed by the suspension of specie payments by the New Orleans banks, who were major players in a cotton-driven national economy.[5] From these two financial centers the panic spread nationwide, leaving the city's banks and cotton dealers insolvent. Coming the year after the city's government had been carved up into three enclaves, the Panic of 1837 ushered in the end of New Orleans's peak period of power and influence, even as other cities' railroad connections took business away from the New Orleans port.

In spite of the depression, or perhaps to combat it, the Mardi Gras parade was repeated in 1838, and it was even bigger. New Orleans reunified politically in 1852, with the English-speaking sector having gained financial and demographic clout. The seat of government moved from the Cabildo to a new City Hall. The Second Municipality had grown in population, swelled by the large numbers of Irish who came to the city following the potato famine, while the French-speaking First and Third had lost population.

New Orleans had a murder rate almost ten times that of Philadelphia and almost five times that of Boston.

> Few other cities in the United States in the 1850s could have matched the level of violence of New Orleans [writes Dennis Charles Rousey]; indeed, the Crescent City may well have been the darkest stain on the butcher's apron. Virtually the dueling capital of the South, a major headquarters for career criminals, site of some of the most intense ethnic strife in the country, New Orleans earned a reputation as one of the most dangerous places in America. . . . In the four years 1857–1860, at least 225 criminal homicides were committed in New Orleans, an annual rate of about 35 per 100,000 of population.[6]

At that, New Orleans was apparently less murderous in the nineteenth century than in the twenty-first, if we contrast a murder rate of 35 per 100,000 population with the 2002 rate of 52.6.

These were not banner years for carnival. The Mardi Gras celebrations became cruder in the 1840s and 1850s as per this item in the *New Orleans Daily Delta* for February 21, 1855:

Mardi Gras Pranks.—Pierre Dufour, a famous Mardi Gras mummer, while charging through St. Charles street last evening at full career on horseback, knocked down a lady and child who happened to be crossing the street, seriously injuring them. He was arrested, taken to the lock-up, and terminated his carnival in one of Captain Moynan's cells. A wild Indian mummer, named John Kelly, rode against a man and then struck him over the head with a huge stick, for which he was arrested. We saw a gentleman give two worthy mummers a sound drubbing on Chartres street for throwing flour on him, and then turned around and swore he could whip any body that would take their part. He was a stout looking individual, and we backed out.

Even as Mardi Gras developed an increasingly bad reputation, several young men from Mobile were setting the style for a new kind of carnival in New Orleans. Page one of the same paper, the same day, described a carnival ball at the largest ballroom in the city, the New Orleans Odd Fellows hall, noting

the sudden appearance in the hall, about 11 o'clock, of the Red Knights, a party of young men from Mobile, it is said, who were dressed from head to foot in a very grotesque, deep red costume. The Knights marched around the room, received the greetings of the "youth and beauty" of our city, and then dispersing among the throng, joined, for an hour or so, in the dance.

The "mystic societies" of New Orleans carnival were modeled on Mobile's. The story as generally told—who knows whether it's true, but we're in the realm of myth here—is that in the early hours of January 1, 1831 (i.e., *not* on Mardi Gras), a group of New Year's revelers in Mobile, led by a young German American cotton broker from Bristol, Pennsylvania, named Michael Krafft, continued their party into the following morning. After liberating some agricultural implements from a dry goods store, they marched down the street playing cowbells dangling from rakes, waking people up with their "rough music," as such percussing with found instruments is called (also known as charivari). This was a ritualized activity with ancient roots, featuring the noisiest possible ambulatory orchestras of such instruments as pots, pans, kettles, bells, rakes, hoes, and whistles as well as the occasional bugle or fiddle.

They were callithumpians, practitioners of a kind of festivity that was broadly popular in nineteenth-century America, and which could serve as a cover for mob action. Describing the 1834 burning of the Ursuline convent in Charleston, Massachusetts, by a group of 150 to 200 anti-Catholics (that is, anti-Irish) in costume, with masks and painted faces, Dale Cockrell writes:

> The rioters were of the sort called during the period "callithumpians," characters in a social ritual that was basically an Americanized mix of the European charivari, carnival, and seasonal "misrule" festivals. Callithumpians were characteristically young, unmarried males who dressed in bizarre costumes, made an unholy racket, and often wore blackface.[7]

Krafft "had witnessed callithumpian rituals in his hometown of Bristol, Pennsylvania," writes Michael McKnight.[8] These Mobile callithumpians called themselves the Cowbellion du Rakin Society, a mockery of French naming and pretension that capitalized on a mania for Masonic-style secret societies, even as the young Mobilians imported costumes from France. Errol Laborde connects the revelry of Mobile via Krafft to the mummers' holiday festivities of Philadelphia, descended from English and Swedish traditions.[9] The New Orleans Mardi Gras thus represents the grafting of the northern European Protestant year-end festive tradition onto southern European Catholic pre-Lenten carnival. By 1837 the Cowbellions in Mobile had begun throwing oranges or candy out to the public as they made their procession. Michael Krafft died of yellow fever in 1839, so he didn't live to see the introduction of themed parades and mule-drawn floats the following year. In 1842 a second mystic society, the Strikers, began parading; a latter-day version of that society still exists in Mobile.

The Mobile festivities were well known in other cities by the time six young Cowbellions from Mobile began parading in New Orleans around 1850, and there were Mobile Strikers in New Orleans too. Three of the Cowbellions were founders of the Mistick Krewe of Comus. Structured along the lines of the Mobile model, Comus was founded in 1857, marking the formal beginning of the Protestant, Anglo-American style of carnival in uptown New Orleans and establishing the krewe system.

The Mistick Krewe of Comus was named for the goblet-wielding Greek god of mirth, the son of Bacchus and Circe. The name was well known from the title of John Milton's masque, which begins with verses in praise of nocturnal revelry. A party club that had the drinking goblet for its emblem, Comus's krewe was also a secret society whose members paraded in anonymous disguise. Beneath its jolly façade, it was a social network. At the same meeting at which the krewe was incorporated, writes James Gill, "the members voted to give themselves a public persona by forming a gentlemen's club. Membership would be identical with the krewe's and provide a cover for its clandestine activities. . . . It was named the Pickwick Club, in honor of the Charles Dickens novel published twenty years earlier."[10] Though the membership rosters were identical, it was permitted to acknowledge membership in the Pickwick, but not in Comus.

The standard tone of much writing about Mardi Gras is that of the courtier acknowledging the sovereign; I will follow here the custom of referring to Comus not as a plural collective, but as "he." Comus kept the details of his first Mardi Gras pageant secret before the fact, and when it was unleashed on the night of February 24, 1857, at the corner of Magazine and Julia in what is now known as the Warehouse District, he astounded the city. First came the *flambeaux*, or torches, carried by black men, that threw dramatic flickering shadows on the float-mounted tableaux and made clear the position of black men in the social hierarchy of Comus. The parade processed to St. Charles with floats that elaborated the theme of "The Demon Actors in Milton's *Paradise Lost*."

With a masquerade, a tableau ball, and a themed torchlight parade, to say nothing of social access to the elite who made up its confidential ranks, membership in Comus swelled beyond the initial eighty-three. The following year, writes Laurraine Goreau, "flaming torches lit 30 resplendent *tableaux roulants* bearing the Gods and Divinities of Olympus, paced smartly by marching bands."[11] The tableaux were presented as staged events during the ball immediately after the parade. Invitations to the krewe ball were distributed mysteriously; to receive one was to be summoned to a privileged sector of society that delighted in secrecy and ritual.

Ten days after Comus's debut, the South was handed one of the low points of American jurisprudence to celebrate when the Supreme Court rendered its decision in the eleven-year-old *Dred Scott v. Sandford* case. Arrived at with improper behind-the-scenes interference by proslavery president James Buchanan, it held that the enslaved Dred Scott, taken by his "owner" into a free state, had no standing to sue for freedom. It meant that Congress had no right to prevent slavery in new federal territories. With that decision, the free states of the North were boxed in; the expanding nation would have slavery, slaveowners could bring their slaves anywhere and keep them, and, more broadly, the decision meant that persons of African descent could not be U.S. citizens. Confrontation was coming closer.

Comus's parade in 1860 was in praise of union, but not the following year. There was a new political party of dangerous radicals: the "Black Republicans." At least that was the inflammatory way the Democrats insisted on identifying them, somewhat the same way the late twentieth-century Republicans gratuitously and disrespectfully insisted on referring to their opponents as the "Democrat Party." The Republicans saw the Dred Scott decision as preparing the way for slave makets in the North; the South considered the Republicans a regional party, and with the election of Abraham Lincoln as president after having not even been listed on the ballot in the southern states, Louisiana voted to secede from the Union on January 26, 1861, with Comus members prominent among the voices for secession. Mardi Gras that year fell on February 12, Lincoln's birthday, and blackfaced krewe members carried "an effigy of Abraham Lincoln riding a split rail."[12]

The war put a stop to Mardi Gras for a time. But because the Union took New Orleans early in the war, the city had a head start on the rest of the country in defining the social conflict between, on the one hand, the determination of people of color to be enfranchised and educated and, on the other, the massive post-Confederate white resistance to the idea of civil rights for black people. As General Benjamin Butler wrote: "We were two thousand, five hundred men in a city seven miles long by two to four wide, of a hundred and fifty thousand inhabitants, all hostile, bitter, defiant, explosive."[13]

Particularly disturbing to the white citizenry of New Orleans was to see colored soldiers in uniform among the troops occupying their city, and therefore in a position of power over them. It was the beginning of that great Reconstruction trope, fearfully and credulously recalled thirty-five years later by Woodrow Wilson: "the white South, under the heel of the black South."

The Confederacy lost the war but won the peace. When the war ended, the business and political class of New Orleans had a broadly popular new mission: to expel the Yankees, destroy the Republican Party, take the government back, and make the ex-slaves into a permanently subservient caste. For that, it would be necessary to organize resistance. Comus already had a clandestine organization at the ready, one whose surviving members now had the bitter experience of combat. It would also be necessary to rewrite history, providing a narrative of corrupt carpetbaggers and bestial Negro rapists as the aggressors and gallant, aristocratic southerners as the victims. Comus could help with that too. It was a brilliant strategy: they countered the progressive linearity of history, in which slavery was finished, with the eternal cyclicality of festival and myth, in which what was will always be.

Comus paraded again in 1866, his antebellum pedigree giving the maskers an air of having always existed. Reid Mitchell writes that Comus's return after the Civil War was "the single most significant event in the shaping of New Orleans Carnival. Its original appearance, if never repeated, would have left it simply another example of the ephemeral antebellum parade. . . . The Comus parade and tableaux created a cultural form through which ideas could be asserted."[14] Until Comus's objective of toppling Reconstruction was achieved, his themes would be highly ideological.

A letter published in Volume 2 of the new journal *The Nation* on January 4, 1866, written by a northerner reporting from Alexandria, Louisiana, gives a sense of the environment in which Comus returned to parading:

> I feel in as much danger as at any time during the war. Everyone goes armed, even the brakemen on the railways wear revolvers. There is a smoldering volcano down here that needs a deluge of cold water before it will be safe to build on. So far as the concession of Negro suffrage from the people of the South is to be expected, there is quite as much chance of Massachusetts adopting slavery as a permanent institution. If these states are not held as conquered territory, they cannot be held beyond the next Presidential election, except the North be willing to receive them back again in the same character (omitting slavery alone) as they assumed before the war; that is, admitting the arrogant assumption of Southern superiority.

Galveston held a masked Mardi Gras ball in 1867, and Memphis had a Mardi Gras by 1872. St. Louis (previously a part of Louisiana) celebrated it, as did Baltimore. The fashion for mummers spread through the South, where it fused with anti-Reconstructionism. The most remembered mummers' society —complete with a whimsical *k* spelling—was a rural one: the Ku Klux Klan, founded by a group of idle Confederate veterans in May 1866 (that was historian Woodrow Wilson's date for it, though other versions of the story put it at Christmas 1865), in the hamlet of Pulaski, Tennessee, a little north of the Alabama border in a region where the white population had been overwhelmingly Confederate. Woodrow Wilson breathlessly described the Klan's founding in his *History of the American People*:

> A little group of young men in the Tennessee village of Pulaski, finding time hang heavy on their hands after the excitements of the field, so lately abandoned, formed a secret club for the mere pleasure of association, for private amusement . . . and one of their number suggested that they call themselves the *Kuklos*, the Circle.
>
> Secrecy and mystery were at the heart of the pranks they planned: secrecy with regard to the membership of their Circle, secrecy with regard to the place and the objects of its meetings; and the mystery of disguise and of silent parade when the comrades rode abroad at night when the moon was up: a white mask, a tall cardboard hat, the figures of

man and horse sheeted like a ghost, and the horses' feet muffled to move without sound of their approach.

It was the delightful discovery of the thrill of awesome fear, the woeful looking for of calamity that swept through the countrysides as they moved from place to place upon their silent visitations, coming no man could say whence, going upon no man knew what errand, that put thought of mischief into the minds of the frolicking comrades. It threw the negroes into a very ecstasy of panic to see these sheeted "Ku Klux" move near them in the shrouded night; and their comic fear stimulated the lads who excited it to many an extravagant prank and mummery.

No one knew or could discover who the masked players were; no one could say whether they meant serious or only innocent mischief; and the zest of the business lay in keeping the secret close.

Ecstasy of panic! Comic fear! According to Wilson, the waves of lynching that were about to sweep the South began as a kind of demented performance art. What he viewed as the originally benign intention of scaring superstitious African Americans for fun by dressing like ghosts soon extended to torture and murder. However, even this was, according to Wilson, no more "lawless" than the Reconstruction government that gave blacks the vote and disfranchised those who had taken up arms against the U.S. government:

Every country-side wished to have its own Ku Klux, founded in secrecy and mystery like the mother "Den" at Pulaski, until at last there had sprung into existence a great *Ku Klux Klan*, an "Invisible Empire of the South," bound together in loose organization to protect the southern country from some of the ugliest hazards of a time of revolution.

The objects of the mysterious brotherhood grew serious fast enough. It passed from jest to earnest. Men took hold of it who rejoiced to find in it a new instrument of political power: men half outlawed, denied the suffrage, without hope of justice in the courts, who meant to take this means to make their will felt. . . .

It was impossible to keep such a power in hand. Sober men governed the counsels and moderated the plans of these roving knights errant; but it was lawless work at best. They had set themselves, after the first year or two of mere mischievous frolic had passed, to right a disordered society through the power of fear. . . . It became the chief object of the night-riding comrades to silence or drive from the country the principal mischief-makers of the reconstruction regime, whether white or black.

The negroes were generally easy enough to deal with: a thorough fright usually disposed them to make utter submission, resign their parts in affairs, leave the country, — do anything their ghostly visitors demanded. But white men were less tractable; and here and there even a negro ignored or defied them. . . . The Ku Klux and those who masqueraded in their guise struck at first only at those who made palpable mischief between the races or set just law aside to make themselves masters; but their work grew under their hands, and their zest for it. Brutal crimes were committed; the innocent suffered with the guilty; a reign of terror was brought on, and society was infinitely more disturbed than defended. . . . One lawless force seemed in contest with another.[15] [paragraphing added]

The Knights of the Ku Klux Klan, with its mystic, faux Greco-Scottish name, spread across Tennessee and beyond. In New Orleans, a Klan-like group called Knights of the White Camellia appeared.

At this point, I should insert a disclaimer: the Mardi Gras krewes and the Ku Klux Klan were quite different organizations that took very different paths, and I am certainly not implying that the present-day successors to those organizations have any connection. But in the early days of the Klan, it was part of a single movement with the krewes—masked, mysticalized, anonymous resistance to Reconstruction, which in turn was identified with race hatred, terror, and repression of the rights of African Americans.

Protestant Mardi Gras had been an antebellum creation, but it was during Reconstruction that it took on its definitive form, both artistically and organizationally.

The South's economy was devastated, but money was being made in New Orleans. Comus's masked ball of Mardi Gras 1868, given in the Theatre L'Opera, astonished all with its high technology: over a decade before Edison's carbon filament bulb, it was illuminated by electricity. The *New York Times* account of it, dated February 29, noted that "The management having recently given 'Le Prophéte,' the electric sun used in that piece was employed in lighting up the theatre, so that everything was resplendent."

A new group appeared in 1870: the Twelfth Night Revelers. Parading on January 6, they provided, as their name suggested, a starting point to the Mardi Gras season that Comus finished. The Revelers (who only paraded until 1876, though they continued to have a masked ball after that date) featured a character from English holiday folklore, played by a prominent citizen disguised with a mask: the Lord of Misrule.

This was a pointed reference that would be obvious to contemporaries. Misrule was the operative metaphor of Reconstruction as seen by southern whites.[16] Carnival turned society upside down, if only for a few days. In the minds of the ex-Confederates, society had been turned permanently upside down to make the natural white aristocrats into subjects, while the savage Negroes, manipulated by unscrupulous northern white profiteers, were given equal or superior social status. Dr. Woodrow Wilson was attuned to the carnival metaphor: "In the states where the negroes were the most numerous, or their leaders most shrewd and unprincipled," he wrote about this era in 1893, "an extraordinary carnival of public crime set in under the forms of law."[17] It seemed to the elite of New Orleans that the Lord of Misrule was running riot throughout the South, and the krewes were determined to mock him and make sure his carnival would last as few days as possible.

The carnival themes of this era display an obsession with proper social order. "The parade of Comus or some other krewe was a king's procession through the city, followed by a stately masque," writes Mitchell.[18] These were public demonstrations of wealth, power, and order, with a serious mien. The plebes were allowed to witness the edifying spectacle of royalty being revered in the street but not to enter the sacred precincts of the masked ball. The burlesque of the Reconstruction carnival was directed not at satirizing the concepts of kingliness and aristocracy but rather at mocking people who failed to respect those concepts.

Logically, the next phase of development of this neo-aristocratic carnival was for the business elite to crown one of its own as king. This was achieved by a new krewe popularly known as Rex, founded in 1872. An offshoot of the city's oldest (1841) gentlemen's club, the Boston (which, in classic New Orleans fashion, was named not for the city of Boston but for a card game), Rex aimed to organize all the "promiscuous maskers" (unaffiliated celebrants) and small clubs into a single big Mardi Gras parade, with a king to reign ceremonially over it. In 1874, the Rex organization was officially incorporated as the School of Design. The first Rex, king of carnival, was banker Lewis J. Solomon, who did a significant amount of the fundraising for it. The theme of the first Rex parade was "The Arabs"; wearing a crown and carrying a scepter borrowed from actor Lawrence Barrett, who was playing Richard III in town, Rex rode a horse down the street, flanked by krewe members in faux-Bedouin robes.[19] Reminiscing in 1921 about that first Rex parade, Solomon recalled that the dukes "were all mounted and wore flowing robes—almost like the Ku Klux Klan."[20]

With Rex, Mardi Gras found its focus. Unlike Comus, Rex wore no mask. His identity was public, and to be chosen as Rex became the highest of civic honors. And unlike Comus, whose fantastical tableaux flickered in the night-time torchlight, Rex had an afternoon parade on Mardi Gras Day. Adopting as his theme song "If Ever I Cease to Love," a show tune from a musical called *Bluebeard* then playing in New Orleans, Rex chose for Mardi Gras its distinctive tricolor standard of purple, green, and gold. A louder chord of colors would be hard to find. (I will forego the routinely told and greatly exaggerated story of the Russian grand duke Alexei Romanov and his role in the first Rex presentation; you can easily find it on the web.) The same year, Mobile too created a king, called Felix.

As New Orleans climbed out of the economic catastrophe of the Civil War, Mardi Gras became a major drawing card for its developing economy of tourism. Nor was that an accident: Mardi Gras intended to show visitors that the city could be both fun and orderly. Exquisitely designed and printed posters inviting visitors to the Rex Parade were posted in train stations around the country.

The Knights of Momus, named for the Greek god of satire and mockery, first paraded on New Year's Eve, December 31, 1872. Created on the model of Comus, with themed parades, floats, and literary and mythological references, they too were a masked knightly society with an anonymous membership, and they too had an associated gentlemen's club, the Louisiana Club.

The Crescent City Democratic Club reorganized in April 1874 as the Crescent City White League. An overtly military organization that invited all white men to participate, it aimed to throw out the Republican regime and subjugate African Americans once and for all. The league called on white schoolchildren to kick black students out of their schools. In rural areas, armed groups confronted Republican officeholders, demanded their resignations point-blank, and murdered some of them, along with troublesome black people. With some twenty-eight hundred men at arms, the White League had two divisions of infantry and one of artillery.

When a shipment of weapons that the White League had purchased arrived at the New Orleans riverfront on September 13, 1874, the crisis came to a head. A large force of policeman and militiamen blocked the unloading. A call to arms against the blockade was published in a newspaper the following morning, and on September 14, a full-scale military confrontation ensued between government forces, which included some three thousand African Americans, and the troops of the White League, backed by thousands of White League sympathizers who answered the call to arms. A pitched battle ensued that lasted ten minutes or so; twenty-seven people died, including eleven city policemen, with the White League the clear victor. It was the largest military confrontation with a state government since the Civil War, to this day. The following day, President Grant—referred to in the *New Orleans Bulletin* as "the thing who disgraces the office formerly dignified by Washington, Jefferson, and Madison"—ordered federal troops to New Orleans to restore the deposed Republican Governor William P. Kellogg to power.[21] From then until 1877, much of Louisiana remained in a state of anarchy, and New Orleans held the status of an occupied territory.

The coup d'état of the Battle of Liberty Place, the heroic-sounding name by which the conflict was remembered, was a turning point in the failure of Reconstruction. It made clear that the Republican government of Louisiana could only survive as long as federal troops propped it up. The example served as a banner for the rest of the South. Though the government was returned to legally constituted authority, no one was ever prosecuted for the successful assault on federal sovereignty. The following year, carnival was suspended.

The White League had triumphed. Carnival had been an organizational conduit that did its part to help reestablish white supremacy. Joseph Roach writes:

> A boast, attributed to a Comus captain by the official historian of the Mistick Krewe, proudly implicates the membership of the men's clubs and secret carnival societies [in the Battle of Liberty Place]: "It is safe to say that every member . . . capable of bearing arms, participated." The centennial pamphlet of the Mistick Krewe lists the coup of 1874 as a historical highlight: "Many Comus maskers took part in the battle." The official historian of the Boston Club, center of the krewe activities of the Rex organization, claims that the plot against the Kellogg government was hatched at the club and quotes approvingly a memoir written in 1899 that states: "The Boston Club party grew into public utterance as an expression standing for the supremacy of the white man and the perpetuation of the white man's institutions." These are boasts, made after the fact, but further research supports their veracity. . . .
>
> This research documents (with names) what many native New Orleanians generally know as a commonplace: that the officer corps of the White League (and a not insignificant number of its rank and file) formed an interlocking directorship with the secret members of the exclusive Mardi Gras krewes and men's clubs, especially Comus-Pickwick.[22]

In 1876, Momus changed its parade day to the Thursday before Mardi Gras, retaining that slot in the festival calendar through modern times. That year, the general election brought in former Confederate brigadier general and krewe member Francis Nicholls as the governor of Louisiana, with his "Redeemer" government. A Republican state government was also sworn in that never took power, but it was clear that the new government in Washington wasn't going to insist on it. The Hayes-Tilden compromise, in which the Republicans capitulated on civil rights for blacks in order to retain the presidency, resulted in the withdrawal of federal troops from the South.

By this point the South had unified politically with the Democrats. It would remain solidly Democrat until the 1960s, when integration flipped the polarity to making the South the Republicans' solid base. But whatever its name, the majority party in the South was the racist party, pure and simple.

By 1883, five of the nine Supreme Court Justices had been appointed subsequent to the Hayes-Tilden compromise; this court, remembered as the "Laissez-Faire court," struck down portions of the Civil Rights Act of 1875 that mandated the "full and equal enjoyment of public accomodations," ruling that Congress had no authority to make such a law because it was a matter for the states. In opening the door for discriminatory legislation all across the South and leaving enforcement of discrimination claims to local governments, it did not merely mean blacks and whites would no longer drink water from the same fountain. It meant blacks could be murdered. The restraints on lynching, which was already in fashion, were removed, and the years that followed were peak years of sadistic ritual. There was no check on the powers of southern sheriffs. The abuses this created led to a massive market of the labor of fraudulently arrested and sentenced black men, under working conditions worse than those of slavery because no one was invested with property rights in the survival of the worker.

As the United States entered a dark period of its history—another one—African Americans became the victims of a collective atrocity of repression and terror. The nation has lived with its consequences ever since. As one court decision after another swept away what protection African Americans had gained, the period badly known as Jim Crow—which lasted for almost another *century*—got under way. In the twenty years between the Hayes-Tilden compromise and *Plessy v. Ferguson*, a racist system was installed, astounding in its extremism, that would endure until the 1960s.

In their struggle to assert themselves as they were being forced into a caste system that intended to keep them permanently servile, impoverished, disfranchised, and uneducated, African Americans responded with a creative explosion. The best-known consequence of that was jazz, but jazz was not the only thing that happened.

16

THE WILD WEST

"Outfit at the bottom of the river, what shall I do?"

—message to Buffalo Bill

New Orleans was back and ready to do business. Rex himself presided over the opening ceremonies.

Ballyhooed as the first American World's Fair, the World's Industrial and Cotton Centennial Exposition was accessible either by rail (a special train ran from Charleston via Savannah with a fare of one cent per mile), by riverboat down the Mississippi, or by ship from the Gulf of Mexico. Held from December 16, 1884 (the opening was postponed twice), to June 2, 1885, the exposition took place on the spacious uptown grounds that had formerly been the plantation of Etienne de Boré, where the first commercially successful sugar crop was grown in Louisiana ninety years before. It coincided with the University of Louisiana being privatized and renamed Tulane University; at the end of the festival, the fairgrounds were divided into Audubon Park (on the riverside of St. Charles), and the beautiful campus that Tulane University occupies to this day (on the lakeside).

The "Centennial" of the exposition's name commemorated the purported first exportation of cotton from America, to Britain in 1784. All the states in the union were represented. Besides their industrial and agricultural products and arts and crafts, some went so far as to send collections of their typical flora and fauna, including menageries—wolves and bears, in the case of the Dakota Territory—that became the foundation of the Audubon Zoo, which dates its beginnings from the exposition. International representatives attended too, but only a few countries participated fully, most prominently Mexico. With an eye to increasing commerce via new railroad connections to the United States and a hoped-for reciprocal trade treaty, Mexico mounted what was practically its own national exhibition.

The undisputed musical star of the exposition was the grand Eighth Regiment Cavalry Band of the Mexican delegation, better known as the Mexican Band. Its presence in New Orleans completed the Gulf of Mexico cultural triangle of Cuba-Mexico-Louisiana; its repertoire, which included *danzas* and *habaneras*, bore the influence of Cuba. A vogue for Mexican music swept New Orleans, and a local music publisher, Junius Hart, inaugurated a "Mexican" series of sheet music.

In the long run, the Mexican Band's presence had a significant impact on the music of New Orleans. An unknown number of band members stayed behind when the exposition ended, which is how New Orleans got its first saxophone player of importance, Florencio Ramos. Between the members of the Mexican Band and other Mexican musicians in town (the Lorenzo Tío family was perhaps the best known), taking music lessons from Mexicans was part of the training of a number of young players who became the first generation of New Orleans jazz musicians over the next two decades.

There was a "Woman's Department" at the exposition, under the charge of Julia Ward Howe, the venerable feminist and author of the words to the "Battle Hymn of the Republic," and there was a section in the north gallery of the government building for "The Colored People" that featured a sofa festooned with silk needlework in honor of Toussaint L'Ouverture, one of several portraits of the great revolutionary on display.[1] But while the exhibits went on in the future Audubon Park, another show fired the imagination of the town.

William "Buffalo Bill" Cody began calling his production Buffalo Bill's Wild West in 1883, after eleven years of intermittent theatrical appearances and productions. Cody was an "Indian fighter" who had been present at Custer's Last Stand, though he had already embarked on his theatrical career by then. His "large company of Indians, cow-boys, Mexican vaqueros, famous riders and expert lasso throwers, with accessories of stage coach, emigrant wagons, bucking horses, and a herd of buffaloes" presented a massive outdoor spectacle that included restaged battles and buffalo hunts as well as trick roping, sharpshooting, and horsemanship.[2] It was styled as a scenic monologue spoken by

Buffalo Bill himself, with the twenty-seven-piece Buffalo Bill's Cowboy Band playing nearly continuously throughout the show, the way circus bands do.

Cody was hardly the first to do a Wild West show—P. T. Barnum had done much to establish the genre—but his famous spectacle helped make the cowboy into an American icon, romanticizing a figure that had formerly been considered violent and disreputable.[3] Henceforth, the western genre would present cattle ranching and the driving of the smelly four-footed product to slaughter as a heroic, nation-building undertaking, with the eating of dead cows enshrined as practically a patriotic act.

Hoping to capitalize on the publicity and the crowds expected to attend the Cotton Expo, Cody brought his show to New Orleans at the end of 1884. The Wild West's extensive use of live firearms was too dangerous under a big top; it required a large, open outdoor space accessible to large crowds. New Orleans had the space to stage the spectacle and the streetcar to get the crowds there. Expectations of success for the show were high, and a special grand finale was mounted for the Cotton Expo: a historically inexact re-creation of the Battle of New Orleans, with Buffalo Bill playing the role of Andrew Jackson, for which, at least, he had the hair.

They opened on December 23, having postponed their starting date twice after losing much of their gear when their chartered riverboat collided with another boat and sank in less than an hour into the Mississippi while on the way to New Orleans. It rained almost constantly during their stay of over three months, depressing attendance and turning the outdoor campsite where they lived into a mud bog.

Tired and discouraged, hoping to sue the riverboat carrier for the loss of all his guns and ammunition, star sharpshooter Captain Bogardus quit in March, even though he was a partner in the show. The nineteen-year-old Annie Oakley, who had been stranded in New Orleans after the circus she had been appearing with folded its tent in the face of the rains, signed on as a star attraction.[4] For her debut with Buffalo Bill, she learned to sharpshoot with a shotgun, as the great Bogardus had done.

"The great West has been reclaimed from the savage," wrote Cody in 1888.[5] Americans took great pride in their expansion across the continent; it was another moment when the United States could imagine itself to be a nation. If that meant genocide of the native population—well, the word *genocide* hadn't been coined yet. In celebrating this expansion, Buffalo Bill's Wild West set the tone and the imagistic vocabulary for the western movies I saw at the Don and the Cane in Natchitoches seventy-five years later. Though Indian wars were still going on in various parts of the West as Buffalo

Bill mounted his spectacle, the conquest of the American natives was presented as a done deal. To play the part of the proud vanquished people, almost a hundred fully costumed Plains Indians appeared with the show, and to judge from their impact on New Orleans they were an important part of it.[6]

As with every traveling show worth its salt, a promotional parade was essential on the first morning the troupe was in town. On the evidence of a 1902 film clip of a Buffalo Bill parade in an unknown city, every little boy in town was there, running down the street alongside the procession.[7] The stars of the over two-hour parade were the phalanxes of Indians that traveled with the troupe in full regalia with feathered headdresses and beaded clothes, carrying long lances.

These were Plains Indians, whose dress did not resemble those of the natives of Louisiana. But their ceremony and grandeur made an impression. The figure of the Indian had long since acquired a mystical significance in Louisiana, where the natives had shown both the Europeans and the Africans the secrets of survival in the strange new swampland. Black maroon communities merged with Indian resettlements; not a few southerners, black and white, had at least a little Indian "blood" (including this writer, who is one-sixteenth Indian on my hillbilly dad's side).

African American cowboys rarely made it into the movies that future generations saw, but in the brief period that cowboying existed there were a significant number of them, including at least one who appeared with Buffalo Bill's Wild West in New Orleans. Billed as "a Feejee Indian from Africa," he rode a saddled elk. His name was Voter Hall.

Voter.

Riding wild elks is a young man's game, so Voter Hall might well have been nineteen years old, like Annie Oakley. I have not been able to find out anything more about Voter Hall, so I am left to imagine the story of a black mother in, say, 1866, when the hopes of Reconstruction were still ascendant, naming her baby . . . Voter.

Mardi Gras was sensational in 1885, featuring the Mexican Band, costumed Indians from Buffalo Bill's troupe, and quite possibly Annie Oakley and Voter Hall. It seems to have been the first carnival in which Becate Batiste, an African American building tradesman in the Seventh Ward of partly Indian descent, took to the streets with his group, the Creole Wild West: a downtown posse of African Americans dressed like Indians. There had long been Indian mummers at Carnival, both black and white, so the Creole Wild West wasn't a completely new idea. But it was a new structure for street performance that had been going on in more informal ways.

Out of the Creole Wild West came the groups that have since become known as the Mardi Gras Indians: small bands of African American men (not a few of them with American Indians in their family tree) who "mask Indian" with clearly defined roles, centering around the figure of the Big Chief. There has been some attention paid in recent years to "the Indians," as they are called in New Orleans, but during their first century of existence they hardly attracted any notice at all, and indeed, at the time the Creole Wild West was created it was one of a bewildering plethora of costumed groups. Few people outside of New Orleans had heard of the Indians until the 1970s, and at that time they were subcultural even within New Orleans; many black New Orleanians thought them scary. The first inkling of them that appeared in mainstream pop culture was the Dixie Cups' irresistible 1965 version of a Mardi Gras Indian song, "Iko Iko," a minor national hit produced by Wardell Quezergue that copied "Jock-a-Mo," a 1953 recording by Sugar Boy Crawford, whose career had been cut short after he was badly beaten by cops in a roadside incident.

The Indians' performance, which is a kind of sacramental street theater, has evolved over the years in a way that stresses its connection to the past even as it transforms to fit the needs of the living community. Today the Indians are an important spiritual resource for black—and not only black—New Orleans.

The most common short-version explanation of why groups of African American men in twenty-first-century New Orleans would wear eight-foot-high hand-sewn "suits" that reference late-nineteenth-century Wild West–style Plains Indian clothing is that it is to honor the Indians who helped African Americans when they were in marronage. But it goes much further than that, given the constant interaction of black and Indian in Louisiana from the arrival of the first ship of kidnapped Africans in Louisiana.

Mardi Gras Indians are, in effect, a black mystic society. It's easy to imagine what Mardi Gras Indian performance *might* mean, but it means what its practitioners need it to mean, and it is as much mystery as it is clear meaning. Becate Batiste left no documentation of his thinking, nor do we have much information about other people who might have constituted the first generation of Mardi Gras Indians. But Batiste and his contemporaries left a deep artistic legacy whose significance eludes simple paraphrase, and that, subsequently informed by the civil rights struggle, has been elaborated by later generations into a complex ritual of affirmation of the right of black men to exist and develop according to their own criteria. Carnival is only the visible manifestation of something they do all year. It's a tremendous commitment to be an Indian—of time, of hard-earned cash, and of responsibility to the community when the suit is not being worn.

It seems clear to me that the Indians' tradition strongly bears the imprint of the displaced culture of Saint-Domingue (the pre-1804 name for the French colony that became the Republic of Haiti). The closest-looking resemblance elsewhere to the Indians' costume is perhaps the Indian maskers of Trinidad carnival, and I believe the reason for this is that both New Orleans and Trinidad are part of that Domingan diaspora. The most typical Mardi Gras Indian rhythm is what the Cubans call *cinquillo* and what in Haiti is called *cata;* widely thought to have come into Cuba from Saint-Domingue, it's practically a marker of the Domingan diaspora. Quarter-eighth-quarter-eighth-quarter: *Ran-ka-kan-ka-kan, Ran-ka-kan-ka-kan,* now sing: *Shallow water, oh mama, Ran-ka-kan-ka-kan, Ran-ka-kan-ka-kan* . . .

Older than western movies, the Mardi Gras Indian tradition became formalized during a period of African American history that was in some respects worse than slavery itself. As the South celebrated its reunification with the North—the birth of a nation, Thomas Dixon called it—that purportedly happy knitting back together of the postbellum United States was achieved at the cost of agreeing to allow African Americans in the South to be forced violently into peonage through lynch-law terrorism, the same way national unity had previously been purchased at the cost of forcing African Americans to be slaves.

At the time of the founding of Creole Wild West, the situation was not yet as bad as it would become: in 1888, about half the registered voters in Louisiana were still African American, and there were African American members of the state legislature.[8] But no matter how vigorously African Americans resisted their own reenslavement, the direction things were going was clear. A series of Supreme Court rulings had chipped away the ability of the federal government to enforce civil rights for African Americans. Emboldened, the southern states passed ever more discriminatory local laws. The culmination of this hands-off approach to white supremacy would be *Plessy v. Ferguson,* which definitively closed the door.

As the black family was increasingly confined to what would later be called a ghetto, the Creole Wild West dressed in the clothes of the conquered Indian nation. I would bet, though I don't know for sure, that they played tambourines as they do today and I bet they also played an iron bell, as the Cowbellions of Mobile did, as Abakuá in Havana and Matanzas do, and as Mardi Gras Indians do today. Singing call-and-response songs that reflected their unique Afro-Louisianan musical heritage, they walked proud through their neighborhoods, where the white krewes never ventured. Over the decades, the Indians created a musical, poetic, choreographic, and theatrical repertoire that has yet to be studied with the attention it deserves. It's a primary living document of unsurpassed flavor with much to teach us about African American music, and it's still alive and transforming on the streets of New Orleans.

Wild West shows, formerly a mass entertainment during the precinematic age of pageantry, are now a curiosity of the theatrical past. But more than a century later, the Creole Wild West is still dressing up like Indians, and still going out to the street during Mardi Gras.

———————

Despite the grandstanding (literally) of the city's white elite during Mardi Gras season, carnival was the property of blacks and whites both, and always had been.

At the turn of the twentieth century, the city's beleaguered colored professional class had their fancy-dress balls behind closed doors like the whites did. But out in the streets, the working-class black carnival created two lasting traditions that evolved in very different directions: the Mardi Gras Indians and the Zulu Social and Pleasure Club. The Mardi Gras Indians adopted a stereotyped image of Native Americans; Zulu adopted a stereotyped image of Africans. But whereas the Mardi Gras Indians are underground, providing an assertive, edgy image of black men as warriors, Zulu is unthreatening and happily mainstream.

The first years of the jazz age were also the era of blacks performing in blackface, most famously Bert Williams and George Walker. Later cultural critics have had a field day probing the layers of contradiction and irony of that phenomenon, but often without noticing that one of its offshoots is still in action in the town where you need a different verb tense to describe a past that hasn't ended. The Mardi Gras parade of the Zulu Social and Pleasure Club, the century-old blacks-in-blackface carnival society of New Orleans, has endured to become the only large-scale blackface event in the twenty-first-century United States. It's the strangest gear in the Mardi Gras time machine.

The proximate inspiration was a skit in a musical revue by a black troupe called the Smart Set that appeared in November 1909 at the Pythian Temple Theater on Saratoga Street (now Loyola) and Gravier. The Pythians were a black mystical society along the lines of the Masons; Louis Armstrong was a Pythian. Making a show of their community's economic power, they had built their own nine-story building, complete with a theater where black people could enjoy a show without being forced to sit in the balcony. When members of a Carnival marching society called the Tramps caught Smart Set at the Temple, they saw a "Zulu King song and drill" which, so goes the legend, suggested a way to style their Canival group.[9]

The Zulu Social Aid and Pleasure Club seems to have made its first appearance on Mardi Gras Day 1910, with William Storey as King Zulu, preceded by a "jubilee" quartet of singers. He wore raggedy trousers and a lard-can crown and carried a banana-stalk sceptre. Zulu was formally incorporated in 1916, one of a myriad of carnival organizations. The function of pleasure clubs, which were fraternal and networking organizations, and social aid clubs, which provided insurance, had overlapped. Neighborhoods had clubs, and professions had clubs, including pimps, whose club had an annual parade and a Pimps' Ball at Economy Hall in the Tremé (which hall was torn down in the 1960s to build Louis Armstrong Park).[10] In Louis Armstrong's 1954 memoir, he recalled the variety:

> All the big, well known Social Aid and Pleasure Clubs turned out for the last big parade I saw in New Orleans. They all tried to outdo each other and they certainly looked swell. Among the clubs represented were the Bulls, the Hobgoblins, the Zulus, the Tammanys, the Young Men Twenties (Zutty Singleton's club), the Merry-Go-Rounds, the Deweys, the Tulane Club, The Young Men Vidalias, The Money Wasters, the Jolly Boys, the Turtles, the Original Swells, the San Jacintos, the Autocrats, the Francs Amis Club, the Cooperatives, the Economys, the Odd Fellows, the Masons, the Knights of Pythias (my lodge), and the Diamond Swells from out in the Irish Channel.[11]

It was perhaps a more distant remove for these Afro-Orleanians to mask Zulu than for Becate Batiste to mask Indian. Whatever African Americans styling themselves as Zulus might be about, it's not about direct heritage. Of all the African nationalities brought to North America on slave ships, it is doubtful that there was one Zulu among them.

The messages are contradictory. At the time Zulu was founded, the independence struggle of the Zulu nation of South Africa had become an international symbol of resistance to colonialism. The Zulus had been in the news for decades, with the Africans routinely referred to in news accounts as "the savages." There was a final uprising in 1906, led by a Zulu chief named Bambaata—yep, like "Planet Rock"'s Afrika Bambaataa, and sometimes spelled *Bambatha*—who was killed by British forces. African Americans of the southern United States were treated as harshly as the Zulus were treated by white Boers; the relative social position of blacks in the two places was comparable until the United States pulled ahead in the 1960s. But meanwhile, on the vaudeville stages of Britain and the United States, the Zulu was a stock comic figure. In dime museums and circuses, a caged "Zulu," eating raw meat, might be displayed next to the Wild Man of Borneo or the Snake Charmer.

Some deny today that Zulu was ever intended as a burlesque of Rex, but it was: the parallelism is there to see, and was frequently remarked on in the past. Rex and King Zulu both arrived with their courts on a boat on Lundi Gras (Fat Monday), though Rex came in via the Mississippi River whereas King Zulu stepped off a tugboat at the New Basin Canal. Rex was already a mockery of royal tradition, but one that took itself seriously. Some contemporary observers see Zulu as a case of inverting stereotypes in order to mock them—that is, that they mocked the white supremacy behind the mockery of Rex, and in doing so mocked the derogatory caricatures of black people that were universal on the popular stage—but that implies that the Zulu members in some way identified with the Africans they caricatured.

Another possibility, I think a likely one, is that they were celebrating their distance from Africa, as upwardly aspiring African Americans often did. W. E. B. DuBois, writing of his attempt to create a Pan-African Congress in 1921, found opposition from "colored members" of the NAACP board "who had inherited the fierce repugnance toward anything African, which was the natural result of the older colonization schemes, where efforts at assisted and even forcible expatriation of American Negroes had always included Africa. . . . They felt themselves Americans, not Africans. They resented and feared any coupling with Africa."[12]

To what degree were the Zulu members satirizing racism (a word not yet coined in 1909), to what degree were they mocking the very idea of royalty, to what degree were they distancing themselves from or embracing the idea of Africa, and to what degree were they merely what we would now call politically incorrect? There are different interpretations, which in their variety almost serve as a Rorschach blot for the interpreter. There's no way we can enter the minds of those working-class people a century ago, who lived under such different conditions. The basic answer is that they were having fun. But the paradox they created still perplexes on the streets of New Orleans today, when Zulu makes some African Americans cringe even as it entertains the masses. Zulu's image manages to be read by many at street level as one of black pride (trading on the signification of Zulu as resistance to white power as per Shaka Zulu); in its early process of institutionalization it received the warm support of the black business community (funeral homes, insurance companies, restaurants, bars), even as its minstrelic caricature made it non-threatening to whites. Carnival societies are social networking organizations, and if there's any mistaking Zulu's place in the black political power structure, the naming in 2009 of former Zulu Queen (twice, in 1988 and 1990) Desirée Glapion Rogers as President Obama's social secretary should make it clear.

Zulu's historically variable route was structured like a second line anniversary parade today, with stops at sponsoring businesses. By 1968, with integration a fact, Zulu was allowed to parade alongside the whites ("not typically viewed as a civil rights victory," as the Zulu centennial exhibit at the Louisiana State Museum dryly noted), preceding Rex along a stretch of St. Charles from Jackson to Canal. Their coconuts (a Hawaiian stereotype, perhaps thrown in to keep it confusing), which they tossed by the bushel beginning in the 1920s, became more elaborate, being drained, hand-shaved of their "hair," primed, painted, and decorated before being thrown. (These days the coconuts, which are the number-one Mardi Gras prize, are handed from the floats to avoid litigatable injuries.) King Zulu's court includes an entourage of comic figures that have become traditions one by one over the years: not only the Queen, but the Witch Doctor, the luxuriously accessorized Big Shot, state functionaries including Mayor and Governor, the loverman Mr. Big Stuff (created in 1973, when Jean Knight's record by that name, produced by Wardell Quezergue, was hot), the Minister of Fun, et cetera.

Probably the peak moment of Zulu's history was in 1949. It was national news when Louis Armstrong, who had left New Orleans in 1922 and had pointedly not returned to play in that segregated town, came back to fulfill his childhood dream of being King Zulu and was received by Mayor deLesseps "Chep" Morrison (though he had to stay in a Jim Crow hotel).[13] He appeared on the cover of *Time* magazine—not in blackface, but wearing a crown—and he blacked up and wore a grass skirt for the parade.[14] By 1960, with the struggle to integrate New Orleans schools traumatizing the town, Zulu's greasepaint embarrassed a generation struggling for collective advancement and equal rights, and civil rights activists called for a boycott of it. The club tried to have a "dignity parade" in 1965, ditching the blackface, the grass skirts, and the coconuts, but it was a flop, and they went back to the old style, retuning the narrative in the process.[15]

Zulu is the only major black Mardi Gras parade in New Orleans. In Mobile today, where there are parallel white and black Mardi Gras Day parades, the black parade doesn't dress up in blackface and grass skirts and throw coconuts. Some of the people who roll with Zulu today are buy-ins, not year-round members of the club. For fifteen hundred dollars, which includes your throws, you can ride on a Zulu float. With that, a whitefaced person can in effect purchase a license to wear blackface.[16] This unfortunately cancels out the Zulu paradox, because white people putting on blackface can never be ironic, no matter what. A more benign interpretation would be what I might skeptically call the "fresh start" theory—that, in the words of my editor, Yuval Taylor, "blackface in New Orleans has ceased to signify minstrelsy and now signifies simply Zulu."

However you look at it, the Zulus have stuck to their image, and the popularity of their parade is indisputable. But the polemic goes on.

Another carnival group that parades today dates from about the same period that Zulu was created, though it was dormant for some decades and was given a new level of visibility in 2003 by Antoinette K-Doe: the Baby Dolls.

Sidney Story, the alderman who wrote the legislation creating the prostitution district in the Tremé, adjacent to the French Quarter, presumably had no idea that his good name would be hallowed in the annals of American whoredom. The working girls of Storyville spread joy and syphilis, the latter resulting in the district's closing down in 1917. Having a major source of contagion in a primary military ship-out point was too much for the surgeon general, especially after medical inspections of inductees for the great war—many undergoing medical examination for the first time in their lives—revealed that 12.6 percent of them were infected with venereal illnesses.[16]

The black underworld didn't shut down, though. It flowed over into a space it already occupied on the other side of Canal Street, a zone known as the Tango Belt. New Orleans was the first city in the world where the word *tango* is known to have appeared in writing—in 1786, referring to black dancing, in an edict by the Spanish governor Estevan Miró—and the word clearly had resonance at a time when the Argentine tango was all the rage. I am indebted to Jack Stewart, a New Orleans musicologist and building contractor who knows every historic jazz building in town and who owns Jelly Roll Morton's former home on Frenchmen Street, for supplying the information that the tango craze (popularized in the United States by Vernon and Irene Castle) arrived in New Orleans in 1913, and for finding the headline from the *New Orleans Item* of January 14, 1914: "Police arrest three women tango fiends."[17] That was the year W. C. Handy's "St. Louis Blues," with its tango beat in the A strain, became a national hit.

All of this may or may not have something to do with the origins of the Baby Dolls. Filmaker Royce Osborn, after researching his documentary *All on a Mardi Gras Day*, told me, "Uptown is supposedly where [it] began—across Canal Street, where they decided to dress as Baby Dolls to show up the downtown Storyville girls."[18] Bawdy girls celebrating and soliciting in New Orleans was nothing new; in 1859, after a licensing requirement for prostitutes was ruled unconstitutional, hundreds of them took to the streets in a victory parade that was, writes Johnson, "one of the lewdest spectacles in American history," with obscene language and nudity.[19] Noah Bonaparte Pais, however, counterposed that Baby Doll founding legend with an assertion by Baby Doll Miriam Reed that the original Baby Dolls were downtowners, founded by a member of her family, Alma Trepagnier Batiste.[20] Whatever the case, other groups followed in the wake of the Baby Dolls: the Gold Diggers, the Zigaboos.[21]

And there were black men who dressed as skeletons, running through the cemetery and waking up the neighborhood on Mardi Gras morning. It's not coincidence that there are black men who dress as skeletons at carnival in Santiago de Cuba too. They're latter-day manifestations of the Haitian lord of the dead, Guédé, who came to New Orleans, perhaps not for the first time but definitively, in 1809, with the Domingan diaspora. The skeletons, who may have formalized their practice around 1930, were still around in New Orleans in 2005.

But with all the carnival elements that went back to the nineteenth century and beyond, there were also aspects that no longer existed. Like Comus's parade, which stopped cold after December 1991, when the black-majority city council passed a desegregation ordinance that placed the burden on the krewes to prove that they did not discriminate in their membership if they were to tie up the public streets and receive public services. The penalty included five months in jail for krewe captains. The firestorm of racial name-calling this provoked can be imagined and has been described amply elsewhere.[22]

Comus and Momus declined to comply with the ordinance and have not paraded since, though they continue to hold Mardi Gras balls. Rex complied by inducting three black members and continued to parade. Proteus withdrew but returned to parading in 1999. Zulu's 375 members already included twenty-five whites.[23]

Comus chose to remain a relic of white supremacy rather than to parade, but he still exists, waiting to return on his terms. "The Confederate caissons," writes James Gill, "which bore Comus floats until the last parade in 1991, sit ready to be wheeled out should he ever reappear in public."[24] He still has his private Mardi Gras ball, at which the customary midnight greeting of Comus and Rex still takes place. Perhaps one day Comus will make his triumphant return, signaling the eternal resurgence of southern tradition—one kind of southern tradition, anyway. For that to happen, the city council would have to have a different composition, and for that to happen, there would have to be a different demographic balance in the New Orleans electorate—a substantial number of the city's black voters moving away, for example. At Mardi Gras 2005, such a thing hardly seemed likely.

The tendency of New Orleans is to turn everything into a tradition, and some of the newer traditions trade on the city's historical crudeness. There was the 1969 surprise-hit movie *Easy Rider*, about two cocaine-dealing bikers (Peter Fonda and Dennis Hopper) on their way to New Orleans for Mardi Gras. The movie's psychedelic centerpiece, shot as pilot footage before the rest of the production, was a decadent acid-trip scene in St. Louis Cemetery #1. For years after, skivey people came to New Orleans who wanted to reenact the sordidness for themselves, the way teenaged Japanese girls invade Prince Edward Island dressed as Anne of Green Gables. The legacy of *Easy Rider* transitioned pretty much directly to the latter-day dominant image of Mardi Gras, namely . . .

As Mardi Gras 2005 was heating up, I found myself at Parasol's, talking to a beefy blond young man on the next stool. He said, "Ah'm So-and-so, from Munn-row [Monroe], Loozyana, and Ah'm here to see some titties!"

"Son," I said, feeling very Louisianan, "you a *long* way from the tittehs up heah."

All year long, when I said to people in other places that I was living in New Orleans, eyebrows would be raised and you'd hear a joke about beads and boobs. It was the overriding image of New Orleans worldwide. But contrary to popular belief, Mardi Gras in New Orleans isn't a display of bare breasts in the street, except between the 300 and 800 blocks of Bourbon Street, and even then, most of the time, if you blink you'll miss it.

A number of companies—most famously Girls Gone Wild, Dreamgirls, GM Videos, Wild Party Girls, et cetera—were in the business of selling compilation videos of breast-flashing at Mardi Gras, as well as videos of . . . oh, never mind. Flashing for beads in New Orleans does not go back to the Phoenicians. It's post–sexual revolution and post–*Easy Rider*. Tit-flashing used to be a motorcycle-mama thing at biker rallies before it became part of the Bourbon Street culture. One of my Tulane colleagues, communications professor Vicki Mayer, who studied the evolution of the phenomenon in New Orleans, told me:

The ritual that's now expressed on the street as "beads for tits" really didn't start until probably the late 1970s, as best we can trace back. The videotaping of flashing for beads really didn't take off commercially until 1988, when the first tapes were distributed, either through the bars themselves or through catalogs. . . . There was a bar on Bourbon Street that made a kind of informal agreement with a commercial videographer to take pictures of women flashing, which, in the case of this videographer, were a lot of his friends and people he would hang out with on a regular basis at Mardi Gras. And then these were packaged and they were displayed in this bar all year long and sold over the counter— fifteen bucks, twenty bucks a tape—and ended up spreading the tradition. . . . This was one of the Johnnie White's bars, on the 700 or 800 block of Bourbon Street. . . . By 1990, there were three or four bars that were playing flashing videos kind of year round. People would come into the bar and actually flash the television set that was playing the video."[25]

Mayer estimated that for every woman flashing in the street, there were at least ten men with video cameras, something confirmed by my own observations. This is, perhaps needless to say, a white people's party; black men getting a hand in the game, so to speak, has been known to spark confrontations.

Elvis's 1958 movie *King Creole* was about a singer in gangster-owned Bourbon Street nightclubs. I don't know who owns all those joints on Bourbon Street today—I've heard stories, but I don't *know*—but if some of those places aren't run by gangsters, they've done a spooky good job of assimilating gangster aesthetics, style, and diplomacy.

Bourbon Street is an alcoholism theme park. It's a fundamental part of New Orleans's brand to be a *zona franca* for messy public drunkenness. There are live cover bands playing high-volume crap-rock at three thirty on Monday afternoon, when booze is cheap and abundant enough to have you passed out by nightfall (HUGE ASS BEERS TO GO, reads the sign a street barker carries). There are walk-up daiquiri windows so you can stumble down the street carrying a triple made with 150-proof rum in a silly green plastic vessel. Fun, no? It's not for children, and you won't feel so great tomorrow. Every day of the year, all day and all night, you can see people careening around there so fucked up they can't walk.

At the bottom of the traveling stripper's list of preferred places to work, Bourbon Street actually manages to be seamier than a real red-light district. All year round, late at night, on the second-floor balconies overlooking Bourbon, female tourists—always white—do what they think they're supposed to do in New Orleans: they perform in an ongoing soft-core amateur shoot, thrusting their cameltoes at flood-footlights while flashing what are sometimes silicone basketballs to the street below, which can be full of hooting people at three-thirty in the morning.

On the evidence of Bourbon Street, what most of us do when we let it all hang out is act like assholes. If you ever wanted to fuck a drunk, fat, pasty-faced person from somewhere else who's waving his or her arms in the air and shouting WHOOOOOOOOO!, this is the place for you. If he or she doesn't puke first. Or maybe even if he or she does.

Bourbon Street is a traveling carny show given a permanent home. It will never stop because it makes so much money for the people who sell the booze, which is not to be confused with the city's overall economic well-being. Still, given that in the Protestant-descended culture of the rest of the United States, unlike most of the rest of the hemisphere, we don't let people carry open drinks into the street, Bourbon Street seems to fulfill some kind of national psychological need.

I was walking on Bourbon Street as the Mardi Gras season heated up, the bacchanalia well under way in mid-afternoon. A middle-aged, tanky-looking white woman was dirty-drunk-dancing in the street with her girlfriend, grinding together and shouting along with a cover-band Billy Joel—is there anything sleazier than a cover-band Billy Joel?—wildly out of tune, at the top of her voice, a look of scary intensity on her face: "I don't care what you say anymore, this is *my! life!*" I don't know who she was, but I immediately made up a story about her: she works all year long in some uptight job in some small- to medium-sized American city. Her coworkers may not realize she's a lesbian. She keeps it buttoned up all year long. For vacation she comes down to Mardi Gras and asserts that it's her life, the best way she knows how, by getting shitfaced in the middle of the day and going out among strangers with her girlfriend. Then she sobers up and goes back to work. I don't know if I got it right or not, but Bourbon Street inspires these stories. Everyone seems to be trying to be temporarily free, if they could only figure out how. Meanwhile they act out New Orleans as they understand it.

I admit I've had fun on Bourbon Street. You can have fun in a disgusting place. But I've had more fun elsewhere.

17

THE END IS NEAR SO DRINK A BEER

During the run-up to Mardi Gras, the Mardi Gras Indians hold their Sunday night practices. These are parties with singing and drumming, battle dance, and drinking, held at whatever neighborhood bar the Indian gang is affiliated with. I went to the Blueprint Lounge on Simon Bolivar (pronounced *Sigh-mon Bolliver*), where I saw a splendid practice by the Wild Magnolias, but the cigarette smoke was so thick I couldn't breathe. In the heavy fog, our party then trundled over to Daiquiri Village, where Hot 8 would be playing.

This was not a tourist event. It was a local, mostly black, mostly younger crowd. Bounce music blasted as people second lined on the dance floor. Here I was assumed to be a music-biz guy rather than a routine customer. I got to talking to the Hot 8's snare drummer. Every band has one guy who's the ambassador, who makes friends for the band. This man was clearly Hot 8's ambassador. He wrote his name and number down for me on a scrap of paper, because you never know who might need to hire a band. I looked at it as he walked away: Dinerral Shavers was his name. Nice guy. (As everyone reading this in New Orleans knows, he was murdered less than two years later.)[1]

On the way home, driving enshrouded in a chilly, dense fog, I heard the record that was electrifying me, probably the great New Orleans hip-hop record of 2005: "Nolia Clap" by Juvenile with Wacko and Skip. "Slow Motion" hadn't disappeared, but here was Juvenile with another killer, and Q-93 was burning it up. In spite of its up-to-date sound, there was a timelessness to it. The track sounded like a dancing skeleton, with graveyard air whistling through the bones.

There were three clearly defined sections, which repeated one after the other. The first section was a rap, under which the main riff was carried by what sounds like cello or double-bass samples, played with heavy bow off the string, staccato. The second section, crosscut-sawing back and forth between two pitches a half step apart, was a shout-out to project people all over town:

Where that Iberville at? That St. Bernard at?
Lafitte? The 8th Ward at?
Y'all hear that Nolia Clap?
Where that Desire at? That Florida at?. . .

Where, indeed, was that Desire at? It no longer existed. The Desire and the adjacent Florida, formerly the largest public housing complex in New Orleans, had been bulldozed years before. But this was a brand-new record, and Juvenile was shouting them out as if they were still there. He was calling out to ghosts. *Where that Desire at? That Florida at?*

Then the release: *Y'all hear that Nolia Clap?* Was the Nolia Clap the hand-clap sample or a gunshot in the street? The line was followed by a scratchy sample of a rhythmic whistle, like a signal between night platoons, in the rhythm that in Cuba they used to call *tango congo*—one bar of habanera alternating with one bar of straight quarter notes.

Y'all hear that Nolia Clap? It made me shiver.

As I turned off Claiborne onto Louisiana, past the Big Man Lounge and the mostly boarded-up Magnolia projects, home of the Nolia Clap, I could see that the Nolia Clap itself was a ghost, punching its way up into the air out of my crunching, maxed-out, factory-standard speakers as I crawled down the dark, deserted, foggy street.

Y'all hear that Nolia Clap?

The partying had been going for days. I monitored it at arm's length so as to be able to continue working.

WWOZ was playing Mardi Gras Indian songs and carnival classics all the time. Turn the radio on in the middle of the day in your car and you might have to pull over and second line by yourself for a minute. I couldn't get enough of Cyril Neville and the Uptown Allstars' "Big Chief Jolly":

Here come the Wild Tchoupitoulas

Yes, we're the Uptown ruler
From way uptown, y'all, in the big 13 . . .

I bopped into Howlin' Wolf on S. Peters Street in the Warehouse District (that's South Peters, not to be confused with St. Peter, which is in the French Quarter) to hear Jon Cleary and the Absolute Monster Gentlemen. Everybody knows Cleary's a fine piano player, but I realized what an underrated singer he is too. I swerved down to the Apple Barrel on Frenchmen on Saturday night to see my old Cajun-Choctaw Louisiana medicine man fave Coco Robicheaux. I tooled up to the Maple Leaf on Oak Street up in Carrollton to catch the Elastic Karma Kings, a good little funk combo I'd learned about from WWOZ. Trombone Shorty got up on stage with them, then Henry Butler sat in on piano. I ordered another beer, of which the Maple Leaf had plenty of choices.

I stayed close to home on Monday, celebrated as "Lundi Gras," the day King and Queen Zulu arrived on a Coast Guard boat and threw their big all-day family party in Woldenburg Park. I didn't go to the Proteus parade in its traditional Lundi Gras night spot. Nor did I see until later the picture on the Homeland Security website showing the Coast Guard fireman Nicholas Reyes, part of a boat patrolling the Mississippi on Lundi Gras, with a big-ass M60 machine gun, under the Crescent City Connection bridge that connects New Orleans with Algiers.[2]

But speaking of hired guns, Mardi Gras season is a marathon for working musicians. Monday night the clubs all had their "A" acts—the Neville Brothers played at the House of Blues—and were packed with people who might stay up all night and begin celebrating Mardi Gras at daybreak, crashing at sundown on Fat Tuesday if they weren't musicians and didn't have a gig that night too.

It was still dark outside when I made coffee, and by the early morning light we were on the interstate over to Tremé. It was early enough that the traffic was still light, but a little later it would be bumper-to-bumper. 'OZ played the record that seemed to catch all the excitement of the morning: James and Troy Andrews's "Talkin' 'Bout the Zulu King." They'd been banging it for weeks. With an alto hook-intro by Donald Harrison Jr. and a propulsive sousaphone bass, it's a perfect little slice of the joy of Mardi Gras day: *Coconut milk / runnin' through the city . . .*

Nothing was happening yet, but under I-10 in Tremé everyone was staking out their positions already, setting up barbecue grills. We were getting closer to lift-off.

The electricity of New Orleans at that early-morning moment—just before it all got under way—was nothing I ever thought I'd experience in the United States. It wasn't just Tremé. No sector of society doesn't participate in

Mardi Gras, and there are celebrations all over. The whole town was synchronized. You could feel that something was about to happen, all across the city.

This is what makes New Orleans different. A substantial portion of the whole town goes out into the street, all at once, in whatever tribal affiliations they feel comfortable with. This is what happens in Salvador da Bahia, in Barranquilla, in Port-of-Spain. It doesn't happen in the United States, except at Mardi Gras in New Orleans. (And, I hasten to add, in Mobile, but on a much smaller scale.)

We didn't have a plan. We'd never done this before, so we didn't have a feel for the day's rhythm. I didn't know what we would or wouldn't run into, but Constance made one thing clear: she wanted to witness the Mardi Gras Indians in action. But the Indians aren't part of official Mardi Gras. They go out on a guerrilla basis, and if you want to see them you have to hunt for them in the backstreets. In a sense, they're marauding. Not sure what to do, we looped back around town, taking it all in, and, since nothing was going on quite yet, we decided to head back home and ditch the car. By the time we got back home, parking on our street was filling up as people flocked up toward St. Charles for Zulu.

This culminating day of two weeks of parades sees the headliners roll: first Zulu, then Rex. Zulu was on its way at eight A.M., and we were there, part of the throng as the parade came along Jackson, turning toward downtown onto St. Charles as they tossed beads, medallions, doubloons, and the most prized throw of Mardi Gras: the Zulu coconuts. I snapped pictures of the Zulu King and waved at Charmaine Neville, riding resplendent on one of the floats as they progressed toward downtown.

Though we only had ever gone downtown by driving before, New Orleans isn't so big you can't walk it. We set out on foot, thinking we'd try to find the Society of Ste. Anne, the rolling freakstravaganza that starts down in the Bywater early in the morning. It was a chilly, damp day, gray but not raining, and most of the businesses were closed. New Orleans musical humorist Benny Grunch has a number called "Ain't No Place to Pee (on Mardi Gras Day)," and we were feeling it. The walk was just long enough that we were getting a little tired, and getting warm for a moment wasn't going to be so easy. But coming through one of those little alleys in the French Quarter we found a tiny bakery that was open. The owner had been up all night making king cakes. We had king cake, still warm from the oven, with coffee, in a Mardi Gras oasis.

As we walked down Bourbon Street, Larisa of the Pussy Footers called to us from a second-story window and waved down. A man on the sidewalk waved at us too, but with a comically huge prosthetic phallus. We ran into the Krewe of Elvis, a mini-parade of Elvis impersonators. Later in the day this block would be full of drunks engaged in beads-for-breasts exchange, but it was still too early for titty-flashers. And there were fundamentalists, who always get up early, which is why I like to get up late. They were already at it, waving their religious-wacko placards—their prosthetic phalli—at the Krewe of Elvis, no less, getting their rocks off on the sinfulness of it all.

We ran into more friends once we got to the Marigny, most of them in costume. The Ste. Anne's parade had arrived, and we hung out in the streets of the Marigny as (mostly white) people played drums (mostly badly) and showed off their costumes—better yet, their characters—as the morning wriggled toward noon. It was the basic carnival experience of hallucinatory otherworldiness: turn your head and something new, strange, and perhaps indescribable filled your eyes before something else distracted you from it. A woman dressed head to toe in parking-ticket orange, her skirt decorated with unpaid tickets. Someone in a giant inflatable sumo-wrestler suit. A woman with a three-foot-high golden scarab beetle headdress. A white-bearded middle-aged man in a pink dress with one leg in a cast, perched on a motorized cart, playing an orchestral kettledrum mounted on wheels as a sidecar. A bald man with a headpiece of martini glasses and a necklace of plastic pot leaves. A devil. A slut. Lots of sluts, actually, of various sexes, some with beards and big, bare, hairy bellies. A sign waving in the air: THE END IS NEAR SO DRINK A BEER.

By mid-day we had arrived at the Backstreet Cultural Museum on St. Claude in the Tremé. It's the former Blandin Funeral Home, turned into a site where Mardi Gras Indian suits are preserved and displayed in the room where they used to lay out the caskets. I like to send visitors there to hear Sylvester Francis give his quick intro-to-carnival tour of the place:

> Carnival starts at six o'clock in the morning. Indians don't come out till twelve. So what we have is skeletons. Groups of mens who dress like a skeleton. Now they dress like that because carnival is a savage day. It's the last day before Lent, so they come out to bless it. To say no rain, no sickness, no death, no killing. So they the first people on the street on Mardi Gras morning. I only been here four years, and by luck, the skeletons done start coming out this building every carnival morning.
>
> After the skeletons get out, this is what we call masquerade. Groups of people who just dress. Anybody. On carnival day you can be what you want to be. You could be Wonder Woman, Superman, whatever.

The skeletons are the first out in the morning. They run through the cemetery in skeleton suits with papier-mâché heads. A reminder of death in the presence of life, they carry bloody joints of meat from the slaughterhouse. There they were, doing their thing on St. Claude amid the masqueraders. The Backstreet whips up a full-strength block party, and this was our hang. We bought beers, ate sandwiches, hung with our costumed friends.

There were the Baby Dolls, led by Antoinette K-Doe, who the year before had begun a troupe based out of the Mother-in-Law Lounge. The oldest Baby Doll was eighty-two, foxy as could be in her baby clothes. At least two of the Baby Dolls this morning had Ph.D.s. Vicki Mayer was Baby Dolling, strutting her stuff with bonnet and bottle, and Helen Regis, an anthropologist at LSU who lives in the Tremé and is the go-to person for second line knowledge, was bonneted up.

A Mardi Gras Indian had appeared—Alfred Doucette, in a splendid tall orange suit, posing for photographers. In my previous book I described the moment this way:

> Then, from a couple of blocks uptown, I heard drums approaching. The first thing I noticed was how good they sounded. It wasn't only tambourines, but a small drum orchestra of various pitches and hefts, played with hands and sticks. Then I heard the chant:
> *Congooooo . . . Congo Nation.*
> *Congoooo . . .*
> The drums slammed a wide-swinging two-bar rhythm, something that would fit with what we call the Bo Diddley beat. It was Congo Nation approaching, with Big Chief Donald Harrison Jr. looking regal in a tall suit of black and gray that extended several feet behind him in a buoyant tail.[3]

At that moment, I stopped being a visitor to New Orleans.

Now I was part of it.

I admit it: I came to town thinking Mardi Gras was bullshit. Weeks of flying beads didn't do much to correct that impression. But this was real. I recognized this region of the soul from my time in Cuba.

The last thing I expected to have in New Orleans was a bona fide spiritual experience on Mardi Gras day. But I know one when I have one.

Constance was right there next to me, feeling it too. Our friends were there, scads of them. Some were people I knew very well, some were acquaintances, some were people I was getting to know, everyone crossing paths. People I've mentioned to you already, and people I haven't had time to introduce you to but I wish I could.

My late friend Arthur Russell had a cult-classic hit record called "Go Bang," the lyric of which went: *I wanna see all of my friends at once / I'd do anything to get the chance to go bang.* Arthur never got to Mardi Gras. But we saw all of our friends at once. We got the chance to go bang. As corny as it sounds, I felt the joy of being alive.

It was feeling like home.

The Chiefs exchanged the greetings of Indian protocol and posed for photographs together with Baby Dolls and Skeletons. We hung for a time, talking to all our friends. We knew a couple of British transplants who lived on the block: Jillian was decked out in a perfect bumblebee outfit, adorned with a Zulu medallion she'd caught, and they invited us to a party in their backyard garden. A little later, we made our way to the Baby Dolls' lair, the Mother-in-Law Lounge.

There was Antoinette K-Doe, still Baby Dolled up, stirring a big pot of beans. Ernie K-Doe—the mannequin, that is—was in his place of honor. The Skeletons were there too, and I wound up talking with one of them, Michael Crutcher, a geographer at the University of Kentucky who's been studying the Tremé for years. He comes down to New Orleans every Mardi Gras to mask skeleton as part of the North Side Skull and Bones Gang, led by Bruce "Sunpie" Barnes, whose importance in the community I was starting to understand. I'd already seen Sunpie play accordion with his fine zydeco band, the Louisiana Sunspots. Now, sitting on adjacent barstools at the Mother-in-Law, I had my first conversation with him. When we spoke about the Skull and Bones Gang, he brought up Guédé before I did.

Though not without its white participants, this was black Mardi Gras. The way Fred Johnson explained it to me:

> There's always been two Mardi Gras. There's been a white Mardi Gras with Rex, there's been a black Mardi Gras with the Mardi Gras Indians, with the Baby Dolls, with the Skeletons. Coming up as a young kid, we never knew anything about going to Canal Street to see Rex. There was so much action and activity going on in our neighborhood until we didn't need to go anyplace else. But how did that happen? That hap-

pened because segregation forced us to be separate and unequal. But in some cases it helped us, because it made us be endeared to each other, and use our strengths and energies and insights.

From the time we arrived at the Backstreet we had been guests on the black side of the carnival street, and we were made welcome. Thank you, Sylvester, thank you, Antoinette. We bid a fond adieu to the Mother-in-Law and crawled back to Frenchmen, where we hooked up with T.R. and Joel. T.R. was emerging from a painful three months with a shattered elbow and a severed humerus, during which we had barely seen him. But his arm was out of the sling, and he was all cheer, with a feeling-no-pain grin.

It was overcast and gloomy after a chilly day, but the party picked up in intensity as daylight began to fade. I stood in the middle of Frenchmen Street, surrounded by a sea of active revelers, taking pictures as fast as I could. Every time I snapped, refocused, and shot again, a different picture appeared before my eyes out of the fantastical dancing texture.

I looked across the revelers toward the darkening clouds and saw another version of the sign bobbing in the air: THE END IS NEAR. It was especially true for people who had been drinking since dawn or maybe since the day before. They were going glassy-eyed, getting really, really loose, and we were getting really, really tired. We'd been on our feet all day and Constance's bad back was spasming. It would have been too much to walk home, plus it was threatening to rain. Somehow I scared us up a taxi. Back in the Channel, only Rocky's Pizzeria was open, running like it was a civil emergency, which in a way it was. Sitting in a booth, calmly eating a pizza—it seemed like a triumph.

We went home and Constance crashed. But I went back out, uptown to the Maple Leaf. I felt like funkin' it up. It was Mardi Gras, but it was also Tuesday night, and that meant Rebirth Brass Band. The place was jammed. Rebirth blew their goddamn brains out.

Two Saturdays later, we headed out across the Twin Span to visit someone I'd been corresponding with. Musicologist Richard Graham lived with his wife, Theresa, in the little Gulf Coast town of Waveland, Mississippi, a forty-five-minute drive east from New Orleans, where they had recently bought a house. Graham had a huge collection of musical instruments—I believe he said four hundred—many of them African. I'd never seen a collection like it. It was a roomful and then some. He could not only play them all but he rocked out on them, laying down a solid groove on his monochord zither. Waveland seemed like a strange place for a musicologist to live, but Theresa had a job there in the paperwork side of the health-care industry. They had room for his instruments, a backyard for their dog, and a happy life together in a lovingly decorated house that was all theirs.

They took us to lunch at a local Mexican joint. Everything looked like it had been put up not too long ago. That's because this humid, low-lying bit of almost-land got flattened and reflattened over the centuries by hurricanes, and in particular had been razed by Hurricane Camille, the strongest hurricane ever to make landfall in the United States. By now, thirty-five years after Camille hit on August 17, 1969, trees had had time to grow back.

After lunch, Richard and Theresa drove us through Bay St. Louis, the first settlement established by Iberville, who founded Louisiana in 1699. There's a little arts-and-antiques scene there, with summerhouses for the rich, the beginning of the so-called Redneck Riviera. As we drove around, they pointed out the high water marks from Camille. We got out and walked around, feeling the tentativeness of the land. We had a lovely day.

Back in New Orleans, the *Times-Picayune* reported that four Marielitos, immigrants from Cuba who had been in a U.S. immigration prison since 1980, had been quietly released from prison and dumped homeless on the streets of New Orleans. The Supreme Court had ruled that 747 Marielitos could no longer be jailed indefinitely, so the Immigration and Naturalization Service was quietly springing them, a few in each city. They drove them from Alabama, where they had been imprisoned, into New Orleans and dropped them off, broke, on Claiborne Avenue for their first taste of freedom after traveling from Cuba to an American prison twenty-five years earlier.[4]

The releases that were being ordered included some Marielito prisoners who had been farmed out to Louisiana parish prisons. That was going to strain those prisons' resources, since they would be losing population. The local jails made money on having federal prisoners—they were a *profit center*—and having a bunch of them set free was going to bring down their bottom line.

"We'll be hurting for money," Barry Patterson, warden of the Pointe Coupee Parish Detention Center, told the *Times-Picayune*'s Keith O'Brien. "It costs you about $1 million to run this jail. We've been budgeting on this."[5]

We hadn't seen Mr. Landlord's wife and baby much lately. One day shortly after Mardi Gras we learned that Mrs. Landlord too had gotten a job in D.C., so they were moving up there. Now their apartment upstairs sat empty. It was just us and the college student in back.

When the sunlight shone in the daytime, the spiral staircase sparkled. It had become a framework for stringing our tons of Mardi Gras beads, which also had a security function. At night it was a snare for anyone who might try to come down it, not that we really thought anyone would. But there was nobody upstairs now, and you could get into our house from up there.

Meanwhile, we had to get over to the House of Blues for Big Chief Bo Dollis's 50th Anniversary Concert with the Wild Magnolias. Dollis is a great soul singer, even though his voice is a multiphonic rasp and even though, or maybe because, his lyrical universe largely consists of Mardi Gras Indian themes. The recordings he's famous for were made in the '70s, released on two LPs and subsequently collected into a CD called *The Wild Magnolias*. Done together with Big Chief Monk Boudreaux, they were state-of-the-art New Orleans funk, with a band led by Wilson Turbinton, better known as Willie Tee. They had a minor R & B radio hit in the '70s with "Smoke My Peace Pipe," which, with its overt pot references, may have seemed like a joke at the time, but the first thing Iberville did with the Houma Indians was smoke the peace pipe. It was a song about diplomacy and chiefly responsibility. As well as about pot.

It was my favorite concert of the whole year. Bo Dollis didn't mask Indian onstage, but two of the band members, including Bo Dollis Jr., did. Listening to the band in a town where musical genre means little, I had an epiphany: the Mardi Gras Indian song tradition is older than jazz, right? It's older than all the commercial forms of African American music we know. When those forms came along one by one, Mardi Gras Indian singing with tambourines— basic call-and-response on the African model, with a local flavor as specific as Louisiana cuisine—was already going on. What this translates to is: you can put any kind of clothes on these songs. It's not wrong to do them as '70s electric funk. They flow into that just fine. In fact, you can put Mardi Gras Indian songs into any style of African American music that came along after Becate Batiste's Creole Wild West got started in 1885 and they work perfectly, because they go back to what's behind all the rest of it, they were there first.

Bo Dollis's show ran something like an old-school soul revue, deploying a string of tricks from the African American stage book. You could hear it by turns as jazz, blues, R & B, rock 'n' roll, funk, or hip-hop without it ever seeming anything but natural. The first number they played was "Iko Iko," also known as "Jock-a-Mo." They played it faster than the song is usually done, but they made the tempo work. The second number was a vamp that went on for something like ten minutes on the words "Rock this town, rock it inside out." That's a Stray Cats song. But how old is that thought? A traveler wrote about New Orleans in 1819: "On Sabbath evening, the African slaves assemble on the green by the swamp, and they *rock the city* with their Congo dances" [emphasis added]. New Orleans was the first town in the United States that rocked, and here was Bo Dollis rocking the town the way Mardi Gras Indians do, which is to say the way Congo Square did. This was New Orleans rock 'n' roll, like I hadn't heard rock 'n' roll in thirty-five years or so. I thought of Larry Williams.

They did a funky electric "New Suit," with Bo Jr.'s iron bell an important element. The song's first line is about the crafting of the Mardi Gras Indians' power: *Every year / for carnival time / we make a new suit*, with emphasis on the last two words. Guest star Rockin' Dopsie Jr. came out with a *frottoir* (washboard) strapped on. That's his ax, and he's a killer on it. Along with his brother Anthony Dopsie on accordion, they played "Sex Machine," faster than James Brown did it, complete with a frottoir solo and breakdancing. Normally, if somebody played a cover of "Sex Machine" I would yawn. But in this case I was looking forward to seeing what they'd do with it. That was the jazz idea: you could play any tune. What mattered was *how* you played it. In this case it was a Mardi Gras Indian zydeco breakdance version of "Sex Machine." It wasn't collage. They were playing right smack in the middle of all those styles that elsewhere are treated as discrete genres, all at once.

Hell, yes, you can rap on top of that. This was black show biz from the late nineteenth through the early twenty-first century all at once. This was living New Orleans, in cyclical time, where once something starts, it doesn't have a beginning, middle, and end, but continues happening. Comus is still waiting for his moment to come back. Husky young black men still learn sousaphone. Fifties R & B is still the shit. Hurricane Audrey is still going on. Gunfights still shake up the streets. Mardi Gras Indians still sing "Two Way Pocky Way."

As we left the House of Blues, walking through the French Quarter back to the Saturn, Constance said what I was thinking.

"Without the Mardi Gras Indians," she said, "all the rest of it would *crumble*."

I had to go back to New York to produce an *Afropop Worldwide Hip Deep* episode about musical happenings in New Orleans, so I missed the St. Patrick's Day celebrations in the Irish Channel, centered on our very own Parasol's. But they don't celebrate St. Paddy's just for one day, so the Saturday before there was a giant block party in our neighborhood, for which we were invaded by women in shiny green dresses and red wigs. On March 17, Constance stayed in the house, avoiding the parade with its crowds, bands, and cabbage throws—though these days they just hand the cabbages off instead of throwing them overhand at your head. If you liked cabbage the St. Paddy's Day parade was a good place to go, because you could come home with all you ever wanted.

Because I was out of town, I also missed one of the year's dramatic moments, the St. Joseph's Night debacle, but I sure as hell heard about it. I've pieced together what happened from some of the many accounts, and I'll begin with the salient quote.

"Take off your fucking feathers or go to jail!"

That ultimatum, spoken by a New Orleans policeman to a Mardi Gras Indian, was given to hundreds of Indians on St. Joseph's Night, March 19, 2005.

Yet another day of significance on the New Orleans calendar, St. Joseph's Day is a Catholic holiday that was widely observed by the Sicilians of the city. The night is a major Mardi Gras Indian event. Geraldine Wyckoff writes:

> The question of when the tradition of the Indians "masking" on St. Joseph's night began remains a mystery. The late Mardi Gras Indian Council Chief of Chiefs Robbe once recalled Indians out on the holiday when he first started masking in 1929. He also knew Indians who hit the streets on St. Joseph's night before World War I.
>
> Most Mardi Gras Indians concur that the custom originated because throughout this predominately Catholic city, which boasts a large Italian population, people enthusiastically observe St. Joseph's Day. Years ago, the streets would be active with folks visiting food-laden altars constructed in the saint's honor at churches, private homes and Italian-owned stores.
>
> "Every corner had an Italian grocery and they'd be celebrating," the late Big Chief Donald Harrison Sr. of the Guardians of the Flame once explained. The late Big Chief Lawrence Fletcher of the White Eagles agreed, adding, "It was an excuse for Indians to mask—it was the only time it was allowed."[6]

Super Sunday—about which, more later—dates back to 1970, and many old-timers see Mardi Gras and St. Joseph's as the two traditional Indian events. St. Joseph's is the only nighttime Indian event, and the dim streetlight shows off a different aspect of the sparkling suits that they spend all year designing and making at a personal expense that can run five to ten thousand dollars, and which can weigh 150 or even 200 pounds. That night in 2005, the uptown Indians took to the streets. Wearing their suits, they walked—some of them for miles—to the place of convergence, historically known as Shakespeare Park and now called A. L. Davis Park. They brought their kids. No, they didn't get a permit, they don't ask for a permit, ever. The Mardi Gras Indians are not about being *permitted* to perform their ritual.

Some two thousand people were in the process of assembling when the police decided to shut the party down. Two dozen squad cars came roaring up Simon Bolivar to shut them down. Apparently someone, perhaps a newcomer in town who didn't know what the Indians were, saw a freaky figure in the street—decorated hatchets, said police spokesman Marlon Defillo—and, feeling threatened, called the police, who responded with an extraordinary action. It was reminiscent of the days of early policing in New Orleans and other southern cities, which was designed to suppress slave rebellion and so depended not on cops walking a beat but on military-style squads that swept the street.[7]

So on the sacred night of holiday, as Indians converged on the park, the police ordered them to remove their spiritually significant suits. A few of the Indians were roughed up, and police actions went on into the night. "You saw police backing up in the middle of the street, driving fast, spinning the cars around, rolling and sliding across their cars," Big Chief Larry Bannock of the Golden Star Hunters told Katy Reckdahl. "I thought they were filming *The Dukes of Hazzard.*"[8]

The next day was supposed to be Uptown Super Sunday, a daytime Mardi Gras Indian parade that normally takes place the third Sunday in March, but it had to be postponed in light of the events the night before.

The police started trouble where there was none. The benign explanation for what happened is that many of the New Orleans police did not know what the Mardi Gras Indians were. A less generous interpretation was that they were trying to provoke something. You don't tell the Mardi Gras Indians to take their suits off any more than you tell a priest to take off his vestments. You just don't. If the police had been deliberately trying to pull a stunt to disrespect the African American population of New Orleans, they couldn't have done it more effectively.

Once again, the community was too smart to take the bait. But people were pissed.

On March 23, a fifteen-year-old was convicted of the 2004 Jazzfest murder of Daniel Breaux. Yeah, the kid was black, and yeah, the victim was white. A bearded fifty-seven-year-old artist and perennial Jazzfest attendee, Breaux was set upon by four teenage boys at the corner of North Orchid and Dupre as he was leaving Jazzfest at the close of its second Saturday. He kept walking when the kids demanded money, and, according to one of the four who copped a plea, fourteen-year-old John Duncan followed him and shot him in the back of the head. As a friend of mine who worked with juvenile offenders once told me: I'd much, much rather have an adult holding a gun on me than a child.

On the night of March 24, Jenard "Nordy" Thomas, a twenty-five-year-old father of three who attended classes at Southern University and worked in a T-shirt shop, was killed by police in the 1500 block of Piety Street. There were ten bullet holes in him, fired from four to six inches away, including one in the back. The police had seen him take a gun out of his glove compartment and put it in his waistband, and said that when they approached him, he ran. They found crack cocaine in his pocket, they said. The dead man's father, who witnessed the beginning of the incident, said the gun was the dead man's mother's gun, that he had tossed it away before the police shot him, and that the police planted the crack rocks. Carrying a gun in the glove compartment is not illegal in New Orleans and, given the general fear of assault in the city, is not uncommon. Carrying a concealed weapon without a permit is illegal, although common. Whatever the case, Thomas hadn't done anything with the weapon, and he didn't start anything with the cops.

Thomas's death didn't register in the city's murder statistics for 2005.

If the police kill you, it's not murder.

18

FRANKLY, I DOUBT ANY OF
IT HAPPENED

I got two pieces of good news at the same time.

I got a Guggenheim fellowship to support my work for the next year. I'd hit the fellowship trifecta, three years in a row. Now I could return to work on the follow-up to *Cuba and Its Music*. I'd expected to be writing a next volume by now, but here I was instead writing about New Orleans. By July I'd be back in New York working on the next Cuba book, on which I'd already put in considerable research time. The other piece of news was also a great honor, though it meant far less money, and none immediately.

Willie Nelson had recorded my song.

Willie fucking Nelson. I mean, how would you feel? Willie and I had spoken over the years about my song "Cowboys Are Frequently Secretly." At one point, when Kinky Friedman was going to make a movie of his novel *A Case of Lone Star*, Willie and Kinky and I were going to sing it for the movie, but it never happened. Now I learned that Willie had recorded it with his band, though I only heard about it via backroom channels and knew nothing of any release plan.

I wrote that song in 1981. I premiered it for an audience of no more than twenty in a SoHo basement performance space called InRoads, accompanied by George Lewis on sousaphone. The next gig I did, someone requested the song. It went on like that, taking on a life of its own from the beginning. I think I have other songs that are far better, but I suppose everyone feels that way when the hit process happens. Not that I had a for-real hit, but it was as close to one as I'm likely to get. "Cowboys Are Frequently Secretly" pondered the phenomenon of gay cowboys:

> Cowboys are frequently secretly fond of each other
> Yeah, what did you think all them saddles and boots was about?

For years people have been saying to me, oh, *you're* the guy who wrote that song! I composed it on the family piano on a visit back to Portales in 1981 at the height of the *Urban Cowboy* plague, with Constance in the room. I was inspired by being back in the Land of Protestant Repression, and by God, I do know how a West Texas waltz should sound. I made a good recording of it in 1984 in Lubbock for an album I made with Lloyd Maines and my band that cost a fuckwad of money and never came out (never mind). Then one night in 1987, my friend Tony Garnier slipped Willie a cassette of the song when they coincided on *Saturday Night Live*. It became a Willie Nelson band bus favorite immediately. Willie started mentioning it in interviews, to my dropped-jaw astonishment. But he'd never recorded it.

The obvious motive for Willie to have recorded it now, after knowing the song for seventeen years, was the forthcoming movie *Brokeback Mountain*. I'd had a friend in publishing send the song to the movie's music supervisor, but they turned it down because it was a funny song and they were making a tear-jerking movie. But you know, the song isn't all that funny. Depends how you do it.

Willie Nelson recording my song? I felt vindicated for all those years I spent singing and writing country songs. I *told* you I knew what I was doing. Just takes people time to catch up. Clearly I was on the twenty-five-year time lag. So I could figure that *Cowboy Rumba*, the album I released in 1999, would be a hit in 2024. I might even live long enough to see it, though it happens faster if you die. Yes, things were definitely looking up. I might even be able to afford to go to the dentist by the time I was seventy-three.

I flew back to New York to go to the Guggenheim reception for incoming fellows. I seem to remember that at the end of the reception, after multiple glasses of wine, I sang "Cowboys Are Frequently Secretly" in its entirety, a cappella, in full voice, to a circle of people. I think.

There were some electrical weirdnesses in the house. Like, I would plug something into the wall on one side of the room and a light fixture plugged into the wall on the other side would switch on. Somewhere between that and the lightning storms, the hard disk on Constance's computer fried out. She had backups on floppy disks—remember floppy disks?—but not everything. After replacing the hard disk and getting her a new surge protector, I tried to find someone who could restore the stuff she didn't have backed up, but I failed.

Meanwhile, the Internet had been out much of the time for two weeks. The router was in Mr. Landlord's side of the house, upstairs in back, and no one lived up there any more. I guess I could have gone up through the hole in the ceiling, but wireless was a new thing to me at the time and I wouldn't have known what to do. Finally we got the guy from Cox Cable to come out and fix it, which took him no more than ten minutes. Not ten minutes after he left, a clueless truck driver turned onto our block and wedged into a tree, taking out the cable to the house across the street. Our elderly German-born neighbor had to cut the truck loose from the tree with his chainsaw. The branches piled up high in front of our house.

In other words, the routine level of dysfunction of the town continued. We sometimes didn't get our mail for the day until after five P.M. The painters no longer came every day, but neither had they finished the job.

The postponed Uptown Super Sunday was held April 3. This is the afternoon the Mardi Gras Indians come out to parade all together, going through the streets of Central City on their way to A. L. Davis Park. I spent the afternoon winding through the streets with them, shooting picture after picture, in tandem with Constance. We worked as a team, running around the event and checking in with each other on the fly, dancing our own pas de deux around the Indians, trying to catch fragments of the splendor of the moment as we paraded through Central City. I think it was the visual high point of our stay in New Orleans, with the bright feathers of dozens of different-colored costumes gleaming in the sunlight.

———

I spent some money at the Louisiana Music Factory, the record store that was still going strong in the French Quarter despite the competition from Tower and Virgin, each a short walk away. Pretty much everyone who was playing in town had a CD out, often without even the formality of a label name, let alone a bar code. There was a whole community of bands ranging from competent to excellent, all of them tight and professional, none of them with record deals. Well, record deals were over, and everybody was rolling their own. I played my new CDs at home, learning the local bands' repertoire the way a fan does, until I went to Seattle, where I gave a talk at Experience Music Project's Pop Conference. I usually give my talks semi-extemporaneously from notes, but I had spent weeks writing this one. It was a tightly packed, if not tightly focused, précis of the ideas I'd been working with all year, themes that were becoming part of *The World That Made New Orleans* and this volume.

There were all kinds of subjects addressed at EMP that year, but New Orleans didn't seem to be on anybody's radar. Few of my fellow music writers were up on the scene that occupied an increasing amount of my listening. No one we'd invited from New York had come down to stay with us in the spare bedroom and check it out. New Orleans could wait.

Meanwhile, there were combos jamming in every bar in the Crescent City. One of the liveliest scenes in the country seemed like one of the best-kept secrets. Hardly anyone who wasn't on the New Orleans wavelength had heard of the Joe Krown Organ Combo. Or Jon Cleary's Absolute Monster Gentlemen. Or Ivan Neville's Dumpstaphunk, Big Sam's Funky Nation, Soul Rebels, Corey Henry and the Young Fellows, Coco Robicheaux, Kirk Joseph's Backyard Groove, Sunpie and the Louisiana Sunspots. These names were becoming bigger and bigger to me. And that's without even talking about the hip-hop scene. This was music history being made in my time and in my face. I couldn't wait to get back home to New Orleans, to see my baby, go on another second line, and listen to those CDs some more.

What did I say? *Back home to New Orleans?* I was hitting my stride, but my stint at Tulane was nearly up. We were going back to New York at the beginning of June.

"Jazzfest starts tomorrow," I wrote a friend. "You can feel the town groaning under the weight of all the heavy musicians." I'd been hearing people talk about the New Orleans Jazz and Heritage Festival, more familiarly known as Jazzfest, since George Wein started it in 1970 as a little tiny festival at Congo Square—albeit with Duke Ellington and Mahalia Jackson appearing—but I'd never been to it.

People all over the country schedule their vacations around this outdoor daytime megablast of music that happens the last weekend of April and the first weekend of May. Bringing in some four hundred thousand visitors, it's a major event for the New Orleans tourism economy.

I'd been waiting for Jazzfest all year. I was planning to hit it the first day, then figure out how to pace myself during the coming musical bacchanal, during which not only was the festival going on but all the clubs in town would have even more music than usual.

The day before Jazzfest began, the painters still had to do the final touch on the job they had started six months before, and it had to be done from inside the house: detail work on the floor-to-ceiling window next to the door. That meant prying out the nails that kept the big window locked from the inside so the window could be opened, after which I would have to renail the window shut. It also meant moving my three-foot stacks of library books away from their spot on the floor in front of the window to clear a workspace. When I got home at the end of the day, I moved the books back into place and started off to the kitchen to get the hammer to renail the window shut.

At some time well after midnight, we were asleep when, as it often did, the light in the passageway outside the window snapped on by my sleeping head. It wasn't our student neighbor in back, though. There were a lot of people passing by out there, and all the voices were male. White boys, with not-local accents. They were going to the landlord's apartment upstairs in back. They had been partying and were none too quiet. Oh, shit, a party rental and he hadn't told us. We settled back to sleep, but then suddenly something I had hoped never to hear again came blasting through the ceiling at very high volume: Bon Jovi's "Wanted Dead or Alive." Now *that* was unforgivable. These couldn't possibly be music fans. They had their boombox set on the floor so that our entire bedroom became a speaker. Oh, great, now we've got a bunch of jocks who've come to New Orleans without their girlfriends to out-drunken-asshole each other in a place where nobody knows them. I picked up the cell phone and called Mr. Landlord in D.C., asking him what the hell was going on. Somehow Bon Jovi got turned down.

To get some sleep we put in earplugs, something Constance usually did but I never do. We dropped off.

Then, because I was wearing earplugs, I didn't hear the crash and thump in the front room.

Constance realized it first. She told me later she thought she was having a nightmare.

She started to scream like I've never heard her scream.

There was someone in our bedroom, looming less than five feet from us.

Time froze.

I reached down under the bedframe and grabbed the Smith and Wesson Browning 1911 model .45 I had bought at Wal-Mart.

Almost before I realized I had done it, I popped the safety, braced the gun with both hands, and squeezed the trigger.

I had never used a pistol except on a firing range. Even in the shadows, despite the recoil, it was too close for me to miss. The shot dropped him, knocking him backward, but then I fired two more times. It was deafeningly loud.

There was blood everywhere.

———

Well, no. And that's why I don't own a gun.

Because if I did have a gun? And if I did keep it within reach of my sleeping form like many people in New Orleans do? That's what I would have done at that moment. That drama has happened over and over again, causing private tragedies galore. After that mini-foray I just now made into action fiction, I should explain that even Wal-Mart wasn't irresponsible enough to sell Saturday night specials in New Orleans, they only sold rifles. The reason I know that was that I had looked at their gun department, because I *had* been thinking—only thinking—about getting a pistol.

Here's what did happen.

I was out of bed very fast and over to the intruder, with Constance behind me, both of us bare-assed and in T-shirts. I shoved him backward toward the bedroom door that opened into the living room.

I was scared shitless for a hot minute, but I quickly realized it wasn't the Angel of Death with lethal weaponry and intent to harm. It was one of those frat-boy party animals from upstairs, so drunk he couldn't walk. Or resist.

He was like, "Whoa! Dude!" Which didn't mean he wasn't dangerous, but at least he wasn't planning to rob, rape, and shoot us. I shoved him backward, repeatedly, pushing him backward a couple of steps at a time toward the front door, shouting curses and threats in his face the entire time as I advanced on him. I don't remember what I said, but it was probably on the order of a stream of what-the-*fuck* [shove] do-you-think-you're-doing-in-here-mother*fucker* [shove]. He never lost his balance and fell on the floor, but neither did he struggle with me. He just let me push him in the direction I wanted him to go as he stumbled backward. I didn't try to hit him. I didn't want to provoke him to respond with a swing at me, since he seemed to be going along with it.

Constance was right there at my back screaming her lungs out, snarling curses and threats—she started the verbal attack before I did—and advancing on him together with me. If I had been him, I would have been far more frightened of her.

The whole thing probably took at the most two minutes, but I really have no idea because time had fragmented into a series of shoves, each one of them an eternity and each one of them lightning fast. I wasn't thinking, I was reacting. In a fair fight at high noon this kid could have beaten me to a pulp. But he was drunk, disoriented, and quite confused, still in party mode, and didn't know where he was, while I was defending my home that I knew my way through in the dark.

It seemed like another episode of that dream I have. The Menace was coming at me. I was doing what I do when The Menace comes at me in my dream. I was snarling at it, cursing it, attacking it, annihilating it. Only this time I wasn't paralyzed and my throat muscles didn't go *auugh*. Words were coming out. I was up on my feet, I was wide awake, my adrenaline was pumping, and I was breathing violently. I didn't pummel him like I do the Menace. I just pushed him back, over and over, toward the door.

The front door was still locked shut. To get him out I had to get the front door unlocked and open while I was pushing him. I did it in flashes—musical training, baby, I got *polyrhythm*—during the beats while he was disoriented from Constance's verbal assault from the other side. Then I gave him one last big shove out the wide-open door, across the threshold through which Jonathan Lorino's murderers had pushed their way in. As I ejected him it occurred to me—I won't call it a thought, because there was no time for thought, but I had this impulse—that I could probably two-handed *throw* him face first off that little stone porch a couple of feet down to those jagged up-pointing brick corners set around the perimeter of the tree. I could have messed his pretty face up. I wanted to. *I wanted to.* But that might take out his eye, or even kill him if he landed wrong. And he had his boys upstairs. How long before they all came down? There were at least ten of them. I hoped they didn't know they could get into our apartment simply by lifting out the circular ceiling plug at the top of the spiral staircase. I was more concerned with being safe, and once the party animal was thrown out the door I slammed it and locked it tight. Then I called 911. Constance kept screaming even after the door was closed.

How did he get in?

Then I saw the knocked-over piles of books in the living room and the wide-open window. He had come home by himself so drunk he couldn't figure out how to get through the gate to the back, so he thought he'd just let himself into the house through the window. He wasn't so drunk he couldn't figure out how to find a window he could open, but he was too drunk to realize someone else lived there and that he was stumbling into a stranger's bedroom. When he came through the window he'd opened, he careened right into Philip Curtin's *The Plantation Complex* and a couple dozen more and kept on going.

I had forgotten to nail the goddamn window shut after the painters had left.

I had meant to do it, never got around to it, and just plain forgot about it by the time I went to bed. Good job, Ned. This was the only night all year that someone could have opened from outside any of the many floor-to-ceiling windows around the house, and someone did. This one and only night, this guy found the only openable window. The only moment at which that particular level of security could have been breached, it was. Had anyone tried the windows on other nights when we were sleeping, hoping to find an unlocked one?

If I had remembered to nail it back shut, he wouldn't have come into our bedroom.

But wait a minute. Someone had been murdered in this house two years before and there was still no working alarm system? There was a sign in front of the house that announced it was protected by a security alarm, but the system wasn't actually connected up and activated. The security system consisted of the sign.

If the alarm system had been working, I would have known he was there before he could get into our bedroom.

I suppose 911 operators are used to the most incredible things, which in this case meant hearing Constance in the background—you've heard the term—screaming bloody murder? She didn't stop screaming for five full minutes after we threw the guy out. I say five minutes, and that seems like nothing, but it was a timeless five minutes as I tried to call my hyperventilating wife back to the world of the nonscreaming. It wasn't until she stopped that I realized: I had caught on immediately that it was one of the party animals upstairs, because I was right on top of him, but Constance can't see in the dark without her glasses at all and wasn't up in his face like I was, so she didn't get that essential piece of information and hadn't readjusted the perceived threat level down like I had as I was pushing him backward, nor had I communicated it to her. She didn't know who it was or what he was doing in our bedroom. As far as she was concerned, she was fighting for her life the whole time. Let the record show that she did not cower shrieking in the corner like girls in '50s horror movies. She was right there on the attack with me.

Since Mr. Landlord hadn't told us anyone was going to be staying upstairs, if we hadn't been awakened by those guys when they came in past our window, and if they hadn't put on Bon Jovi so loud, and if this guy had then wound up in our bedroom without my knowing there were people upstairs, I would have been considerably more frightened, and my response might have been less measured and more violent.

We still didn't have any pants on.

Constance had ripped up her larynx screaming. She wouldn't be able to talk normally for two weeks.

"Ned," she croaked, "we're getting out of here."

Two cops came to investigate our call. I gave them as accurate an account of what happened as I could. They asked if the intruder was black. We said definitely not, he was one of these guys from the vacation rental that had just arrived upstairs. They banged on the door of the landlord's apartment in back, and a young man came down the stairs who gave his name as—I'll call him Neil.

Since I hadn't actually seen the intruder go into their apartment, there was no hot pursuit, and the police couldn't enter the premises. So as long as the party animals kept their boy inside and upstairs, he was going to be safe.

Constance was still hyperventilating and shaken. Looking around in our house, one of the cops commented to Constance how nice the beads and statuettes looked that we had on the spiral staircase, obviously trying to calm her down. She explained that she put them up there to trip intruders.

Was the security alarm on? asked one of the cops, indicating the these-premises-protected-by sign in front of the house. It's never been turned on, I said, there's just a sign. It's against the law to have a sign, said the cop, without having an alarm activated. I'll tell my landlord, I said.

Now that the police were there, a small agglomeration of neighbors gathered and watched as young Mr. Neil, the police, and I conducted a conversation that was none too calm on my part. Before I had been focused on having my wife be safe. Now I got angry. In response to a question about how many were staying in the vacation rental, Neil replied that there were ten. One of the cops asked if one of them had just come into the house or if they'd heard anything. Neil looked down his nose—up on the steps, he was higher in the air than us—and calmly said, "Frankly, I doubt any of it happened."

My jaw dropped. He wasn't just denying their involvement. He was asserting we had made it all up. The home invasion had never happened. We were delusional. My wife was hyperventilating from a bad case of the vapors.

Then the horror of it hit me. This kid was . . . a *Republican*.

Not that I checked his voter registration. But only a Rove-era Republican could lie that effortlessly, that breathtakingly, with that patrician scorn for the hysteria of the lower types. It was the classic airy Republican dismissal: *nonsense*. That's absurd. Poppycock. Et cetera.

Now I was pissed. You want to know what didn't happen? I didn't grab my K and shoot your boy stone cold dead when he came into our motherfucking bedroom, that's what didn't happen.

By now neighbors had assembled. "I vould have *schott* him," said our elderly German neighbor. He wasn't talking tough, just stating a fact. He'd been living in the Channel for a long time, and he wasn't one to mess around. That kid, whoever he was, doesn't know how lucky he is to be alive. Not only did he find the only open window the only night it was open, he also found the only house on the block where the residents weren't prepared to splatter first and ask questions later.

The same guy, or perhaps another one of them, had tried to push into Jennifer's locked door in back. She'd been crazy with her final term papers. Fortunately, Ray had been there with her. She was still shaky.

If Wal-Mart had sold pistols, and if I had dropped the party animal, I could have gotten off. Kill an intruder inside your house in Louisiana and the law is not only on your side but they might even give you a medal. And besides, hardly anybody ever gets convicted of murder in New Orleans, of anybody. But this was a member of the ruling class, so there would have been some kind of consequences. My life would have gotten a whole lot more complicated.

And *that's* why I don't own a gun.

I insisted that Mr. Landlord boot the party animals immediately, since that was unacceptable behavior by any yardstick, but he told me he couldn't do it unless I pressed charges.

On the Richter scale of traumatic things that happen in New Orleans, this little police incident wasn't even a tremor. The cops left and we finally dropped off to sleep about seven, exhausted.

When we woke up, there was a crowd scene outside. The painters were out there again. I thought they were done. No, they'd never be done. The party animals were assembled in front of our porch too, slouching around, presumably waiting for their rides to Jazzfest. There were more than ten of them. I knew which one it was, partly from his height and his build. I looked him in the eye and he kept as stone a face as possible, but some kind of silent communication passed between us. It *was* him. He wasn't as good a liar as Neil. He couldn't quite lie with his eyes, plus he must have had a bad hangover. I shot him a look that said, you don't have the balls to come up and apologize, do you? I'm such a softie that I would have accepted a forthright admission and an apology and wouldn't have pressed charges.

Of course he didn't know that, so he played it safe. I couldn't press charges, because you *don't* make a positive ID on someone unless you really are sure. And I had no corroborating physical evidence. I kept thinking, that kid would look a lot nicer with a couple of open cuts on his face. And then I would have been able to press charges. I spoke briefly and stiffly with Neil, who'd had a conversation with Mr. Landlord. He gave me one of those non-apology apologies, one of those if-anything-did-happen conditional things, and they promised to keep things down.

I didn't go to Jazzfest that day. I went to Tulane to start closing up my office. On the way home I stopped at Wal-Mart and bought a baseball bat, which I placed leaning up against the corner of our bedroom within reach of my pillow. "The next person who invades our bedroom gets a baseball bat across the face," I wrote Mr. Landlord.

We started making plans to go home. It wasn't going to be that fast a process, though. There was a lot to do. Meanwhile, Jazzfest was going on.

I had the weirdest thought: well, at least now I know how my book ends.

I was wrong.

19

THE STRAIN OF THE FESTIVAL

I don't know if I possess the stamina to endure the incredible, constant strain of the festival.

—Brian Jones

Like many things in New Orleans, the sprawling, dusty Fair Grounds Race Course is older than jazz.

Its management claims it's the oldest racing site in the United States in continual operation. The track was built in 1872, but races were going on at the site twenty years before that. Racing continued during the Union occupation, while the Civil War was raging elsewhere. Fats Domino's father supported his family by working there as a groundskeeper, and Fats himself worked there briefly as a stable boy.[1] Jazzfest, which takes place there, has to be the largest music festival in the United States. It occupies two weekends of the year, plus set-up and tear-down time. The rest of the time the track is devoted to gambling, which is where the real money is.

For Jazzfest, a number of themed stages are erected all around the huge racetrack area. There are long rows of stands selling high-calorie regional food, to be eaten in the heat and washed down with endless beers. Enormous lobster-red sunburned breasts bounce in their haltertops. Some of the stages are open under the broiling sun, while others offer shade in tents. Besides the rays, there's the dust, which, speaking as an allergy sufferer, is a disincentive. But there are big misting areas where you can stand in front of giant fans that blow a cooling mixture of tiny water droplets and air.

The grounds are so large that you can easily spend a lot of your day shuttling from one stage to another. The fundamental musical experience of Jazzfest is grazing, like at a buffet. Wandering around, you can't fail to hear something good somewhere. You catch a number here and a number there, stopping in for about as long as you'd listen to a song on your car radio before deciding whether to stay tuned or move on. You hear immortal figures who are all too mortal, blowing their hearts out across the way as you're walking in the other direction because you just gotta pee. When something really grabs you, you stop and check it out and maybe you make a discovery. And the ones you really wanted to hear, the ones you'd been hoping someday you could catch? Everyone else wants to hear them too, so it's not for the claustrophobic.

The programming is overwhelming. For thirty-five dollars—half the price it would cost for a good seat to see any one of the headliners in an auditorium—there were seventy-two different artists scheduled to play on Saturday alone, shutting down by dusk. I could only hear a handful. It's the sadness of the all-you-can-eat buffet—you *can't* eat it all and it doesn't make sense to have one bite of everything, so you still have to choose.

Every kind of popular music of the region is represented, with a conspicuous underrepresentation of hip-hop. There was, however, a new stage in 2005 for traditional folkloric New Orleans music—mostly Mardi Gras Indians and brass bands—and the first thing I saw there was the best I saw at Jazzfest. Big Chief Donald Harrison and the New Sounds of Mardi Gras was a glorious, world-class Mardi Gras Indian Afro-jazz-funk big band of maybe fifteen people, some of them in feathers, including Harrison, who wore the grand Indian suit I'd seen him wear at Mardi Gras. I'd been studying that suit in the pictures I'd taken, and now I admired other details of it from the perspective of the stage. As he opened his arms he looked like a majestic gray bird, exulting with wings spread wide.

There was some occasional second lining, but second lining in Jazzfest is understood to be at best a re-creation, because second lining is about the street, and the street is precisely what Jazzfest is not. Helen Regis, who has been going on second lines for twenty-five years, speaks of Jazzfest as a "gated community." As the ligature between the New Orleans music community, which is by and large composed of poor people and comes up from the street, and the big money of the tourist industry, Jazzfest is in a continual point of tension. Some people in New Orleans love to hate on it, particularly musicians, for whom exploitation by the tourist industry is an ongoing concern and who feel slighted by the attention given to imported big names.

What second lining in the street meant was brought home by something that happened the first day of Jazzfest. "Papa" Joe Glasper, owner of Joe's Cozy Corner, had been jailed on March 11 to await sentencing on his murder conviction stemming from the shooting after Tuba Fats's funeral. The year-long stress of a pending murder charge had taken its toll on Glasper, who was in poor health, and on April 22, the first day of Jazzfest 2005, he died in Orleans Parish Prison.

When word of his death filtered out to the neighborhood, an impromptu event began outside Joe's Cozy Corner, the way such events have been happening since before anyone can remember. Rebirth, who in other years played at Joe's every Saturday, stopped by on their way to Jazzfest to play a few numbers. Eight patrol cars screeched to a halt in front of the bar, topknots whirling, and fifteen officers ordered the citizens to disperse, threatening them with jail.[2] There was anger, but, once again, no confrontation erupted. The people just took it.

In New Orleans, where music does not become obsolete, the legacies of elder performers are alive and continuing rather than nostalgic. During Jazzfest, the dense array of legends can set you to meditating on the connections between them. There was eighty-five-year-old Dave Bartholomew, founding father of rhythm and blues/rock 'n' roll, leading a big band in front of tens of thousands of sun-broiled people. He did his 1957 proto-skank number that was such an influential hit in Jamaica in the pre-ska days, covered again in 2004 by Dr. John: "The Monkey Speaks His Mind," which turned the ape libel on its head to examine humankind from the monkey's point of view, affirming that

> Yes, man descended, the worthless bum
> But brothers, from us he did not come

Made huge by the video amplification at either side of the stage, Bartholomew held a large stuffed monkey in his hand as he intoned the words.

The day closed with the big deal of Jazzfest 2005, a reunion of the four Meters—Art Neville on keys; Leo Nocentelli, guitar; George Porter Jr., bass; and drummer Zigaboo Modeliste—on the consumer-electronics-branded corporate stage. Bearing one of the best band names ever, this was New Orleans's legendary instrumental funk quartet, founded in 1967 (Art Neville's younger brother Cyril joined in '75 as a fifth member) and audibly modeled on Memphis's Booker T and the MGs. They fine-tuned their ensemble in the '60s as the house band at a Bourbon Street bar called the Ivanhoe, which was so small that only four musicians would fit in the space allotted for the band. Let a band play somewhere every night and they'll get good. If they started out as good as these guys were, they'll get great. The Meters had a big R & B hit, now a standard, called "Cissy Strut" in 1969. Their bitter business wrangles with Allen Toussaint and Marshall Sehorn, to whom they were under contract until they disbanded in the 1980s, are legend, and in 1994, a different version of the band took the name the Funky Meters.

But this wasn't the Funky Meters, this was the Meters. To see them on a mega-stage was the inverse of what the Ivanhoe experience must have been. The press of the crowd was too intense for me. I heard a couple of numbers, then negotiated my way home on a beautiful afternoon. I rested up, and that night I took Constance to the House of Blues.

Outside the realm of Jazzfest proper, New Orleans lights up at night as all the clubs in town lay on extra programming. So two nights after we repelled our home invasion we went to hear the Neville Brothers, whom I had never heard live.

Little Rascals Brass Band opened, and they were hot. Then there they were—Art, Aaron, Charles, and Cyril. Art Neville, walking with a cane after back surgery, was playing his second big show of the day after an afternoon with the Meters. They reproduced the sound of *Walkin' in the Shadow of Life* perfectly, and they played what must have been their stock set, some of it consisting of covers ("Drift Away"?), and they played "Fiyo on the Bayou."

And then I heard that opening augmented chord I'd been waiting for.

I gasped. I was finally, for the first time, going to hear Aaron Neville sing "Tell It Like It Is" live. The time tunnel opened. I was sixteen again, in Portales, recalling Louisiana and shutting it out of my mind again even as I let in the triplets that went as far back as my musical memory can reach. As the tune kicked in, I started to scream and hyperventilate. Music can do that to you. You don't *know* how I love that record, and there it was, alive. It was Aaron Neville's crowning career achievement, from thirty-eight years before. For which record he received no money at all. I can't imagine what it's like to have to sing and play a song as many times as they've had to do that one. But I dare say that song is even more of a time tunnel for Aaron Neville than it is for me.

Back at home, the party animals were relatively quiet. No one had acknowledged the seriousness of what had happened two nights before. I was still pissing mad.

On Sunday, I saw Jazzfest from the point of view of the touring performer.

The weakest thing about Jazzfest's booking is the Latin component. With only a tiny Latin community, New Orleans doesn't really get Latin music, so instead of meaningful Latin jazz or heritage performers, Jazzfest winds up booking a few big pop Latin showbiz names out of context into a bloc one afternoon, and that's it. On the other hand, those big names can be good. In 2005 one of them was Víctor Manuelle, the Puerto Rican salsa superstar whose romantic heartthrob image might lead a casual observer to underestimate his musical intelligence and his capacity to improvise perfectly formed rhymes for days on end. His publicist was my pal Blanca Lasalle, who was coming to town with him, so I fired up the Saturn to go to the airport Hilton way out in Kenner, where the band was staying, then traveled from there to Jazzfest with them on their bus.

Here's what the twenty Puerto Ricans saw: the airport. The inside of the hotel. The inside of the bus. Some concrete. Some strange-looking houses. Entering the racetrack in the bus. Getting out of the bus onto a catwalk that led directly into a white tent city, one of which tents they remained in. Emerging from the white tent to step out onstage and play to pretty much every Latin music lover from whatever country of origin who lived within miles.

While the band was in the dressing womb, I poked my head out and heard something I recognized floating in from over at the next stage. It was "Sea of Love." Not only that, it was the original singer, Phil Phillips, singing it. Holy shit, it was the real "Sea of Love," being sung live. I went out and scouted around for a minute and wound up hearing a couple of numbers by Cyril Neville and the Uptown All-Stars. Neville had played the House of Blues with his brothers the night before. No matter: Jazzfest is a marathon. He was rapping, presumably referring to the St. Joseph's debacle. I remember it as: *Rex and Momus / Do what they wanna / Mardi Gras Indian / Get off the corner.* Such are the wonders of New Orleans speech that it rhymed.

Back in the wings, I watched Víctor Manuelle sing his many hits, songs I've heard him sing many times, in clubs, in Carnegie Hall, and on the radio in every Spanish-speaking country I've been to. He was the only Latin artist of any importance I saw all year in New Orleans, and he parachuted in. The city's not on the Latin circuit at all. It's the other great tradition. Then the Ricans left the stage and waited in the tent until they got back into the bus for the hotel. They had a four A.M. lobby call for a six A.M. plane, so they stayed in. That was their Jazzfest. Getting on the plane was their day job. I liked my Jazzfest better than theirs.

All this great music that I hadn't gotten to hear all year was available in the dense concentration of the Jazzfest time-compressor. It had taken me all these months to rev up to the point where I could live New Orleans this intensely. It had never seemed so interesting. But we didn't want to be in New Orleans anymore. I never wanted this music to end, but I wanted to get back to my next book about Cuba, and we wanted out of that house.

I realized: you don't really love New Orleans until you've hated it.

The Monday night between the two Jazzfest weekends is Piano Night. That's WWOZ's big fundraiser, held at Generations Hall, a two-level structure big enough to hold a couple thousand people. Two stages were set up in different parts of the building which, despite its modern interior, was built in the early 1820s as a sugar refinery. On the smaller stage, a piano. On the bigger stage, two pianos. Damn near every pianist in town does a shift, along with whoever's visiting. There are a lot of good pianists in New Orleans, and on Piano Night you can take their measure laid out next to each other. Larry Seiberth played beautifully. The Joe Krown Combo, Hammond B-3 organ in tow, sounded just like their record and made me appreciate Krown as a composer. There was an especially fine set by the duo of pianist Tom McDermott and thirty-year-old clarinet virtuoso Evan Christopher, who played Creole-style numbers by Jelly Roll Morton and Sidney Bechet, ragtime by Scott Joplin, and a Brazilian-style *chôro* of McDermott's. The two had played together so much they seemed like one player, Tom breathing when Evan breathed.

The honoree at that year's Piano Night was Allen Toussaint, one of the greatest living record producers—"Mother-in-Law," Lee Dorsey's hits, all the best stuff by Irma Thomas, "Lady Marmalade," scads more—a distinguished piano stylist in the New Orleans tradition and the very picture of the finely dressed, well-spoken New Orleans creole. When I interviewed him in '92 I thought: this man sings when he speaks. I stood overhead on the balcony, listening to him do some of his many hits by himself, where slaves had sweated before an open sugar-boiling fire 150 years before. A rotating cast of pianists played the second piano in duo with him, which at one point included Dr. John and Marcia Ball playing four-handed.

And there was David Torkanowsky, Jon Cleary, "Papa" John Gros, and . . . Henry Butler. Who is in a class by himself. Butler had a gallery opening, concurrent with Jazzfest, of his photographs. Which might not be so remarkable, except he's been totally blind since childhood. He's one of those guys who doesn't let anything stop him.

Besides the other things Henry Butler is, he's a serious Longhairian. The essential repertoire of Piano Night is the Professor Longhair canon. All New Orleans pianists are expected to be able to interpret Professor Longhair (born Roy Byrd in Bogalusa), the great spirit who found a way to bring elements of the Cuban thing into the florid Louisiana style, complete with habanera bass and claves. At Piano Night, whatever else gets played, you will hear "Tipitina," "Big Chief," and "Go to the Mardi Gras" more than once, each composition tackling a different slice of New Orleans pianistic style with a different compound rhythm, and each pianist bringing out something different in it.

I went home late and rested up, trying to save some energy for the next night.

There was Leslie, from New York. What was she doing here?

Oh, right. Leslie is a roots-rocker. There's a whole circuit of people who come into town not for Jazzfest but for the Ponderosa Stomp. Taking its name from a 45 by Lazy Lester, who plays the festival every year, the Stomp was the creation of a fez-wearing character named Dr. Ike, who is in real life Dr. Ira Padnos, an anesthesiologist and vinyl freak. In classic New Orleans fashion, Dr. Ike formed a secret society, the Mystic Knights of the Mau Mau, that produces the Stomp. In an overwhelming two nights going from five P.M. to five A.M. each night, on an upstairs stage and another simultaneous one downstairs, the Stomp presented an astonishing array of still-surviving sexagenarian-or-more legends of the regional first-generation rock 'n' roll scene, including swamp-pop, old-school New Orleans R & B, and rockabilly, with no small presence from Memphis. These were not just call-a-booking-agent oldies packages: Dr. Ike had to find many of the performers and in some cases coach them on what repertoire to play.

This fourth annual Ponderosa Stomp took place at the Mid-City Rock 'n' Bowl, a two-level bowling alley that shared a strip mall with Family Beauty Supply and Thrift City in a low-lying part of town. With a bandstand on the second floor, as well as a short-order kitchen and a bar, you could bowl, dance zydeco, eat an alligator po'boy, and drink beer all at the same time. There was another stage downstairs.

Once again, the problem was the suffocating smoke. The downstairs area boasted perhaps the densest nicotine cloud I had encountered in New Orleans. The music was so much fun that I tried to ignore the air quality, but I wound up taking frequent oxygen breaks to join the considerable party of fellow airheads accumulating out in the Rock 'n' Bowl's spacious parking lot. Which is how I found myself talking to a tall, skinny, bearded guy who turned out to be Paul Cebar, the Milwaukee singer-songwriter. He comes down in his van every year during Jazzfest. I'd heard him on *Prairie Home Companion*. He'd read my book, heard the *Afropop Worldwide Hip Deep* show I'd produced on New Orleans, and knew *Cowboy Rumba*. We hit it off immediately.

We checked out Dale Hawkins (Mr. "Suzie Q") from Shreveport. There was Ace Cannon—how great is that?—down from Memphis with a darn good little combo. The surviving members of Elvis's band—Scotty Moore on guitar and D. J. Fontana on drums—played the early Elvis repertoire, with Memphian Billy Swan ("I Can Help") filling in on the Elvis parts, though it's understood with a thankless task like this that the voice is only a cipher. The real point was to watch Scotty Moore, the guy who played the guitar part on "Blue Moon of Kentucky," cut #1 on *A Date with Elvis*, playing the part live in front of me. Behind him, D. J. Fontana showed you exactly what kind of drummer Elvis had: a solid one.

I'm one of those people who like to walk into a roomful of strangers and just start talking, maybe because I lived for so many years in a town where everybody had known everybody else their whole lives. I swam in the party, hanging out with friends old and new. There was Dan Rose and Peggy O'Neill, with some friends of theirs who'd come down from Detroit for the Stomp. They were friendly but gave off a slightly weird vibe, for reasons I found out later. I hadn't seen John Swenson, the veteran music journalist who also writes for the *Racing Form*, in ages. Cheap chic was everywhere. I saw a young woman in a skirt that displayed her leg tattooed like an aquarium, the entire skin surface water-blue, with fishes swimming around it. I was stupid enough to ask her if she was going to do the other leg too. Well, duh.

Up till now, the music hadn't even been very loud. But that changed. Cebar and I were hanging out downstairs when Link Wray came on. One of the most influential electric guitarists for the later loud-rock generation, Link Wray and his Ray Men had an all-time hit in 1958 with the crunchy, distorted, proto-psychedelic guitar instrumental "Rumble." You can't imagine the Who without "Rumble." Wray was about to turn seventy-six, making him the oldest bona fide punk I'd ever seen. He wore a leather jacket, looking like a '50s juvenile delinquent turned denture-wearer. His only facial expression was a scowl. Part Shawnee Indian, he'd been living in Denmark for twenty years or so, and he sounded for all the world like a loud European art-guitar band, though of course the influence ran the other way round. Most people tune their guitars silently now with electronic tuners, right? Not Link Wray. He had his much younger second guitarist—his son, it turned out—play through the amp while he tuned out loud to it, with the amp wide open. He didn't even get it close to in tune before he kicked off the first number, which was a timbral excursion into the harmonics generated by thick-gauge metal strings at high volumes. Think MC5, the Stooges, Johnny Thunders.

"He's like your ornery grandpa who won't turn his amp down!" laughed Cebar, who by now I seemed to have known for years. Despite rocking out, Wray brought his domestic drama onto the stage with him in the form of his chunky, longhaired Danish wife, Olive, about whom there are many stories, who stood onstage with him, bizarrely holding a plastic tambourine in the air and whacking it amusically against the heel of her hand the entire time, like something out of *This Is Spinal Tap*. She had been doing this since 1997, when she debuted as a tambourine nonplayer alongside Wray on *The Conan O'Brien Show*.[3]

I'd known "Rumble" forever, but I'd never seen Link Wray play before. Nor would I again; he died a little more than six months later. He went out distorting.

I hadn't had this much fun in . . . well, maybe since Mardi Gras. Upstairs in front of the bowling lanes, I saw Classie Ballou, from Baton Rouge and now living in Waco, playing a Gibson SG just like mine. I'd never heard of him before, but I recognized the riff he played when he started doing "Just a Little Bit." It was the guitar lick the Beatles used at the beginning of "Birthday." Classie Ballou was the guy who came up with that lick, playing with Rosco Gordon on "Just a Little Bit." Herbert Hardesty, best known as Fats Domino's longtime sax man, was onstage with him.

And up came Rudy Ray Moore, better known as Dolemite, the dirty-talking comedian from party records and, later, blaxploitation films. He came onstage looking like a pimp from one of the lesser southern cities, resplendent in rhinestone-studded shades and ceremonially encrusted walking cane.

"I ain't gonna get no pussy tonight!" he shouted. Now there's an ice-breaker for you.

"You know why I ain't gonna get no pussy tonight?" Pause. He pointed out a guy in the front of the audience. "Cause *you* done ate it all up!"

He sold Dolemite souvenir walking canes from the stage for ten bucks. You know I bought one, handed the money right up to the man onstage. It's been a personal power object for me ever since.

And then it was time for the surprise hit of the evening.

"How do you perform solo when all your hits are based on overdubbing your own voice in octaves?" asked Cebar, still laughing, as I cracked open another beer. Brenton Wood went for the higher octave when he came out to sing "The Oogum Boogum Song," "Gimme Little Sign," and "Baby, You Got It."

I had always thought of Brenton Wood as being from Los Angeles, but no, it turns out he was born in Shreveport before moving to Compton as a child—the LA-to-L.A. migration that so many New Orleanians made during the years of white supremacy. He was great, plus he played his album tracks. Brenton Wood's hits were on an independent label called Double Shot, which had only one other hit group, and a one-hit wonder at that: Count Five. Presumably because the label owned the publishing, Brenton Wood recorded a version of the Count Five's hit. Which is how it happened that a sixty-three-year-old black man from Shreveport in a brown pinstriped zoot suit came to sing "Psychotic Reaction" in a bowling alley in New Orleans, complete with double-time freakout break. On guitar was Alex Chilton, a Memphian living in New Orleans, whose brush with permanent-rotation supermarket immortality was singing "The Letter" and "Cry Like a Baby" with the Boxtops, and on keyboards was Mr. Quintron. Cebar and I were howling. When Brenton Wood finally left the stage, we shouted, "Do 'Oogum Boogum' again! Do 'Oogum Boogum' again!" in unison at the top of our voices.

He did "Oogum Boogum" again.

I was getting hoarse. My bronchs were on fire from the intense tobacco haze. Lady Bo was starting up—Bo Diddley's female second guitarist for many years, she was the first woman to be regularly hired as a musician by a major rock 'n' roll group—but I was done.

I pointed the Saturn back to the Irish Channel and wheezed my way home.

I would have to miss Blowfly.

————

By day, I was packing. I blew off the second night of the Ponderosa Stomp because I couldn't face another night of breathing smoke. As it was, my chest burned when I inhaled, and Constance had come down with a bad cold. I didn't get to see Archie Bell play "Tighten Up," or Barbara Lynn, Roy Head, Nathaniel Meyer, or Plas Johnson.

Our neighbors from further down Constance Street, Dan and Peggy, did go to both nights of the Ponderosa Stomp, but they'd had a freaked-out week, courtesy of the drug dealers that infested their block. Dan told me the story:

We had friends in from Detroit, Sandy and Jim, who showed up in a rental car with out-of-state plates. The night before the Ponderosa Stomp, they pulled up around midnight, dropping us off. The drug dealers were there. We got out of the car, the drug dealers got out of our way, and we went into our house. Then we started hearing all this gunfire, and tires squealing.

They were shooting at Sandy and Jim. I don't know if it's because they assumed that they were coming to buy drugs and they weren't so they got angry, but evidently they emptied off a whole clip. It was dark and we couldn't tell. Their tires squealed, and they took off like a bat out of hell. The drug dealers ran after their car, shooting as they were driving away.

Once I heard the tires squealing and the gunshots, I got really frightened for Sandy and Jim. I looked out the window and I could see that they were moving down the street. It sounded like the car was getting away, but I went out of the house to see if I could see their taillights fading off into the distance, or did they get hit and were slowly coming to a stop? I saw them fade off, and then I ran back in the house because I didn't feel like getting shot myself. By that time the drug gang kind of all scattered, maybe because they had drawn a lot of attention to themselves and I'm sure they would expect the police to be showing up in the near future, from a buncha shots going off.

The police did show up, maybe five minutes later. But nobody was shot, so they didn't even knock on doors and ask questions of people, which in other cases they did. We actually had policemen jumping over the back of our fence chasing them one time—all of a sudden you hear all this commotion in your backyard and this policeman is pushing you out of the way, leaping over fences. A lot of times they could get a little bit verbally hostile to us. Like, when they want to get information from local people and local people are afraid to give information because they don't want to get the snitching thing going on.

At that point we were so upset about it we were like, OK, this is about the fourth shooting we've experienced in a handful of months here. If we had a shooting maybe once a year, that wouldn't intimidate and make us feel like we want to leave, but after they started shooting at our friends we were like, no, we can't have this, this is really dangerous for us, and we need to start asking around and getting inquisitive about finding a new place to live. But the Ponderosa Stomp was upon us! And we had Sandy and Jim in from out of town.

Then the second day of the Stomp, in the afternoon before we went out, we were sitting in our house, just talking about how terrible this is and how upset we are about the fact we're getting chased out of our neighborhood. Even if we're not being chased out directly, it's an indirect chase-out. And we start hearing shots go off again, and this time even louder. About four or five shots popped off, and I look out the front window and there's this guy, just fallen off his bike. Right in front of our house, in broad daylight. Shot down, he's got two or three bullets in him. He's lying in the street bleeding. Like, literally ten feet maybe from our house directly in front. And his seemingly eight-month pregnant teenage girlfriend, with her belly stuck so far out, she's on her knees with him, and she's wailing, and it was just such a horrible sight to see and feel. It shot electricity through us, and made us feel like, we have to leave immediately. From what we were told, he was one of the local drug dealers. I couldn't see his face real well, the way he was contorted on the pavement in the middle of the street, so I couldn't tell. It looked like somebody I recognized that used to hang out, so the rumor made sense. It was some sort of retaliation thing. I don't know if it was a jealousy issue, or a rival drug gang, or—I've heard both rumors, and I never really found out the truth.

The police were there relatively quickly, but it was a long time before an ambulance came to get that kid bleeding on the street. And that made me really sad. 'Cause he was probably anywhere from fifteen to twenty years old, and there was his girlfriend, maybe mother of his child, wailing in there, and that ambulance seemed to take forever. I would say, I'm sure it was a half an hour, even though when you're in those situations, time gets surreal. But it seemed like the ambulance took a long time. I found that discouraging and depressing and sad and worrisome. Because, you know, he's some family member to some people.

But Dan and Peggy and their friends from Detroit weren't about to miss the second night of the Ponderosa Stomp. And this is what I learned, above all when I was in Cuba, and I saw it reconfirmed in New Orleans: just because you're dancing doesn't have to mean you're happy. It's how you go on living in spite of everything. As it turned out, despite the agony of waiting for a slow ambulance, the teenaged drug dealer didn't die, and as such, the shooting merited very little newspaper space. Just another scary incident.

Jazzfest started up again the next day, Thursday, April 28, but I went on with my packing marathon instead. I was going out that night, though, because the Mothership was landing. George Clinton and P-Funk weren't part of the Jazzfest schedule, but they were coming into town anyway, to play at TwiRoPa Mills, a huge club in the Warehouse District.

I'd sailed past TwiRoPa any number of times on my perfectly calibrated nocturnal speed-route back from downtown, but I'd never been in it. The large former twine, rope, and paper factory was on a dark stretch of Tchoupitoulas by the levee, downriver from our house on the other side of Wal-Mart.

The Jazzfest week was turning into not only a musical experience but an architectural one. Every one of these repurposed spaces I'd been in—the Fair Grounds Race Course, Generations Hall, Mid-City Rock 'n' Bowl, TwiRoPa—had a story to tell that wrapped around the music. P-Funk might have played the same notes anywhere, but their music felt different when they played in New Orleans. They were on the sacred ground of funk and they knew it. George Clinton told me as much the one time I interviewed him, in 1993. P-Funk spent a lot of time on the road, and they made sure to hit New Orleans a couple of times a year, where their music was understood and where they were challenged to do their best.

I'm an immoderate P-Funk fan and hadn't seen the band in a while. I turned around and there was Ariana Hall—turns out she's a P-Funker too; I might have known. But mostly it was college kids, a new generation of funkateers. P-Funk did not disappoint, playing tunes old and new. After all I'd been through, up and down, that week, there he was: George Clinton, right in front of me. Who says gods don't still walk the earth? Clinton to my mind is the only successful lineal descendant of Frank Zappa. Not in the musical substance, which comes from somewhere much different than Zappa's, but in building on the genre of musically virtuosic, toilet humor–laden theatrical extravaganza that Zappa pioneered back in the days when Clinton was an LSD-taking hippie—white hippies would have called him a "spade"—and taking it to places Zappa could never have gone. James Brown apart, Clinton was the greatest living exponent of funk, one of the great American musics, and an American poet whose verses should be remembered in the twenty-second century. Now sixty-three and road-toasted, he actually did very little on stage; he was the ringmaster of a giant traveling circus that at one time had over sixty members and still had more than twenty. Nobody could have been getting paid very much.

It was like a commedia dell'arte somewhere in northern Nigeria. There was Gary Shider in a diaper—the first character on stage, a reworking of the figure of Eleguá, if you will, called Starchild in the P-Funk sagas. And there was his enemy, Sir Nose D'voidoffunk, who in the 1979 *Gloryhalla-stoopid* turned Starchild into a mule. Along with Rumpofsteelskin and Mr. Wiggles the Worm, they were the stock characters in a mythology Clinton

338   THE YEAR BEFORE THE FLOOD

had defined, the Harlequin and Scaramouche of a musical, lyrical, metaphysical edifice constructed on top of a maybe Kikongo-English word enthusiastically taken up by African Americans, probably as early as the seventeenth century, that referred to body odor, and I do mean *funk*.

I hope to write a volume someday about Clintonian metaphysics. George Clinton's funk is an entire Afrocentric universe, with devastatingly perfect blue-note intonation, busy-texture rhythm, dance moves, dirty jokes, preposterous singalongs, stoned multiple entendres, and what in Zen are called koans: *How'd you get all you got into what you ain't wearin' on you?*

They opened with "Bounce to This," a new tune to me. Was George leading with that one because New Orleans is the bounce town? For that matter, TRU (Master P and his brothers) had a track called "Bounce to This" on their 1999 album *Da Crime Family*. By the end of it I was bouncing.

With the Mississippi River right outside at her back, the honey-voiced lead singer Kendra Foster, in her sexy gold dress, was a perfect Ochún, goddess of love and rivers, only singing funny lyrics:

> *Fat cat record executives, step to this*
> *Thought I was sleepin', came creepin', look what you missed*
> *Ooh, you couldn't resist, and now you're pissed*
> *Thinkin' it was over . . .*

Most of the time, though, there's no single lead voice identified with P-Funk. There's a communal vocal sung by the whole troupe, and the next line might be taken by anyone in the circle. The lack of intelligibility in big-chorus vocals is compensated for by extended repetition, the way talking drums repeat the message to ensure communication, giving you time to hear the phrase out: *Make my funk the P-Funk . . .*

There were pink people in the band, the way there usually are in the later incarnations of popular black bands. As Clinton beamed, his full-grown granddaughter—named Sativa, no less—rapped in praise of large, erect penises on a number from the ten-year-old overlooked masterpiece *T.A.P.O.A.F.O.M.* (The Awesome Power of a Fully Operational Mothership):

> *No itsy bitsy teeny penis type of pecker poker pusher ever penetratin'*
> *   a puss-eh!*
> *She like it hard!*
> [chorus:] *Hard as steel and steel gettin' harder . . .*

And my favorite, from *Motor Booty Affair*:

Psycho-alpha-disco-beta-bio-aqua-do-loop
A motion picture underwater starring most of you loops

I always wondered about that one. When I studied computer programming in between R & B concerts that summer when I was sixteen, I learned about "DO loops." If you wanted to be ready for the future in 1967, you learned to write FORTRAN programs, of which DO loops were a basic component. Then and now, loops—cyclically repeating actions—are basic to programming languages. Back in the day they were called DO loops, from the "DO" command they used. If you screwed up writing your little program—a keyboarding error, say—it could get caught in an "infinite DO loop" and the computer would repeat the steps helplessly, endlessly, until the mainframe operator finally terminated it and your tall stack of punch cards was returned to you in disgrace.

How did George Clinton know about DO loops, I wondered. Did he perhaps learn some FORTRAN, back in the prehistory of P-Funk? There's always been an undertext of logic to his poetics, and it's audible in the music as well: funk is based on loops. I was getting loopy. The smoke was killing me. I wondered how Clinton could stand this level of exertion—that band plays *loud*, though they only went for about two and a half hours instead of the four I've seen them do before—in an environment of pure nicotine, when you gulp for air as you're singing and what you take in is pure poison.

I had always admired that Lee Dorsey tune, written and produced by Allen Toussaint: *Ev-e-rythang I do gon' be funky / From now on*. But under the strain of the festival I was starting to realize that it might indeed even be possible to be such a thing as *too funky*. Indeed, that's the oldest complaint in New Orleans music: *Funky butt, funky butt, take it away*, a plea to open the windows in a crowded, stinky dancehall. That night, as I made my funk the P-Funk, I wondered how funky the DO loop could get.

The next afternoon, still P-Funked out and still coughing, I went to a Jazzfest panel with Earl Palmer, Cosimo Matassa, and Art Neville. During the Q-and-A round, when the interviewer mentioned Neville's house on Valence Street, a little ways uptown from our house, Neville answered: "I still live on the block I was born on, and I'm gonna be there till the water comes." *Till the water comes.* There was no question of what he was talking about.

During this part of the New Orleans calendar, you bang from one dense experience into another. As I was leaving the panel I ran into Mark Bingham, an old guitar-playing, music-composing pal from back in the day in New York (whom you already met in the "Whips and Ice" chapter). He had moved to New Orleans in the fall of 1982 and had seen the town go through twenty years of changes. Besides playing music, he'd always done engineering and producing. His first recording gig in New Orleans was a live album of Mardi Gras Indian songs by Big Chief Monk Boudreaux and the Golden Eagles—bang, welcome to New Orleans, Mark, here's the real deal. Mark wound up being the proprietor of a recording studio, Piety Street Recording. I hadn't looked him up all year. Which seems incredible now, but there were scads of people I never looked up. I lived uptown in the Irish Channel and the Tulane orbit, and he existed in a different reality, that of the Bywater and the realm of the working musician. And maybe I was avoiding going near recording studios, the way a rehabbed alcoholic stays out of bars. At the track with Mark that day was his significant other, Shawn Hall, and they invited me to visit. That's two more friends I have in New Orleans. It was getting to be a long list.

I stopped in at one of the tents and found myself talking to Victor Harris, Spirit of Fi-Yi-Yi, one of the most important figures in the Mardi Gras Indian community. I wandered over to the big automotive-sponsored stage where Randy Newman was singing from the piano, all by himself, to a vast crowd. Though he's from Los Angeles, his Louisiana connection is bona fide: his father's family had three Hollywood composers in it, but his mother's family was from New Orleans. He knew the town as a child, and he's always kept up with it. He's the only contemporary American songwriter I can think of to have addressed directly the topic of the slave trade (in "Sail Away": *Sail away, sail away / We will cross the mighty ocean into Charleston Bay*).

Newman launched into his thirty-one-year-old song that had long since become an anthem in New Orleans: "Louisiana 1927," about the great flood of that year. I'd heard it any number of times that year already, in various versions. Many more people would soon get to know the song:

Louisiana, Louisiana
They're trying to wash us away

We knew perfectly well what he was talking about.

Within twenty-four hours I'd been caught up in the presence of George Clinton and Randy Newman both, spoken with Earl Palmer, met Fi-Yi-Yi, and meditated on the weight of their legacies. And I'd caught the cold Constance had. I felt like shit. I didn't return for the last two days of Jazzfest. It defeated me. I missed Isaac Hayes, Ike Turner, B. B. King, and 483 others. I started asking around to see if anyone I knew wanted to take over the remaining sixty-four months of payments on the Saturn.

There were people upstairs in the party rental apartment this weekend too, but they kept quiet. And I had my baseball bat.

I hoped to be out of that house in two weeks.

There was another parade coming up.

20

SUPER SUNDAY

Bayou St. John occupies a unique place in the city's psychology. It's a long, thin tongue of sluggish water that sticks into land from Lake Pontchartrain, connecting with what geologists call Esplanade Ridge, which is more or less what the street map calls Esplanade Avenue. In prehistoric and colonial days, Esplanade Ridge was the only land that stuck up out of the muck of the swamp. At the other end of Esplanade from the Bayou is the French Quarter, the old colonial city built on the high ground of the side of the natural levee of the Mississippi River. The ridge thus furnished a portage trail that could connect the Mississippi to Lake Pontchartrain, which in turn connects to the Gulf of Mexico. It was the best available way to get goods from the river to the ocean.

The Bayou St. John was the first part of modern New Orleans to be cleared by the colonists, even before the cedar swamp along the levee was cleared to build the city proper beginning in 1718. As the terminal of the lake route to the city, it was the city's main harbor before the invention of the steamboat.

It was also a voodoo spot back in the day. After the city of New Orleans restricted gatherings of black people in 1817 to certain times and places, the voodoos moved their dances out to Bayou St. John and various places on the shore of Lake Pontchartrain. Though by the 1870s or so these voodoo ceremonies had become heavily touristed, a host of, shall we say, folkloric spiritual associations still adhere to the place, as per the name of the big voodoo holiday: St. John's Eve.

I had come to Bayou St. John for the Tamborine and Fan Super Sunday parade, which assembled there before parading down Orleans Avenue. It used

343

to start uptown, but some of the old-timers thought it needed a little fiyo (fire) on the bayou, meaning, says Tamborine and Fan's Jerome Smith, "that the emotional excitement of the gathering would have a greater impact by that water." Besides the historical resonances, the Bayou St. John was a practical starting point for a big parade. That old portage trail provided a straight shot in the direction of riverside for the parade's multiple bands, many of whom might have to get on down there to another gig afterward.

Tamborine (without a "u") and Fan pointedly doesn't style itself as a Social and Pleasure Club, though they have an affiliate Social and Pleasure called the Bucket Men. The organization explicitly represents the consciousness of the civil rights movement as applied to New Orleans street tradition. Beginning informally in 1966 and formalized two years later, Tamborine and Fan was "an outgrowth of the Mississippi Freedom Schools," according to Jerome Smith. Smith knew Schwerner, Chaney, and Goodman, and he cites as his mentor Lorraine Hansbury, author of *A Raisin in the Sun* and *To Be Young, Gifted, and Black.*

In creating Tamborine and Fan, says Smith, "we combined education and those rituals that have social significance in the neighborhoods." With activities year-round, the organization is focused on the consciousness of the community's children. They have a football team, but, to participate in it, the boys have to have library cards and bring them to the game or they don't get to play. They have regular meetings at the Martin Luther King monument, at South Claiborne and Martin Luther King, where guests are told to bring their favorite quotes from King's work, which the children copy into their notebooks. The kids learn the lyrics to "Strange Fruit."

The Tamborine of the organization's title refers to the Mardi Gras Indians, whose characteristic instrument is the tambourine. The Fan represents the second line, where costumed marchers carry plumed fans. These two distinct traditions come together at Super Sunday, a pan-tribal parade begun by Tamborine and Fan, with Mardi Gras Indians, brass bands, and a second line. Smith told me that Super Sunday

> was an outgrowth of a conversation with a local photographer by the name of Marion Porter, who worked for the *Louisiana Weekly*. I had come home from some demonstrations and even at that time, we were speaking about how the neighborhoods were being ruptured by the intrusion of the expressways. And he thought that I should make an effort to pull folks together, because many of the things that [used to be] happening in the neighborhoods were not happening because people were being scattered all over, even way back then.

Super Sunday, then, began as a cultural act of resistance to aggression, architectural and otherwise, against the black community. It was first celebrated with a rally in 1969 and a full-strength nighttime parade across town in 1970. Back then, no one outside New Orleans had heard of the Mardi Gras Indians, and they were subcultural even in their home ground. "We broke the door open," Smith told me. It was the beginning of a new era of consciousness in the practice of the local traditions, as the tradition of marching in a parade coalesced with the newfound power of marching for justice.

> We all came out of [the civil rights movement]. Several of us had been in jails and been beaten and been involved in the struggle. Initially the city said no. And we refused to accept that. So they tried to stop us on that night. But we didn't stop. We marched from St. Bernard and Claiborne, up Claiborne, all the way back to Orleans and Rocheblave, and then we came all the way to the Municipal Auditorium. The neighborhood was so powerful and the discipline was so great.

Over time, uptown has developed its own Super Sunday, and there's one on the West Bank. But Tamborine and Fan has done a Super Sunday every year since 1970, and the influence of the parade has helped unite the Indians around the concept of competitive suiting as an alternative to intertribal violence, while the world has slowly become aware of the Indians' existence in the meantime. Big Chief Alison "Tootie" Montana is generally credited as a central figure in this transition; he was one of the founders of Tamborine and Fan and its Super Sunday parade.

For their 2005 parade, on May 8, Tamborine and Fan had four brass bands and a large complement of Mardi Gras Indians of various tribes, decked out in all the different colors you can dye plumes. The event had been three times postponed because, Smith told me, they had to be careful with the weather with so many children involved in the parade. You can't have children out there for four hours if it's going to rain, because some of them will get sick the next day.

The event began on the banks of the Bayou with a church service to give it a spiritual grounding, complete with a gospel choir. As the day's players assembled, I saw faces I recognized. There was Sunpie, all Skull and Bones–ed up, and Antoinette K-Doe. Hot 8 stood along the Bayou, with the horn players in a horizontal rank. I said hi to Dinerral Shavers, his snare drum strapped in place. I'm sure he didn't remember me, but I remembered him. Mardi Gras Indians arrived one by one. Then, as the energy gathered on the bank of the Bayou St. John, I turned around and found myself face-to-face with . . . Tony Garnier.

This is what second lines are for. I hadn't seen Tony in years. He's one of my favorite people. He lives in New York but spends most of his time on the road with Bob Dylan. He played bass in my band in the '80s in New York—when he had time, that is, because he played with a lot of bands. He first became known for playing in Asleep at the Wheel during their peak moment in the 1970s, when they had the same eleven people for five years. When I met him, he was playing around town with Robert Gordon. I had already written a song called "Disappear into the Cracklin' Sound," thinking, I'd like to get the bass player from Asleep at the Wheel to play this. When I got him on it, he played it even better than I had imagined it. When we toured together in 1985 playing in Peter Gordon's band, we spent a memorable evening hanging out at the Hell's Angels clubhouse in Paris, not to mention Hanky Panky's tattoo parlor in Amsterdam.

Tony's grandfather, D'Jalma Garnier, was a musician in New Orleans— he led the Camelia Brass Band in the 1920s—and Tony knows how to make a roux. He's a working musicologist who always had the cassettes of the good stuff back when it wasn't easy to hear older popular music. He taught me a lot, especially about how to feel a shuffle. Tony's the guy who gave Willie Nelson the tape of "Cowboys Are Frequently Secretly." Since 1989 he's been with Dylan, far and away the longest-running musician to work with him. He's the perfect bassist for Dylan. He loves the same old American music Dylan loves, and he's a discreet, self-effacing player, with no desire to be the guy in front. He can't hardly be coaxed to play a solo, but when he's in the band it rocks harder. Weirdly, this is something I share with Bob Dylan: we've both been made to look and sound better by having Tony Garnier standing behind us. I think the steadying influence of Tony Garnier was a significant factor in Bob Dylan's renaissance during the '90s. Tony's probably too modest to agree.

Tony was talking to Dr. Ike and carrying baby Lucas in a little sling. He looked so happy.

As the Indians assembled, I watched two of them get in each other's face, like you do if you're ready for mortal combat. They were performing their ritual. It was theater, all right, but with an edge. People gathered in a circle. Sunpie slapped a tambourine while another skeleton stilt-walked. Another was disguised behind a papier-mâché mask and raffia hair. A mature African American woman in a lime-green baby doll outfit, playing a silver flute, danced on all fours on the ground, in the middle of a circle.

And then it rolled. A group of boys pranced down Orleans Avenue with the grandeur of Rebirth behind them, dressed like the men in uniform khaki shorts, powder blue suspenders, starched white shirts, red bow ties, and straw hats with white bands. They were carefully tended by watchful adults who made sure they stayed hydrated and took brief rests. It was no easy task supervising a passel of youngsters on a second line, but they did it. I wanted to pin a medal on every one of those adults, not that they needed my praise. The kids were getting a serious shot of love along with a lesson in self-respect. While they had their fun, they were learning the power and the multiple meanings of the second line and were being given an inoculation against the self-hatred at the root of New Orleans's endemic murder crisis. I've seen it in Brazil, in Colombia, in Puerto Rico, in New Orleans: the traditional culture is a bulwark against the hell of the streets. I think the people who do this work are heroes.

I took pictures, but documentation of a second line is inadequate to represent the social and sensory experience. As thousands of people second lined past the Lafitte projects, Rebirth played a specific call that there ought to be a proper name for but isn't. It's a lick everyone in the community knows, the one that starts off Bill Sinegal's "Second Line": *da-dat DWEEE-dat*—and on the *and* of the third beat, thousands of people shout *Hey!*

That exuberant *Hey!* was so much more than a good-time shout. This community shouting *Hey!* was the whole that was more than the sum of the individual heads that were its parts. The community knew things that it had to be assembled together in order to know, and that was expressed in that *Hey!* Above all, it celebrated survival in black space.

With a few exceptions, most notably the work of Helen Regis, remarkably little scholarly attention has been paid to second lines despite their cornerstone status in African American cultural tradition. It's like the way people ignored the rumba in Cuba. What attention there has been has largely been paid to the music, which is understandable, but there's so much more to a second line than the tunes.

The parade picked up people as it rolled along. Black horsemen and horsewomen rode, mounted high in the air. When we passed the Lafitte projects, people cheered from the balconies. I wouldn't normally have cared to walk this route by myself. But as part of this crowd of thousands, I could. Among the other things it is, a second line is a ghetto pass. Much of what I've seen of the projects, I saw while going on second lines. But that wasn't just true for me. Helen Regis speaks of second lines as "producing neighborhoods":

Each Sunday afternoon parade . . . creates a four-hour pedestrian route through distinct neighborhoods. It connects neighborhoods separated by social and geographic distance, such as the historically anglophone "uptown" and historically francophone "downtown" areas. The route also transcends more recent notions of "turf" based on localized entrepreneurial "crews" or "gangs" engaged in the drug trade. Children in New Orleans grow up thinking about neighborhoods in these terms. The parades empower participants to walk through terrain that they might otherwise perceive as hostile, dangerous ground where (other) drug dealers are in charge. The clubs that sponsor these parades are quite explicit about their role as an alternative force on these streets. The Lady Buck Jumpers' signs claim to be "taking it to the streets," and members recollected after a particularly successful parade, "we *owned* the streets."[1]

Today Tamborine and Fan owned the streets, and they came in peace. My last second line of the year was an event about consciousness. Codes within codes. Layers beneath layers.

I was seeing a kind of civil rights demonstration. Literally: the African American community was demonstrating its civil right to assemble in the street. It was demonstrating its right to exist, projecting a vision of itself as having order and structure, and having fun in the process.

As Americans increasingly stay in their cells and communicate by message, second lines insist on the reality of physical presence. That was the essence of life in New Orleans, a place where you see your friends face-to-face frequently and where, accordingly, you have a lot of friends. In New York, I see even my best friends only every few weeks or months. Living in New Orleans, we saw our friends all the time, had dinner with them, went on second lines with them. Maybe less work gets done that way. But it's a more human way to live.

I was learning to appreciate the skill with which Rebirth negotiated the pivot onto Claiborne, going under I-10, regulating the parade's movement with their tempo. The concrete caverns beneath the trestles have become a part of the sonic environment of the second line, because the bands know the exact spots under the elevated highway where the big echoes and reverb are, and they often pause in the space to play a number in place for the sheer joy of sounding big. Jon Cleary told me:

> The highlight, the point of ecstasy, is when the second line crosses Claiborne Avenue. There are only two things the interstate is any good for. One is getting somewhere fast. And the other is making the bass drum sound big and fat when the second line goes underneath. All of a sudden there's a palpable sense of the excitement level being notched up a good fifty percent, and people start shouting as they approach this thing,

because they know, as soon as you get underneath with the band, the volume doubles and the bass drum gets big, big, big. It's the biggest echo chamber in New Orleans.

We passed the Mother-in-Law—hello, Antoinette!—and as we moved toward a series of high concrete interchanges I looked up and saw daredevil marchers way up on the overpass, so high in the air they looked tiny, compelling the crowd's attention as they pranced above it all. This too is part of a second line: incorporating the surrounding area as part of the theater of action, whether jumping up to slap the stop sign in rhythm or climbing as high in the air as you can get.

When the parade broke up, I had to get back to my car. It had been a beautiful second line—once again—and all over Tremé, the afterparty was getting under way.

Oops. My car was back up by the Bayou St. John. Some parades go in a loop, so you wind up back where you started. Not this one.

It was a long walk, a little tense. My ghetto pass had expired, and the sun was sinking low. A project chick from Chicago who was visiting town—that's what she told me—came up and started walking down the street alongside me, talking to me, and asked me to buy her a beer when we passed a little grocery store. I did, and she went away. I let the *Hey!* keep ringing in my ears.

Five days later, it was Friday the thirteenth, which seemed like the right night for a good-bye party. Chris and Ladee were kind enough to host so that we could see our friends one more time. We ate Voodoo Bar-B-Q takeout and had a farewell toast.

Once again, I had to move away from Louisiana.

I bubble-wrapped seventy-one boxes with books, CDs, photographs, and everything else. With her bad back, Constance spent three days on her hands and knees cleaning the place. It wasn't that dirty, but that's how she is. I said, he's not going to give us back our deposit, whether you do this or not. It's not about that, she said, and by God, we left the joint clean.

I shipped out the two pallets' worth of boxes with the same freight company that had brought the stuff to town in August. The driver remembered me. I was going to drive home solo with a Saturnful of stuff, so I put Constance on a plane for New York. Her first night back in our apartment, all by herself, with a securely bolted door and windows, she had a good night of sleep, something she hadn't been having in New Orleans. "I didn't realize," she e-mailed me, "how tense I was. I felt safe for the first time in months." Chris and Ladee helped me load up the car and waved as I drove away.

Mr. Landlord stiffed me on the one-month security deposit, with no accounting of why. I knew he would.

We were further in debt than we had been a year before.

I hadn't been in New York three months when someone bought me a plane ticket back to New Orleans. I was delighted.

21

A Murdery Summer

The tension stemming from the St. Joseph's Night debacle came to a dramatic denouement on June 27 when, in a remarkable show of unity, both uptown and downtown Mardi Gras Indians gathered for a nighttime meeting at City Hall to hear community concerns about police misconduct toward the Indians.

The house was packed. The most prominent speaker was the retired Chief of Chiefs, eighty-two-year-old Alison "Tootie" Montana, Big Chief of the Yellow Pocahontas and a grand-nephew of Becate Batiste, who had founded the Creole Wild West 120 years before. Montana had masked Indian for over fifty years. In the classic Mardi Gras Indian style, he had made his living in the building trade, as a lathe operator, and his knowledge of architecture entered into the construction of his suits. He was known for his elaborate three-dimensional creations with needle and thread. In May, the New Orleans Museum of Art had screened *Tootie's Last Suit*, Lisa Katzman's documentary about the making of his swan-song suit for Mardi Gras 2004. He was universally credited as a major figure in the transition from violent physical beefing to competitive esthetic suiting, a transition that had taken the Indians years to arrive at (and that hip-hop still needed to make). But that didn't mean he wasn't ready for battle. He'd complained about police harassment of the Indians for years.

The dozen or so Chiefs in the audience were asked to rise, then they came up to the podium. They flanked Montana as he made an emotional, unscripted speech recounting years of harassment. An eyewitness wrote:

Tootie astutely blew holes in all of Mayor Nagin's exhortations by describing the police violence he has seen and experienced over his many years as Chief of the Yellow Pocahontas Tribe. He spoke about police tightening their billy-club straps as the Indians approached and his tribe's strategy of simply walking through lines of police attempting to block their path. He spoke about a cop repeatedly trying to swing a club at his ten-year-old relative's head and the young boy just barely missing a brutal skull injury. His last words were "This has got to stop," and he turned from the podium, slumping towards the floor.

The other Chiefs caught him as the whole room gasped.[1]

Big Chief Tootie had suffered a heart attack. His son, Big Chief Darryl Montana, rushed to his side. Two student activists began giving him CPR. There was a defibrillator in the building, but it was kept behind a locked door. As is typical in New Orleans, the ambulance was slow: it took twelve minutes for EMTs to arrive, though Charity Hospital was only two blocks away. Councilman Oliver Thomas led the room in prayer, and the assembled Indians began to sing their anthem, "My Indian Red"—with emphasis, I was told by someone who was there, on the words "we won't bow down." They finally took Montana on a stretcher to Charity Hospital, where he was pronounced dead.

It was like a Viking dying with his sword in his hand. Big Chief Tootie had, as an Indian song had it, "died on the battlefield," fighting for his people, refusing to bow down, insisting on the value of Mardi Gras Indian culture to a city that had tried to stop it.[2] It was the most sensational event in years of tense relations between the culturally aware black community and the city government, and it instantly became one of the legends of Mardi Gras Indian lore. His wake was scheduled for July 8 at the city-owned Mahalia Jackson Theater, with services the next day at St. Augustine's, burial at St. Louis Cemetery #2, and, of course, a jazz funeral.

But first Tropical Storm Cindy came ashore, terrifying New Orleanians when it slammed into town on July 5. After a day of rain, a violent windstorm started about ten P.M. that went on for five or six hours with gusts up to seventy miles an hour. The electricity went out for a quarter million people, the biggest blackout locally since Hurricane Betsy forty years earlier. When the power goes out in New Orleans, the fear of crime becomes electric, and in some places power stayed out for days. Traffic signals went dark. The streets were full of tree limbs and even entire oak trees that had been uprooted. Fifty trees were torn out of City Park alone. The *Times-Picayune's* web server went down, and they published a skeletal page with only a summary of events. With four inches of rain having fallen that had nowhere to drain to, because every drop in New Orleans has to be pumped out, some streets flooded. A number of homeowners faced expensive repairs.

There had been no massive evacuation for a mere tropical storm. The state didn't put contraflow into motion. A July 12 *Gambit Weekly* article noting the problems that were apparent in the wake of Cindy cited an estimate by the New Orleans Council on Aging that ten thousand elderly city residents had no means of evacuation.

Meanwhile there was a second storm out there, stacked up right behind. With 135-mph winds, Hurricane Dennis packed a lot more punch than Cindy. It was the earliest in the season that there had ever been four named storms. In Cuba they didn't hesitate to evacuate 1.7 million people for Hurricane Dennis in a day and a half, but New Orleanians, though shaken from the thrashing Cindy gave the city, were torn whether to evacuate or not.

Big Chief Tootie was to be buried on Saturday. I would have gone back to New Orleans for the funeral, but it looked as though Hurricane Dennis might arrive on Sunday. Two heavy-duty storms in a week made travel in and out of the city impractical. Going through with the jazz funeral on schedule might well mean not evacuating, but of course they went on with it, with Father Jerome LeDoux officiating at St. Augustine's. Out in the street, hundreds of tambourines played.

In the end, Dennis blinked. The storm weakened and curved, making landfall near Pensacola on July 10. Six days later a stronger storm formed: Emily, which made landfall twice on Mexico's Gulf Coast. In the next six weeks there were Franklin, Gert, Harvey, Irene, and José, none of which posed any problem to New Orleans.

During that time, Felipe Smith came to New York to do some library work, and we had a Dominican-style dinner at El Cibao on Clinton Street. With the season already under way, I remember we talked about hurricanes and how they usually curve before they get to New Orleans. I mentioned that I felt I'd left a lot of things in New Orleans unfinished. He smiled and said, "One thing about New Orleans—when you do come back, everything'll still be right where you set it down."

That was the one thing Felipe Smith ever said to me that turned out to be wrong.

It had been, wrote a New Orleans blogger, a "murdery summer."[3]

Murdery. A word to describe social weather. It's been a rainy summer. It's been a windy summer. It's been a murdery summer.

And other crimes as well. In June, two young men robbed and raped a forty-nine-year-old woman in her office at Tulane, sending a chill of fear throughout the university. On the morning of July 11, a New Orleans police officer pulled a female bicyclist over on the pretext of a traffic stop, drove her to a remote spot by the Industrial Canal, and raped her. She reported the crime immediately afterward, and he was reassigned to desk duty until he was indicted six weeks later.

A rash of four domestic murder-suicides killed ten people in a week, though six of the dead—two love triangles—were in St. Bernard Parish and so didn't add to the New Orleans murder count. Someone sprayed a group of people with bullets, wounding at least eight, at a child's birthday party in Central City on July 17. Later that night, four people were shot, though not killed, in a club at five fifteen in the morning. Three days later a fourteen-year-old honor student whose nickname was "Lady" was found raped and strangled with her housecoat in her Seventh Ward home. That same day, a man was found lying dead on Prytania Street in the Garden District and another man was discovered murdered in New Orleans East. On the twenty-third, two out-of-towners were booked for standing on a second-floor walkway at the Economy Motor Lodge on a seedy stretch of Tulane Avenue and shooting at people walking beneath I-10.

On the twenty-fourth, Trymaine Lee wrote an article in the *Times-Picayune* about the uptick in violence that was headlined, "Whole Neighborhoods in Fear." An auto repairman was stabbed to death by his son on July 27. Three men were gunned down in separate incidents within a half hour on July 30. On Sunday morning, July 31, a man was murdered in front of the Lafitte projects on his twenty-eighth birthday. "Put the guns down," his sobbing mother told Lee. "Put the guns down . . . you're killing your own people." On August 1, a fifty-five-year-old gay man in the Marigny was murdered, apparently by a trick, who stole his Mercedes. On August 2, a man was murdered at Flood and Royal in the Lower Ninth Ward and another on Jackson Avenue in Central City. That same day on North Robertson, as the Genesis Baptist Church choir was rehearsing, a man burst in through the front door, taking refuge after being wounded by a gunshot. By the time the annual Night Out Against Crime got under way that evening, eight people had been murdered in four days. New Orleans was at 173 murders for the year, up from 158 for that date a year before, not counting anyone killed by the police.

It was a murdery summer in New Orleans, all right. The blogger had used that word in writing about a bizarre, bogus AP report. Though it was unsubstantiated, no one seemed to question it:

NEW ORLEANS—Last year, university researchers conducted an experiment in which police fired 700 blank rounds in a New Orleans neighborhood in a single afternoon. No one called to report the gunfire.

This is the kind of misinformation that gets blogged, quoted, forwarded. The mysterious lack of specificity—what university? what neighborhood?—was a pretty obvious tipoff. After I called the New Orleans police department to find out who the unnamed "university researchers" were, I got a courteous callback on my cell phone from police spokesman Marlon Defillo, who had attained local celebrity status owing to the number of times the police had to talk to the press in New Orleans. He advised me that no one in the police department knew anything about it, adding, "We're just as mystified as you are." When I said, "It sounds like a hoax, then?" he declined to speculate, but said, "If we're gonna fire seven hundred rounds in a neighborhood, believe me, I would know it." It was an urban legend, but that it could appear and be believed was indicative of something.

On August 3, I got back to New Orleans. In the early hours that morning, a gunman had burst into Nick's Bar on Tulane Avenue and sprayed the place, killing one person and wounding another. But I was in a good mood.

I had paid my credit cards down, then splurged a little to take Constance on a modest vacation that was luxurious for us. We'd never done anything like it, but July 25 was our twenty-fifth wedding anniversary and we felt the need to celebrate. We hopped in the Saturn and drove to the original French colonial cities, which aren't that far from New York: across the border to Trois-Riviéres, then up the river to Montréal, and on to Québec City for a four-day holiday. Seeing the dramatic point where the St. Lawrence River opens up into the bay put that other French colony of Louisiana in perspective. After all, Louisiana was colonized by Canadians working for the French. We were in Iberville land. We ate wild boar crêpes. On the day of our anniversary, we went to the Québec library. That night, in the Hotel Chateau Frontenac's top-floor bar with its spectacular panoramic view, we drank a champagne toast to another twenty-five years.

This time I'd bopped down to New Orleans by myself because I'd been invited to give a talk at Satchmo Summerfest. A year before, I had been admiring the presenters from afar, and now I was one. I bunked at T.R.'s, and for a few days we ran together as I got into the Bywater experience for the first time. It was a whole different New Orleans, living downtown. Felipe drove in from New Orleans East to see me, and we went for drinks at Markey's, next to the Country Club, around the corner from Mark Bingham's studio on Piety Street.

The big news was that New Orleans's Democratic Congressman William Jefferson had been busted with ninety thousand dollars in marked hundred-dollar bills in his freezer, giving him the nickname "Dollar Bill" and making him the political legend that his lackluster fifteen-year career in the House of Representatives had failed to do. Even more locally, Funky Butt was going to be closing down.

Everyone was freaked out about crime. We went to a party at a fabulously restored house near T.R.'s place, where the talk was about the serial killer who'd murdered fourteen gay men in Houma. And, of course, the lousy hurricane protection. After the violent season of 2004, the Bush administration had responded with the largest single-year funding cut ever for the New Orleans district of the Army Corps of Engineers. An item in *New Orleans City Business* noted that "the New Orleans district, which employs 1,300 people, instituted a hiring freeze last month on all positions."[4]

Everywhere I turned I ran into a friend. Satchmo Summerfest was great. Ellis Marsalis gave the keynote: "I don't think Louis Armstrong was deprived at all," he said, "and I don't think *he* thought he was deprived." Keith Weldon Medley in his talk pointed out that Armstrong had fewer civil rights than his parents. I sat and chatted with him for an hour while we signed books. Jack Stewart talked about the Tango Belt, the black vice district uptown from Storyville in the 1910s. John McCusker, who's been researching the life of Kid Ory, spoke about early jazz in the river parishes.

Cherice Harrison-Nelson, a schoolteacher who in 1999 created the Mardi Gras Indian Hall of Fame in the New Orleans public schools and is a daughter of the late Big Chief Donald Harrison Sr., appeared with her mother, Herreast, and her son Brian. The young man sat politely with his mother and grandmother and gave a student-ish Powerpoint presentation about the Indians. But then he disappeared and a few minutes later burst into the room via the back door, fully suited up as a Mardi Gras Indian and shouting and singing. The transformation was astonishing. He had gone from boy to man in a flash. He was now a Big Chief. I went on next, giving a talk about the Cuban influence in jazz that Jelly Roll Morton called the "Spanish tinge."

This was a community you would want to belong to. Outside, there was music on the grounds of the Mint. Cherice's brother Donald Harrison Jr., probably the musician who had most impressed me during my year in New

Orleans, appeared with his band, going from hard bop to funk. I ran into Richard Graham, the musicologist we'd visited in Waveland with his amazing collection of instruments, throwing a frisbee to his dog. WWOZ was broadcasting live from the grounds, and T.R. was on the air for his shift as a DJ; I stopped by to talk on air for a few minutes about the Spanish tinge, and we played Louis Armstrong's 1931 version of "The Peanut Vendor," which is in swing time instead of Latin time, and in which Satchmo sings the song's key word as "Marie" instead of *maní* (peanuts).

In my time living in New Orleans, I'd focused on working more than socializing, so there was a long list of "you gotta meet" people I hadn't met. At her home on Dante Street, I met my scholarly hero, Gwendolyn Midlo Hall, who did pioneering work with the research that led to her book *Africans in Colonial Louisiana*. I popped down to Frenchmen Street, ran into some friends, and someone introduced me to traditional jazz clarinetist Dr. Michael White, one of the nicest people you'd ever care to meet. Marilyn was there. Ina Jo Fandrich, who wrote that book on Marie Laveau. Soon I was sitting in the bar called d.b.a. in the middle of the afternoon, hanging out with a bunch of old and new friends. Dan Storper from Putumayo, who was living down here now. Joel came downtown and we hung out at Mimi's into the night, eating a New Orleans version of tapas and drinking mugs of beer.

We hit Sweet Lorraine's on St. Claude, where T.R. advised me not to linger on the sidewalk but to go straight into the club. We cruised ten blocks down to the Saturn Bar, created back in space-age 1960s when it looked like NASA was going to set up operations in the area and the aerospace workers would need a lounge. I hadn't been to the Saturn Bar during my year of living uptown. It was a bizarre time-out-of-time place, dark, almost devoid of customers, full of mysterious, random junk. Down front, O'Neil Broyard, the proprietor, tended bar in a small pool of light. We went to the upstairs level, which was deserted and which, I have it on good authority, had on occasion served as a setting for various scandalous hijinks. There was a grungy leopard-print booth. Spare machine parts lay around everywhere. The walls were festooned with dingy, cheesy artworks by local drunk painters of some time ago.

Prior to 1960, the upper area had been the gallery and the main floor had been an amateur boxing ring where human cockfights took place. Broyard (a nephew of Anatole Broyard) had been one of the boxers, then turned the place into the Saturn Bar. During Hurricane Betsy, a giant turtle washed up into the bar. Broyard kept it as a pet, keeping it in the stall where boxers had once showered. When it died in the early '70s, he pulled it out of the shell and made soup, then hung the shell on the wall, putting a neon rim around it.

On Saturday night, T.R. and I went to see one of my local favorites, the longhaired Cajun-Choctaw swamp-blues growler Coco Robicheaux, on his regular no-cover Saturday gig at the Apple Barrel—a smoky little dive that has no real P.A. system, so you can never quite catch what Coco is saying. On break, as we were talking with Coco, he said something I didn't get, and then added: "I'm lucky to be alive!"

I said, well, we all are. No, he meant something more immediate. He opened his shirt and showed us a long cut along his rib, where the skin had been broken. He had been walking home a couple of nights before when along Elysian Fields he saw a man dragging a woman by her hair. Coco intervened.

I did that once in New York, when I was much younger, stepped in when I saw a man brutalizing a woman. It's one of the easier ways to get your ass killed, because the guy's already hyped up and you're challenging his masculinity. In the middle of the night on a deserted avenue, the guy whipped out a long knife and lunged at Coco. "I looked in his eyes," said Coco, "and I saw a *dead man*." The knife missed him by that much, just slicing his shirt and breaking the skin. That was no kitty scratch on Mr. Robicheaux's torso.

Coco Robicheaux

It was getting late, maybe two thirty, and we were walking down French-men back to the car when T.R. said, "Let's just stick our head in d.b.a. for a minute and see what's going on there." Corey Henry and the Young Fel-lows were beginning a set—a snazzy little five-piece combo with a trombone instead of a lead singer.

So what if it was late? We didn't leave until the set was over. The whole room was dancing. They played "Let's Stay Together." The dancers sang the words of the song, and no one wanted it to end, so they stretched it out for a long time. It made me dance, made me sing, and made me a happy member of a pulsing mass of people. I've had this experience many times, but mostly in Havana and points south. Rarely have I had it in the United States, except sometimes in the salsa world, because I can't have it dancing to records, it's got to be a live band that can respond to the dancers in turn. But in New Orleans, this could happen on an ordinary hot Saturday night.

The next day, Sunday, my last day in town, I got T.R. to drive me on a mission. I had planned all year to go by Fats Domino's house on Caffin Avenue, but I had never gotten around to it. T.R. kindly drove me over and waited while I jumped out and quickly snapped some pictures of Fats Domi-no's mansion, the one that was profiled in *Ebony*, the one that cost an astro-nomical two hundred thousand dollars in 1960.[5] I could care less about going to Graceland, I've never bothered. But this was *Fats Domino*, and he still lived there, in the Lower Ninth Ward, baby, where he'd outlived Elvis by twenty-eight years and counting.

We stopped the car on a few of the neighborhood corners so that I could photograph street signs that said "Piety" and "Desire." Because I had finished my song:

I imagine all those po'boys still alive
Elysian Fields is full of ghosts, they grope at me when I drive
Those governors and generals, and Frenchmen who once thrived
In the perfume and the fever, and in 2005

I lived between Piety and Desire
On my one hand a blessing, on the other hot hellfire
By day I'd sweat, by night I'd perspire
Right at home between Piety and Desire

I added a coda:

Sobriety's overrated, but I'm preachin' to the choir
In my crib between Piety and Desire.

The last thing I did before I went home was go to a Sunday afternoon welcome party for my successor as a Tulane Rockefeller Humanities Fellow. The Afro-Peruvian singer and folklorist Susana Baca was going to be in residence for the fall semester, splitting the chair with her husband, Ricardo Pereira, who would take it over in the spring. I had played Baca's *Ecos de Sombras* album many times—it's sensual music, slow, tense, restrained like a coiled spring that always seems about to snap, with nylon-string guitar and the slaps of the *cajón*, the wooden box drum that produces a remarkable crack when it's smacked hard, in a three-against-two meter that allows for maximum rhythmic suspense.

Baca's Peruvian paisano in the music department, ethnomusicologist Javier León, hosted the party where I felt like a fan, enjoying the privilege of hanging out with Mrs. Baca, getting tipsy from red wine as we listened to Celina González, the great Cuban country singer. Hearing Celina brought back a flood of memories. We were listening to ¡*Que Viva Changó!*, a CD compilation of Celina's music that I'd put out on Qbadisc and better known to me as 9004. I'd done everything to make that album except record the music, which, since it was made by Cubans, would have been a felony under United States law. I'd made the licensing deal, picked the tunes, supervised the transfers in Havana and brought the tape back, done the mastering, taken the picture on the back cover, and got drunk on Celina González's patio in Marianao one memorable hot afternoon in 1994. All those memories popped up as we listened to Celina sing. Susana Baca traveled to Cuba long before I did, and I tried to imagine what she brought to hearing Celina. She was so excited to be in New Orleans, and was already talking about Mardi Gras.

People kept saying to me, we've got to find a way to get you back here.

I found myself thinking, but I can't get hired on at Tulane. I don't have a doctorate. I don't teach. I don't *want* to teach. I've got my life in New York, and I can't deal with all these hurricanes and murders. But . . .

Maybe I could have a second base here. Maybe . . .

Maybe I kind of belong here.

Maybe New Orleans is somehow home.

The Saturn was waiting for me in JFK long-term parking. I had planned to sell it at year's end, but I'd grown attached to it. I had gotten to like the idea of having a car in New York, despite the hassles. It would make possible things I'd never been able to do and give me more freedom of movement. And as long as I had it I was still connected to New Orleans. Since I controlled my own schedule, I figured I was flexible enough to deal with parking my car on the street in my neighborhood, which entails waiting twice a week for an hour or two in the middle of the day because of alternate-side-of-the-street parking.

When I went out to move the car on the morning of August 9, there was a ticket on my windshield. My safety sticker had expired. It was the anniversary of my buying the car, and the sticker had expired that very morning. The revenue-producing parking-law enforcement officer hadn't wasted a minute in writing me up. Seventy-five bucks. Shit. Better go get a new sticker. But then, when I turned on the ignition, the "service engine soon" light came on. I got my sticker, but it cost two hundred and change by the time the repairs were done, plus the ticket. Damn. The problem turned out to be . . .

Rats.

Have I mentioned that SoHo is disgusting? I live in a neighborhood where the sidewalks have been colonized by restaurants, and restaurants bring rats. I don't get why people want to eat sitting out on the street in New York anyway—do they think they're in Paris?—but there they are, blocking my way as I shlep to the supermarket, sitting on the piss-stained sidewalks as a waiter brings them another glass of expensive wine to be savored along with the perfume of *eau de garbage*. Late at night, when they leave, and they set out the mountains of garbage bags full of half-eaten meals? Yuck. The garbage trucks compact it, squeezing out the putrid essence onto the street. Then there's the pizza parlor, a neighborhood institution that serves tourists oily slices all day long, the scraps of which they deposit in open garbage cans by the park benches, so that at any time of day or night there are overflowing rat banquets sitting on the sidewalk.

Rats had crawled up under the hood of my car while it was parked on the street and chewed up the hoses and belts. I suspect they were using the rubber like chewing gum, maybe sharpening their teeth on it or something. Long story short, it happened twice more. The second time, the mechanic's report read "seafood parts in engine." I don't even want to *think* what that was about. I tried mothballs under the hood in a sock. The third time it happened, the Saturn place in Long Island City had gone out of business and I had to go to the Saturn place in Bay Ridge, which charged me twelve hundred dollars. Elijah Wald suggested I might as well make a blues out of it:

I got rats in my Saturn / And I can't drive my car . . .

I went to the Blue Note with Harry Sepúlveda to see eighty-seven-year-old Israel López "Cachao," creator of the mambo and the most influential bassist of the twentieth century, who was up from Miami.

Cachao walked with difficulty, but he negotiated the Blue Note stairs gamely and played his ass off. We sat directly in front of stage left, where three Puerto Ricans were holding forth: Jimmy Delgado on timbales, Richie Flores on congas, and Jimmy Bosch on trombone. They'd been doing gigs with Cachao for years; he even had a *descarga* in his repertoire in honor of Bosch, "Jimmy en el Trombón." It was a smoking set of music, and the two Jimmys and Richie were explosive. I said to Harry, "The Puerto Ricans are driving this train." Harry laughed and said, "It's the same train." We hung out in the dressing room between sets and I managed not only to ask Cachao a few history questions while he chilled but also to arrange to come to Miami to interview him for the book I was going to write. In all this time, I had never interviewed Cachao.

I waited a couple of weeks to call him, to let him get settled again after his traveling while I got my stuff together. I figured I could drive down. Then, as I was getting ready to call, it seemed like not the right moment because a hurricane was bearing down on Miami.

They were up to K by now, so this one was called Hurricane Katrina. It made landfall in Florida at seven P.M. on Thursday, August 25, a Category One storm that killed eleven people and left a million without electricity before pushing on west.

I never saw Cachao again. I never interviewed him. He died on March 22, 2008. Nor did I ever write that book. Hurricane Katrina blew it away. Not that I stopped working, or writing.

The August 23, 2005, issue of the *Gambit Weekly* carried an editorial entitled "The Scream." Noting that the city had exceeded two hundred murders already for the year, that if New Orleans had New York's crime rate the number would have been thirty-six, and that New Orleans was on track to hit three hundred murders by year's end, it said:

"New Orleans, the city we were born to love, lay in a pool of blood— again—last week. Raped by hate. Beaten, stabbed, strangled and bludgeoned to death by violence. She screamed for help, over and over, just as she has always done, year after year."

On Friday, August 26, as Hurricane Katrina crawled out from Florida into the Gulf of Mexico, a jury convicted Karla Frye of negligent homicide in the thrill-killing of Shawn Johnson at the Courtyard Marriott. Frye, a deranged twenty-two-year-old from Mobile whose nickname was Never and who carried a doll around with her, was an accomplice; her boyfriend, Kriss Lane, who actually killed Johnson, still awaited trial. His nickname was Worry, and he claimed to be a Satanist, complete with a pentagram tattooed on his back. Never and Worry had been arrested in Florida after someone overheard someone bragging about killing a man in New Orleans.[6] Frye was held over for sentencing. Another accomplice, Benjamin Anthony, pled guilty that day.

Meanwhile, I had a bit of business to take care of, not worth mentioning except that it was the last bit of business. I needed a password while I finished up my project so I could continue to use the Tulane library website with its restricted scholarly databases that aren't available on the free web. From my office in New York I called Sue Inglés, the bureaucracy wrangler at the Stone Center, to see if she could finagle me a password. But I waited until five thirty to call, and she was gone for the weekend. I left a detailed voicemail for her explaining my request. It was Friday, August 26.

New Orleans should have already been evacuating. That day, Governor Kathleen Babineaux Blanco asked President Bush to declare a state of emergency, and the following day he did. That gave the federal authorities all the authorization they needed to deploy their resources.

Hurricane Katrina was a very large storm, and it looked to be headed straight for New Orleans. I spent some time Saturday calling my friends, making sure they had evacuated and finding out where they had gone. All over the place is where they went. Talking to Marilyn in Dallas, I said, "It sounds kinda like you might not be going back for a while."

"Don't say that," she shuddered. All day long, I was in a black depression. I knew what could happen.

Saturday was the dormitory move-in day for Tulane students for the new academic year. They dropped their things off and evacuated. Some were bused to Jackson State University in Mississippi. They wouldn't return that semester. It was supposed to be the largest freshman class in Tulane's history.

On Saturday, August 27, in the Bywater, at St. Claude off Montegut, thirty-four-year-old Tracy Bridges's home was invaded and she was shot. She was the last murder victim in New Orleans, the year before the flood.

By Monday morning, Sue Inglés had other things on her mind than my computer password. She wouldn't be back at work any time soon. For that matter, the 504 area code was about to stop working and all the Tulane e-mail addresses were about to vanish. The books I'd used in the basement of the Howard-Tilton Library were about to drown.

As were a lot of people, many of them elderly.

It was a very murdery summer.

On Friday night, T.R. went a few blocks over to Sugar Park Tavern, having decided to evacuate first thing in the morning. People were watching sports on cable. No one was talking much about the hurricane. About eight o'clock the next morning, he called a bunch of his friends. As he recalled it, he said:

> "Hey, I've never evacuated before, but obviously school's gonna be closed for a couple of days, might as well get outta here."
>
> And they're like, "What are you talking about?"
>
> "Well, turn on the news, man, this is gonna be a pretty big storm." All of my friends had evacuated last year for Ivan, and they said, never again. I said, "Look, man, you better take a look at this, 'cause they're saying it's gonna be kinda heavy."
>
> My attitude was, if I don't leave right now, I'm not leaving, because I'm not gonna spend the weekend before the semester starts sitting on a goddamn highway. I gotta get out of here, 'cause otherwise I'm gonna stay, and I know campus is gonna be closed until probably Tuesday or Wednesday.
>
> I went ahead and gassed up the car. My brother was living in Louisville, it would be easy to stay at his place. Stopped at the Dreamland Barbecue in Tuscaloosa. Happened to tell the old fella behind the counter I was running from a hurricane down in New Orleans.
>
> He says, "Aw, really? Hurricane? Wow."
>
> "Yeah, but I'm sure it's nothing," I said. "I'm going to Louisville just on a lark. I'll be driving back through here in two days. I'm gonna stop and get some more of these ribs, more of this banana pudding."
>
> He says, "All right, man, I'll see ya in a couple of days."

PART III

FAST DYNAMITE, SLOW DYNAMITE

Lower Ninth Ward, February 2006.

Lakeview, with chopouts in the roof, February 2006.

22

FATS DOMINO'S BOOK OF
KNOWLEDGE

American Negroes have always feared with perfect fear their
eventual expulsion from America. They have been willing
to submit to caste rather than face this.

—W. E. B. DuBois, 1940[1]

W as New Orleans . . . gone?
And did we still have a United States without New Orleans?
On September 2, with New Orleans underwater and George
W. Bush about to travel there, he referred to it as "that part of the world."
Not that part of the country. That part of the *world*. It wasn't just a slip of the
tongue. New Orleans wasn't part of the country he presided over. He wasn't
my president.

The same day Bush said that, an *Army Times* article referred to the population of New Orleans as an "insurgency":

Combat operations are underway on the streets "to take this city
back" in the aftermath of Hurricane Katrina.
"This place is going to look like Little Somalia," Brig. Gen. Gary
Jones, commander of the Louisiana National Guard's Joint Task Force
told *Army Times* Friday as hundreds of armed troops under his charge
prepared to launch a massive citywide security mission from a staging

area outside the Louisiana Superdome. "We're going to go out and take this city back. This will be a combat operation to get this city under control."

Jones said the military first needs to establish security throughout the city. Military and police officials have said there are several large areas of the city are in a full state of anarchy.

Dozens of military trucks and up-armored Humvees left the staging area just after 11 A.M. Friday, while hundreds more troops arrived at the same staging area in the city via Black Hawk and Chinook helicopters. . . .

While some fight the insurgency in the city, other carry on with rescue and evacuation operations. Helicopters are still pulling hundreds of stranded people from rooftops of flooded homes.

Insurgency.
Little Somalia.

I'm not going to describe in detail what happened to the city of New Orleans and its people. You've heard about it. It's important to lay that story out, even though there's much we don't know, but it would be another whole book.

In the terrible weeks and months after August 29, 2005, my little record collection that I'd pulled together at live gigs and the Louisiana Music Factory took on a whole new meaning. I couldn't listen to those records without shuddering, and I couldn't stop listening to them. The music revealed new meanings in the new circumstances.

I can tell you something I learned—something obvious, really—that I'd already observed looking at history and even experienced during 9/11 but now saw confirmed. After a great rupture, what we want is a sense of continuity with the past. New conditions will create new music, but that's a slow process. In the near term, we want to reassure ourselves that something endures from the life we used to know. The new thing has to grow out of the old thing. That was the great survival feat of kidnapped Africans: they managed to hold onto their musical essence in their prison across the ocean and, with time, make something new out of it. That music was much more than entertainment.

I listened to the Neville Brothers' version of the Melodians' 1972 song based on Psalm 137:

> By the rivers of Babylon where we sat down
> And there we wept when we remembered Zion

But the wicked carried us away
Captivity required from us this song . . .

With the city underwater and its population dispersed, it was easier to get angry than to feel the emotions Aaron Neville's multitracked voice called up as he caressed those words.

Every morning, after absorbing the latest horrible news over coffee, before I went out the door, to get the strength up to go outside, I paused to listen to "Walk with the Spirit," the first cut on Coco Robicheaux's 1994 masterpiece *Spiritland.* A minor-key gospel-rock song with baritone sax and organ, sung in Coco's blowtorch shout, as nonspecifically applicable to Native American spirituality as to Pentecostalism or vodou, it was as close to prayer as I needed to be:

Sometimes I walk all by myself
I don't want to talk to no one else
And I cloooose my eyes
And I feel the spirit rise . . .

I let that song flow through me as I closed my eyes and I felt the spirit rise. Then I wiped my eyes and went about my day. I did that every day for weeks, a little invented ritual that helped me get through. At night I played "Handa Wanda," and "Big Chief Jolly," and "Talkin' 'Bout the Zulu King," and "Kingdom Come," and "Marie Laveau," and "I Want It (You Got It)," and "Nolia Clap," and "Slow Motion," and "Work That Thing," and the rest of my short stack of New Orleans CDs, over and over.

We wondered if the music we were listening to might be all that was left of New Orleans.

———

I got back to New Orleans in February 2006, just in time to see the State of the Union speech on TV at Chris Dunn's. The Democratic congresspeople stood stone-faced. The sound on the TV was off. "It looks like the Politburo under Stalin!" gasped Idelber. All the apparatchiks, applauding out of fear.

Predictably, the loss of an American city five months previously was not a theme of the address, nor was the malevolent incompetence of the Homeland Security bureaucracy mentioned. New Orleans made an appearance in the speech when the chief executive announced that eighty-five billion dollars in federal aid had been committed to the "people of the Gulf Coast and New Orleans." Anyone who'd been paying attention through 9/11 knew damn well that kind of money wouldn't get to the people of New Orleans.

I hadn't heard from Richard Graham since he e-mailed me right after the hurricane. I still haven't. His house, and all his collection of instruments, recordings, first editions, and everything else, and pretty much the whole town of Waveland blew away. I do know they got out alive. Richard, if you're reading this, e-mail me.

Chris and Ladee and the kids were fine. Six-year-old Isa seemed to have dealt pretty well with all the moving around and the destabilization, probably because they gave her so much love at home. But there was one night when she asked, out of the blue, about nothing in particular, "Is this a dream?" She was laughing, she might have been joking, enjoying being able to articulate the distance between waking life and dream-state. But she must have asked that question ten times that night. "Is this a dream?"

The next morning, Chris took me on a four-hour excursion to the Lower Ninth Ward and Lakeview, two of the most spectacularly destructive flood-points out of one hundred thousand square miles of damage.

The Lower Ninth would have gone underwater anyway, because the levees that overtopped in neighboring Chalmette would have inundated the Lower Ninth as well. But the Industrial Canal breach caused sudden, violent flooding, knocking out a pumping station. People were caught by surprise in a wall of water. Hurricane Katrina didn't kill them. They had ridden that out. The storm was over. They died on a clear, sunny day, under blue sky, like the morning of September 11, 2001—I remember it well—in New York City. Many of them were old. They were the ones who in 1965 had been young and strong enough to rebuild their neighborhood after Hurricane Betsy.

Somebody's shirts were still neatly hanging in the closet, but the outside wall was ripped clean off the house. Somebody's rusted filing cabinet, with a DVD of *The Horse Soldiers*. Somebody's house—and this was a neighborhood where people owned their homes—had been pulled right off its foundation and set down again on top of an inverted truck. This went on for as far as you could see. Homes carried blocks and blocks away from their foundations, then set down, sometimes disintegrating into matchsticks, sometimes retaining their form and structure, only warped, like those watches in the Salvador Dalí painting. I always suspected that if you could walk through that melted-watches Dalí landscape you would smell rotting bodies.

You can take a picture of a house surreally plunked down on top of an upside-down car. What you can't take a picture of is blocks and blocks of it. You can't take a picture of a whole neighborhood turned into a ghost town. It's too big and enveloping. Nor can you take a picture of what's not there.

Those warped and splintered houses had had people in them. A few probably still did.

It had happened five months ago and nothing had been picked up. Not all the premises been searched for bodies yet, because not all the premises were accessible. The ghosts hovered overhead, angry at not having been given the burial that spirits demand. Hundreds of jazz funerals were in order.

The barge was still there. The barge that went through the breach in the floodwall and hoved up on land. It was a giant strongbox, inside a thick iron casing with square corners. I couldn't measure it, but maybe two hundred feet long, forty wide, thirty high? Weighed eighteen hundred tons, I was told. It sat there on what was now dry land, literally dropped in on top of a school bus that it cut in half. Were there people crushed under it?

They were going to have to cut the monolith up and take it out in pieces, but no one was at work on it. One nonuniformed man was guarding it because, he said, fully aware of the absurdity of what he was saying, it's evidence. Mostly it seemed that what he did was take questions from visitors, which is to say tourists. Some two to three hundred people a day were coming by, he said. It was Gray Line's most popular tour; they were charging money to take people there, some of whom viewed it from inside the bus window. Once one hundred bicyclists showed up. Someone had erected a sign: TOURISM HERE IS *PROFANE!*

Anyone who was in any of these houses near the breach was dead. "You can maybe survive floodwaters," said the guard, who'd had weeks to sit and think about it, "but not rushing waters, and not when it collapses around your ears like that. There's no way."

There was a block where all the other houses were gone save one at 1700 Deslonde, painted bright blue. By chance I ran into the owner of the house, an articulate young woman named Dolores Cager, at an event later that evening with the Hot 8—six of them, anyway—at the Sound Café in the Bywater. She had inherited the house from her grandmother, who with an eleventh-grade education nevertheless managed to be a homeowner.

Why was her house still standing when the ones around it were smashed? "I do not know," she said. "I have to say, by the grace of God." I asked Dolores Cager about her evacuation experience. "I evacuated on Sunday," she said, "the day that they called for the evacuation. And right after they called for the evacuation, they closed all the interstates down. If you wasn't already currently on the interstate, you were basically stuck down here. And they had a gas shortage also."

Having lost her possessions, Cager leased the house to Common Ground, an organization cofounded by Algiers-based community organizer Malik Rahim. It was now the Blue House, their neighborhood headquarters. Common Ground volunteers lived there round the clock without electricity or running water, using it as a distribution center for food, water, and tools. People were begging for trailers from the Federal Emergency Managament Agency (FEMA) and getting no answer.

We went to Fats Domino's house, in another part of the Lower Ninth. It was still standing, but it had taken eight feet of water, up to the chandeliers. Someone, thinking Fats had died, had graffitied it: *R.I.P. FATS . . You will be missed*. Some of his family's possessions were sitting out in the street, weather-beaten, five months after the flood. There was Fats Domino's ceiling fan, trashed in the street. There was Fats Domino's toaster, his bottle of A-1 Steak Sauce, his Book of Knowledge. When a salvage crew from the Louisiana State Museum arrived the following month, they took out both of Fats's grand pianos (one subsequently was put on display at the Cabildo Museum) and the Wurlitzer electric baby grand that he kept at the foot of his bed, along with what was described as a "huge" jar of pickled pig's feet.[2]

We drove up to the other Ground Zero, to the London Avenue Canal breach by the Lake Pontchartrain side of town, where the cataclysm took a much different form. A moonscape of sand had pushed up from below, engulf-ing cars and solid brick houses. This was where the floodwalls were breached because the pilings weren't driven in deep enough, and through which Lake Pontchartrain came flooding into the city. The storm surge that pushed out beneath the floodwalls pushed it upward too, burying the area around the breach with the soft weave of sand and peat that had formerly been way under-ground. We walked over buried cars. These were what to a person of my income bracket were expensive houses. I saw a golf club, rusted and partly buried.

In the house nearest the breach, there were two holes in the roof: chop-outs, hacked open from the inside, by people trying to escape. The house was full of sand. I walked up to it, standing on a high shelf of sand, and looked down into the front window. I saw a wheelchair.

That night the weather was freaky. I was staying uptown, sleeping in Joel's study, when I was awakened at two thirty in the morning by a very loud thunderclap close at hand. Lightning flashed in the windows, blinking constantly, like a failing fluorescent light. The sky was illuminated, and the thunder rolled continuously, with occasional triple-forte timpani blasts. I was in a semi-dream state, so I don't know how long it lasted, maybe half an hour? I think it was the most violent thunderstorm I've ever been in. Three torna-dos touched down that night, one of them damaging a concourse at Louis Armstrong International Airport.

T.R. had come back to his house in October. For weeks he lived in it without electricity, playing his saxophone for hours a day, hanging out with his cat. During my February 2006 visit, he described his experience to me:

> I came to the city for twenty-four hours on September 14, and at the time I thought it was over. I thought I'd never live here again, nobody would. I thought it was gone, just hopeless. Without ever even consciously making the decision in any kind of deliberate way, I found myself thinking about my New Orleans life and talking about it in the past tense— "Oh, yeah, this is where I used to hang out, this is where I used to do this and that."
>
> Three weeks later, I moved into my house to start taking care of repairs. My house was inhabitable, no reason not to come back to it— well, I suppose I could have invented all kinds of reasons, but it was time to come home if I was going to come home. I came back on October 10, and it was a very anxious time. Because the city was—not stone empty, but close to it. Not a lot of people around. I knew one or two people in this end of town, and we would walk up to Washington Square Park and get free meals at night, and there would be a handful of people standing around, everybody like they'd seen a ghost, like they'd been hit by a truck or something, just sort of standing, staring into space, eating some gruel served out of a big kettle, and just looking around.
>
> The silence, I guess, was probably what was the most unnerving. There was simply no sound. There were no birds, no squirrels, no dogs, nothing. Occasionally you would hear a helicopter. And the silence was piercing. I would sit on my front stoop, and there would be not a living thing moving. And it occurred to me: this city has not had silence like this in three hundred years. It's *dead*. It has *died*. And there's no reason to believe, there's no evidence to stimulate any kind of hope, that it would come back.
>
> It was very, very hard living here in October and November. I left in early December for almost a month, and when I came back, it had gotten a little bit easier in terms of, electricity goes out less often, and I've got a grocery store on this end of town, and it feels like it's better than it was, but there's simply no denying that essentially, the sources of the city's culture are *gone*. Basically everything north of me and everything east of me is *gone*.
>
> This is a peninsula. I live on the edge of town. This hasn't been the edge of town since 1875. It's spooky. Driving at night, when you go out

toward the lake to that one grocery store that's open—there's electricity right up here along the river, and then there's another little bit of electricity right there on the lake, where that grocery store is, but for the thirty-five blocks in between, it's as dark as being out in the middle of the ocean. When you sit there at an intersection and look out—when you sit on St. Claude and look north, it's like you're standing on the beach at night looking out to sea. There's *nothing.* There's not anything moving out there. It's pitch dark. And if you do see a pair of headlights, it's like seeing another boat out in the ocean—way, way, way out there you can see a little bitty light twinkling, coming toward you. And you know that on August 27 it wasn't like that. This was a thriving, crackling, zooming, bustling population—very poor, but not dead. And a lot of it's like Chernobyl out there now.

Little by little, electricity became stable, reliable. Five months into this thing, I'm still not getting any mail. There's heavy traffic on Magazine Street and St. Charles, and Frenchmen Street's jumpin' on the weekends, but other than that, there's not much here. It's just destroyed.

The federal government's not a presence here in any way. I haven't seen any sign of 'em.

Of the city's 117 public schools, forty-seven were severely damaged. All of them were closed.

The African American struggle for social justice, whether in the years of Reconstruction or the second Reconstruction of the 1960s, always emphasized two things: black enfranchisement and access to public schools. Now both were under attack.

In her influential 2007 book, the Canadian journalist Naomi Klein coined the term *shock doctrine* to refer to the way otherwise unacceptably radical social and economic changes are pushed through by free-marketeers in moments of crisis. Klein took as one of her prime examples what happened to the New Orleans public schools at this moment. In the introduction to *The Shock Doctrine*, she cites a December 5, 2005, op-ed in the *Wall Street Journal* by ninety-three-year-old Milton Friedman, who had been pushing privatized education for decades: "Most New Orleans schools are in ruins, as are the homes of the children who have attended them. The children are now scattered all over the country. This is a tragedy. It is also an opportunity."[3]

That was one of the refrains of the postflood period: this is an opportunity. It was an opportunity to keep the black voting bloc from coming back in its preflood numbers. It was an opportunity to weaken the Democrats. It was an opportunity to close down the housing projects. It was an opportunity to create a laboratory for privatizing schools. It was an opportunity for politically connected contractors to make a ton of money. It was a golden neocon opportunity.

One day in October, when the schools were all still closed, many school employees found out they would be losing their jobs by turning on the five o'clock news. The Louisiana state legislature had fired all the city's public schoolteachers *en masse*—four thousand public schoolteachers and thirty-five hundred other workers.[4] Besides saving money, it was a shot at breaking the back of the union, prior to restructuring the schools in a way the union would find unacceptable. The teachers' union, not coincidentally, was the most powerful union in the state and practically the backbone of the Democratic Party in Louisiana. A mass exodus of experienced teachers followed.[5] The New Orleans public school system would be divided into two tiers. One consisted of charter schools, which were integrated, and the other, called the Recovery School District (RSD), was effectively all black. Guess which was set up to be the winner and which the loser.

The housing projects were sealed up tight. It had taken years of effort to close down the St. Thomas and put in a Wal-Mart. Now, to many— certainly to real-estate developers—it seemed as though the hand of Providence had emptied all the projects overnight. In the often-quoted words of Rep. Richard Baker, a Republican real estate millionaire from New Orleans who represented Baton Rouge in Congress: "We finally cleaned up public housing in New Orleans. We couldn't do it, but God did." There were a whole lot of people who were determined that they never reopen. Some of the projects, especially Lafitte, were located on desirable land, if there was such a thing in a city whose survival was so uncertain. It would be a popular move, even among some African Americans, to bulldoze the projects. But they were people's homes, and many of those people had nowhere else to go.

Driving at night up Louisiana toward Claiborne through a sea of darkness, I suddenly realized, holy shit, we're passing the Magnolia projects. I didn't recognize it. It was completely dark. Not a soul stirring. Nor were the stoplights working. It turns out to be a complicated thing to get a destroyed system of synchronized stoplights back up and running, and it takes money. There was an emergency grant to help with that, but it was only one item on a long checklist. The city had had to be dewatered and the dead bodies collected. Debris lay everywhere, and the city had three working garbage trucks. Air testing and water-supply testing had to be done. The power and utility grid had to be rebuilt. The sewage system had to be made functional. The city had to do this with some three thousand fewer employees than it had before; many of those who remained were emotionally devastated, and many were living in improvised circumstances. Three hundred seventy-four city buildings were severely damaged or destroyed, including the Mahalia Jackson Theater. The city had to get a new computer system. And they had to get a recovery plan in place as well as a for-real workable civil defense system in time for next year's hurricane season.

The federal government did not send New Orleans a check and say here, fix it. All those billions of federal dollars spent on the Gulf Coast? Much of it went to the immediate aftermath of the storm—debris removal, troops and mercenaries, emergency supplies, levee repair. The federal money that was sent to Louisiana was just that—sent to Louisiana, not to New Orleans. The law was written so that federal money went to the state first, where the legislature was controlled by upstaters who had no political motivation to get New Orleans rolling again. If they were Republicans, they had a strong partisan motivation to obstruct Blanco. Freeing the money from the state would prove as problematic as getting it from the feds. Meanwhile, dollars were being sent in greater per capita amounts to Republicans Trent Lott and Haley Barbour's Mississippi, where the casinos went back into action.

FEMA, which is mandated by the Stafford Act to help the city with infrastructural repairs, made the city apply on a project-by-project basis to be reimbursed. At a time when the city's treasury had imploded and its credit rating had cratered, the Bush administration said, ask our permission, then go borrow money on the capital markets, and we'll reimburse it after you've spent it, if you fill out the forms right and if we haven't changed our minds. New Orleans was running on borrowed money.

My Tulane posse might not be much use in a gunfight, but in a battle of wits they're the ones I'd want at my back. A number of them had passed through New York at some point during their enforced leave, but it was reassuring to see them all in New Orleans again. Most faculty and long-term employees at Tulane had continued to get paychecks during the fall semester when the university was closed, providing they committed to return, so they'd had a much easier time of it than the people who lost their homes, their livelihood, their communities, possibly a family member, and, in short, their identities.

New Orleans had become a two-class system: those who did, and those who didn't, flood. Most of the Tulane faculty was in the latter category. Felipe Smith was one exception to that. Much of New Orleans East had been destroyed, and Felipe's house took five and a half feet of water in the first floor. Having lost three vehicles as well as mementos, heirlooms, appliances, and furniture, his family had moved into temporary quarters in the Irish Channel. Fortunately, he got a quick insurance settlement—others would wait years, or never receive one—and was able to begin the multiyear process of rebuilding. Which was an agonizing experience, given how difficult it was to get capable, honest contractors, much less induce them to come way out of town to a severely damaged New Orleans East, where even fast food was a twenty- or thirty-minute drive each way and where there was less than a full governmental commitment to rebuilding the neighborhood's infrastructure. Between dealing with that and the increased workload at Tulane, he was juggling two full-time schedules.

Tulane had reopened for the spring semester, but it had been restructured prior to reopening. They didn't cut out the football team, though football is a revenue drain, perhaps because the board would not have approved. But some departments abruptly lost their graduate programs. Spanish and Portuguese kept its doctoral program, but the Ph.D. program in English was closed out. No one could say why. It was clear that the specific cuts were made hastily, in improvised circumstances, with little access to facts and figures. They seemed like dartboard decisions.

As part of the restructuring, some tenured faculty were dismissed, which earned Tulane censure from the American Association of University Professors, and so were staff. Full professors put in twelve-hour days teaching three classes or even four. Some worked without teaching assistants, since graduate programs had been slashed. Maybe you don't think teaching is really work. Try it. The good thing was that some 80 percent of the freshman class had returned to Tulane after spending the fall semester elsewhere, and those students must have been getting a hell of an education from those people, in that place, at that time.

My friends at Tulane didn't have an easy time; no one did. They'd all had their lives turned upside down, and they were all still stunned—though, being articulate people, they expressed their situation with great clarity. They still had jobs, which was no small thing, but their scholarly work—their research, their writing—had largely to be put on hiatus, and that's what academic careers are based on. You don't publish, you don't advance in the profession, and most of them would have no chance to publish in the coming few years.

Changes were necessary, and some of the changes seemed positive. The university, which formerly cultivated a reputation as the "Harvard of the South" (though the phrase has also been tossed around for Rice, Vanderbilt, and Duke) and had something of a fortress mentality with respect to the community around it, became redefined as a community-interested institution. Students were required to take courses in New Orleans culture and put in time on community service. Cynics wondered how much of it was dictated by trying to reposition Tulane, already the largest employer in the city, to seem like a player in the rebuilding of the town when money started to flow. But actively encouraging students to connect with New Orleans and its culture was unquestionably a good thing, and Tulane had faculty members who were not only equal to the task but had been waiting for the chance.

Not a few of the faculty had taken their jobs at Tulane in the first place because they wanted to be in New Orleans, and they were committed to trying to stay—if there was a real New Orleans to remain in, instead of what Felipe described to me when I visited him in the Irish Channel: "I fear that New Orleans could become an Epcot—a kind of simulacrum of an Afro-Creole culture with European, Caribbean, and other world cultural influences, where African Americans are embraced and welcomed to the extent that they visually enhance that presentation, but whose presence within the city is otherwise not necessarily considered desirable."

Loyola, next door to Tulane, came back. The University of New Orleans, by the lakefront, soldiered on; they even managed to have a fall semester in spite of everything. Marvalene Hughes, the president of historically black Dillard, had only been on the job since July when her campus, next to the fatally breached London Canal, was covered with high water that came in from three directions. They ran the college out of a hotel, reopening on January 9 with offices and student housing in the Central Business District Hilton Riverside. The other two historically (and historic) black colleges, Xavier and Southern, were trashed, but through heroic effort, they and other colleges in the area managed to reopen.

On Bourbon Street, on a Wednesday night, the entire daiquiri-and-T-shirt tourist apparatus was cranked up full blast, but the crowd was sparse, and it was about 90 percent men. The city had gone back to its 1875 boundaries and its 1745 gender balance.

In the low-lying Mid-City area, the Banks Street Café had started having music by candlelight before the electricity came back on. Now the power was back, but the Banks Street was the only place on the block, or the next block, or the block on the other side, with lights on. The street was deserted, and deathly quiet except for the electric band thumping out of the Banks Street. Nearby, the Rock 'n' Bowl was dark.

On Thursday night I went to Vaughan's, in a dark part of the Bywater. Outside it seemed dead, but inside the bar was buzzing. Kermit Ruffins, back from Houston, held forth as he did before, with the same set-ending joke about taking a reefer break. I found myself standing next to a friend who said to me, kind of out of the blue, "my uncle was in a tree in Biloxi for three days." I said, "That's a long damn time to be up in a tree." She said, "No food, no water." People were just blurting out things like this, apropos of nothing. We partied on.

Five months after New Orleans was destroyed, it reminded me of nothing so much as Havana. Power outages in whole neighborhoods were a common occurrence. Mail? Forget about it, at least if you lived in the Bywater. Appointments had to be rescheduled constantly because life was being improvised day to day. Rubble everywhere. People standing in long lines to get bureaucratic things done. And, just like in Havana, there was a sense of being in a place under embargo by Washington, D.C., a hostile colossus to the north.

The fun in New Orleans was Havana-style. You'd hear by word of mouth that at such-and-such a place at five P.M. there was going to be a little combo, and when you got there, there was a passel of word-of-mouthsters hanging out, catching up with their social network in a building with plaster chunks missing from the front, forgetting their troubles for a little while. The music was a necessary amenity, as important to the social event as the food and the beer. You're not consuming the music, you're all in it together. Maybe you know some of the musicians. They're on the same level as you, still trying to get their houses gutted while they perched wherever they could. Music has a different meaning in that situation.

Also like Havana, the water pressure was low. Driving upriver from downtown on February 3, I saw helicopters flying back and forth dangling slings full of water below them. They were fighting a losing battle to save the ninety-one-year-old Coliseum Theater at Camp and Melpomene, an old-style movie house that last showed a film in 1976. I'd driven past it every time I drove downtown, the year before the flood. But there wasn't enough pressure in the hoses to put the fire out. The next day several houses burned in the Marigny, leaving eleven homeless.

The clincher on making it seem like Havana was when I went to see Fred Johnson of the Black Men of Labor Social Aid and Pleasure Club. Johnson had me meet him at Powell's Place, which was drummer/vocalist Shannon Powell's home on St. Philip Street, right across from Louis Armstrong Park, which is to say not far from Congo Square. With most of the restaurants in Tremé closed, the Powells had opened one in their home, cooking up soul food at popular prices. It was exactly a *paladar*—the food speakeasies that in the early '90s sprang up in Cuban homes and became a part of Cuban culture. We walked through Shannon Powell's living room and out to the concrete patio in the back. I bought a Shannon Powell CD called *Powell's Place*.

It felt like Havana because I ran into magnificent, soulful people everywhere I went. They had to be there because it was their place. They were defending their home by living in it.

The waves of immigration that changed the complexion of the United States beginning in the 1960s had never come to New Orleans. The people who were there, most likely their grandparents were there too. The place with the flimsiest ground in the country had the most deeply rooted people. Fred Johnson told me:

> I'm a New Orleans native, born and raised here. And if I was on flat zero, the place I would want to be is the place I know best. I can navigate on the streets of New Orleans. I know where the food places are, I know where the money places are, I can make my way on the streets of New Orleans. I'll make it anywhere I go, but I think that it's much more convenient for me to make it here, because this is my turf.

Only a few of the musicians were back at that point—5 to 10 percent, I guessed. But whoever was there was real true flavor. I saw a lot of love. And that's what I remember about Havana, what so inspired me during the Special Period in the early '90s, as terrible as it was. When no one else cared about Cuba, the people—for all they bickered—were there for each other. They might not have seen it that way, but that's what I saw coming from outside: how they kept it together. And when the world had turned its back on Cuba, people without enough to eat were dancing—not because they were happy but because that's how they kept sane. It was an essential music that could only have been played there, in that place, at that moment.

It's not a fair comparison, of course. For one thing, Cuba had a functional government. There were doctors in Havana but not in New Orleans. Don't even mention hurricane preparedness.

And Havana, militarized though it was, didn't feel like it was being occupied by mercenaries.

I said to David Freedman, "I don't see a whole lot of evidence of the U.S. government here." He answered:

You know what we *have* seen? And this has probably been one of the most Stephen King moments of this whole episode. We've seen a lot of people in quasi-military uniforms—gray shirts and dark gray pants, and patches on their shoulders. But they aren't part of the official government. They're hired military-type people. And we're not sure *who* they report to. But we know they carry guns, and they have a lot of attitude. I can tell you, going down to the SBA office just down the street at St. Charles Avenue was one of the scariest moments of my being back here. Because they looked like Americans, they talked English, they were clean-cut, and they had these uniforms that—I don't know any military branch of our government that has that kind of uniform.

Who *are* these people?

Who are *we*?

What country am I in?

You know, I felt like I didn't belong here. You have to experience it to really know what I'm talking about.

I'll tell you another story. I was in the French Quarter, and this guy hit my car from behind. Just tapped me, punched a couple of holes in my bumper. So I got out, looked at it, and I said, "I'd like to see your driver's license and your insurance." He wouldn't show it to me.

And I said, "Well, I'm not movin' my car, and you can't go anywhere till you do what you gotta do, which is, you gotta show me your insurance and your driver's license, so if I have a problem—I don't know if I will, but if I do, I gotta know who I deal with."

He wouldn't do it.

He had a black T-shirt, black pants, crew cut, very clean-cut. He looked like an American, and he talked English, but I don't know—it was weird. That's all I can say, it was weird. He said, "Well, now I've gotta file a report."

"Well, lots of luck," I said. "If you try and call a policeman in New Orleans for a little thing like this, it's gonna be six hours before anybody shows up, if they show up at all."

He said, "Not a problem." He picked up the phone and called the police chief of our city! Called him by his first name! Said, "I have a little problem here. You need to send out some police." Fifteen minutes later the police were there! I mean, you can't get police to come out for a *murder* in fifteen minutes! And he never did show me his license. He never did show me his insurance. I did get a police report. I'm not sure what I can do with it.

But this is where I grew up, here in New Orleans. I was born here. And I felt like, all of a sudden, the rules had changed. This guy never identified himself. *Who is he?* That can call up the police chief and not identify himself when he hit somebody with his car?

I dropped in to see Coco Robicheaux, still playing his Saturday night gig at the smelly old Apple Barrel on Frenchmen. Instead of tourists, the place was full of beefy young soldiers of fortune, some of whom had acquired a curious species of blond girlfriend with vinyl-like hair and suspiciously large breasts, and who didn't seem to be from New Orleans either. Their idea of relaxing in a bar was a little different than mine. One of the men standing next to me punched one of his buddies in the chest as a drunken kind of fun, with a whoomp that would have flattened me. It wasn't that far from my head. That kind of shit in a bar makes me nervous. I said to him politely, "Please don't do that." He looked at me wordlessly, with a puzzled expression. I thought, it would be easy to get my head beaten in.

I went driving around on a warm Sunday afternoon, winding up at the Iberville Projects, across from the French Quarter.

This is someplace I never went before the flood, because it had a reputation for being unsafe. But it was perfectly safe to be there that Sunday. There were no people. It had been empty of people for five months. There were No Trespassing signs but it was wide open. I could have walked into it and no one would have challenged me. There was a bicycle up on one balcony, a barbecue grill on another. The residents had left quickly. This is relatively high ground, and the buildings were undamaged. There was no apparent reason why people couldn't move back in.

I walked all the way around the projects and never saw another person. The New Orleans projects are low-rise, typically three stories, and extend horizontally. They consume a lot of otherwise valuable real estate throughout the city. These acres would be worth a lot—if the city had reliable protection from flooding and if it weren't the home of so many poor people.

As I faced the Iberville ghost town, I had my back to St. Louis Cemetery #2. New Orleans's above-ground cemeteries—necessary because the water table is so high—are often referred to as "cities of the dead." Some of them are adjacent to the projects, which kind of function as cemeteries for the living. I had never been in St. Louis #2, because it had a reputation as a good place to get jacked. It's an island, stuck between the Iberville on one side and the elevated I-10 on the other. There are notices from the Archdiocese on the cemetery walls disclaiming responsibility for what might happen to you, which in normal times was that you might get mugged by project kids who grow up with the cemetery as their playground and know every nook and cranny. It was about three P.M., with bright winter sunlight already at a low angle. According to the posted hours, the cemetery had closed at noon. But the gates were wide open. I walked in. There wasn't a living soul around.

For a half hour, maybe forty-five minutes, I was alone in St. Louis Cemetery #2, just me and the dead. Not the unquiet, unfuneraled dead of the Lower Ninth Ward, but the properly buried ones whose bodies had been cut loose with music. The difference was easy to feel. If I had heard a human voice I would have jumped out of my skin, but there was nobody the whole time I was there. Some of the tombs were in fine shape; others were crumbling, as they no doubt had been for a long time. Earlier in the day, a woman had told me how upset she was to see a scumline on the tomb of her father. But there were no scumlines in St. Louis #2, which hadn't taken water.

I looked down and saw the tomb of Claude Tremé (d. 1828), the planter for whom the Tremé is named. I walked on and there was the tomb of drummer Paul Barbarin (1899–1939), in which are also buried Danny (1909–1994) and Louisa "Blue Lou" (1913–1999) Barker, guardian spirits of twentieth-century New Orleans music. And over there was the tomb of Dominique You (1775–1830), businessman, pirate, and associate of the brothers Lafitte.

All of them—the pirate, the planter, and the musicians—told me they were *pissed* at what had happened to their city. Their anger was coming up from the ground. I could hear them because, like T.R. said, New Orleans had never been so quiet, not since 1718. I looked up and saw a tomb on which was inscribed the word SILENCE.

This city should have had people living in it by now, rebuilding their lives. Popeyes was offering nine bucks an hour, Santa Fe wages, but there was no place for workers to live. The exiles didn't have a place to stay if they came back. The children didn't have schools to go to. Charity Hospital was closed and might never reopen. The city was freaking out and there were only a handful of mental health professionals. The FEMA trailers, temporary solutions that cost more than fixing the houses would have, had been purchased and stockpiled, but they weren't yet being given out in New Orleans. When they finally were, they turned out to be gas chambers, exuding formaldehyde and causing respiratory problems that were especially bad for babies and old folks.

It's almost like someone somewhere said: let's do everything possible to keep *those people* from coming back. No wonder there is a deeply rooted belief that the levees were blown up. Just like it's an ineradicable folk belief that the flooding of the Lower Ninth with Hurricane Betsy in 1965 was the result of dynamited levees. I have seen absolutely no evidence to support either of those claims. But no matter, because in another way they *were* blown up. Talking about this with Felipe, he said: "There's fast dynamite, and there's slow dynamite."

The fast dynamite goes boom. The slow dynamite was what America's urban poor had been experiencing over the last forty years. The slow dynamite was the neglect of the city's people and of the protection the city needed against the ravages of the wind, the rain, and the oil companies that cut thousands of canals into the wetlands. The slow dynamite was MR-GO, the Mississippi River Gulf Outlet, that had flooded the Lower Ninth with Betsy in 1965 and now had taken out the Lower Ninth and New Orleans East the next time it was tested, forty years later.

———————

The following day I went by the Backstreet Cultural Museum on St. Claude. It's not far from the French Quarter, and it's on high enough ground that it wasn't flooded.

I hadn't been overcome by emotion once the whole trip. But that moment came when I pulled up in my car outside the Backstreet and saw Al Morris sitting out front, like he used to do. Al was sixty-six, and he was a Skeleton. "I've been a Skull since I was seven years old," he told me. He remained on the block the entire time after the storm hit, taking care of things. I asked him if he was going out this year, and with a broad grin he told me, "At five thirty I come out of the casket." I asked him what Indians were around, and he said, "Vic Harris was just here." Victor Harris. Also known as Mandingo Warrior. Also known as the Spirit of Fi-Yi-Yi. One of the authentic culture heroes of New Orleans. Mardi Gras was going to be deep.

That block is dominated by the presence of St. Augustine Catholic Church, where free people of color once paid for pews so enslaved people could talk to God. Homer Plessy and civil rights lawyer A. P. Tureaud were parish members, as were Sidney Bechet and Tootie Montana.[6] Dedicated in 1842 and still in constant use, St. Augustine was still standing but not looking its best. The metal cladding had been peeled off the bell tower by the storm, and it suffered rain damage inside. I walked around the church and saw the Tomb of the Unknown Slave, which honors slaves buried in unmarked graves.

Most memorial sculpture is kitschy or just plain awful, but this is a fine and noble work of art. A large, heavy rusted cross of iron links was set at an angle in the ground, with manacles and weights hanging off it, and little grave-top crosses planted in the earth around. It intends to be, as the dedicatory plaque says, "a constant reminder that we are walking on sacred ground."

New Orleans is a deeply spiritual town. A person who's lived there all his or her life, speaks one of the peculiar local dialects, and has gone to the same church for fifty years isn't going to feel comfortable in exurban Texas. They'll trickle back in when they can. The way to stop them is to get rid of their churches. On Thursday, February 9, the archdiocese announced that it could no longer afford to support St. Augustine Parish and would be merging it with neighboring St. Peter Claver Parish. No longer needed would be St. Augustine's seventy-five-year-old priest, Father Jerome LeDoux, a historically conscious spiritual leader whose pulpit was a cypress stump, literally representing the community's roots. Taking away their parish was going to be a serious blow. Activists subsequently occupied the sanctuary for twenty days, and the Archdiocese ultimately kept the parish open, but Father LeDoux was moved to Fort Worth.

I drove past another kind of cemetery. The space on Claiborne underneath the I-10 trestles was packed full of automotive bodies, blocks and blocks of them. Ruined, abandoned cars had been brought there, one by one, the dead, driverless vehicles sitting there in the quiet dark. As the sky turned gray and clouded up, I tuned in Keith Hill's blues show on WWOZ.

They say New Orleans is a place where the blues isn't in quotation marks. Now all those songs about deep water, about wind and rain, about how you can't find your baby or your way home, had ceased to be metaphors and became lived experience once again. Under weeping skies in this mostly deserted city, a line as corny as *If you're looking for a rainbow, there has to be some rain* sounded like the truest thing in the world.

I went to the French Quarter. Much of it was open for business, but there were no customers. After lunch in a big, empty café, I went to the Louisiana Music Factory, the record store in the French Quarter that sells mostly local product. Tower and Virgin were shut, like a lot of the chain stores in the neighborhood, but this homegrown business was open.

The store's central stage area, where bands play, was empty. There was no one in the store except for me, two guys who worked there, and a middle-aged African American man who very politely went up to the counter and explained that he hadn't been able to play a piano for weeks and could he please play the old upright on the bandstand for five minutes? If it wasn't possible, he understood perfectly. The piano wasn't really in playing condition, the younger man explained apologetically, and the older man said thank you and walked on out into the street.

As I made a purchase I said, "Who was that?"

"I don't know his name," said the man behind the register. Pause. "I hear he's a pretty good piano player, though."

Furious Five in action, September 28, 2008.

CODA

I n the second week of Barack Obama's administration, the closing of
MR-GO began. For the three and a half years since the flood, the channel had remained open. Wetlands restoration to protect the city's downriver exposure hadn't even begun—though with subsiding land and rising sea
levels, maybe even that wouldn't be enough to buffer the city from the next
big one.

What happens to New Orleans—and as I write this, it's still an open question—is a test case. If, as presently seems possible, the world's coastal cities
oceanside and riverside are inundated by rising sea levels, we will lose nothing
less than the living record of civilization, which grew up alongside river banks
and seaports. Our history and culture as a race—I mean, human race, *homo
sapiens sapiens*—is bound up in the continuing legacies of our port cities.

When I began writing *The World That Made New Orleans*, I never imagined it would be seen as an argument for "why we need to save New Orleans,"
as the first newspaper review put it.[1] But the reviewer was right. Suddenly, telling the city's history had acquired a sharp point. Whatever the economic argu-
ments pro or con for the city's continued existence, we need to preserve the
city for cultural reasons. Not for tits, beads, and public drunkenness, but for
something more profound—which means we need to study and teach people
about the culture of the possibly vanishing coastal city of New Orleans. This is
a battle we will be fighting the rest of our short lives, possibly in many places.

A full history of the criminal negligence that attended the flooding of
New Orleans has yet to be written. How did it happen that the Bush administration chose not only not to help but to proactively keep rescuers out of
the city when it was in turmoil? What were they thinking when they let

New Orleans writhe in agony for days and did nothing to save its people? How much of it was deadly incompetence, and how much was by design? In 2009, a credible article by Robert Draper charged that army search-and-rescue helicopters stationed only two hundred miles away remained idle at the insistence of Secretary of Defense Donald Rumsfeld, who was engaged in a turf war with the Department of Homeland Security.[2] As I write this epilogue, a thoroughly documented answer is hidden behind a curtain of secrecy; documents pertaining to the federal response to Hurricane Katrina that Congress requested have not been provided. But whatever the case, the incompetence was itself by design, the logical consequence of the radical Republicans' commitment to make government ineffective.

The rogue presidency of George W. Bush never recovered from the reality-television pictures that outraced his spin machine. Two pictures of him were particularly damaging. One, the Nero moment, was when he posed holding a guitar while an American city drowned on his watch. The other was of him looking out the window of Air Force One as he flew over the devastation on the way back from his belatedly terminated vacation. That was the George W. Bush I knew: the absentee president who'd spent September 11, 2001, running and hiding while we in lower Manhattan breathed in the vaporized dead from the World Trade Center. From 9/11 to the New Orleans flood to the crash of 2008 was one big presidential vacation.

The failure of New Orleans was complicated, and represented the conjuncture of a number of different forces, including serious failures on the part of the mayor and governor, who were quite possibly on the receiving end of more anger locally than even the Bush administration. But any accounting has to note that unlike the governors of Mississippi and Alabama, Mayor Nagin and Governor Blanco were Democrats, and therefore were to be excluded, rather than cut in, by the syndicate mentality of the Bush administration, which put party over country to a degree unprecedented since the Civil War. The failures of Governor Blanco and Mayor Nagin cost lives and impeded the recovery. But the Bush administration was monstrous. In thinking about what happened to New Orleans, one should never lose sight of the fact that a sizable African American voting bloc was dispersed to the four winds and its return obstructed. For the Bush regime, that was a desirable outcome.

George W. Bush should have been removed from office. The Democrats chose not to confront him and his gang directly but to wait it out. It cost the country dearly. With no government to stop them, the doors were left wide open to the looters who ransacked the economy, culminating in the crash of '08. Fuck taking a box of Pampers, steal fifty billion dollars. For their final act, the Bushists crashed not only the U.S. but the world, in a global economic Katrina. They didn't merely let it happen; they got up every morning for eight years, working hard to create the conditions for it to happen, packing slow dynamite around the levees of the world economy. For reasons of their own, they did to us all what they did to New Orleans, leaving us with multiple systems failing around us, all at once, leaving it to someone else to try to rebuild from the ruins.

The destruction of New Orleans shredded Bush's aura of invulnerability. After that, there was no way even right-wingers could pretend he was anything but bad news. It was the turning point of his presidency.

New Orleans paid the price for that moment of truth.

New Orleans came back, unevenly. There was a rebuilding party going on, but not everyone was invited. By summer 2008, according to demographer Greg Rigamer's estimate, the city had 72 percent of its former population but only 63 percent of its former African American population. More than a third of black New Orleanians remained in exile, either trying to get back home or building new lives elsewhere.

New Orleans was a smaller, less black city, with a white-majority city council. By 2009, Louisiana had a religious-right Republican governor, Bobby Jindal.[3] As of December 2008, when the embarrassing, indicted African American congressman William Jefferson was defeated in an surprise-upset, low-turnout runoff that many voters didn't seem to know about, New Orleans elected its first Republican congressman since Reconstruction: the previously unknown Anh Cao, who represented the political maturation after two generations of another diaspora, New Orleans's Vietnamese community, which had a strong base in the devastated New Orleans East. Cao campaigned not on the radical Republican hobbyhorses of gay marriage and abortion, but on promising to work for wetlands restoration and flood protection.

Nobody knows where all the people who were moved out of the toxic FEMA trailers went. FEMA was supposed to provide contact information for them to the state of Louisiana. It didn't. A 2008 study of the health of 261 still-displaced "Katrina children" in Baton Rouge found them "the sickest I have ever seen in the U.S." in the words of Dr. Irwin Redlener, the study's director.[4] Forty-two percent of the children had respiratory disorders, some of them likely from the trailers. Forty-one percent were anemic. More than half had mental health problems. They had missed years of school that could never be replaced. Another study found Louisiana to have the schoolchildren

least prepared for college; still another found the state to have the lowest
level of public health in the country. New Orleans had 179 officially recognized murders in 2008, out of a population estimated at over three hundred
thousand. Austin, with more than twice as many people, had twenty-three.

Three years after the flood, a third of the houses in New Orleans remained
vacant. In the Lower Ninth Ward abandoned, blighted, dead homes sagged
by the hundreds as the weeds around them grew higher. Only 11 percent of
the population had returned to that neighborhood, the home of Fats Domino,
the first rock 'n' roll star.

It's still an open question: with so much of the black community gone,
where will the next generation of New Orleans music come from?

In July 2008, I wrote a piece in the venerable jazz magazine *Down Beat*
that tried to answer editor Jason Koransky's question about New Orleans:
"Who's there?"[5]

It was a downbeat piece, all right. I had expected to write a more optimistic one, but then I started interviewing New Orleans musicians. Most of
the musicians you've heard of were back, though less so the rank and file.
Everyone was enthusiastic about the music they were making, but the collective toll of stress was evident, and not everyone was optimistic about the
future of the city. It was as if the music of New Orleans could be literally the
spirit that survived the body. I turned the article in the day before the third
anniversary of Hurricane Katrina, when two million or so people evacuated
for Hurricane Gustav. The levees held. But Gustav was a smaller storm than
Katrina, and made landfall as a Category Two. What would happen next
time, or the time after that? New Orleans still hasn't been squarely smacked
by a major hurricane.

But despite the obstacles, great music was happening. Out of that same
visit to New Orleans, I programmed an episode for *Afropop Worldwide* of postflood music—electrifying stuff from a transcendental time. Postflood New
Orleans compared only with two other moments I had experienced in my life:
New York during its bankruptcy crisis of the '70s, and Havana in the Special
Period of the early '90s—great music cities where there was creativity amid
chaos, gloom, depression, and poverty. When you and everyone else in the
band have lost your houses and music is what you have to survive with, you're
going to play with some feeling. When a trumpet player drives six hours each
way from Houston to make his weekly bar gig in New Orleans, the way musicians in Soul Rebels did, you can feel his commitment in every note. And the

music was being listened to by people who didn't take it for granted. It had a big job to do to combat the depression everyone was suffering, and it rose to the challenge.

I hope I've successfully conveyed that New Orleans was a great music city the year before the flood. I'm writing this sentence in 2009: let me assure you that the music continues. It was a great music city then, and it's a great music city now.

In spite of everything, it was an exciting time to be in New Orleans.

Second lines had never seemed more essential.

We exist, they said. We will not stop being ourselves. We will not give up our culture. We will not go into exile.

On the fourth Sunday of September 2008, the Young Men Olympian Junior Benevolent Aid Society's anniversary was marked by a mighty second line on a hot, sunny day. The YMO first paraded in 1884, so they've been out in the street in three different centuries. As the parade rolled through Central City, it picked up people, the way second lines do. This is a big club, with six divisions—I counted only five in the street, but I mostly hung at the back of the parade, trying not to get trampled by the police horses that impatiently push the rear along. Each division came suited in its own color, with its own brass band.

When you're in it, you can't see how far it stretches. Three thousand people? Five thousand? More? I have no idea. There was a city there.

The parade paused in front of Lafayette Cemetery #2 on Washington Avenue. With the above-ground tombs as their backdrop, men and boys of the division called the Furious Five proceeded to do a high-energy circle dance in the street. They wore orange and white outfits, some with white eyemasks and orange bandanas over their noses and mouths that made them into faceless ceremonial figures. Africa was alive—not merely preserved, but transformed to suit the present-day needs of the community. Some people in adjacent neighborhoods and communities might not consider having Africa be alive as something desirable, but in African American New Orleans it meant nothing less than the will to live.

At a rest stop on Dryades Street, there was a battle of the bands between Rebirth (with the Furious Five) and Hot 8 (parading with the Untouchables). Both bands had kept working, playing a busy schedule of second lines and funerals. But everyone, marchers and bands alike, had been through hell. There were a lot of funerals in a town with so much stress and depression, and so few doctors and hospitals. Charity Hospital had been closed since the storm and was not scheduled to reopen.

Hot 8 had blown the breath of life back into the second line, playing the first one after the flood on October 9, at the jazz funeral for chef Austin Leslie, in a mostly empty city. But snare drummer and cofounder Dinerral Shavers was murdered on the evening of December 28, 2006, while trying to rescue his stepson from a tense situation on enemy turf. The murder shocked the city and traumatized the students at L. E. Rabouin High School, where Shavers had organized the school's first-ever marching band. The Hot 8 filled the snare drum position and kept working. Another Hot 8 musician, Terrell Batiste, lost both legs after being hit by a car in Georgia, but he continued second lining in a wheelchair, trumpet in hand. But the Hot 8 had been working on their skills, getting together with traditional clarinetist Dr. Michael White. He'd lost a lifetime's collection of vintage clarinets and jazz historical material in the flood, but he was going forward, teaching the Hot 8 about traditional New Orleans–style jazz. Nothing was going to stop the Hot 8, or Dr. White, both of whom in their different ways knew what the stakes were for New Orleans culture.

Facing off across the packed-out intersection, the Hot 8 and Rebirth duelled playing the fanfare: *da-dat-DWEEEE-dat*, answered by the crowd: *hey!* They played it against each other, Rebirth at a faster tempo and higher pitch, and each band's crowd trying to out-*hey!* the other. It wasn't a contest, it was music. Everybody won.

Funerals are for the dead, but second lines are for the living. At one point I heard some people chanting that Rebirth chant: "*Reeee-*birth! *Reeee-*birth!"

Were they supporting the band, or shouting to their city? It was the same thing.

We need a second line for this whole hurting country. But only New Orleans has it.

And the second liners shouted: "*Reeee-*birth! *Reeee-*birth!"

AFTERWORD

A s this book was in copyedit, Terry and Thatcher McElveen came to trial for the murder of Jonathan Lorino. By then they had been in prison for six and a half years, and Terry McElveen was already serving a thirty-year sentence for a separate armed robbery conviction. Theirs was one of thirty preflood murder cases still awaiting resolution in Orleans Parish.[1]

Their mother, who collected the eighteen-thousand-dollar Crimestoppers reward for having turned them in, had been arrested as a material witness prior to the trial. According to her, Thatcher said before the two left the house, "We're going out for cigarettes. We don't care if we have to kill somebody to get them," and when they returned, their clothes were bloody.[2] The jury took less than two hours to convict them of second-degree murder, with a mandatory life sentence.

Jonathan's father, Tony Lorino, was in the courtroom when the guilty plea was read. He had been to every hearing in the case over the last six and a half years, more than 135 court dates.[3]

In the early hours of Mardi Gras morning 2009, Empress Antoinette K-Doe died of a massive heart attack at the age of sixty-six, perhaps another victim of the postflood stress.

She went to join the other saints: Marie Laveau, Buddy Bolden, Mahalia Jackson, Oretha Castle Hailey, Danny and Blue Lou Barker—and Ernie K-Doe. But as anyone knew who'd ever seen her sitting with the mannequin at the

Mother-in-Law's outdoor tiki bar, she'd been in communication with Ernie all along. The mannequin version of Ernie rode in her funeral procession.

A few months later, I asked Antoinette's daughter Betty if she knew how to make a Burn, K-Doe, Burn. Betty shook her head sadly. "She took it with her," she said.

I'm looking forward to knocking back a Burn, K-Doe, Burn in the celestial branch of the Mother-in-Law Lounge, though hopefully not soon.

Oh, yes. The dead like to have a drink once in a while. That's why we pour them a little from time to time.

ACKNOWLEDGMENTS

I want to thank all my friends. To those who appear in these pages, I say: I hope you don't mind. To those who don't appear in these pages, I say: I hope you don't mind. But to everyone I say, thank you all.

As I hope this book makes clear, I have great friends, and lots of them. A few of them are named in this book. Even a book this long is necessarily selective, and many close friends as well as acquaintances who might have danced through this limited number of pages had to remain offstage. It would be impossible to name them all here, and I won't recite again here the names of the people named in the text. But to all my friends I say thank you, and please don't worry that future conversations with me will wind up in some book somewhere.

Everyone thanked at the end of *The World That Made New Orleans* is hereby thanked again, since these two books are one project. As noted in the text, my stay in New Orleans as a Tulane Rockefeller Humanities Fellow was an initiative of the Stone Center for Latin American Studies and the Deep South Humanities Center. I can't imagine that any other community of academics would have welcomed me in the way the Stone Center and my Tulane posse did. To all the people at the Stone Center—especially Thomas F. Reese, Valerie McGinley Marshall, Sue Inglés, and everyone else—thank you. And thank you to Ariana Hall of CubaNola Collective, who first alerted me to the fellowship's existence.

I spent my year in New Orleans saying hi every day to the gracious and helpful staff at the Howard-Tilton Library, and I want to shout them out again, and especially to Dr. Hortensia Calvo and the staff at the Latin American Library; and to Dr. Bruce Boyd Raeburn and Lynn Abbott at the Hogan

Jazz Archive; and the staff of Tulane's Louisiana Collection, as well as to Bob
Black of the Natchitoches Parish Library.

I would especially like to thank the John Simon Guggenheim Foundation, of which I was a Fellow in 2005–06, during the period that New Orleans
was destroyed, a catastrophic event that transformed my life and work and
through which the support of the Guggenheim Foundation was critical. I
benefited in the writing of this book from research previously done at the
New York Public Library as a fellow at the Cullman Center for Scholars and
Writers. Support from the estate of Keith Burnett, the Hal Fishman Fund,
and the Freeze Foundation is also gratefully acknowledged.

Robert Farris Thompson's friendship and vision were a great help to me in
thinking about this material, and I received a great deal of time and thought
from Garnette Cadogan. Valuable criticisms and suggestions were made by
Jeff Chang, Marianne Greber, Gwendolyn Midlo Hall, T. R. Johnson, Jennifer Kotter, Janis Lewin, Dave Marsh, Bruce Boyd Raeburn, Elijah Wald,
and Daniel Wolff. A special thanks to Ron Robboy, who did on-the-ground
research in San Diego and more. Very special thanks to David Rubinson, T. J.
English, Mark Bingham, and Bob Holman. And thanks to Larry Blumenfeld,
Jon Caramanica, Charles Chamberlain, Robert Christgau, Dan Dawson,
Henry Drewel, Freddi Evans, Kevin Fontenot, Joyce Jackson, Lisa Katzman,
Rob Kenner, Ivor Miller, Robert Morales, Royce Osborn, Tatjana Pavlovic,
Ann Powers, Greg Samata, Donna Santiago and Tony Ciaccio, Ben Socolov,
Will Socolov, Theresa Teague, Beverly Trask, and Eric Weisbard. I would like
to thank my longtime *Afropop Worldwide* colleagues Sean Barlow, Banning
Eyre, Georges Collinet, Mike Jones, and Misha Turner.

I would also like to thank the musicologists, ethnographers, anthropologists, and journalists not otherwise mentioned whose work I've learned from
and cited, especially those who took the trouble to do firsthand documentation of the rich musical material all around them when nobody else seemed
to care. This list includes Connie Atkinson, Jason Berry, Thomas Brothers,
John Broven, Mick Burns, Rick Coleman, Jeff Hannusch, the late Tad Jones,
David Kunian, Keith Spera, and Geraldine Wyckoff. One of the threads of
this book is a dialogue with the daily newspaper, and I'd like to thank the
hardworking reporters of the *New Orleans Times-Picayune*, whose work I have
so frequently drawn on here, including Paul Purpura's ongoing coverage of the
C-Murder case, as well as the various other media in New Orleans, including
Gambit Weekly, *Louisiana Weekly*, and *Offbeat*. A special acknowledgment is
due the fine work of Katy Reckdahl.

This is my third book with editor Yuval Taylor and publisher Chicago Review Press, to whom I am indebted for having a career as an author. I am thrilled that they have continued to encourage and publish me. Thanks to Mary Kravenas, Michelle Schoob, and Jen Wisnowski. My agent, Sarah Lazin, was, as always, wonderfully supportive and crucial to making this book become reality.

Portions of this work appeared in a different form in *Bomb*, *American Legacy*, *Oxford American*, *Offbeat*, and *Downbeat*, and thanks to Betsy Sussler, Audrey Peterson, Marc Smirnoff, Alex Rawls, and Jason Koransky.

Thanks to all the musicians, Mardi Gras Indians, Skeletons, Baby Dolls, and second liners of New Orleans, and to everybody who supports them.

I acknowledge the suffering of the families and loved ones of the murder victims, named or unnamed, whose stories appear in this book, and in particular the family of Jonathan Lorino, whose story appears here only because telling it was unavoidable.

This is the third book I have written expanding my conversations with the late Robert Palmer, who started me out right in New Orleans.

And first and last, thank you, Constance.

NOTES

Introduction

1. Russell.
2. *Legacy of Shame*, 6–7.
3. Haygood and Tyson.
4. A fantasy trilogy: Ash, Constance. *The Horsegirl* (1988); *The Stalking Horse* (1990); *The Stallion Queen* (1992), all published by Ace, New York.

Chapter 1 : Jump Jim Crow

1. Grant, 61.
2. Denison, 1.
3. Fairclough, 276.
4. See Chestnut and Cass, 220. The Natchitoches Public Library was desegregated pursuant to a special board meeting on August 4, 1964, one month after the passage of the Civil Rights Act.
5. Interview with Cleveland Presley, Louisiana State Museum Civil Rights Oral Histories, http://louisdl.training.louislibraries.org/cdm4/item_viewer.php?CISOROOT=/LOH&CISOPTR=18&CISOBOX=1&REC=2.

Chapter 2: Are You a Yankee or Are You a Rebel?

1. Baker, Liva, 15.
2. Smith, Felipe, 1998, 49.
3. Presentation at Satchmo Summerfest, 2005.
4. *Southern School News*, September 1954.

5. A definition of the term *nigger-lover* was given in John Dollard's *Caste and Class in a Southern Town* (1937), as paraphrased by Felipe Smith: "independent-minded whites who did not observe ceremonial distance." (Smith, Felipe, 1998, 106).

6. *Southern School News*, December 1960.

7. Bass, 112.

8. Liebling, 48.

9. Liebling, 65.

10. Transcribed from film footage: http://www.youtube.com/watch?v=Qy8ImPFWZRA.

11. Starr, 103.

12. Fontenot, 53.

13. Berry 2003.

14. Liebling 1960b, 105.

15. *Southern School News*, August 1960.

16. *Southern School News*, December 1960.

17. Jerome.

18. *Southern School News*, December 1960.

19. Steinbeck, 195.

20. *Southern School News*, October 1961.

21. *Southern School News*, January 1962.

22. *Southern School News*, May 1962.

23. Mohl.

24. Levin.

25. Mohl.

26. Kuzenksi, 5.

Chapter 3: The Good Darkey

1. Wilson 2002, v. 5, 21.

2. "Detective Sergeant Wilson Victim."

3. Blackmon, 4.

4. See Blackmon.

5. Taylor, 190.

6. Barrier, 155.

7. Clips of Bosko cartoons can be found on YouTube.

8. DuBois, 730.

9. DuBois, 730.

10. Smith, Felipe, 1998, 137.

11. Barry.

12. Agee.
13. Croce, 24–26.
14. Included on the Kino DVD edition of *The Birth of a Nation*.
15. Ransom, 14.
16. See Chapters 17 and 18 of *The World That Made New Orleans*.

Chapter 4: Made Out of Mud

1. Laird, 115.
2. Laird, 124.
3. Hannusch, 119–124.
4. See Smith, Felipe, 1998 for a discussion of the revenant in southern race romances.
5. DuBois, 488.
6. Palmer.
7. Coleman, 17.
8. In a conversation at Jazzfest 2005.
9. Broven, xxi.
10. Scherman, 16.
11. Scherman, 44.
12. See Coleman, 27; Hannusch, 99.
13. Scherman, 91.
14. Hurtt; Coleman, 295.
15. Quoted in Smith, Felipe, 1998, 134.
16. Guralnick responded forcefully to the Elvis-was-a-racist meme in an op-ed in Guralnick 2007.
17. For my summary of the substantial Cuban influence on rock 'n' roll, see Sublette 2007.

Chapter 5: Tell It Like It Is

1. See *The World That Made New Orleans* for an account of the degenerate amateur composer Philippe II, Duc d'Orléans, and his role in founding the city.
2. Broven, 197.
3. Hannusch, 117.
4. Neville Brothers and Ritz, 251.
5. Hannusch, 339.
6. Barnes.
7. *New Orleans Weekly Pelican*, April 2, 1887.
8. Guillory, 5.

Chapter 6: Constance Street

1. Spain, 86.
2. See Smith, Felipe, 1998, for a discussion of "white" and "black" space.
3. Schleifstein.

Chapter 7: Ivan the Terrible

1. Quoted in Smith, Michael P., 145–146.
2. Cable, 120–121.
3. Guralnick 2005, 523.
4. Guralnick 2005, 549.
5. Guralnick 2005, 156.
6. "Three Children at School Arrested for Weapons Offenses."
7. Perlstein 2004.
8. Schleifstein and McQuaid.
9. Fischetti.
10. Powell.
11. For an account, see Hallward.

Chapter 8: Elysian Blues

1. DeLillo, 275.
2. Ingham, 1245.
3. Kunian.
4. Johnson, 241.
5. The late Rodolfo Cárdenas.
6. Mullener.
7. Quoted in Patel, 233.
8. Dylan, 187–88.
9. Chase, 82.
10. See *The World That Made New Orleans*, 93ff.

Chapter 9: The Kalunga Line

1. MacGaffey, 426.
2. Keynote address at Satchmo Summerfest, August 4, 2005.
3. Library of Congress interview, 1648b.
4. www.youtube.com/watch?v=05WCrH-kCgA.
5. This scene was witnessed by Helen Regis, who described it in Regis 2001, 756.
6. The story is told in Filosa 2004.
7. Satten.
8. Young 2004.

9. Young 2004b.
10. Bone.
11. Reckdahl 2004.
12. Weston.
13. Lee.
14. Armstrong 1954, 225.
15. Varney 2004.
16. Rioux and Philbin.
17. Raeburn, 8.
18. Brothers, 140–141.
19. Shapiro and Hentoff, 31–32.
20. Library of Congress interview, 1658a.
21. Barker, 26.
22. Marquis, facing page 23.
23. Bechet, 64.
24. Reproduced in Marquis, 127.
25. Marquis, 112–113.
26. See Streatfeild for an extended treatment of the early history of cocaine.
27 Perry, Mark, 71.
28. Streatfeild, 126.
29. Brothers, 110.
30. Library of Congress interview, 1642b.

Chapter 10: Creative Destruction

1. Schumpeter.
2. Babalola, 164.
3. Dr. John, 31.
4. Kenney, 41.
5. Bair, 1.
6. Bair, 6.
7. I borrow the term *ghetto-industrial complex* from Kaplan.
8. *Substance Abuse and Treatment Needs*, 1-4, 1-5.
9. Marriott, 72.
10. Perlstein, 1999, 1999a.
11. Perlstein, 1999b.
12. Kane and Abel.
13. Wade, 86.
14. Wagner.

Chapter 11: Whips and Ice

1. See *The World That Made New Orleans*.
2. Vargas.
3. Rankin, Kenny. See also Cohn.
4. Williams, 96. Apparently Juvenile's words, though the attribution is unclear.
5. "Bounce Back."
6. Williams 1998.
7. I thank Kandia Crazy Horse for the phrase *performative negritude*.
8. Powers.

Chapter 12: The Day of the Dead

1. Herz, 309.
2. Young 2004c.
3. Start with Fitrakis et al, *What Happened in Ohio?*
4. Interview with Mara Liasson, National Public Radio, www.npr.org/templates/story/story.php?storyId=1123439.
5. Marqusee.
6. Jamail.
7. Marqusee.
8. Marqusee.
9. www.brennansneworleans.com/ma–noeyeopener.html.
10. Young 2004d.

Chapter 13: The Blizzard of '04

1. He wrote an autobiographical sketch: "How I Became Felipe Smith," Smith 2003.
2. Varney and Young.
3. Finch.
4. Varney 2005.
5. Jensen 2005.

Chapter 14: King Kong

1. Assmann, 13.
2. Armstrong, 225.
3. www.piersystem.com/go/doctype/425/4761/&offset=20.
4. I am indebted to Joseph Roach for applying the term *noblesse oblige* to the krewe parades.
5. Spain, 88.

6. McPherson, 567.
7. Rankin, David, 418.
8. Rankin, David, 423.
9. Christian, 254–255.
10. "Shrove Tuesday. New-Orleans Mardi Gras." February 26, 1873, 1.
11. Gill, 53.
12. For more about "the cultural construction of time," see Assmann, 13–19.

Chapter 15: The Heart of the Pranks
1. Quoted in Rankin, David, 434.
2. Winston, 221.
3. Ted Widmer's *Martin Van Buren* is a highly readable and mercifully brief biography.
4. Rousseau, 457.
5. Rousseau, 482.
6. Rousey, 80, 89.
7. Cockrell, 168.
8. McKnight, 409.
9. Laborde, 52–53.
10. Gill, 51.
11. Goreau, 352.
12. Gill, 58.
13. Quoted in Gill, 65.
14. Mitchell, 67.
15. Wilson 2002.
16. James Gill's excellent book, which has been a useful source for this chapter, is titled *Lords of Misrule*.
17. Wilson 1893, 268.
18. Mitchell, 98.
19. Laborde, 25.
20. Quoted in Mitchell, 56.
21. Taylor, 204.
22. Roach, 261.

Chapter 16: The Wild West
1. Fairall, 376-80.
2. Cody 1917, 307.
3. Reddin, 68.

4. Kasper, 32.
5. Cody 1888, 307.
6. Cody 1917, 311–312.
7. www.youtube.com/watch?v=n4wWCE9HN5k.
8. Medley 2003, 91.
9. Abbott and Seroff, 112.
10. Brothers, 200, 212.
11. Armstrong, 224–225.
12. DuBois, 755.
13. Mitchell, 148.
14. See Mitchell, 188–189.
15. This was pointed out to me by Felipe Smith, whose insights about the subject of Zulu I gratefully acknowledge.
16. Brandt, 77.
17. In a presentation at Satchmo Summerfest, 2005.
18. Pais.
19. Johnson, 236–237.
20. Pais.
21. Gill, 171.
22. See Gill; Roach.
23. Rohter.
24. Gill, 280.
25. Sentences resequenced from different interview segments for continuity; see also Mayer.

Chapter 17: The End Is Near So Drink a Beer
1. Filosa 2006b.
2. www.piersystem.com/go/doc/425/62360/.
3. Sublette 2008, 301.
4. O'Brien 2005.
5. O'Brien 2005a.
6. Wyckoff.
7. See Rousey.
8. Reckdahl 2005b.

Chapter 19: The Strain of the Festival
1. Coleman, 17, 265.
2. Reckdahl 2005.
3. McDonough. I found the O'Brien performance at www.wraysshack3tracks.com/downloads.html.

Chapter 20: Super Sunday

1. Regis 1999, 479.

Chapter 21: A Murdery Summer

1. Paxton.
2. Material in the preceding paragraphs appears in a different form in Sublette 2008, 303–304.
3. http://neworleans.metblogs.com/2005/08/19/new-article-about-new-orleans-homicide-rate/.
4. Roberts.
5. Coleman, 203.
6. Filosa 2006.

Chapter 22: Fats Domino's Book of Knowledge

1. DuBois, 777.
2. Jensen 2006.
3. Friedman.
4. "All New Orleans Public School Teachers Fired."
5. American Federation of Teachers.
6. Medley 2005.

Coda

1. Lozaw.
2. Draper.
3. Jindal.
4. Carmichael; the study is *Legacy of Shame*.
5. Sublette 2008a.

Afterword

1. Rodríguez.
2. Filosa 2009.
3. Rodríguez.

REFERENCES

Abbott, Lynn and Doug Seroff. 2007. *Ragged But Right*. University Press of Mississippi, Jackson.

Adler, Constance. 2001. "Neither Wind Nor Rain." *Gambit Weekly*, May 15.

Agee, James. 1948. "D.W. Griffith, Remembered." *The Nation*, September 4.

"All New Orleans Public School Teachers Fired." 2006. *Democracy Now!* June 20. http://www.democracynow.org/2006/6/20/all_new_orleans_public_school_teachers.

American Federation of Teachers. 2007. *No Experience Necessary: How the New Orleans School Takeover Experiment Devalues Experienced Teachers*. http://www.aft.org/presscenter/releases/downloads/NoExperReport_07.pdf.

Armstrong, Louis. 1954. *Satchmo: My Life in New Orleans*. Prentice-Hall, New York.

Ash, Constance. 1988. *The Horsegirl*. Ace Books, New York.

———. 1990. *The Stalking Horse*. Ace Books, New York.

———. 1992. *The Stallion Queen*. Ace Books, New York.

Assmann, Jan. 2002. *The Mind of Egypt: History and Meaning in the Time of the Pharaohs*. Trans. by Andrew Jenkins. Metropolitan Books, New York.

Avelar, Idelber. 2004. *The Letter of Violence: Essays on Narrative, Ethics, and Politics*. Palgrave Macmillan, New York.

Babalola, Adeboye. 1989. "A Portrait of Ogun as Reflected in Ijala Chants." In Barnes, Sandra T., ed., *Africa's Ogun: Old World and New*. Indiana University Press, Bloomington.

Bair, Asatar P. 2007. *Prison Labor in the United States: An Economic Analysis*. Routledge, New York.

Baker, Jean H. 2004. *James Buchanan*. Times Books, New York.

Baker, Liva. 1996. *The Second Battle of New Orleans: The Hundred-Year Struggle to Integrate the Schools*. HarperCollins, New York.

"Bar Owner's Prison Death Was Natural, Coroner Says." 2005. *New Orleans Times-Picayune*. April 24.

Barker, Danny. 1998. *Buddy Bolden and the Last Days of Storyville*. Continuum, New York.

Barnes, Dick. 1967. "S.F.'s Hashbury Combos Rock Convention Hall." *San Diego Union*, July 24.

Barrier, Michael. 1999. *Hollywood Cartoons: American Animation in Its Golden Age*. Oxford University Press, New York.

Barry, Richard. 1915. "Five Dollar Movies Prophesied." *New York Times*, March 28.

Bass, Jack. 1981. *Unlikely Heroes: The Dramatic Story of the Southern Judges of the Fifth Circuit who Translated the Supreme Court's Brown Decision into a Revolution for Equality*. Simon and Schuster, New York.

Baumbach, Richard O. Jr., and William E. Borah. 1981. *The Second Battle of New Orleans: A History of the Vieux Carré Riverfront-Expressway Controversy*. Preservation Press, University, AL.

Bechet, Sidney. 1960. *Treat It Gentle*. Hill and Wang, New York.

Bergreen, Laurence. 1997. *Louis Armstrong: An Extravagant Life*. Broadway Books, New York.

Berry, Jason. 2003. "Long Remembered." *Gambit Weekly*, March 25.

Blackmon, Douglas A. 2008. *Slavery by Another Name: The Re-enslavement of Black Americans from the Civil War to World War II*. Doubleday, New York.

Bone, Black Dog. 2004. "Soulja Slim." *Murder Dog.* http://www.murderdog. com/january_articles/souljahslim/souljah_slim.html. Accessed July 2005.

"Bounce Back." 2006. *Scratch,* April.

Brandt, Allan M. 1987. *No Magic Bullet: A Social History of Venereal Disease in the United States Since 1880.* Expanded edition. Oxford University Press, New York.

Brothers, Thomas. 2006. *Louis Armstrong's New Orleans.* W. W. Norton, New York.

Broven, John. 1983. *Rhythm and Blues in New Orleans.* Pelican Press, Gretna, LA.

C-Murder. 2007. *Death Around the Corner.* Vibe Books, New York.

"C-Murder Indicted for Murder; Wrongful Death Suit Expected." 2004. Associated Press story in *Louisiana Weekly,* March 11, 2002.

Cable, George Washington. 1880. *The Grandissimes.* Charles Scribner's Sons, New York.

Carmichael, Mary. 2008. "Katrina Kids: Sickest Ever." *Newsweek,* December 1.

Chase, John. 1960. *Frenchmen, Desire, Good Children . . . and Other Streets in New Orleans.* Pelican Publishing Co., Gretna, LA.

Chestnut, J. L. Jr., and Julia Cass. 1990. *Black in Selma: The Uncommon Life of J. L. Chestnut, Jr.* Farrar, Straus and Giroux, New York.

Christian, Marcus B. 1945. "The Theory of the Poisoning of Oscar Dunn," *Phylon* (1940–1956), 6: 3 (3rd Qtr.).

"The Cocaine Habit Among Negroes." 1902. *British Medical Journal,* November 29.

Cockrell, Dale. 1996. "Jim Crow, Demon of Disorder." *American Music* 14: 2 (Summer).

Cody, William F. 1917. *Life and Adventures of "Buffalo Bill."* Stanton and Van Vliet, Chicago.

———. 1888. *Story of the Wild West and Camp-Fire Chats, by Buffalo Bill.* R. S. Peale, Chicago.

Cohn, Nik. 2002. "Soljas." *Granta* 76.

Coker, Cheo Hodari. 2005. "Compton's Most Wanted." *Vibe*, February.

———. 2003. *Unbelievable: The Life, Death, and Afterlife of The Notorious B.I.G.* Three Rivers Press, New York.

Coleman, Rick. 2006. *Blue Monday: Fats Domino and the Lost Dawn of Rock 'n' Roll.* Da Capo, New York.

Croce, Arlene. 1966. "D.W.G. Returns." *Rally* 1: 1, March.

Cunningham, Cheryl V. 1982. *The Desegregation of Tulane University.* Master's thesis, University of New Orleans.

DeLillo, Don. 1985. *White Noise.* Viking, New York.

Denison, Edward Fulton. 1985. *Trends in American Economic Growth, 1929–1982.* Brookings Institution Press, Washington, DC.

Dennis, Michael. 2002. "Looking Backward: Woodrow Wilson, the New South, and the Question of Race." *American Nineteenth-Century History,* 3: 1, Spring.

Department of the Army (United States). 2005. *Army Band Section Leader Handbook.* Publication TC 12–44. www.us.army.mil.

"Detective Sergeant Wilson Victim." 1919. *Washington Post,* July 22.

Dixon, Thomas. 1903. *The Leopard's Spots: A Romance of the White Man's Burden—1865–1900.* Doubleday, Page, New York.

———. 1905. *The Clansman; A Historical Romance of the Ku Klux Klan.* Doubleday, New York.

Dollard, John. 1937. *Caste and Class in a Southern Town.* Institute of Human Relations, New Haven.

Draper, Robert. 2009. "And he shall be judged." GQ, July.

Dr. John. 1994. *Under a Hoodoo Moon: The Life of Dr. John the Night Tripper.* St. Martin's Press, New York.

DuBois, W. E. B. 1986. *Writings.* Library of America, New York.

Dunn, Christopher. 2001. *Brutality Garden: Tropicália and the Emergence of a Brazilian Counterculture.* University of North Carolina Press, Chapel Hill.

Dylan, Bob. 2004. *Chronicles, Vol. 1.* Simon and Schuster, New York.

Fairall, Herbert S. 1886. *The World's Industrial and Cotton Centennial Exposition: New Orleans, 1884–1885.* Republican Publishing Company, Iowa City.

Fairclough, Adam. 2000. "Brutality and Ballots, 1946–1956," in Vincent, Charles, ed. 2000. *The African American Experience in Louisiana: Part C: From Jim Crow to Civil Rights.* The Louisiana Purchase Bicentennial Series in Louisiana History. Center for Louisiana Studies, Lafayette.

Filosa, Gwen. 2004. "Bar Owner Killed Man in Self-Defense, Jury Told." *New Orleans Times-Picayune,* December 7.

———. 2006. "'Goth Murder' Suspect Gets 45 Years in Jail.'" *New Orleans Times-Picayune,* June 7.

———. 2006b. "Two Die in New Orleans Shootings." *New Orleans Times-Picayune,* December 29.

———. 2009. "Mom due to testify against sons charged with murdering college student in Fourth Street apartment." *New Orleans Times-Picayune,* March 4.

Finch, Susan. 2005. "Student's Death Called 'Lynching.'" *New Orleans Times-Picayune,* January 8.

Fischetti, Mark. 2001. "Drowning New Orleans." *Scientific American* 285: 4, October.

Fitrakis, Robert J., Steven Rosenfeld, and Harvey Wasserman. 2006. *What Happened in Ohio?* New Press, New York.

Florence, Robert, and Mason Florence. 1997. *New Orleans Cemeteries: Life in the Cities of the Dead.* Batture Press, New Orleans.

Fontenot, Kevin. 2008. "Sing It Good, Sing It Strong, Sing It Loud: The Music of Governor Jimmie Davis." In Lornell, Kip, and Tracey E. W. Laird. *Shreveport Sounds in Black and White.* University Press of Mississippi, Jackson.

Friedman, Milton. 2005. "The Promise of Vouchers." *Wall Street Journal,* December 5.

Gill, James. 1997. *Lords of Misrule: Mardi Gras and the Politics of Race in New Orleans.* University Press of Mississippi, Jackson.

Gilmore, Glenda Elizabeth. 1996. *Gender and Jim Crow: Women and the Politics of White Supremacy in North Carolina, 1896–1920*. University of North Carolina Press, Chapel Hill.

Goreau, Laurraine. 1968. "Mardi Gras." In Carter, Hodding, ed. 1968. *The Past as Prelude: New Orleans 1718–1968*. Tulane University, New Orleans.

Goudeau, D. A., and W. C. Conner. 1968. "Storm Surge over the Mississippi River Delta, Accompanying Hurricane Betsy, 1965." *Monthly Weather Review*, 96: 2.

Grant, Ulysses S. 1999. *Personal Memoirs*. Modern Library, New York.

Grunwald, Michael, and Manuel Roig-Franzia. 2005. "Ivan and the Big Uneasy." *Washington Post*, September 15.

Guralnick, Peter. 2005. *Dream Boogie: The Triumph of Sam Cooke*. Little, Brown and Company, New York.

Guralnick, Peter. 2007. "How Did Elvis Get Turned into a Racist?" *New York Times*, August 11.

Guillory, Barbara Marie. 1974. *Black Family: A Case for Change and Survival in White America*. Ph.D. dissertation, Tulane University.

Hallward, Peter. 2007. *Damming the Flood: Haiti, Aristide, and the Politics of Containment*. Verso, New York.

Hannusch, Jeff. 1985. *I Hear You Knockin': The Sound of New Orleans Rhythm and Blues*. Swallow Publications, Ville Platte, LA.

Haygood, Wil, and Ann Scott Tyson. 2005. "'It Was as if All of Us Were Already Pronounced Dead.'" *Washington Post*, September 15.

Herz, Henri. 1866. *Mes voyages en Amérique*. A. Faure, Paris.

Highsaw, Robert B. 1981. *Edward Douglass White: Defender of the Conservative Faith*. Louisiana State University Press, Baton Rouge.

Hryhorchuk, John. 2002. "Tulane Senior Murdered at Off-Campus Home." *Tulane Hullabaloo* 93: 3, September 13.

Hurtt, Michael. 2004. "Backtalk with Fats Domino." *Offbeat*, June.

Ingham, John N. 1983. *Biographical Dictionary of American Business Leaders*. Greenwood, Westport, CT.

Jamail, Dahr. http://dahrjamailiraq.com.

Jensen, Lynn. 2005. "Galatoire's Diner Recalls 'Awful Display.'" *New Orleans Times-Picayune*, January 6.

———. 2006. "Ain't That a Shame." *New Orleans Times-Picayune*, March 15.

Jerome, Richard. 1995. "Keeper of the Flame." *People* 44: 23, December 4.

Jigsaw. 2004. "Master P: Big Business." *allhiphop.com*. Accessed December 27, 2004.

Jindal, Bobby. 1994. "Physical Dimensions of Spiritual Warfare." *New Oxford Review*, December.

Johnson, Phil. 1968. "Good Time Town." In Carter, Hodding, ed. 1968. *The Past as Prelude: New Orleans 1718–1968*. Tulane University, New Orleans.

Jones, Bomani. 2004. "Africana Masterpiece: *Doggystyle*." http://archive.blackvoices.com/articles/daily/mu20040305snoop.asp.

Kane and Abel. 1999. *Eyes of a Killer/Behind Enemy Lines*. St. Martin's Griffin, New York.

Kaplan, Erin Aubrey. 2005. "These People." *Los Angeles Times Magazine*, July 24.

Kasper, Shirl. 1992. *Annie Oakley*. University of Oklahoma Press, Norman.

Kenney, William Howland. 2005. *Jazz on the River*. University of Chicago Press, Chicago.

King, Martin Luther Jr. 1994. *Letter from the Birmingham Jail*. Harper, San Francisco.

Klein, Naomi. 2007. *The Shock Doctrine: The Rise of Disaster Capitalism*. Metropolitan Books/Henry Holt, New York.

Kunian, David. *Meet All Your Fine Friends: The Dew Drop Inn in New Orleans*. Radio documentary, WWOZ, New Orleans.

Kuzenksi, John C. 1995. "David Duke and the Nonpartisan Primary." In Kuzenski, John C., Charles S. Bullock III, and Ronald Keith Gaddie, eds. *David Duke and the Politics of Race in the South*. Vanderbilt University Press, Nashville, TN.

Laborde, Errol. 2007. *Krewe: The Early New Orleans Carnival from Mardi Gras to Zulu*. Carnival Press, Metairie.

Laird, Tracey E. W. 2008. "Beyond Country Music," in Lornell, Kip, and Tracey E. W. Laird, *Shreveport Sounds in Black and White*. University Press of Mississippi, Jackson.

Landphair, Juliette. Undated. "Sewerage, Sidewalks, and Schools: The New Orleans Ninth Ward and School Desegregation." http://www.virginia.edu/history/graduate/southcon/southcon.97/landphair.html. Accessed January 2005.

Lee, Trymaine. 2005. "Block Party Turns Violent." *New Orleans Times-Picayune*, May 24.

Legacy of Shame: The On-Going Public Health Disaster of Children Struggling in Post-Katrina Louisiana. 2008. The Children's Health Fund and the National Center for Disaster Preparedness, Columbia University Mailman School of Public Health, New York, 6, 7.

Levin, Jordan. 2009. "Miami's Overtown Was Once a 'Mecca of Music.'" *Miami Herald*, January 31.

Lewis, Peirce F. 2003. *New Orleans: The Making of an Urban Landscape*. 2nd ed. Center for American Places, Santa Fe, NM.

Liebling, A. J. 1960. "A Reporter at Large." *New Yorker*, May 28.

———. 1960a. "A Reporter at Large." *New Yorker*, June 4.

———. 1960b. "A Reporter at Large." *New Yorker*, June 11.

Link, Arthur F. 1970. "Woodrow Wilson: The American as Southerner." *Journal of Southern History*, 36: 1, February.

Lornell, Kip, and Tracey E. W. Laird. 2008. *Shreveport Sounds in Black and White*. University Press of Mississippi, Jackson.

Louisiana Coastal Wetlands Conservation and Restoration Task Force and the Wetlands Conservation and Restoration Authority. 1998. *Coast 2050: Toward a Sustainable Coastal Louisiana*. Louisiana Department of Natural Resources, Baton Rouge. http://www.lca.gov/net_prod_download/public/lca_net–pub–products/doc/2050report.pdf. Accessed February 2005.

Lozaw, Tristram. 2008. "The Heartbeat Behind the Tragedy." *Boston Globe*, January 22.

Luster, Michael. 1996. "Hayride Boogie: Blues, Rockabilly and Soul from the Louisiana Hill and Delta Country." http://www.louisianafolklife. org/LT/Articles_Essays/creole_art_hayride_boogie.html. Accessed July 2005.

MacGaffey, Wyatt. 1976. "Oral Tradition in Central Africa." *International Journal of African Historical Studies*, 7: 3.

Marquis, Don. 2005. *In Search of Buddy Bolden: First Man of Jazz*. rev. ed. Louisiana State University Press, Baton Rouge.

Marqusee, Mike. 2005. "A Name That Lives in Infamy." *UK Guardian*, November 10. http://www.guardian.co.uk/world/2005/nov/10/usa.iraq.

Marriott, Rob. 1998. "American Gothic." *Vibe* 6: 4, May.

Matthews, Bunny. 2003. "Wish You Were Here, Dawl!" *Offbeat*, July.

Mayer, Vicki. 2007. "Letting It All Hang Out: Mardi Gras Performances Live and on Video." *TDR*, 51:2, Summer.

McDonough, Jimmy. 2006. "Be Wild, Not Evil: The Link Wray Story." *Perfect Sound Forever*. http://www.furious.com/PERFECT/linkwray6.html.

McKnight, Michael. 2005. "Charivaris, Cowbellions, and Sheet Iron Bands: Nineteenth-Century Rough Music in New Orleans." *American Music* 23: 4, Winter.

McPherson, James M. 1982. *Ordeal by Fire: The Civil War and Reconstruction*. Knopf, New York.

Medley, Keith Weldon. 2003. *We as Freemen: Plessy v. Ferguson*. Pelican, Gretna, LA.

———. 2005. "Famous Parishioners." http://www.staugustinecatholic church-neworleans.org/hist-famous.htm.

Mitchell, Reid. 1995. *All on a Mardi Gras Day: Episodes in the History of New Orleans Carnival*. Harvard University Press, Cambridge, MA.

Mohl, Raymond A. 2008. "The Interstates and the Cities: The U.S. Department of Transportation and the Freeway Revolt, 1966–1973." *Journal of Policy History* 20: 2.

Mohr, Clarence L., and Joseph E. Gordon. 2001. *Tulane: The Emergence of a Modern University, 1945–1980*. Louisiana State University Press, Baton Rouge.

Mullener, Elizabeth. 2005. "Wal-Mart Fails to Live Up to Disastrous Billing." *New Orleans Times-Picayune*, March 13.

Neville Brothers and David Ritz. 2000. *The Brothers*. Little, Brown, Boston.

O'Brien, Keith. 2005. "Recently Released from Prison, Cuban Refugees Who Came to the United States in the 1980 Mariel Boatlift Are Left to Fend for Themselves." *New Orleans Times-Picayune*, February 16.

———. 2005a. "Six Weeks After Cuban Refugees Were Ordered Released, Many Remain Locked Up." *New Orleans Times-Picayune*, March 3.

Oliver, Paul. 2008. "Jerry's Saloon Blues: 1940 Field Recordings from Louisiana." In Lornell, Kip and Tracey E. W. Laird. *Shreveport Sounds in Black and White*. University Press of Mississippi, Jackson.

Ozersky, Josh. 2002. Introduction to Wilson, Woodrow. *A History of the American People*. Barnes and Noble World Digital Library, New York.

Pais, Noah Bonaparte. 2009. "Rally of the Dolls." *Gambit Weekly*, February 16.

Palmer, Robert. 1979. *A Tale of Two Cities: Memphis Rock and New Orleans Roll*. Institute for Studies in American Music, Brooklyn, NY.

Patel, Raj. 2008. *Starved and Stuffed: The Hidden Battle for the World Food System*. Melville House, Brooklyn, NY.

Paxton, Kate. 2005. "Chief 'Tootie' Montana Dies of a Heart Attack at City Council Meeting." New Orleans Independent Media, June 28. http://neworleans.indymedia.org/news/2005/06/3515.php.

Perlstein, Michael. 1999. "N.O. Man Admits to 8 Murders, Drug Kingpin Gets Life Term." *New Orleans Times-Picayune*, January 15.

———. 1999a. "Drug Kingpin Has No Regrets at Sentencing; Pena to Spend Life Behind Bars for Drugs, Murders." *New Orleans Times-Picayune*, March 12.

———. 1999b. "Rap Twins: Feds Wanted Master P." *New Orleans Times-Picayune*, July 23.

———. 2004. "Chilling Tale Emerges from Scene of Killing." *New Orleans Times-Picayune*, September 14.

———. 2005. "Criminal Court Mired in Minor Cases." *New Orleans Times-Picayune*, August 24.

Perry, Imani. 2004. *Prophets of the Hood: Politics and Poetics in Hip Hop.* Duke University Press, Durham, NC.

Perry, Mark. 2004. *Grant and Twain: The Story of a Friendship That Changed America.* Random House, New York.

Plyer, Allison, and Denice Warren. 2004. "Change in the Irish Channel." Greater New Orleans Community Data Center. http://www.gnocdc.org/articles/IrishChannel.html. Accessed March 2005.

Portré-Bobinski, Germaine, and Clara Mildred Smith. 1936. *Natchitoches: The Up-to-Date Oldest Town in Louisiana.* Dameron-Pierson Co., New Orleans.

Powell, Alan II. 2005. "3 LaPlace Men Plead Innocent to Murder." *New Orleans Times-Picayune*, May 3.

Powers, Thomas. 2004. "Secret Intelligence and the 'War on Terror.'" *New York Review of Books* 51: 20, December 16.

Presley, Cleveland. Interview. Louisiana State Museum Civil Rights Oral Histories. http://louisdl.training.louislibraries.org/cdm4/item–viewer.php?CISOROOT=/LOH&CISOPTR=18&CISOBOX=1&REC=2.

"Promoting Mitigation in Louisiana: Federal Emergency Management Agency and the State of Louisiana." 2002. Federal Emergency Management Agency report. http://www.fema.gov/txt/fima/performance.txt. Accessed February 2005.

Raeburn, Bruce Boyd. 2009. *New Orleans Style and the Writing of American Jazz History.* University of Michigan Press, Ann Arbor.

Rankin, David C. 1974. "The Origins of Black Leadership in New Orleans During Reconstruction." *Journal of Southern History* 40: 3 (August).

Rankin, Kenny. 2000. "Terrance 'Gangsta' Williams." *F.E.D.S.* 2: 7.

Ransom, John Crowe. 1930. "Reconstructed but Unregenerate," in Twelve Southerners, *I'll Take My Stand: The South and the Agrarian Tradition.* Harper and Brothers, New York.

Reckdahl, Katy. 2004. "Why?" *Gambit Weekly*, August 17.

———. 2005. "Stopping a Second Line." *Gambit Weekly*, May 3.

———. 2005b. "St. Joseph's Night Gone Blue." *Gambit Weekly,* March 29.

Reddin, Paul. 1999. *Wild West Shows.* University of Illinois Press, Urbana.

Regis, Helen. 1999. "Second Lines, Minstrelsy, and the Contested Aspects of New Orleans Afro-Creole Festivals." *Cultural Anthropology* 14: 4, November.

———. 2001. "Blackness and the Politics of Memory in the New Orleans Second Line." *American Ethnologist* 28: 4.

Rioux, Paul, and Walt Philbin. 2004. "Body Found in Freezer Is N.O. Man." *New Orleans Times-Picayune,* October 23.

Roach, Joseph. 1996. *Cities of the Dead: Circum-Atlantic Performance.* Columbia University Press, New York.

Roberts, Deon. 2005. "Corps Budget Faces Record $71.2 Million in Cuts." *New Orleans City Business,* June 6. http://www.neworleanscitybusiness. com/viewStory.cfm?recID=13197.

Rodríguez, Maya. 2009. "Father of Slain Son Recounts the Long Road to Justice." WWL-TV, March 14. http://www.wwltv.com/topstories/stories/ wwl031408mljustice.363d731d.html.

Rogin, Michael. 1985. "'The Sword Became a Flashing Vision': DW Griffith's 'The Birth of a Nation.'" *Representations* 9, Winter 1985.

Rohter, Larry. 1992. "Bias Law Casts Pall over New Orleans Mardi Gras." *New York Times,* February 2.

Rose, Chris. 2009. "Antoinette K-Doe's Funeral Proved Why We Live and Die in New Orleans." *New Orleans Times-Picayune,* March 8.

Rousey, Dennis Charles. 1996. *Policing the Southern City: New Orleans, 1805–1889.* Louisiana State University Press, Baton Rouge.

Rousseau, Peter L. 2002. "Jacksonian Monetary Policy, Specie Flows, and the Panic of 1837." *Journal of Economic History* 62:2, June.

Russell, Gordon. 2005. "Information, Rules Elusive at Arena." *New Orleans Times-Picayune,* September 22.

Satten, Vanessa, 2005. "Soulja Slim: Life Goes On." *XXL* #66. January/February.

Scherman, Tony. 1999. *Backbeat: Earl Palmer's Story.* Smithsonian Institution Press, Washington, DC.

Schleifstein, Mark. 2005. "Preparing for the Worst." *New Orleans Times-Picayune*, May 31.

Schleifstein, Mark and John McQuaid. 2002. "Washing Away." *New Orleans Times-Picayune*, June 23–27.

Schumpeter, Joseph. 1942. *Capitalism, Socialism, and Democracy*. Harper and Brothers, London.

Shapiro, Nat, and Nat Hentoff. 1955. *Hear Me Talkin' to Ya: The Story of Jazz as Told by the Men Who Made It*. Rinehart, New York.

Simpson, Doug. 2004. "C-Murder Trial for Murder Begins." Associated Press story in *Louisiana Weekly*, September 22, 2003.

Smith, Felipe. 1998. *American Body Politics: Race, Gender, and Black Literary Renaissance*. University of Georgia Press, Athens.

———. 2003. "How I Became Felipe Smith." In Rahier, Jean M., and Percy Hintzen. *Invisible Others: Active Pretences in the U.S. Black Community*, Routledge, New York.

Smith, Michael P. 1994. *Mardi Gras Indians*. Pelican Publishing Company, Gretna, LA.

Spain, Daphne. 1979. "Race Relations and Residential Segregation in New Orleans: Two Centuries of Paradox." *Annals of the American Academy of Political and Social Science*, Vol. 441, *Race and Residence in American Cities*, January.

Starr, S. Frederick. 1985. *New Orleans Unmasqued*. Édition Dedeaux, New Orleans.

Steinbeck, John. 1997. *Travels with Charley*. Penguin Books, New York.

Streatfeild, Dominic. 2001. *Cocaine: An Unauthorized Biography*. Picador, New York.

Sublette, Ned. 2004. *Cuba and Its Music: From the First Drums to the Mambo*. Chicago Review Press, Chicago.

———. 2007. "The Kingsmen and the Cha-Cha-Chá." In Weisbard, Eric, ed., *Listen Again: A Momentary History of Pop Music*. Duke University Press, Durham, NC.

———. 2008. *The World That Made New Orleans: From Spanish Silver to Congo Square*. Lawrence Hill Books, Chicago.

———. 2008a. "New Orleans: Three Years After Katrina." *Downbeat* 75: 11, November.

Substance Abuse and Treatment Needs Among Entering Louisiana Prison Inmates, 2001. 2001. State of Louisiana Office of Addictive Disorders Report. http://www.dhh.louisiana.gov/offices/publications/pubs-23/ Prisoner%20Study.pdf.

Taylor, Joe Gray. 1968. "New Orleans and Reconstruction." *Louisiana History* 9: 3.

"Three Children at School Arrested for Weapons Offenses." 2004. New Orleans Police Department press release, September 10. http://www. cityofno.com/pg-50-49-press-releases.aspx?pressid=1910.

Twelve Southerners. 1930. *I'll Take My Stand: The South and the Agrarian Tradition*. Harper and Brothers, New York.

Vargas, Ramon Antonio. 2009. "Lil' Wayne Saved by Alert Off-Duty Cop." *New Orleans Times-Picayune*, April 9.

Varney, James. 2004. "Murders Rock Family." *New Orleans Times-Picayune*, October 22.

———. 2005. "Parents Sue Razzoo over Son's Death." *New Orleans Times-Picayune*, January 12.

Varney, James, and Tara Young. 2005. "3 Bouncers Arrested in Student's Death." *New Orleans Times-Picayune*, January 7.

Wade, Carlton. 2005. "True Crime." *The Source* 188, June.

Wagner, Peter. 2003. *The Prison Index: Taking the Pulse of the Crime Control Industry*, Section III. http://www.prisonpolicy.org/prisonindex/prison industry.html.

Weston, Kelly. 2004. "Tempers Flare at Scene of Police Shooting." WDSU, August 4. http://news.infoshop.org/article.php?story=04/08/04/9149518.

White, Adam, and Fred Bronson. 1993. *The Billboard Book of Number One Rhythm and Blues Hits*. Billboard Books, New York.

Widmer, Ted. 2005. *Martin van Buren*. Times Books, New York.

Williams, Ted. 1998. "Hot Boys Nasty!" *Murder Dog* 5: 5.

Williams, Ted, and Black Dog Bone. 1998. "Cash Money Records: Big

Tymers Get the Party Started." *Murder Dog* 5: 5.

Wilson, Joseph. 1999. *Mutual Relation of Masters and Slaves as Taught in the Bible*. Academic Affairs Library, University of North Carolina–Chapel Hill, NC. http://docsouth.unc.edu/imls/wilson/menu.html.

Wilson, Woodrow. 2002. *A History of the American People*. Barnes and Noble World Digital Library, New York.

———. 1893. *Division and Reunion: 1829–1889*. Longman, Greens, and Co., New York.

Winston, James E. 1924. "Notes on the Economic History of New Orleans, 1803–1836." *The Mississippi Valley Historical Review* 11: 2, September.

Wyckoff, Geraldine. 2008. "Yet Another Tradition and Celebration Unique to Our Culture Approaches." *Louisiana Weekly*, March 10.

Young, Tara. 2004. "The Cost of Death." *New Orleans Times-Picayune*, February 15.

———. 2004b. "The Art of the Funeral." *New Orleans Times-Picayune*, February 15.

———. 2004c. "Man Held Toddler as He Shot Rival, Say N.O. Cops." *New Orleans Times-Picayune*, October 26.

———. 2004d. "Motorized Mayhem." *New Orleans Times-Picayune*, December 14.

INDEX

left overleaf: Walter Ramsey, trombonist and leader of Stooges Brass Band, outside Juicey's Lounge on Seventh Street in the Irish Channel, at the Prince of Wales anniversary parade, October 17, 2004.

top: The Prince of Wales comes up Tchoupitoulas.

bottom: Fred Johnson of Black Men of Labor, February 2006.

right overleaf: Outdoor opening pageant of the Pussyfooters' Ball, in front of the Country Club in the